THE BASQUE SERIES

BOOKS IN THE BASQUE SERIES

A Book of the Basques
by Rodney Gallop

In a Hundred Graves: A Basque Portrait
by Robert Laxalt

Basque Nationalism
by Stanley G. Payne

Amerikanuak: Basques in the New World
by William A. Douglass and Jon Bilbao

Beltran: Basque Sheepman of the American West
by Beltran Paris, as told to William A. Douglass

The Basques: The Franco Years and Beyond
by Robert P. Clark

The Basques:
The Franco Years and Beyond

OTHER BOOKS BY ROBERT P. CLARK

Development and Instability:
Political Change in the Non-Western World
(Dryden, 1974)

Power and Policy in the Third World
(Wiley, 1978)

The Basques:
The Franco Years and Beyond

ROBERT P. CLARK

University of Nevada Press
Reno, Nevada

Basque Series Editor: William A. Douglass
University of Nevada Press, Reno, Nevada 89557 USA

Printed in the United States of America
Designed by Dave Comstock

Library of Congress Cataloging in Publication Data

Clark, Robert P.
The Basques, the Franco years and beyond.

(Basque series)
Bibliography: p.
Includes index.
1. Basque Provinces — History — Autonomy and independence movements. 2. Nationalism — Basque Provinces. I. Title.
DP302.B53C55 946'.004'9992 79-24926
ISBN 0-87417-057-5

THIS BOOK IS DEDICATED TO TWO BASQUES:

Dr. Vicente de Amezaga y Aresti, who lived and died in exile for his dream of an autonomous Basque country; and his grandson, **Bingen Amezaga Zubillaga,** who may one day see the dream become reality.

Contents

Preface

I know of few areas of scholarship as highly charged with political implications and as fraught with political landmines as the one that is the subject of this book: the course of Basque nationalism since the conclusion of the Spanish Civil War, in 1939. Even if it were in fact possible for an outsider to disengage himself from the normative dimensions of the subject (a disengagement I consider neither possible, necessary, nor indeed desirable, given the circumstances), he would quickly become aware that every study of the complex questions dealt with here is sooner or later seized upon by partisans in support of, or refutation of, one or another of the several positions taken by Basques and Spaniards. Therefore, I find it necessary at the outset of this book to alert the reader to my own predispositions, to describe how I came to hold such opinions, and to indicate how my attitudes have influenced my approach to this question.

First, as to attitudes and opinions. I believe that the positions adopted by Basque nationalists generally, and by the Basque Nationalist Party in particular, are entirely legitimate, defensible and justifiable in the context of a modern industrial society. I do not find regional autonomy to be contrary to the social, economic or political needs of an industrialized Spain. More to the point, however, I believe in the legitimacy of the expression of these political interests through organized political parties and other institutions, and in the right of the inhabitants of the Basque provinces (collectively or separately) to decide for themselves what should be the appropriate way for them to organize their relationships with the rest of Spain.

One cannot take a stand on the question of Basque nationalism, however, without confronting the ethical obligation to make known his feelings about the role of violence in political struggle. Having seen the effects of guerrilla warfare, urban insurgency and political instability first hand in Asia, Latin America and Europe, I am convinced that violence brutalizes both the target and the agent, and thus is never supportable by outside opinions. The plight of Basque nationalists during the Franco era is a clear example of those too-frequent cases, however, where the institutionalized violence directed by the State against citizens must be weighed in the ethical balance. In short, was the violence done by the Spanish government against Basque nationalists of sufficient magnitude and duration as to justify ETA's insurgent actions of the late 1960s and 1970s? In my opinion, the answer is an unequivocal "Yes." Intransigence breeds intransigence; and the historical record will show that the Basque nationalist movement endured extraordinary pressures for nearly thirty of General Franco's thirty-nine years in power before its adherents struck back with violence. When a people are subjected to extraordinary pressures, heroic counter-measures are needed simply in order to survive. Once we enter the post-Franco period, of course, the legitimacy of ETA as a revolutionary force becomes much fuzzier. In defense of ETA, one must observe that the spiraling violence and counter-violence of the Franco era bred a generation of revolutionary Basque youth whose commitment to the life of the gun cannot be switched off as one would a lamp just because a new regime is in power in Madrid. (A qualifier to the preceding sentence: it seems likely that most of the ETA militants of the late 1970s were too young to have actually felt the force of Spanish oppression during the 1950s, so it is hard to say how much of ETA's current activity is a residue of the earlier years, and how much stems from events of the day.) On the other hand, no matter how one might describe its effects, the parliamentary system in Spain works at least well enough to have embraced the legitimate aspirations of all the nonviolent Basque nationalist groups, including the Basque Nationalist Party. Whether or not the Party will be able to secure these aspirations through the new democratic system is of course an important question; but a negative answer is no justification for ETA to continue its war against the agents of Spain and Spanish capitalism. Virtually every Basque political party has denounced ETA's violence (as well as the counter-violence of the Guardia Civil), so in stating my opposition to ETA's insurgency following the 1977 parliamentary elections, I am really echoing the opinions of many Basques.

We are all, of course, the products of prior experiences. Whether or not these experiences make us their prisoners or their beneficiaries depends on whether or not we allow ourselves to be blinded by them or informed, and especially whether or not we continue the systematic search for confirming or refuting data. In my own case, my marriage to the daughter of an exiled Basque nationalist political and intellectual figure gave me a near-unique window into the lives of the people who populate the movement. These countless personal contacts have been supplemented by two trips to the Basque country, the first for ten weeks in the spring and summer of 1973, the second for a month during the winter of 1978-1979. During these visits, I was welcomed into the homes and offices of many Basques of all political persuasions. A number of them talked with me of their intimate lives as participants in the resistance. My principal hope here is that I have been faithful to their views and respectful of their privacy. As much as I would like to be able to thank them all publicly here, I shall not do so, since their being listed here might be considered by some as an indication of their agreement with, and approval of, the contents of this book, which is by no means always the case.

In my attempt to deal both sympathetically and analytically with the contemporary Basque nationalist political scene, I have inevitably been drawn into an analysis of the economic and social class aspects of the movement. The approach of the book is not derived from Marxism; but I do make the assumption that where one stands in relation to society's modes of production and consumption has a great deal to do with one's political beliefs and actions. While not definitive to the exclusion of all other influences, classes do have an impact on the expression of the ethno-nationalism, especially those like the Basques' which are rooted in a heavily industrialized society. Thus, a central theme of this book is the clash between class and ethnicity within the Basque political universe. The other theme, of course, has to do with the struggle between Basques and Spaniards. Full liberation of the Basque people depends on the outcome of both struggles.

This completes, I think, the inventory of the author's attitudes about which the reader must be aware. In concluding this already too long preface, I wish also to thank the institutions that supported my visits to the Basque provinces: the University of Chattanooga Foundation of the University of Tennessee at Chattanooga, for the 1973 trip; and the Center for Research and Advanced Study of George Mason University, for the trip in 1979. Obviously, neither organization is responsible for any of the contents of this book. And, of course, I must express my gratitude to my wife and her family who, I'm sure, could not understand why it took me so long to absorb the full details of a political struggle which for them possessed the clarity and immediacy of one's daily life itself. If their forebearance has been rewarded with a book that has meaning for them as well as for its English-speaking audience, then the delay will have been justified.

Robert P. Clark

March 1979
Burke, Virginia

Prologue

"THE NABARA"

On the evening of March 4, 1937, five Basque trawlers weighed anchor in the French port of Bayonne and started their nine-hour journey across the Bay of Biscay to the waiting Basque government in Bilbao. One ship, the cargo trawler *Galdames,* carried a precious treasure: some two hundred important Basque and Spanish citizens, over half of whom were women and children; and the whole of the new Basque nickel currency. The other four — the *Nabara,* the *Guipuzkoa,* the *Bizkaya* and the *Donostia* — were part of the armed trawler fleet the Basques used to escort cargo vessels through the dangers of the Spanish blockade.[1]

By this time, the Spanish Civil War was in its eighth month, and the Basques had been reduced to a shrinking semi-circle surrounding the industrial port city of Bilbao. The Spanish rebel navy of General Franco had established a blockade (albeit a rather porous one) on the northern coast of the peninsula in December 1936; the aerial bombardment of Bilbao had begun the next month. Food was now severely rationed; fuel and ammunition were in short supply; and the exemplary Basque police forces were being tested in the maintenance of public order.

In an effort to break through the blockade thrown up before Bilbao by the Spanish rebel cruiser *Canarias* and her sister ships, the Basques equipped a fleet of fishing trawlers with modest armament and communications, staffed them with civilian crews made up principally of fishermen from the Basque seaports, and sent them out to do battle with forces incomparably larger, better equipped and staffed with German-trained crews.

On the morning of March 5, the *Galdames* and her four escorts emerged from the misty Bay of Biscay to discover the *Canarias* in the act of seizing a neutral merchant vessel en route to Bilbao. The Basques and the *Canarias* promptly made for each other's prizes. While the *Canarias* forced the captain of the *Galdames* to run up the white flag, the Basque trawler *Guipuzkoa* took the merchant vessel under tow and steamed for Bilbao. Left behind to engage the *Canarias* were the *Nabara* and the *Bizkaya* (the hopelessly outclassed *Donostia* had broken off the fight early).

The battle raged through most of the day. Against the most modern cruiser in the Spanish navy were deployed two tiny fishing boats, each armed with two four-inch guns. By three in the afternoon, the *Guipuzkoa,* with fire threatening the munitions locker, withdrew to Bilbao. The *Nabara* continued the battle until seven in the evening, when the ship's guns ran out of ammunition, the engines were destroyed, and the broken hull was slipping rapidly into the sea. Of the original crew of fifty-two aboard the *Nabara,* only fourteen were still alive by this time, all of these wounded, many seriously. Laboriously, the fourteen lowered the ship's life boat into the water and tried to reach the shore. As the *Canarias'* boat moved to intercept, the *Nabara* crew began to throw hand grenades at them, but to no avail. The fourteen were imprisoned, but spared the firing squad as a tribute to their heroism. The other thirty-eight had gone down in the Bay of Biscay.

As news of the *Nabara*'s heroic struggle against impossible odds reached the outside world through George Steer's book, *The Tree of Gernika,*[2] British poet C. Day-Lewis was moved to write his poem "The *Nabara,*" in tribute to the Basques, and their commitment to the struggle for freedom.[3] The poem begins with these lines:

Freedom is more than a word . . .
. . . She is mortal, we know, and made
In the image of simple men who have no taste for carnage
But sooner kill and are killed than see that image betrayed.

The struggles of the tiny *Nabara* on that cold March day reflect in microcosm the refusal of the Basques to give in to the overwhelming pressures of military force, coercion and numbers. Today, more than forty years after the *Nabara*'s battle, after Guernica, and after Franco, Basque nationalism survives, a tribute to man's ability to keep his spirit free even in the midst of dictatorship. This book is about the Basque struggle for freedom. As we shall soon see, that struggle took two forms. The simpler, more dramatic struggle pitted Basque against Spaniard, and political liberty was the goal. At the same time, the Basques carried on an equally arduous if less romantic struggle to define for themselves what it means to be a Basque in an age when primitive ethnic nationalisms like theirs are threatened with extinction by modern industrial life. In a way, the crew of the *Nabara* faced the easier of the two foes.

PART ONE

Basque Nationalism before 1939

Chapter One

THE BASQUES: AN INTRODUCTION

As the Pyrenees Mountains descend westward into the Bay of Biscay, they intersect the rugged Cantabrian Range, which runs several hundred kilometers west along the north coast of the Iberian Peninsula. Within the range, mountain peaks soar to more than 2,400 meters, then plunge sharply into the Bay of Biscay, leaving scant littoral for the region's inhabitants.[1] The brisk, cold winds from off the sea bring abundant rains to the region, making it one of Spain's lushest agricultural areas, although a difficult one to exploit because of the hilliness of the terrain.[2] To the south of the mountains, the terrain levels off quickly, and rugged peaks give way to gently rolling hills and plains. Beyond these plains lies the Ebro River, flowing roughly south and east toward Spain's Mediterranean coast.[3] Within these natural boundaries — the Pyrenees Mountains, the Bay of Biscay, and the Ebro River — live the Basques, a people whose resistance against cultural absorption has made them prototypical of ethnic nationalism in Western Europe (see Map 1).

The Basque People

The Basque provinces of France and Spain occupy about 20,600 square kilometers, about the size of the American state of New Jersey.[4] As of 1970, some two and a half million people made their home in this region. It would be misleading and inaccurate, however, to refer to these people as "the Basques" without pointing out various ways in which they are differentiated into a number of smaller sub-groups. One of the central themes of this book has to do with the struggle of Basques to determine for themselves which of the social fault lines within their society will be fundamental and lasting, and

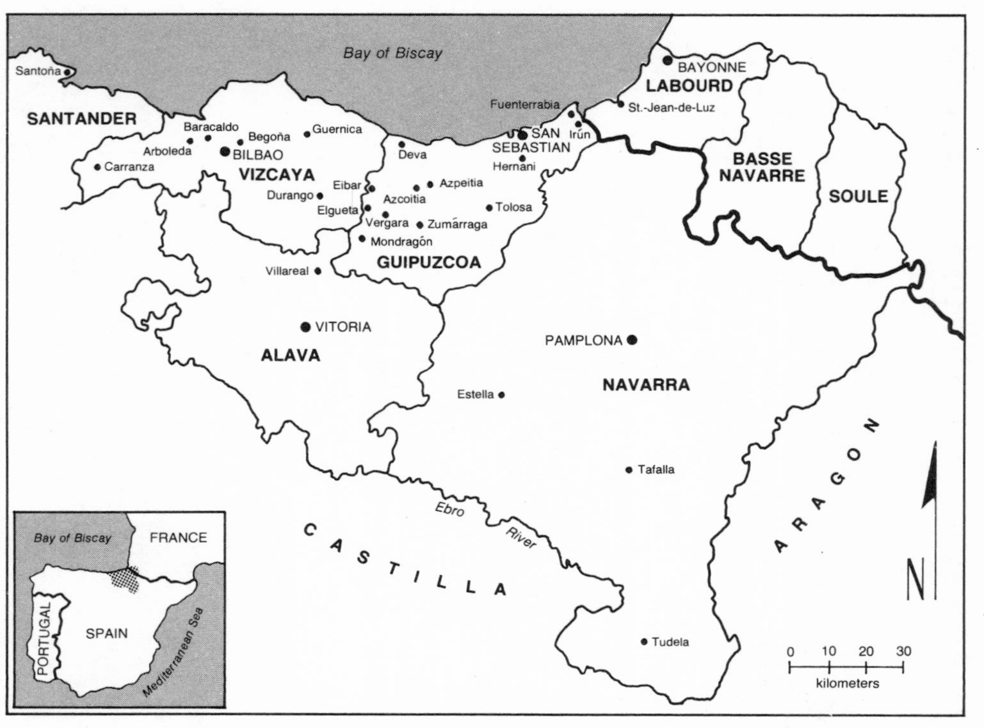

Map 1. The Basque Region.

which are nothing more than superficial overlays that will disappear with time. The fact that the French and Spanish governments and peoples are far from being disinterested observers, and have their own ideas of the correct solution to their respective versions of "the Basque problem," makes the struggle that much more intense and complicated, and the stakes that much higher.

The most visible dividing line among the Basques is the international boundary that separates the three French provinces of Labourd, Basse Navarre and Soule from the four Spanish provinces: Alava, Guipúzcoa, Navarra and Vizcaya. The Spanish provinces make up about 85 percent of the entire Basque region; Navarra by itself accounts for slightly more than half of the territory. To the north of the line that follows generally the crest of the Pyrenees to the mouth of the Bidasoa River live about 200,000 French Basques. On the Spanish side of the frontier live somewhat more than 2.3 million people, or more than 90 percent of the total Basque population. To many Basques, the line, established in 1512 and generally accepted as authoritative by France and Spain ever since, is nevertheless an artificial boundary, no less artificial for all of its durability. The clandestine movement of people and goods across the frontier is regarded as normal commerce by local residents; and villages in the proximity of the border have close ties with their neighbors on the other side.[5] Basque nationalists perceive the seven provinces as forming one integral ethno-nation, referring to the French provinces as "Euzkadi Norte," and the Spanish provinces as "Euzkadi Sur." Nevertheless, it can not be denied that the international boundary has played an important role in the development of a modern Basque consciousness. Negatively, the boundary has caused the two fragments of the Basque collectivity to learn a different second language, so that communication among Basques across the boundary became more complicated and awkward as use of the Basque language declined. On the positive side, however, the international frontier has made it possible for the Basque Resistance to survive "in exile" without actually moving out of their homeland, and by remaining within striking distance of Spanish targets.

For the sake of completeness, this account will touch on the French Basques from time to time. The central focus, however, must remain the Basques on the Spanish side of the boundary; and here, we find significant sources of division that are just as solid and just as enduring as the international boundary, even if they are less visible.

Coastline, mountains and plains have all played their part in shaping various aspects of the Basque culture. To the north of the mountains, topography and climate conspired to direct the people outward toward the sea, rather than south to the peninsula's central plateau. The ocean beckoned; and the sturdy oak trees that grew abundantly throughout the mountains provided the timber for seagoing vessels before the age of iron-sided ships. A maritime culture, adventurous and daring, was the consequence. The mountains served to shelter these hardy folk from alien others, from those who would invade their land and submit them to foreign rule. More than once would these mountains slow, then stop, the advance of strangers bent on conquest. In contrast, the southern plains fostered the growth of a cattle and farming economy and culture, one that had little interest in dealing with the outside world. To this day, these differences persist and sharply intrude into the political calculations and cultural aspirations of both Basques and Spaniards.

The 1970 census of the Spanish population shows about two and one third million persons residing in the Basque provinces. Only about one and a half million of these were born in the province in which they resided. In other words, only about 65 out of every hundred persons living in the Basque provinces were living in the province of their birth. The other 35 had migrated from another Spanish province. These figures are not uniform across the region. In Alava, Guipúzcoa and Vizcaya, where in-migration has been going on at a higher rate for a longer time, the respective percentages of indigenous populations are 58.9, 65.2 and 60.6. In Navarra, in-migration has been neither so large nor so early, so the percentage of natives there is somewhat higher: 81.6. In any event, when one refers to the populations of the Basque provinces, he must take care to specify whether or not the reference is to the ethnic Basque or non-Basque, of whom there are many, and whose number is increasing.[6]

One of the central characteristics defining Basque ethnicity is language. Genetically transmitted characteristics that set Basques apart, such as blood type or Rh negative factor incidence, are too subtle and diffuse to be used as a device for separating Basques from non-Basques in real-world political and social settings.[7] Language must serve as the most overt distinguishing feature of Basque ethnicity. However, because of a set of intricate political and social pressures that have interplayed over the past several generations, and which will be discussed in detail in Chapter 6, the use of the Basque language, Euskera, has been declining. While there are no exact figures on the extent of Euskera usage today, reliable estimates indicate varying levels of mastery of the language by between 450,000 and 600,000 in the four Spanish provinces. These data would represent between 30 and 40 percent of the Spanish ethnic Basque population; the remainder are incapable of using Euskera as a functioning medium of communication beyond understanding simple phrases or sentences. Euskera usage varies considerably across the four provinces. Yrizar estimates that usage in Guipúzcoa has extended to more than 43 percent of the population; in Vizcaya, the figure is about 13 percent. In the two interior provinces, Alava and Navarra, the figures decline markedly to less than one percent and eight percent, respectively.[8]

Moving beyond language, however, anthropologist William Douglass has observed that Basques themselves perceive considerable differences between and among the characters and personalities of Basques from various districts and provinces. To cite Douglass: Vizcayans are seen by other Basques as "extroverted and haughty;" Navarrese are described as "introverted and distrustful;" persons from Alava are "aloof and severe;" peasants from the interior of Vizcaya think the fishermen from the coast are "loud, pretentious busybodies," while the fishermen return the favor by viewing the peasants as "sullen, shrewd, and tight-lipped;" persons from northern Navarra see southern Navarrese as "violent and hot blooded;" the urban Basque sees the rural Basque as "rustic and backward," while the farmer sees the city dweller as "shiftless and untrustworthy."[9]

Much of this book however, focuses on social and economic criteria for defining the "we" and the "they" of a Basque world view. But we ought not leave this overview of the Basque provinces without some brief comment on differential socio-economic developments, especially as they have traditionally set apart the more industrial, urbanized and liberal coastal areas of Bilbao and San Sebastián from the more rural, agrarian and conservative interior provinces of Alava and Navarra.

In 1973, according to the survey conducted by Amando de Miguel, the economically active population of the four Basque provinces consisted of ten percent employed in agriculture, 13 percent as unskilled labor, 38 percent in skilled labor and service jobs, six percent as craftsmen, 28 percent as mid-range administrative and technical personnel, and six percent as professional or executive level managers.[10] Within the region, however, industrial development has proceeded at drastically different paces, and has taken off from fundamentally different bases. The coastal provinces of Vizcaya and Guipúzcoa were centers of commerce, trade and manufacturing as early as the sixteenth century;[11] and industrialization, led by iron, steel and shipbuilding, was well established in the Bilbao and San Sebastián areas by the last two decades of the nineteenth century. In Alava and Navarra, by contrast, the economies remained predominantly agrarian until after the Spanish Civil War. In recent years, the Vitoria and Pamplona areas have been the scene of rapidly growing industry, made possible by the influx of migrant labor from other parts of Spain.

The percent of the economically active population employed in agriculture is usually taken as one of the key benchmarks of the industrialization of a particular society. Self-sustaining industrial growth is usually marked by a decline in the agrarian sector to below one quarter of the total active population. In 1950, the percent of the active population in agriculture was already below 25 percent in Vizcaya and Guipúzcoa (19.4 and 20.5 percent, respectively), but nearer one half in Alava and Navarra (42.2 and 54.8 percent, respectively). By 1970, dramatic industrial growth throughout the region had caused these percentages to decline even further: 5.1 percent in Vizcaya; 6.9 in Guipúzcoa; 10.6 in Alava; and 26.2 in Navarra. Of the four provinces, only Navarra still was significantly agrarian; and the trend was clearly toward the industrialization of that region as well.[12] While the industrial labor force was growing at a modest rate of three to four percent annually in Vizcaya and Guipúzcoa during the twenty years after 1950, in Alava the increase was more on the order of ten percent per year, and in Navarra the increase was closer to six percent annually.

Along with the rise in the industrial labor force has come increased urbanization throughout the four provinces. Vizcaya and Guipúzcoa are among the most densely populated provinces in Spain. In the thirty years after 1940, Guipúzcoa has grown in population density from 166 persons per km² to 316 persons per km², an increase of about three percent per year; in Vizcaya, the increase has been from 232 to 471, or more than three percent per year. Since 1950 Alava has begun to manifest somewhat the same rate of urbanization: from 39 persons to 67 persons per km², an annual increase of about three percent. In Navarra, the increase did not begin to be noticeable until about 1960, but since that time the density of that province has increased at the rate of 1.8 percent annually, and it appears to be rising.[13]

All of these developments have given rise to a socioeconomic class structure that has come to have crucial importance for the direction of politics in the Basque provinces. With due allowance for the complexities of classification, as well as for the ever present differences across the provinces, it seems that the Basque provinces are characterized by a class structure composed roughly of ten percent small farmers, peasants or farm laborers; 15 percent small shopkeepers, artisans, etc.; 25 percent middle class (professionals, intellectuals, administrators, etc.); and 50 percent industrial labor (both skilled and unskilled).[14] We shall encounter repeatedly throughout this book instances in which social class structure interplays with language and ethnicity to shape and turn the political allegiances of particular individuals. To enter into detail now would be premature. It is enough now to observe that this interplay has done much to affect the successes and failures of the Basque nationalist movement, not only during the pre-Civil War period, but afterward, when the movement went into exile and underground. In the brief period since Franco's death, it is apparent that the same issues are still around to bedevil the Basque elites who are attempting to shape an ethnic awareness out of a mass population that shares only a portion of that elite's convictions, attitudes and — most important — economic interests.

The Origins of the Basques: From Prehistoric Times to 1512

Visitors to the caves of Santimamiñe, a short distance from the historic Basque city of Guernica, in the province of Vizcaya, climb some 500 meters to the cave entrance, and descend to find the remnants of a civilization at least 20,000 years old.[15] Although the exact origins of the Basque race remain obscure, the drawings discovered in these and other nearby caves suggest that the Basques may be directly linked to one of Europe's truly ancient cultures.[16] Some authorities have argued that the present-day Basques are the direct descendants of these ancient cave painters; others have asserted that the Basques moved into the area relatively recently (between 5,000 and 3,000 B.C.), absorbing the original tribes in the process. Even this latter interpretation would place the Basques in their present homeland sometime before the arrival of Indo-European speaking tribes in western Europe.[17]

There is little consensus about the origin of the name "Basque." García Venero asserts that it is of pre-Celtic origin, and comes from the word *bascunes,* which means "those from the heights," "the mountain people," or "the haughty."[18] Rodney Gallop tells us that Roman historians before the birth of Christ were writing about a tribe living in or near what is now the Basque country, and which spoke a language that their neighbors could not understand. This tribe was called by various names, including Vascones, and was first mentioned by Livy in his description of the Sertorian War (77-74 B.C.). However, Gallop continues, since the Vascones could have been either the Basques or the Gascons, it is impossible to locate the Basques at this particular place and time in history with any degree of certainty.[19]

Sometime between the years 1000 and 500 B.C., the original inhabitants of the western Pyrenees were visited by the Celts, cousins of the people who were at about the same time colonizing parts of the British Isles. These primitive contacts were the first chapter in the 2,000-year-long story of the Basque people and of their struggle to keep their culture alive in the face of almost constant challenge from beyond their borders. Many Celts remained in the Basque region; many others passed through the area en route to less resistant peoples to the south and west. Although they had an impact on Basque civilization, they could never call the region theirs in any meaningful sense. Other pre-Roman waves of visitors to the Iberian Peninsula, such as the Phoenicians, Greeks and Carthaginians, never even touched the remote Basque region.

About two hundred years before the birth of Christ, the first legions of Rome entered the Iberian Peninsula to engage in combat the declining Carthaginians. Roman conquest of the eastern, coastal areas of the peninsula came easily; domination of the mountainous regions to the north was rather more difficult and required more time. Early Roman reports spoke of fierce resistance from tribes in the north, but these were most probably the Cantabrians to the west, and not the Basques. Roman domination of the Basque region was never complete, not only because of the Basques' resistance to foreign rule, but also because the Basques' land was uninviting to outsiders and offered little incentive for conquest. Basque revolts, while irregular, occurred frequently enough to remind Rome that its dominion over the region was a shaky one indeed.

The impact of Roman colonization, while indirect, had important linguistic and social ramifications. The Basque language absorbed a considerable number of new words from Latin, especially in areas with commercial or agricultural application, such as farming implements. Young Basque men were recruited for Rome's military legions; and their return often brought new information about the outside world. Romans built roads through the area to facilitate administrative control and mining operations; but the practical result was to break down local barriers to communication. Many Basques lived in population clusters that today we might call reservations, and thus huddled together they sought to defend their linguistic distinctiveness in the face of foreign influence.[20] In any event, during the third century of the Christian era, Roman control over the Basques began to weaken; and by the middle of the fourth century, the Romans' fortifications and military installations were under assault and crumbling.

Early in the fifth century, Roman domination of the peninsula was shattered by the invasion of several Germanic tribes, last of which were the Visigoths. From about 406 until 467, the Visigoths swept over the remnants of the Roman Empire on the peninsula, which they would rule for some 250 years. As the Romans withdrew from the Basque country, the peasants erupted in what was probably the region's first socio-cultural revolution.[21] Under Roman control, local land owners had become extremely powerful because the Imperial regime depended on them to collect taxes, regulate commerce and recruit troops for the Legion.[22] These local strong men had seized increasing power, acquired major landed estates, and reduced their workers to a state approaching serfdom. With the destruction of the Roman Empire, and its support for this oppressive land ownership system, the peasants seized the land and redistributed it among themselves. The rebellion went further. Place names were changed to reduce Roman influence, and to reassert native identification.

Visigoth control over the Basques was always incomplete and tentative, even though the city of Pamplona was occupied by the Visigoths for a time. In an attempt to assert Visigoth dominance, their monarch Leovgild (568-586) constructed a fortified outpost which later became the city of Vitoria, capital of the Basque province of Alava.[23] Throughout the fifth century, Basque military forces conducted a series of raids and skirmishes against the Gothic armies and fortifications. While the Goths were usually the victors in these battles, they were unable to subdue the Basques, partly because of the rise in Basque militancy and internal unity, and partly because of the intense disarray within the ranks of the Goths. In addition, the Goths themselves had to contend with pressure from the

Franks, who occupied the region north of the Pyrenees, and, later, from the Moslems who had entered the peninsula in the eighth century. In the year 711, the Visigoth King Roderic found himself in Navarra laying seige to the rebel city of Pamplona when word reached him of the Moslem invasion of Gibraltar. Breaking off his struggle with the Basques, the Visigoth leader traveled south to meet the invaders from North Africa, thus ending Gothic pressure on the Basques from the south.

The Goths were actually only one of the threats to the Basques during this period. Like the Goths to the south, the Franks laid claim to that portion of the Roman Empire north of the Pyrenees, and thus felt that they had a right to sovereignty over the Basque region as well. By the middle of the sixth century, the Basques were caught between these two powerful and antagonistic forces. Obviously outclassed militarily, they survived during this period by playing one power against another, and by eschewing permanent alliances with both. Since the mountainous Basque heartland was a formidable obstacle to both Frank and Gothic forces, the Basques were able to defend their stronghold rather effectively. Indeed, during this period Basques began to descend to the plains and grazing lands on either side of the Pyrenees. It was at about this time that they began to establish a more or less permanent presence on the northern side of the Pyrenees. According to Douglass and Bilbao, the immediate motivation for their expansion was probably the desire to secure grazing space for their livestock, as their traditional grazing areas in southern Navarra were at that time in the hands of the Goths.[24] Counter-pressure from the Franks was usually sufficient to dislodge the Basques from their new lands; but the fighting was intermittent rather than constant. The Franks, like the Goths, saw little incentive for launching a large-scale invasion of the Basque region. The Franks seldom attacked the Basques, and only when the latter posed a threat to their southern flanks.

In the year 602, the Franks determined to restore their control over the region between the Loire and the Pyrenees. After subduing the Basques militarily, the Franks imposed on them a new political entity, the Dukedom of Vasconia, and installed as the ruler of this area a Gallo-Roman named Genialis. It is not clear how far the Dukedom of Vasconia extended south of the Pyrenees. The fact that the present-day provinces of Alava, Guipúzcoa and Vizcaya are referred to as the *Provincias Vascongadas* suggests that these regions may have been incorporated within the dukedom. On the other hand, given the traditional difficulty of controlling the Basques, it seems likely that the authority of the duke declined proportionately to the distance south from the Pyrenees. In any case, the establishment of the Dukedom of Vasconia marked a crucial watershed in Basque political development. From the seventh century on, Basques to the north of the Pyrenees were gradually incorporated into a broader political and economic world through the links between the Frankish kings and the successive rulers of Vasconia. In subsequent centuries, the ruling line of Vasconia would provide continuity in the relations between northern Basques and wider circles beyond their realm. To the south, however, the Goths remained unable either to conquer the Basques, or to absorb them into their society through some sort of similar arrangement. During the seventh century, Basques to the south of the Pyrenees lived in an almost constant state of warfare with the Goths. With the arrival in Iberia of the Arabs, the surviving Gothic leaders retreated to Asturias and Cantabria, from where they sought to organize a resistance.

Moslem domination of the Iberian Peninsula came swiftly, and was long lasting (the last of the Moslems were expelled in 1492, nearly eight hundred years after their arrival); but it was not complete. Several times during the eighth century, first in 718, and later in 732, Moslem forces entered Pamplona en route to the land of the Franks across the Pyrenees; yet, by the latter third of the eighth century, Pamplona had been returned to Navarrese control. Between 718 and 722, and again between 792 and 816, the Arabs assaulted the still resisting Kingdom of Asturias to the west of the Basque region, where the descendants of the Visigoths had gathered. Thus, the reconquest of the Iberian Peninsula for Christianity had its origins in two separate areas: the Kingdom of Asturias under King Pelayo, and the emerging Kingdom of Navarra.

As Rafael Altamira points out, the expulsion of the Moslems from the northern regions of Iberia was only a prelude to a lengthy struggle over possession of the Basque region, a struggle that led eventually to the integration of the various Basque provinces into a larger political unit by 1512.[25] As the Asturians, to the west, and the Navarrese, to the east, expanded southward to drive out the Arabs, they began to covet the relatively undeveloped lands that lay between them: Guipúzcoa, Vizcaya and Alava. (The present-day names of the three Basque provinces began to appear in documents about the eighth or ninth centuries.)

The emergence of the independent principality of Pamplona early in the ninth century must rank as one of the most important developments in pre-modern Basque political history. As Payne tells us, this was the first organized state in Basque history.[26] The Kingdom of Navarra was proclaimed by its king, Sancho Garces, in 905; and, for the next two centuries, Navarra played a key role in the politics of the Iberian Peninsula. The military prowess of the Navarrese had been demonstrated by the rout of the army of the Frankish King Charlemagne in the famous battle of Roncesvalles in 778. The diplomatic success of the kingdom was also great. Caught between the Christian and Arab worlds, and occupying a strategic location along one of the major communication routes between these two world religions, Navarra was able to play off one force against another. Through a judicious combination of alliances and dynastic marriages, the Navarrese rulers steadily increased their territory. At the height of Navarrese power (at the beginning of the eleventh century), the kingdom included nearly all of the present-day Basque country, the Dukedom of Vasconia as far north as Bordeaux, all of the Pyrenees including most of Cataluña, and all of Castilla la Vieja. Moreover, for perhaps the first time a large body of Basques were governed by a native regime that was not only effective but responsive to local economic and political needs. Local governing bodies arose. It is at about this time that self-governing representative assemblies, called *biltzar,* began to take control over the affairs of local Basque communities, well before the establishment of the famous *fueros* that guaranteed local autonomy over local matters. A mercantile class began to form, and trade began to expand. It is little wonder that today many Basques assert that Navarra was the first organized political expression of Basque ethnicity.[27]

The decline of Navarrese power began with the death in 1035 of their ruler Sancho El Mayor. The kingdom was divided among the sons of the deceased king; and the process of dynastic fragmentation was set in motion. The territory of Navarra was separated into three jurisdictions, each with its own ruling elite. To the east, the Kingdom of Aragón and to the west, Castilla proved to be vigorous heirs to the power of Navarra. They expanded southward in the reconquest of the peninsula from the Arabs, while Navarra stagnated, and soon became a landlocked backwater. As a consequence, the three western Basque provinces, Alava, Guipúzcoa and Vizcaya, eventually came under control of Castilla. In 1076, following the assassination of the Navarrese king Sancho de Penalen, there ensued a breakdown of civil order which prompted certain political factions to invite the kings of Aragón and Castilla to intervene in Navarrese politics. The result was the eventual absorption of much of the former Navarrese territory into the spheres of influence of the two adjacent kingdoms.

The process of separation of Navarra from the western Basque provinces began in 1200, when the King of Castilla, Alfonso VIII, captured the city of Vitoria and thereby conquered the province of Alava. Guipúzcoa was brought into the kingdom at the same time by means of a pact whereby the Guipuzcoans accepted the protection of Castilla. Significantly, the annexation of both of these provinces by Castilla was conditioned on the respect for, and guarantee of, their local autonomy and the continued effectiveness of local laws. In 1076, the Lopez de Haro family line brought Vizcaya into association with the crown of Castilla. For three centuries, Vizcaya was loosely connected with Castilla through the personal and family ties represented by this lineage. In 1379, the *señorío* (seigneury) of Vizcaya was joined by marriage to the Kingdom of Castilla; and Vizcaya, while remaining independent of Castilla, now recognized the personal leadership of the Crown within the limits of its own local autonomy and custom. The process was completed in 1512, when Ferdinand, King of Aragón, conquered all of Navarra, including that portion to the north of the Pyrenees, then known as the sixth merindad of the Kingdom of Navarra, now known as the French province of Basse Navarre. It was originally Ferdinand's intention to retain control over the French portion of Navarra; but his successor, Charles V, found the region too remote to be easily defended, and withdrew his forces south of the Pyrenees in 1530, leaving the northern Navarrese to their own devices, and to the mercy of the French.[29]

These developments brought to a close the period of Navarrese ascendency over the Basque region. The significance of these changes was apparent in both the ethnic and economic dimensions of Basque life. The delimitation of the international boundary between France and Spain hardened the separation between northern and southern Basques and Navarrese that had begun with the decline of the Roman Empire. The changes also greatly affected Basque economic development. The coastal provinces of Vizcaya and Guipúzcoa now found themselves to be central outlets for the expanding trade between Castilla and the outside world, especially that with the Western Hemisphere. Navarra, cut off from these outlets to the sea, suffered economic decline; Vizcaya, Alava and Guipúzcoa, astride the trade routes, prospered. The expansion of Castilla also stimulated an increase in the merchant marine of the coastal provinces, and brought new impetus to the iron industry of Vizcaya. With Castillian expansion came increased demand for sailing vessels and experienced crews, as well as for the iron weapons needed to conquer the people of the New World, and the iron farm implements needed to work its lands. Basques had already established themselves as expert sailors through their achievements as whalers; and this skill lent itself to the expansion of Spain's naval power and maritime prosperity during the fifteenth and sixteenth centuries. Royal policies during this period sought to stimulate both the maritime and ironsmith sectors of the Basque economy, with major repercussions for Basque society, at least in the three western provinces. Navarra shared little in this general economic change, and remained primarily a precapitalistic agrarian region with little industry and little contact with the outside world.[30]

Foral Laws and Regionalism: From 1200 to 1800

From the beginning of the thirteenth century to the end of the eighteenth, the predominant tension in all of Spain was that between unification and regional separatism. Of this general problem, the Basque case was but one example; the monarchy that emerged from the union of the royal families of Castilla and Aragón faced incipient resistance from Galicia, Asturias and Navarra, to their north, as well as Valencia, Granada and Sevilla, to their south (to say nothing of their possessions in the New World). Regionalism was linguistic and cultural, as well as political; psychological, as well as economic. The peninsula's various regions each possessed their own special laws, their own political institutions, their own folk customs (art, music, dress), and, important in the Basque case (and others), their own language. Moreover, the peoples of the diverse regions neither felt themselves to be part of a larger domain, nor were they inclined to contribute resources — money, or troops — to defend other constituent segments of the Kingdom of Castilla.[31]

In the face of such powerful centrifugal forces, only one institution sufficed to hold together the nascent state: the ancient *fueros*, or foral laws. The *fueros* dated from as early as the seventh century, and stemmed from the Visigothic effort to codify and systematize the legal rights of free Christian males. At about the same time, representative assemblies of freemen began to meet more or less regularly in remote villages in the Cantabrian Mountains; from their deliberations emerged a tradition of self-government, and a respect for local authority, matched by suspicion of rule from abroad. For several hundred years, until about the tenth century, the *fuero* concept developed along these two separate lines: the one descending from grants of local authority made from above, the other ascending from the healthy exercise of municipal democracy. As the *fueros* changed from an oral tradition to a written code, binding both center and periphery, sometime between the eleventh and the thirteenth centuries, the separate strains merged to yield Spain's particular approach to reconciling centralism and separatism. As Elena de la Souchere writes: "These codes . . . amounted to a synthesis between the written Romano-Germanic law (*fuero juzgo*) which the sovereigns tried to impose, and the popular *fueros* which they were obliged to recognize."[32]

Beginning about the middle of the twelfth century, the codification of the *fueros* spread systematically throughout the Basque provinces. In the province of Guipúzcoa, the earliest *fuero* was granted to the city of San Sebastián in 1150, not by the King of Castilla, but by the King of Navarra, under whose control the province remained at that time.[33] Upon being integrated into the Kingdom of Castilla, in 1200, the province was subjected to expanding protection of *fueros* granted by the Castillian monarch to a growing list of municipalities. Similarly, the first *fuero* in Vizcaya was granted in 1150 to the town of Durango, again by the King of Navarra. The process had been essentially completed by the end of the fourteenth century, when the entire province was integrated formally into the Kingdom of Castilla.[34] The same was true for Alava.

Inasmuch as foral law tried to specify what was a very complex relationship between central and regional authority, and between the rights of the state and those of the citizen, the codes were often tangled and confused. The encrustations of centuries of written tradition around additional centuries of oral agreements further complicated these relationships. Each municipal government cherished its own peculiar *fuero* so that one would have to describe literally hundreds of individual *fueros* for the complete picture to emerge.

With due respect for such complexity, however, foral law can be described as containing the following elements. First, several institutionalized structures emerged within which the growth and development of the *fueros* would take place. The first of these was the local governing council, composed of the elected representatives of free males in the community. These councils, named variously *Cortes, Juntas* or *Hermandades,* were virtually sovereign within their provinces. They had the sole power to tax property within the province, they had sole authority to mobilize soldiers from the province, and they reserved the right to review the central government's laws as they affected the province before those laws could go into effect. This last provision, called the *pase foral,* amounted to a veto over the king's edicts; indeed, it was not unknown for local governments to bring down a monarch for violating the *fueros*. In addition, citizens had recourse to the governing councils to right wrongs done to them by the central government; in the Basque country, a man condemned to death by the king could have his case reviewed, and his life spared, by local authorities. These councils possessed unusually wide permission to criticize the monarch, especially when the latter's behavior transgressed the *fueros*. Finally, an ascending monarch had first to travel to the Vizcayan city of Guernica, and swear his obedience to the *fueros* beneath the famous oak tree of that city, before his sovereignty extended to Vizcaya province. The oak tree apparently was selected as the symbolic location for the ceremony because it was the meeting site for the assembly of locally elected representatives of the province. Inhabitants of other Basque provinces expected similar demonstrations of loyalty from the monarch.

In addition to the local governing council, the *fuero* was institutionalized through the person of a *corregidor,* the appointed representative of the king in each province of his realm. The *corregidor* functioned in all three political roles: as a judge in cases of conflict between regional and central authority, as an executive in administering regal mandates in the province, and as a legislator when he met with the councils to draft amendments to the legal codes. To be sure, provincial councils exercised significant control over these officials; the councils set his term of office at three years, and the council of Guipúzcoa even insisted that the appointee be a native of their province. Nevertheless, the *corregidor* was a constant reminder that the province was not sovereign, and that there did exist a higher authority, even if its limits were narrowly circumscribed.

Even in their limited, early form, the civil rights of both individual and province as guaranteed by most foral laws were substantial. As the rights developed through the Middle Ages, they anticipated by several hundred years those liberties for which American colonists would struggle in the American Revolution. No freeman, for example, could be subject to corporal punishment, or imprisonment without trial. One's home could not be violated by the state. Freedom of the accused on bond was permitted; and imprisonment for debt was prohibited. In some provinces, separation of powers (the cornerstone of American constitutional democracy) was practiced five centuries before James Madison wrote the principle into the United States Constitution. The *fueros* were used to guarantee that newly-freed former serfs be full members of the society, with all rights and privileges. At an institutional level, the *fueros* served primarily to isolate the provinces from central rule. Troops of the central regime, for instance, could not enter the provinces without permission of the local council; public offices in each province were reserved to citizens of the province; and each province kept the right to determine itself whether it would send troops to assist a neighboring province under attack.

Above all, foral democracy was a state of mind, a refusal of each local group to consider itself affected by happenings in other parts of the peninsula. Rafael Altamira has observed of this phenomenon:

> The different kingdoms united in the person of Charles I did not consider themselves by mere virtue of that fact to be fused and molded into a single political entity and a single nation. The only homogeneous group which seems to have felt an aspiration for such a Peninsular solidarity was Castile. . . . The rest, although recognizing one King over them all, were very far from feeling nationalistic or political aspirations in common with Castile nor with any other one realm.[35]

While foral law was a shaky solution to the tension between centralism and regionalism, it was at least a solution that prevented the shattering of the Spanish state during its difficult transition from a medieval to a modern political order. So long as Basques, Navarrese, Catalans, and so forth, were not required to think of themselves as Spanish, they were willing enough to pay limited homage to the Spanish Crown.

In the three-hundred-year period following 1512, however, a number of dramatic developments were to unfold that altered permanently the tenuous links between and among the several component regions of the Iberian Peninsula.

The first of these was the discovery of the New World and the consequent expansion of the Spanish Empire. The impact of this development on Basque social and economic structures can hardly be exaggerated. Spanish interests in the Western Hemisphere demanded high levels of commercial intercourse and a skilled and energetic mercantile class. Such a class arose readily in the coastal Basque provinces of Vizcaya and Guipúzcoa. For the first time, there was a Basque elite whose economic interests were identified with a strong and vigorous Spanish state. The thrust of Spanish Empire abroad brought increased demand for weapons and farm implements made of iron; and the ore deposits of Vizcaya began to assume the dominant position in the Basque economy that they have occupied to this day.

Out of all this economic ferment, a new economic class began to exercise influence in Basque politics. Their new wealth was based on the iron ore and related manufacturing of Vizcaya, and on the commercial skill of the maritime leaders, particularly in Guipúzcoa. Called *jauntxos* (Basque for "little lords"), these men were destined to alter fundamentally the ways in which Basques lived and worked.[36] With their new found wealth, the *jauntxos* began to expand their control over the farm land of the region, particularly in Navarra, and to force the peasants either to leave the land and move to the city (a process necessary for industrialization to proceed), or to work the land as tenants. The decline in large estates at about this same time combined with the shift in land ownership to produce instability among the peasant class. More serious, however, were the new economic elite's efforts to have transferred the customs duties collection stations from the Ebro River, where they had been located out of respect for regional autonomy, to the national ports, such as San Sebastián. In brief, the issue that was being raised had to do with the price of imported goods. As long as imported products paid no duty until they left the Basque provinces and crossed the Ebro

River, the peasants could buy at low prices, but the new commercial and industrial elite had little incentive to expand production. With the customs collection points moved out to the national boundaries, prices of imported goods within the Basque provinces would rise, and the protected Basque industry could develop. Of course, the peasants resisted this move since it was clearly against their interests. In 1717, the king declared the customs stations transferred to the boundaries, an act that generated a bloody uprising of Basque peasants known as the *matxinada*. The duty stations were withdrawn to the Ebro River as a result of this protest, and did not return permanently to the national boundaries until 1876. Nevertheless, the lines of economic interests were beginning to be drawn as the Basque region edged slowly toward industrialization, economic modernization, and the differentiation of class interests that these changes imply.

The second major development that shook the foundations of Spanish regionalism was the French Enlightenment. Followers of Voltaire began to appear in Spain, criticizing the Church and all institutions designed to suppress human happiness and economic production. As George Hills notes:

> All [Spanish Voltairists] agreed that a greater number of men should have the means to be happy in this world — more men should have wealth and a reserve of wealth in order to enjoy life. To that end they preached revolution, a revolution from above, maintaining that it was the duty of the king, his Ministers, and the enlightened to encourage all human activity calculated to produce more wealth, and to suppress all that did not.[37]

For Basques, the expansion of Spanish Empire, with its attendant demands for trade, commerce and industry, provided the material incentives for economic development; eighteenth century liberalism offered the philosophical justification for growth. French positivism meant more than economic growth; it meant as well science, learning, technology and urbanization. In 1766, the new Basque commercial and political elite formed the Basque Society of Friends of the Country, whose first self-proclaimed goal included these objectives: "To cultivate the inclination and the taste of the Basque nation toward science, letters and fine arts; to banish idleness, ignorance and their fatal consequences; and to tighten more the union of the three Basque provinces of Alava, Guipúzcoa and Vizcaya." It was, according to García Vernero, the first use ever of the term "Basque nation."[38] The most visible symbol of these trends was the founding of the Royal Seminary of Vergara in 1776 as the university extension of the Society of Friends.[39]

It would be premature to talk at this point of nationalism, either Basque or Spanish. Nevertheless, eighteenth century economic liberalism did argue for the suppression of all activity that did not produce more wealth, and regional autonomy was clearly in this category. As many other developing countries have discovered, one of the first steps toward economic modernization is the reduction of internal barriers to trade and the movement of goods and people. In the Spanish case, such a philosophy led inevitably to a stronger central government in Madrid, and to even greater tensions between this government and the historically autonomous regions. The eighteenth century witnessed the first steps in the long and arduous process of Spanish political and economic centralization. At the beginning of the century, in 1714, attempts to secede by Cataluña during the War of Spanish Succession were crushed ruthlessly by the Spanish Crown. And, at century's close, in the midst of still another war, that with France in 1793-95, the Basque province of Guipúzcoa sought to separate herself from Spain, with like results. In 1795, Spanish centralists urged the Prime Minister, Godoy, to take advantage of the end of the war to destroy the *fueros,* and to take complete control of the Basque economy. Godoy hesitated, not wishing to incur the wrath of the Basque bourgeoisie; but the hesitation was only temporary. Centralization would be attempted again in a few years.

French influence also spread through the Basque country by force of arms in the eighteenth century. From 1701, when the House of Bourbon ascended the throne of Spain, and started, thereby, the War of Spanish Succession, to 1814, when the last of the Napoleonic invaders were driven from the peninsula, Spain was in an almost constant state of war. On two occasions, in 1720 and in 1793, French forces occupied the Basque provinces, and sought to extend their rule across the Pyrenees.

In the latter instance, the French were aided materially by Basques from Guipúzcoa who steered the province into a "protectorate" relationship with the French Republic. At the Peace of Basle, in 1795, the French withdrew, leaving the Guipúzcoanos to the mercy of the Spanish, many of whom, as we noted, urged the severest of reprisals. As the French departed, however, they left behind the organizational machinery of a political underground, complete with clandestine operations, communications, and life style.

The Carlist Wars and the Loss of Autonomy: From 1800 to 1876

The nineteenth century saw a marked decline of the *fueros* as a protection of regional freedoms and privileges. In a formal and very vivid sense, the foral system came to an end in 1876 as a consequence of the Second Carlist War. More fundamentally, however, the erosion of the Basque provinces' regional autonomy stemmed from the significant social and economic changes that were just beginning to occur in Vizcaya and Guipúzcoa. Through the middle years of the century, there began to arise in the larger Basque cities economic and social groupings that saw little advantage in a continuation of Basque localism, and much to be gained by being part of a larger Spanish political and economic unit. By the time the foral system was destroyed by the Carlist Wars, these groups were in a position to take maximum advantage of the potential for industrial growth in the Basque region.

From 1808 to 1814, Basques fought alongside other constituent groups of the Spanish kingdom against the invading troops of Napoleon. The French First Consul, in an effort to consolidate his southern flank, had sought the abdication of Spain's King Ferdinand VII, in 1808, and his replacement by his brother, Joseph Bonaparte. Spain's War of Independence was the consequence, and it was to change totally the face of Spanish politics. Six years later, when Ferdinand returned to rule after Napoleon's defeat, he found not royalist Spain, but a new constitutional regime based on the liberal organic law of 1812 passed by the Cortes of Cadiz.

The passage of the Constitution of 1812 was the first phase

of the struggle between liberals and traditionalists that would enflame Spanish passions until the mid-twentieth century. During the war, liberals had taken advantage of the absence of Spain's ruling house to create a centralized, representative regime that would not permit organic groups which were not subject to its laws equally with all other groups. This belief took shape as an attack not only on the Church, and its tax-free lands, and on the universities, traditionally autonomous, but on the various regions which for centuries had enjoyed special privileges and status. It was in this way that the Constitution of 1812, and the liberal ideology which produced it, created the next threat to the freedom of the Basque provinces.[40]

The Basque provinces sent to the Cadiz deliberations delegates who proved to be unwilling to challenge the new constitution's incursions into the region's traditional rights. In the Basque cities of Bilbao and San Sebastián, a growing liberal sentiment actually welcomed the 1812 document as the final, logical extension of Basque insistence on individual liberties. The 1812 Constitution, they insisted, was merely the *fueros* of Vizcaya applied to the entire nation.[41]

Apparently Ferdinand VII agreed with this proposition, for at his earliest opportunity after his return to power, in 1814, he annulled the 1812 Constitution, and reestablished an absolutist monarchy. For the next nineteen years, until his death in 1833, Ferdinand set about to establish firmly the principle that he — as sovereign — could withdraw the foral privileges, just as he had the authority to grant them. And though his messages to the Basque envoys asserted his belief in foral protection for Basque liberties, his actions served slowly but steadily to reduce this protection to the constraints of Spanish nationlism, either absolutist or constitutional.

During this period, controversy over foral privileges usually focused on two questions. For centuries, the Kingdom of Castilla, and later the government of Spain, had placed their customs collection stations on the south side of the Ebro River, rather than at the points of entry into the nation. Goods traveling into the Basque ports of Bilbao, San Sebastián, Pasajes, or others, paid duties to the provincial governments; duties were paid to Spain only when the merchandise left the

Basque provinces. In 1815, a Royal Commission established to investigate smuggling recommended moving the customs houses out to the national boundaries and ports, a proposal which met with great hostility in Bilbao. In 1820, after the liberal revolution against Ferdinand, the Spanish moved the customs houses to the boundaries; but they were returned to the Ebro after the conservative counterrevolution of 1823.

The second major issue had to do with the responsibility of the Basques to contribute troops to Spain's defense. As late as 1806, the provincial government of Vizcaya informed Madrid that it was not bound to send soldiers beyond the town of Luyando, some thirty kilometers south of Bilbao. In 1818, however, and again in 1820, Ferdinand and the Cortes imposed on the Basques the requirement to supply as many troops to Spain's national defense as did other provinces, adjusted of course to reflect differences in population.

Ferdinand's position throughout these controversies set the tone for national government proclamations in later years: while the *fueros* may indeed have received royal confirmation in earlier times, they could only be maintained in a modern nation to the extent that their existence did not prejudice the general interests of the nation, its system of unity or of order, or the royal prerogatives of the sovereign authority. It would be difficult to imagine a more nationalistic, liberal pronouncement on political unity from a Spanish monarch of this epoch. Spain was not the only thing changed by the War of Independence; the returning King Ferdinand had become modernized as well.

Upon Ferdinand's death in 1833, the forces of traditionalism took concrete shape in support of his younger brother, Don Carlos, and in opposition to Ferdinand's infant daughter Isabella and his widow, the Regent María Cristina. The tension between liberal reformers and the defenders of tradition was about to break out into open warfare, the First Carlist War (1833-1840). The complex origins of the war were at least fourfold. There was, to begin with, controversy over royal lineage, coupled with a belief held by many that the female Isabella had not the right to ascend the Spanish throne. The special role played by the Catholic Church in Spanish politics likewise provoked considerable opposition. Economic factors were not unimportant as well, particularly in the Basque provinces, where liberals and conservatives were divided not only by ideology, but by interest and geography as well. Finally, there was a supreme struggle over the relative power of the central government and the provincial *juntas,* which took shape as a debate over the continuation of foral privilege.

With the outbreak of hostilities in 1833, the growing split in the Basque provinces between liberals and traditionalists finally emerged as a crucial dimension of the war. Carlists drew the largest part of their support from the rural areas and small towns of Navarra and Alava and the interior regions of Guipúzcoa and Vizcaya. For many of these peasants and small farmers, land ownership was the crucial issue. As the liberal economic elite of the coastal cities had grown in power, many of its members had acquired large tracts of land in Navarra and Alava. Aided by the government's policy of disentailing both Church properties and communal lands, these new landlords sought to bring agrarian capitalism to what was essentially a pre-capitalist society. To do this, they had to upset the traditional forms of land ownership and of social relationships in the two agrarian provinces. Thus, the issues of land ownership and Church prerogatives coincided. The small farmers and peasants of Navarra supported the Carlist cause as the best way for them to defend themselves against the modernizing alliance of the Basque coastal urban elite and the Spanish government.[42] The modernizing cities of San Sebastián, Vitoria and Bilbao, on the other hand, remained in the camp of Isabella, and supported the liberal solution to the war. These liberals, representative of the growing business, mercantile and intellectual classes of the Basque cities, accused the Carlists of using the latter's concern for the *fueros* as a disguise for their real intentions: namely, to establish an autocratic monarch who would repeal individual liberties and seek to take Spain back to the Middle Ages. The Carlists, in turn, accused the liberals of selling out to the Spanish for money, and a privileged place in Madrid's post-war government. When the war in the Basque provinces came to a close, with the Accord of Vergara, in 1839 (peace would not come to Cataluña until a year later), the Carlists were furious with their fellow Basques from the large cities for having betrayed their *fuerista* heritage. Some sixty or so years later, when Basque nationalism began to emerge, the recrimination and bitterness engendered by the Carlist Wars would return, and Navarra would shun participation in the nationalist movement. And a full century later, in 1936, militarists such as Generals Franco and Mola would discover some of their greatest support came from Navarra, while their strongest opposition was found in Vizcaya and Guipúzcoa.[43]

From the close of the First Carlist War, until the end of the century, the foral guarantees enjoyed by the Basques were steadily diminished by acts of successive Spanish governments, whether liberal or conservative, monarchical or republican. To many Basques, the entire process seemed much less obvious than it does to observers with the advantage of hindsight; but the ambiguity surrounding the loss of these guarantees appears to have been deliberately fostered by contradictory promises made by ensuing regimes in Madrid.

The reduction of the *fueros* to an historic curiosity began as early as 1837, when the progressive General Espartero pledged to the Basques that their ancient privileges would be guaranteed after the Carlist War. Five months after his pledge, the provincial foral councils were abolished by the new radical constitution. In October 1839, after Vergara, the Cortes passed a law which apparently guaranteed foral privileges, but which added the proviso that confirmation of the Basque and Navarra *fueros* was done "without prejudice to the constitutional unity of the Monarchy."[44] Exactly one year later, portions of the Basque areas rose in revolt against the progressive government of the now-Prime Minister Espartero, apparently with the objectives of securing the return of the Regent María Cristina to the throne, and of reestablishing the *fueros*. The revolt, called "La Octubrada," was quelled easily by Espartero, who took advantage of the disruption to withdraw completely all foral guarantees from the Basque provinces.

Even when power passed into the hands of more conservative governments, such as that of General Narvaez, in 1843, the *fueros* remained virtually nonexistent. A change in constitution, from the centralist document of 1837 to a more moderate organic law of 1845, likewise failed to rectify the situation. The customs houses remained along the national boundaries; and the Crown continued to press the provincial councils on the questions of taxes and troop contributions. Finally, in 1856, with the passage of a centralizing law on public education, Madrid sought to bring regional educational systems under national control for the first time. Municipal governments asked for continuation of their right to name teachers to local schools, arguing that teachers of Basque children must know how to speak the Basque language. The petition was rejected, and cultural autonomy began to slip away from the Basques, just as they were losing economic and political autonomy.

In the face of these challenges, the Basques began to develop tactics to resist further encroachment on their freedom. The long debate over resistance revealed several different opinions within the Basque community on how best to defend themselves from the Spaniards. A "compromise" line appeared as early as 1839, when Basque provincial governments met in Bilbao to devise a common front against Madrid. At this meeting, delegates accepted a uniform judicial system for the enforcement and application of laws, and a reduction of the foral mechanisms to purely administrative matters. Economic questions would be dealt with by means of a *concierto económico,* or economic pact between the provinces and the national government. This strategy was answered by the "rebellion" line of 1841, when Basques revolted to bring about a change in the Spanish government which they deemed to be favorable to their regional aspirations. This strategy was tested again from 1873 to 1876, when the Second Carlist War erupted. As in the first war, however, Basques were divided, with the more traditional Navarrese joining the Carlists, and the liberal strongholds of San Sebastián and Bilbao defending the central government.

About mid-century, however, a new "passive resistance" line began to appear. Basques who followed this line argued that rebellion would achieve nothing more than provoking Spanish leaders into elimination of all guarantees. Compromise, on the other hand, would end just as surely in the suppression of the *fueros*. The only path which lay open to them was that of passive resistance, or civil disobedience. Basque provincial foral councils continued to meet alongside the Madrid-appointed governing bodies, as a constant reminder of the need to respect provincial sensibilities. In 1859 and 1860, while Spain was engaged in a war in North Africa, the Basques moved so slowly in supplying troops and money to the war effort the war was over before their troops were introduced into combat. In 1876, following the Second Carlist War, the Basques finally lost all foral privileges, including those dealing with troop contributions and taxation. The provincial juntas met first to issue a public proclamation denouncing the step, and a second time in clandestine session where they agreed to resist passively any measure designed to put this law into effect.[45]

Despite the actions of the Cortes in eliminating the *fueros*, the economic privileges enjoyed by the Basques lingered on in the form of the *conciertos económicos*, the first of which was promulgated in 1878. According to these economic agreements between Madrid and the provinces, the provincial governments would be charged with the responsibility of determining the taxes which would be levied, and the way in which these taxes would be collected. Each province would then remit a certain sum to Madrid, depending on bilateral agreements negotiated between the two governments. The results were favorable, both politically and economically. In a political sense, the act of conciliation defused rising anti-Spanish sentiment in the Basque country, and the compromisers defeated the intransigents in the general elections of 1879. Economically, the effect was to lay the base for the spectacular industrial boom which was about to hit the major Basque cities. In Vizcaya, for example, industry taxes were slight; the costs of government were borne by regressive sales taxes. At the same time, the Spanish government assisted Basque industry and mining with protective tariffs.

As the century drew to a close, the Basque provinces seemed closely linked to Madrid both politically and administratively. Carlism had been defeated militarily; and the *fueros* had been beaten down into mere symbols of what they once were. Economically, the union seemed beneficial, at least to the rising bourgeois industrial class of Bilbao and the other burgeoning cities; and the new economic elite was inclined to regard traditional cultural heritages as anti-modern and therefore to be eschewed. An observer of the Basques in the period from 1875 to 1890 could hardly have expected the upsurge of separatist spirit which lay only a few years ahead.

Chapter Two

THE EMERGENCE OF BASQUE NATIONALISM: 1876-1936

The Bourbon Restoration, covering the monarchies of Alfonso XII and XIII, endured almost fifty years, from 1876 until the military dictatorship of Miguel Primo de Rivera, established in 1923. Politically, this was a period of stability, as the two monarchical parties — Liberals and Conservatives — alternated in power in an attempt to replicate the British parliamentary system. In other fields, however, Spain underwent major changes. The inability of the Restoration politicians to stay abreast of the important social, cultural, economic and psychological developments among their people eventually produced the downfall of the carefully balanced political order.

In the Basque provinces, the most significant changes were those that flowed from the spectacular industrialization of Bilbao and, later, San Sebastián and other major cities.[1] Fed by the rich deposits of low phosphorous iron ore in Vizcaya, and financed largely by foreign capital, the growth of heavy industry in and around Bilbao transformed the life of the Basques not only economically but socially and politically as well. Among these changes was the emergence of nationalism as a powerful force in Basque politics.

It is not always clear why complex political phenomena like ethnic nationalism wax and wane through historical periods. At least three sets of explanations have been advanced to explain why Basque nationalism became so significant between the end of the Carlist Wars and the beginning of the Second Spanish Republic.

Anglo-American scholars, and others who write in English,

are inclined to explain Basque nationalism as a response to the dislocating effects of the industrialization and modernization processes in Basque society in the late nineteenth century. In his book *Basque Nationalism*, Stanley Payne writes that Basque nationalist sentiment was "born of the intersecting of traditionalism and modernization, and of the need to adjust to and achieve the latter while preserving as much as possible of the former."[2] Rodney Gallop, who wrote in the 1930s, notes the following in his *A Book of the Basques:* "A more conscious pride of race has grown up among those [Basques] whom circumstances have compelled to face the disintegrating and denationalising influences of modern civilization."[3] After examining a number of alternative explanations for Basque nationalism and finding them all wanting in some way or other, Milton da Silva concludes a 1975 article by suggesting that political modernization did not erode ethno-nationalism in the Basque region, but rather sharpened and "modernized" it.[4] Similarly, a recent analysis of French Basque nationalism suggests that it is fundamentally a phenomenon associated with the modernized elite of the region, who have found in its doctrines a way to deal with the social and political changes in their communities.[5]

Basque nationalists, however, see their movement as emerging from other quite different sets of conditions depending upon whether or not they perceive Basque nationalism as primarily a class issue or an ethno-linguistic question.

Class Interests and Basque Nationalism[6]

With the destruction of the *fueros* in the Basque provinces after the Second Carlist War, in 1876, the way was opened for industrial capitalism to establish itself in Vizcaya and Guipúzcoa. After 1876, the customs duties collection stations were moved out from the Ebro River to the national boundaries, where they have remained ever since. This development, coupled with the advent of high protective tariffs in Spain, made it possible for formerly uncompetitive Basque heavy industry to prosper behind customs barriers. In 1891, taking their lead from Barcelona's mercantile class, the Bilbao steel interests joined the powerful protectionist National League of Producers. By 1906, Spain had the highest tariffs in all of Europe.[7]

Among other things, the *fuero* of Vizcaya prohibited the extraction and exportation of the province's natural resources. Blocked by this prohibition, the province's iron and steel industry had remained in a virtually pre-capitalist state, unable to export its principal raw material abroad. Spanish markets were simply too underdeveloped to offer much demand for Vizcayan iron ore. After 1876, with the foral law eliminated, British capital flooded into Vizcaya in order to exploit the province's ore deposits and to develop accompanying industries, especially ship building and railroads. In the 1860s, the total iron ore production in Vizcaya was at about the level of a quarter of a million metric tons annually. In 1876, this figure doubled to almost half a million tons; in 1877, production doubled again to more than a million tons; and by 1899, Vizcaya was producing nearly six and a half million tons of ore, more than 80 percent for British markets. Of the 180 million tons of iron ore imported by Great Britain between 1874 and 1914, 130 million came from the Iberian Peninsula, nearly all of which came from Vizcaya. It is not at all an exaggeration to observe that when industrial capitalism came to the Basque country, it came in the form of British investment.

The first article of the 1876 law abolishing the *fueros* contained the following passage: "The duties that the Constitution has imposed on all Spaniards to present themselves for military service when the law calls them, and to contribute in proportion to their abilities to the expenses of the State, will be extended, as the constitutional rights are extended, to the residents of the provinces of Alava, Vizcaya and Guipúzcoa, in the same way as to the rest of the nation."[8] Despite the explicit requirement that the Basque provinces must share equally in the financial support of the Spanish government, the provincial assemblies of the three provinces refused to participate in the levying or collection of Spanish taxes. The consequence was that the three assemblies were dismissed by Madrid, and replaced with representatives supposedly less intransigent on the taxation issue. Shortly after, on February 28, 1878, the first *concierto económico* was signed. This document, the result of negotiations between the Spanish government and the new provincial assemblies, called upon the provinces to collect taxes and to remit their receipts to Madrid. The taxes would be based on overall sums agreed to by both parties: the national government and the provincial assembly. The distribution of the tax burden by these economic agreements is revealing for what it tells us about the allocation of political power in those days. Without question, the most heavily taxed items were farm land and livestock, which bore between 66 and 69 percent of the total tax burden. Highly regressive sales taxes on such staple consumer items as flour and salt accounted for ten to 12 percent. In all, clearly regressive taxes accounted for 88 to 90 percent of the tax quotas; industry's share of the load ranged between five and seven percent. There was no income tax, or tax on wealth. In the case of Alava, the *conciertos económicos* were regularly renewed and are still in effect. The agreements of Vizcaya and Guipúzcoa were officially abolished on June 23, 1937, four days after the fall of Bilbao to Franco's troops. Although the 1937 decree has been abolished by the new Spanish Constitution, nothing has replaced the abolished *conciertos económicos,* so Vizcaya and Guipúzcoa remain under the same tax system as they were during the Franco years. During their period of maximum impact, however, from 1878 to the 1920s, the provincial economic accords did much to stimulate the growth of heavy industry, especially in Vizcaya and Guipúzcoa.

Industrialization brought with it major social changes which led to increasingly sharp differentiations in the Basque political scene. By the turn of the century, there were at least four discernible social and economic groupings at work in Basque politics. As the social and economic underpinnings became more complex, the political party structure reflected this change by splintering into at least eight tiny but highly competitive parties.[9]

The socio-economic group most resistant to change continued to be the traditionalists of Navarra and Alava provinces. Here, not only the small farmers but the peasants who worked the land rejected modernity, and avowed their allegiance to the ancient monarchy and to the Catholic Church. Carlism was the dominant political force here, and would continue to be for decades to come. Political leaders from the area wanted to return to the protection of the *fueros,* but they wanted to do it within the context of a traditional not a liberal Spain. They opposed the rise of the nationalist spirit in Bilbao as much as in Madrid, because the nation soon came to rival the Church for men's loyalties, and this they could not accept. As late as 1936, "A journey to Navarre," Hugh Thomas wrote, "was indeed still an expedition into the Middle Ages."[10]

The chief political opponents of the Carlists during the 19th century were the liberal, upper class bourgeoisie of the coastal cities. The liberalism of these men was not accidental; their introduction to political life had come in the First Carlist War when the Madrid government relied heavily on loans from the merchants of San Sebastián and Bilbao. Henceforth, the business classes of these cities would be tied tightly to the fortunes of the Spanish government.[11] These linkages were strengthened as the century wore on through central government investments in railroads and public works, and, as we saw earlier, through the protective tariff. While these merchants and industrialists built their political power on their ability to exploit the *fueros* issue among the lower classes, particularly as regards taxation and military service outside their community, these bourgeois gentlemen were not separatists, or even advocates of autonomy. They maintained representatives in Madrid to insure the favorable treatment of their interests; and they used the threat of incipient Carlist revolt as leverage against the Crown on more than one occasion. It was easy for the enemies of the mercantile class to ridicule these men; and their interest in preserving regional freedoms could easily be explained by their desire to keep the central government from intervening in the rapidly increasing labor disputes which were shaking the area. But they provided the entrepreneurial leadership and capital to stimulate the economic prosperity which has marked the urban zones of the Basque provinces since the 1870s.

The third political grouping was just beginning to emerge in shadowy outline by the time of the Bourbon Restoration; but as the industrial boom proceeded apace, it brought about the creation of a class of intellectuals, professionals, and lesser bourgeoisie who were to play a key role in the development of Basque nationalism. The economic basis of this grouping was more complex than that of either the farmers and peasants of Navarra or the industrialists of Bilbao. The industrial boom of Vizcaya and Guipúzcoa after 1876 tended to foster the growth of a financial and manufacturing elite which rapidly accumulated a large share of the region's industrial wealth. As a consequence, a number of the members of the bourgeois sector, the *jauntxos* from earlier days, fell into some degree of decline. Smaller firms were absorbed or driven out of business by the large industrial combines. Traditional Basque-owned companies found they could not compete with the giants of Bilbao, who had the assistance of large amounts of British capital. Thus, as industrial growth accelerated, the bourgeois class tended to split into two discernible groups: the smaller but more successful oligarchy, which was liberal and opposed to Basque localism; and the lesser bourgeoisie, who resented the intrusion to their disadvantage of both Spanish political control and British capital. The decline of this sector of Basque leadership was reflected in the shift of their sons from industry into the professions. These were the men who handled the increasingly complex administrative and informational network generated by industrialization. They were lawyers and doctors, journalists and teachers, artists, composers, and writers, the providers of services, such as transportation, communication, design, and planning. They were the "second generation" of the industrial boom, in both a biological and a metaphorical sense. The co-founders of the Basque Nationalist Party, for example, Sabino de Arana y Goiri, and his brother Luis, were the sons (and grandsons) of industrialists (shipbuilders) who had begun to experience hard times by the period of the Second Carlist War. Sabino studied law (although he never received his degree), and apparently his only employment was in journalism (he wrote for, and edited, newspapers and magazines). Luis was an architect by training. This pattern was apparently typical of the nationalist movement in its early days.[12]

Finally, industrialization brought to the Basque provinces a labor movement built on a rapidly growing working class. The labor movement came late to Spain; workers' associations were granted juridical existence only in 1887, and the right to strike was guaranteed only in 1909. However, once introduced into the Basque country, especially in Bilbao, the organization of workers grew rapidly to become a major political power, not only in the region, but throughout Spain in general. The Spanish Socialist Party, founded in 1879, and its organic trade union, the UGT (*Unión General de Trabajadores*), founded in 1882, spread quickly to Bilbao; and it was there, in 1890, that iron and steel workers began one of the first strikes in Spanish history. The issues were familiar ones to the labor movement: reduction of the work day to ten hours; elimination of company-owned stores and barracks; better compensation for injuries suffered on the job. The strike became violent, martial law was declared, and the military commander of the Basque region was dispatched not only to quell the disturbance but to mediate the dispute. The strike's solution lasted only so long as the troops were on duty; with their withdrawal, the owners rejected the agreement, and conditions remained as they had been before the strike. Thirteen years later, in 1903, the same companies were struck to achieve virtually the same benefits sought in 1890.[13]

In Spain, in general, and in the Basque country in particular, the place of the labor movement in the political order was complicated by the organic presence of a major union within each of the principal parties of the left. Thus, the Anarchists' link with the labor movement was through the CNT (*Confederción Nacional de Trabajadores*); the Socialists', through the UGT. In Vizcaya and other Basque regions, in addition, the Catholic *Solidaridad de Obreros Vascos* (founded in 1911) became strong, especially among the railroad workers. The marked nationalism of the union, linked informally with the Basque Nationalist Party, made it possible to attract members away from the more Spanish-oriented socialist and anarchist unions, both of which felt that Basque nationalism was a cover for the protection of the Church and for the industrialists. In later years, the nationalist movement would try to make itself felt through the mechanism of the general strike, not as an economic weapon but as a political device.

In the early 1890s, then, on the eve of the formation of the Basque Nationalist Party, the social and political forces in the Basque provinces were only marginally favorable for the nationalist movement. All manner of things have been seen to divide some men from others: money, land, religion, language, race, and so forth. At this point in their history, it can fairly be said that only a very few Basques really perceived the major dividing lines in their society as running along the Ebro River. For some, the major division was between owners and workers; for others, it was between Catholics and atheists. The number of nationalist militants was to grow, of course; and at the height of the movement, in 1933, the Basque Nationalist Party could claim perhaps as much as 30 to 40 percent of the vote throughout the region. But the overwhelming vote for autonomy registered in the plebiscite of November 1933 masked real and continuing schisms in Basque society. No doubt many non-nationalists voted for autonomy in the belief that in an autonomous Basque state they could advance or protect their economic or religious interests better than they could as part of greater Spain.

Language and Ethnicity: Sabino de Arana and Basque Nationalism to 1923

Until recently only a relatively small percentage of Basques perceived Basque nationalism as essentially a class phenomenon, such as I have described in the preceding section. The majority of Basque nationalists saw their movement as the intersection of two historical lines: the resurgence of an interest in the ethnic characteristics and language of the people, despite efforts to suppress such characteristics; and the driving personality of the founder of Basque nationalism, Sabino de Arana y Goiri.[14]

Sabino de Arana y Goiri, was born in a suburb of Bilbao on January 26, 1865, the sixth and last child of Santiago de Arana Ansotegui and Pascuala de Goiri Acha. Both his father and his grandfather were industrialists who had specialized in the construction of ships, barges and lighters; but Sabino was to show little interest in continuing the family's participation in manufacturing. The elder Arana was devoted to the Carlist cause and donated considerable amounts of money to advance the movement; but he manifested his hostility toward Basque nationalism by speaking only Spanish in the home. Since the schools of Bilbao likewise did not teach the Basque language, Euskera, Sabino did not learn the language until well into his teens.

As we so frequently discover when we examine in detail the early lives of great persons, Sabino's childhood and adolescence were stormy and turbulent. In 1873, when the boy was eight years old, Santiago de Arana went into exile in southern France to escape reprisals against him for his Carlist sympathies (Bilbao sided with the liberal Spanish government, it will be recalled); and the family did not return to Bilbao until 1876, when Sabino was eleven. The change affected the health of both father and son. Santiago de Arana suffered ill health more or less continuously until his death in 1882, when Sabino was seventeen. The youngest Arana was in ill health throughout his teenage years; at the age of fifteen, he almost died of consumption, and he suffered an attack of jaundice two years later. Even as a boy he had already acquired something of a reputation as a mystic; and his almost miraculous recovery from consumption was said to be accompanied by a mystical religious experience connected with his praying before a statue of the Virgin of Begoña. Ill health continued to plague him throughout his life. His marriage in 1900, at age thirty-five, did not result in any children and he died of the extremely rare Addison's disease in 1903, at age thirty-eight.

Until his father's death, Sabino de Arana had adhered fairly closely to the Carlist line, in all likelihood out of deference to his father's position in politics. At the age of seventeen, however, following Santiago de Arana's death, Sabino was taken by his mother to live in Barcelona, apparently because of the boy's poor health. While in Barcelona, Sabino exhibited little interest in his studies. He explored first medicine, then law, but failed to complete his college degree. His stay in Barcelona coincided with the growth of Catalan nationalism, with its emphasis on the linguistic and cultural underpinnings of political separatism. The influence of the Catalans, plus exposure to the nationalistic ideas of his older brother Luis, converted Sabino to a devoted follower of Basque nationalism. He dedicated the bulk of his time in Barcelona to learning Euskera and Basque history. In 1888, when he was twenty-three, Sabino returned to Bilbao to work determinedly for the cause of Basque freedom until his death, fifteen years later.

In the last two decades of the nineteenth century, Basque ethnic sentiment was extremely weak. Cultural, ethnic and linguistic heritages had been forgotten or were derided as anti-modern; and political autonomy was subordinated to the benefits of economic prosperity. Sabino was faced, then, with a massive challenge in the art of what we would call today "consciousness raising" among the Basque people. Accordingly, his strategies would be global, encompassing virtually every phase of Basque life that could possibly have an influence on what was essentially a political movement.

Sabino's first objective was to revive Euskera as a functional language, and to carry on political communication using the language as a distinctive medium. He worked assiduously to publish grammars, text books, and history books in Euskera. He wrote and published newspaper and magazine articles in Euskera, when the government permitted it; and he coined political terminology in a language which had almost died out by the time modern political communication came into being. He created the word *Euzkadi,* derived from the word for the Basque language, Euskera, to denote the new ethnic nation; and he coined the Basque Nationalist Party slogan *Jaun-Goikua eta Lagi Zarra* ("God and the Old Laws"). These were the first verbal political symbols Basques had ever used in their native tongue. Both politically and psychologically, the Basque language has played a central role in Basque political history since the 1890s. Sabino's influence stemmed from his recognition of the value of a distinctive Basque language in the struggle for political separatism.

Apart from his work in advancing the study of Euskera, Sabino made many other important contributions to the symbolic repertoire of nationalism. He designed the Basque flag, for example, during a recruiting visit to Pamplona, and asked a Navarrese woman from an important local political family, the Irujos, to sew the first of these banners, as if to reassert his desire to include Navarra in the nationalist camp. In 1894, along with his brother Luis he founded the first *Centro Vasco,* a cultural propaganda office which also served as a sort of folklore center and informal club for nationalists. In just a few years, *Centros* had spread not only through the Basque provinces, but to cities in North and South America and the Philippine Islands where Basques had migrated.

But the most important contribution of Sabino de Arana to the Basque nationalist cause lay in the political organization, the Basque Nationalist Party (PNV, for *Partido Nacionalista Vasco*). The PNV traces its origins back to the year 1895, when Sabino and a handful of supporters organized a political "bureau" in Bilbao, to contest elections first in the provincial capital, and later throughout Vizcaya province. By means of astute electoral coalitions and alliances, the bureau was able to compensate for its early weakness and lack of popular support; and its first electoral victory was scored by Sabino himself in 1898, when he was elected to the Vizcaya provincial government. In 1899, nationalists contested city elections in Vizcaya, and five were elected in Bilbao. In 1906, a nationalist was elected to be mayor of Bilbao. Following Sabino's death, the loosely organized bureau reconstituted itself as a more or less formal political party called *Comunión Nacionalista Vasca* (CNV). In just a few years, the party began to present candidates for election to the Cortes from all the Basque provinces.

Most of the advances in nationalist strength, however, came only after the death of Sabino de Arana, when the leadership of the party passed to more pragmatic leaders. Sabino himself was sentenced to jail terms of several months on two different occasions for crimes of a propaganda nature (his second jail term was occasioned by an inflammatory telegram he sent to President Theodore Roosevelt congratulating him on United States' liberation of Cuba from Spanish rule). When he emerged from jail the second time, the bureau office had been closed, the party was out of money, and his supporters could not have numbered more than several hundred. In an interview from jail, Sabino left many with the impression that he was prepared to abandon the struggle for autonomy, and accept Spanish domination. But he repudiated this impression, and was at work again in the provincial and national elections of 1903 (in which no nationalist candidate won) when death ended his career.

It would be impossible to exaggerate the importance of Sabino de Arana's contribution to the ideology of Basque nationalism. Ever since 1893, when he published the seminal *Bizkaya por su independencia,* all interpretations of nationalist ideology begin by tracing their heritage from his work. The ideology can be summed in these six principles:

One. The paramount role of the Catholic religion. The first-named ingredient in the new slogan of the Basque nationalist movement was God, *Jaun-Goikua,* or "Lord of the Heights," as He was called in Euskera. From the beginning, the nationalist movement reflected Sabino's devotion to the Catholic Church, as well as his intention to use the nationalist cause to combat anti-religious forces on both the political right and left (bourgeois mercantilism, and proletarian socialism). Even though the Basque nationalist movement is regarded as one of the earliest Christian Democratic parties in Europe,[15] the priorities of politics and religion are different for the Basques. Although they are advocates of the separation of Church and State, Basque nationalists feel strongly that the government must protect the Church from its opponents, while permitting religious freedom for those who seek it. But the integrity of the Church came first, political freedom, an important (but unequivocal) second. An important statement of Basque nationalist philosophy published in 1906, *Ami Vasco,* put it this way: "Between seeing Euzkadi in full exercise of its rights, but separated from Christ, and seeing her as in 1901 [i.e., an integral part of Spain], but faithful to Christ, the Basque Nationalist Party would opt for the second."[16]

Two. The union of all Basques. Prior to 1890, Basque political movements, such as Carlism and the *fuerista* parties, had concentrated only on those Basque provinces in Spain, that is, south of the Pyrenees. In order for Sabino to press home his case for the racial and linguistic character of nationalism, however, he had to make the Basque nation coterminous with the Basque culture, of which there was a significant portion outside of Spain. Thus, Euzkadi was defined as the union of all the Basque provinces, Vizcaya, Guipúzcoa, Alava and Navarra, in Spain, and Labourd, Basse Navarre and Soule, in France. Still another new slogan, *Zazpiak Bat*, "Out of Seven, One," was created to reflect this new unity. Even today, the three French provinces are called "Euzkadi North," and the Spanish Basques in exile there maintain that they are still in their homeland.

Three. The racial nature of nationalism. Among the most controversial aspects of Basque nationalism is found the assertion that Basques are racially different from all other peoples, especially those that inhabit the Iberian Peninsula. Support for this claim may be found from history (the relative isolation of Basques from the racial mixtures which have characterized the remainder of the peninsula), and from medical surveys which reveal that Basques have an extraordinarily high incidence of Rh negative factor blood. From this assertion (which obviously can be seriously contested), Sabino concluded that each racial type deserved to rule itself, and to establish its own particular political order. Non-Basques were not to be allowed to settle in Euzkadi, or to be employed there; and Basques were to be encouraged to marry within their race. Today, racial definitions of nationalism have tended to give way to ethnic distinctions; and ethno-nationalism continues to be one of the most potent forces in world politics. But, in the context of nineteenth century Europe, the Basque emphasis on race as the source of nationhood does not seem surprising or out of place.

Four. Race is defined by language. The complex interplay between race, language, politics and psychology as exemplified by the Basque experience deserves its own separate treatment; and we must postpone such discussion until a later chapter. We can only note here that Sabino relied heavily on the linguistic uniqueness of the Basques as the key defining factor of Basque racial character. *Ami Vasco* introduced the theme through the catechism technique of question and answer:

> "What is Basque nationalism? The political system that defends the right of the Basque race to live independently of all other races.
>
> "What is the basis of this system? The distinction that exists between the Basque race and the rest that people the earth.
>
> "How can you prove it? . . . I have told you before that the difference in race is proved by the difference of languages. Thus it is that the Basque language differs radically from all the rest of the languages. So the race differs also from all the remaining races."[17]

Given the difficulty in discovering identifiable, surface characteristics of Basques which marks them as truly unique, Sabino fell back on the behavioral attribute which does indeed separate Basques from all the rest of the people on the earth: their language. In more recent times, Basque nationalist leaders have tended to be less intransigent than Sabino on both issues: the racial nature of Basque nationalism, and the linguistic definition of race. Considering the decline in the use of Euskera, they really had little choice but to move more toward ethnicity, or a culturally transmitted feeling of "Basque-ness," to define political issues along nationalist lines. One gets the feeling, however, that race and language are still powerful emotional dimensions of Basque politics, and lie latent just below the surface of political rhetoric. Judging from the policies of the Franco government toward the Basque language, many Spanish politicians of that period evidently felt threatened by these ideas and sought (with only partial success) to suppress them.

Five. The struggle for separation should be nonviolent, and should follow parliamentary tactics if possible. We have few overt pronouncements of Sabino to cite as evidence for this principle; but we have only to look at his life and his conduct to realize the central role of nonviolence in the nationalist movement. From the beginning, Sabino portrayed an almost sublime faith in the workings of the democratic process. If

Basques could only learn of their history, their culture, and their language, and if they had the freedom to vote for candidates who pledged to protect these things, then Basque nationalism would triumph at the ballot box, and in the parliament. What should the movement do, however, if the central government repressed this right, and denied Basque nationalists the opportunity to vote for their cause? Then, argued Sabino, Basques must not engage in open rebellion, but simply continue the slow, steady pressure of cultural resistance, wearing away the chains of tyranny. After all, they had been struggling for a thousand years to maintain their culture intact. The true value of a culture is seen, he thought, in its ability to survive the centuries, and to defeat its antagonists by simply outliving them. As we shall see, some Basques in the 1960s became impatient with this prescription, and began to question the nonviolent road to independence.

Six. The tentative nature of internal political organization. Perhaps in an effort to span as many socioeconomic classes as possible with the nationalist movement, Sabino avoided writing any prescriptions about what form Basque self-government would assume after separation. We can infer from other things he said, and from actions taken to organize the Republic of Euzkadi during the Civil War, that nationalists had in mind some kind of parliamentary democracy, with a moderate emphasis on social justice and the redistribution of wealth. The Basque Nationalist Party appeared to be cut from the same mold as the later Christian Democratic parties in Europe and Latin America. It was hardly a radical ideology as far as internal politics was concerned. The reluctance of the movement's leaders to discuss in detail the economic, social and political policies to be pursued once independence was secured meant, however, that more impatient, radical groups would surely challenge the PNV's right to speak and act in the name of the Basque nation.

During the thirty-year period, from 1893 to 1923, the growing popularity of Basque nationalism was accompanied by political action on two fronts. Violence erupted at irregular intervals, and represented both militant nationalist protest and labor troubles of an economic nature. The first mass demonstration in favor of regionalism occurred in Bilbao on August 16, 1893, and spread to San Sebastián on August 27. Troops were called in to suppress the rioters; and the death toll ran to about ten for the two incidents combined. Strikes, lockouts and labor violence continued throughout the period, with major incidents registered in 1903, 1906 and 1910. Unrest following World War I, and the successful Bolshevik revolution in Russia in 1917, caused the conservatives to fear oncoming social change, and to withdraw their support from the nationalist movement. The political left, in turn, made a major effort prior to 1923 to infiltrate the nationalist party and its subordinate groups.

The Basque nationalist movement concentrated most of its effort on electoral competition, both at the provincial and at the national level. Starting from a position of marked weakness, the CNV registered major electoral victories from 1914 to 1918. Aided by the economic impact of World War I, and by the propaganda for self-determination stimulated by the war, the nationalist movement gained an absolute majority of the seats in the provincial government of Vizcaya, and began to elect a growing number of delegates to the Cortes. In 1918, of the twenty delegates allotted to the four Basque provinces (including Navarra), the CNV won seven seats: five (of six) from Vizcaya, and one each from Guipúzcoa and Navarra. The rising strength of the nationalist party led provincial delegations to begin to present demands for autonomy to the Spanish government, to which in 1918 the Conservative Prime Minister Antonio Maura replied:

> Decentralization? All that you want. Administrative autonomy? As much as belongs to the region, as much as you are capable of enjoying. An approach to political sovereignty? Never. None, not even the slightest bit. From an eagle watching over its young, you must not strip even one single feather from its wings, not even one of its claws.[18]

Of such demands, nothing was heard from the Cortes. The delegation of Basque nationalists to Versailles to ask for aid from the Big Four likewise returned empty-handed.

As the economic prosperity of the World War turned to the depression of peacetime, and as fear of communism spread throughout Spain, the nationalist movement fell on hard times. In the parliamentary elections of 1919, the CNV returned three delegates to Madrid; in 1920, the number dropped to one. Persistent demands from more radical nationalists for the party to become more aggressive and to eschew electoral deals with right-wing parties led, finally, to a split in the movement. After a stormy meeting of the CNV leadership in San Sebastián in 1920, a new party was created, the Basque Nationalist Party, the first formal organization to carry that name. In 1923, then, when King Alfonso XIII turned over power to the military dictatorship of Primo de Rivera, the Basque nationalist cause was divided once again.

From the Dictatorship of Primo de Rivera to the Civil War

When King Alfonso XIII asked General Miguel Primo de Rivera to form a new government, and abrogated the Constitution of 1876, the Basque nationalists were confronted for the first time in their history by a regime which considered regional separatism as not only bad but actually treasonous. Only a few days after Primo de Rivera was installed in office, in September 1923, he issued a decree which outlawed any act which might tend to undermine the concept of national unity. Flags other than the Spanish banner were prohibited, and Spanish was to be the only official language. The Cortes was dissolved, constitutional guarantees were suspended, and the country was declared to be in a state of war.

Most importantly for the future, however, the dictatorship of Primo de Rivera left a philosophical legacy of centralism which informed the fascism of a later era, as promulgated by his son, José Antonio. Whereas the dictator had come to power with mild sympathy toward the Catalan separatists, by 1925 this feeling had completely reversed itself, and regional sentiments of all varieties were ruthlessly suppressed. In the short run, Primo de Rivera's anti-regional policy was no doubt in response to pressures from the army to keep the social order under control. As time went on, however, the policy became dignified by an intricate theory, based on the idea of the state as an amalgamation of social organisms into one global organism. Just as the human body could not be rent asunder and survive, so the social organism which was the nation likewise would perish if divided. As Raymond Carr wrote,

> Inevitably, the dictatorship saw its greatest enemies in those forces which threatened the unity of the nation. More destructive than party politicians, who put party above country, were regionalists whose aspirations had engendered separatism. . . . The region, as a political unity, was neither socially nor historically "real": it was the creation of a minority of separatist intellectuals who had exploited legitimate grievances against bad government and played on the excessive individualism which was the primal political sin of Spaniards. . . . To the dictator, regionalism meant folk-lore, country-dancing, regional literature, and home crafts — politically safe, attractive to tourists, and a proof of diversity in unity.[19]

Six years after the dictatorship fell in 1930, Basque nationalism would be assaulted by General Franco's rebels in the name of the theories of Primo de Rivera.

Confronted thus by repression and ideological hostility, the Basque nationalist parties withdrew from conventional political activity. The newly formed PNV became a clandestine political movement; its newspaper, *Aberri,* was closed by the regime shortly after taking power. The CNV withdrew from all political action and, in effect, ceased to exist. The only nationalist party involved in the recurring conspiracies against the regime was the more radical, left-oriented, anti-clerical *Acción Nacionalista Vasca* (ANV), a dissident separatist group whose origins could be traced back to 1910.

On the whole, however, Basque nationalism survived during the dictatorship as a cultural rather than a political phenomenon. Just as Sabino had counseled, during times of repression Basques could retreat to the mental sanctuary of their ancient culture and outlive any Spanish political force which chose to range itself against them. If the use of Euskera was suppressed, Basques turned to art and music for nationalist expression; and Basque painting moved decidedly in the direction of political art during the 1920s. We must also mention here the growing use of Basque mountain-climbing societies, called *mendigoitzales,* as a haven for nationalist militants. The mountainous Basque hinterland had long been the scene of this vigorous sport; but during the dictatorship, these societies took on a definitely political character. High atop some remote mountain, the Basque alpinists could meet safely, far from Spanish police scrutiny, and discuss politics freely. Soon the organizations began to resemble paramilitary groups; they would become the core of mountain guerrilla forces in the years ahead. Beginning in 1921, radical nationalists began to infiltrate the *mendigoitzales* and to turn them to political purposes. Throughout the terrible years of Primo de Rivera, these mountain-climbing societies were practically the only nationalist groups which showed the ability to survive and grow. The lesson would not be lost on later resistance fighters.

The government of Primo de Rivera fell in early 1930. The monarchy sputtered on, through political turmoil and economic unrest. In August, leaders of the principal antimonarchical parties met in San Sebastián with their counterparts among the Catalan nationalist groups to formulate their opposition to Alfonso XIII. This group would later become the Provisional Government of Spain. In order to secure the support of Barcelona in the uprising, promises were made of regional autonomy. Although the Basque nationalists did not attend the meeting because of its "left" inclination, they were later to call in the promises made to the Catalans. The fall of Primo de Rivera had brought about a slackening of political suppression; and the nationalists moved back into public activity by agreeing to a reunification of the two wings of the party, thus healing the split of 1920. ANV remained apart, however, because of its anticlerical stance. In November, the rejuvenated PNV held its first national assembly in Vergara. Their newspaper returned to the streets, and the party began to ready itself for the inevitable parliamentary contests.

On April 14, 1931, Alfonso XIII, dismayed by the failure of monarchical forces to carry the country's major cities in municipal elections, abdicated the throne, and the Second Spanish Republic was proclaimed. Thus was ushered in a period of six years of intense political activity by Basque nationalists, marked by alternating sentiments of euphoria and disillusionment, and culminating in the outbreak of the Spanish Civil War.

From the beginning of the Republic, the Basques were caught in a dilemma without adequate solution. If they were committed to gaining independence without violence (a commitment which weakened quickly as the decade wore on), then they had to rely on the political good will of the Cortes to vote them such status. Since they constituted such a tiny portion of any of the three separate Cortes which sat during that period, the PNV deputies had to develop intricate coalitions around a matter which essentially was not a core issue for any group but themselves.[20] Moreover, the ideological position of the PNV consisted of two dissonant features: staunch defense of the Catholic Church, and regional separatism, coupled with a vigorous attack on social injustice. Because of the former, the left opposed regional autonomy; because of the latter, the right did also. Thus, from 1931 to 1933, and from February to July 1936, when the Cortes was dominated by parties of the left, the PNV suffered because of its pro-Church position. From 1933 to 1936, when the right was in control of parliament, the Basques' role in labor unrest (particularly the October 1934 rebellion) destroyed any hope they might have had to secure support from that sector. Within the Basque provinces themselves, the same dilemma was reproduced in smaller scale: Navarra and Alava deserted the nationalist cause out of fear of the unleashing of uncontrollable social forces among the proletariat of Bilbao and San Sebastián; in those cities, on the other hand, the Socialist, Communist and Anarchist parties and labor unions continued to chip away at the strength of the PNV, and to criticize the party for its collaboration with exploitative capitalism. In a country increasingly split over religious and economic issues, centered parties like the PNV, representing a rather primitive form of Christian Democracy, were simply pulled to pieces by forces beyond their control. Indalecio Prieto, leader of the Socialists, declared he would never allow the establishment of a "Vatican Gibraltar" in the Basque country;[21] from the right, Finance Minister José Calvo Sotello (his assassination in 1936 was to be the *cause célèbre* of the army rebellion) uttered his famous "Better a Red Spain than a broken Spain."[22] The nationalist cause never had a chance.

From 1931 to 1936, the focal point of the Basque nationalist movement was the Autonomy Statute, the law which was to give them the legal independence they had enjoyed prior to 1839.[23] The San Sebastián agreement had guaranteed it; the new Republic's Constitution made it a right of all the regions of Spain, with these words: "if one or various contiguous provinces with common historical, cultural and economic characteristics decide to organize themselves into an autonomous region in order to form a politico-administrative nucleus, they shall present their Statute in accordance with the conditions set forth in Article 12 [of the Constitution]. . . . Once the Statute has been approved, it should be the basic law of the politico-administration organization of the autonomous region, and the Spanish State shall recognize it and support it as an integrating part of its juridical ordinance."[24]

The new generation of PNV leaders who had come to prominence with the municipal elections of 1931, such as the young, soccer-playing mayor of Guecho, José Antonio de Aguirre, apparently entertained the idea of declaring the region to be autonomous unilaterally, without benefit of parliamentary approval. Following the Catalan lead, the mayors of Vizcaya met in Guernica on April 17, 1931, when the Republic was only three days old, to discuss the possibility. The rapid collapse of the Catalan challenge before determined Madrid power forced the PNV to back off from this position, however; and the chosen strategy, even after the Civil War began, was a parliamentary one.[25]

The draft Statute of Autonomy went through three distinct versions in its tortuous history, and an even larger number of modifications. The initial version drafted by a group of intellectuals called the Society of Basque Studies, was tentatively approved by the mayors of the four provinces in late May 1931, by a vote of 485 to 97, and formally by all the Basque town councils meeting in Estella in June. After amending the draft to accommodate concerns of the Navarrese, supporters carried the day, 427 to 155. Support for the project was already beginning to erode, especially in the more traditional, Carlist areas of the region. Upon submission to the Cortes in November, however, the draft Statute was declared unconstitutional because of its assertion that Euskera would be the official language of the region and that the Basque State would have the right to negotiate with the Vatican the exact status of the Church in the region. Both of these provisions were contrary to stipulations in the new Constitution, to be promulgated in December.[26]

In late December 1931, then, the Basques initiated the second commission to draft an Autonomy Statute, buoyed by the knowledge that the Cortes had shortly before approved autonomy for Cataluña. In Navarra, however, there were ominous stirrings of a renascent Carlism. It was common knowledge that arms were being smuggled across the French border into Navarra, and that the Carlist militia, the *requetés,* were practicing in paramilitary formations. The PNV went to great lengths to keep Navarra in the union of Basque provinces, but to no avail. When the Autonomy Statute was presented to the assembly of municipal leaders in Pamplona in June 1932, it was accepted by Alava, Guipúzcoa and Vizcaya, 218 to 14 (23 abstentions). Navarra's delegates, however, rejected the draft by a vote of 101 to 123 (with 35 abstentions). From this point on until 1936, Navarra diverged from the nationalist path, and was an important center of support for the anti-Republic uprising under General Mola.

The third commission concentrated on a draft which left open the possibility of Navarrese adherence, but which basically was a union of only three provinces. The new commission began its work in October 1932, and took almost a year to complete its task. In the meantime, the pace of social change had risen in Vizcaya and Guipúzcoa. The communists had formed their own nationalist group, a communist-nationalist newspaper appeared on the streets, and a radical new splinter group began to form within the PNV itself. The more conservative nationalists in Alava province then began to slip away from the coalition, much the same as in Navarra. In August 1933, an assembly in Vitoria approved the third version of the draft Statute by a vote of 239 to 28, but the vote from Alava was

Chapter Three

THE BASQUES IN THE SPANISH CIVIL WAR: FROM 1936 TO 1939

Civil War and Autonomy: July to October 1936

Under Generals Sanjurjo, Mola, and Franco the rebellion of dissident units of the Spanish army against the Republic reached the mainland on July 19,1936. In a matter of hours, the war split the Basque provinces into two opposing camps. The struggle of the next twelve months bore remarkable resemblance to earlier battles between the liberal modernizers of the coastal industrial cities and the tradition-bound *fueristas* of the mountainous rural areas. This time, however, the Carlists and their allies were destined to win, and the result was a prolonged attempt to eradicate the last vestiges of Basque nationalism from Vizcaya and Guipúzcoa.

By the end of the day on the 19th of July, Pamplona and Vitoria were in the hands of the rebels, while Bilbao and San Sebastián had declared themselves in defense of the Republic. The alignment of Basque provinces into enemy camps was the product not only of underlying political, economic and social forces, but at least in two instances of rather random twists of fate as well. But in all cases the decisions made by key actors in the drama of July 19 were to seal the fate of hundreds of thousands of innocent bystanders during the next year.

There seemed little doubt that the conservative rebel forces would capture Navarra and Alava provinces from the beginning. One of the key leaders of the rebellion, General Emilio Mola, commanded the Spanish army garrison in Pamplona, and could count on the enthusiastic support of thousands of Carlist *requetés*. Earlier in the year, in what Brian Crozier calls "an unaccountable error of judgement," Spanish Prime Minister Manuel Azaña had recalled Mola from his post in Morocco, and had assigned him to duty in Pamplona, ostensibly as punishment for siding with right-wing groups emerging within the army. While the assignment may in fact have been a demotion, it placed Mola in a crucial location, in the heart of anti-Republican Carlist country, an area already seething with conspiracy against the regime.[1]

Not much urging was necessary to propel Navarra into the rebellion. Hills observes that the people of Pamplona were "wildly enthusiastic" in their support of Mola;[2] and Raymond Carr cites the following description of the tumultuous welcome Pamplona gave the rebellion:

> On the evening of the 18th July, lorries hired by the mayors began to arrive from the villages far and near, crammed full with young and old of Navarre who responded to the call with indescribable enthusiasm. Each lorry, as it circled the main square of Pamplona received an ovation from the crowds which, at the sound of bugles, appeared at balconies hung with flags. . . . Music and applause.[3]

At the outset of the war, Navarra contributed some 8,400 Carlist volunteers; by September, the number had grown to 20,000 in a province where the number of adult males probably did not exceed 100,000.[4] Of course, opposition to the rebellion in Navarra and neighboring Alava was crushed ruthlessly.

In Vizcaya and Guipúzcoa provinces, matters were rather more complicated. To be sure, in both provinces the strongest single political force was that of the Basque Nationalist Party (PNV); and the position of the Party would be crucial in the impending struggle between left and right. From the beginning, the PNV aligned itself with the Republic, although the decision was made with the understanding that the Party was choosing the less undesirable of the two alternatives. On July 19, *Euzkadi,* the Party's newspaper, published the following declaration by the Party's central bureau:

> Before the events which are developing in the Spanish state, and their painful repercussions which could affect

> Euzkadi and its destiny, the Basque Nationalist Party . . . declares that today it ratifies solemnly that, given the struggle between the people and fascism, between the Republic and the Monarchy, its principles carry it without doubt to come down on the side of the people and the Republic, in consonance with the democratic and republican regime that was peculiar to our People in its centuries of liberty.[5]

While the complex issues of Church and autonomy undoubtedly were raised in the Party discussions of this declaration, in the end the PNV sided with the Republic principally because of the autonomy question. Strongly Catholic Basques naturally were repelled by the anti-Catholic excesses of the left; the later defense of Vizcaya and of Bilbao would be complicated greatly by tension between these two forces. On the other hand, the pro-Church position of the rebel generals Franco and Mola did not emerge clearly until November 1936; and, by that time the Basques had their own autonomous government. Therefore, as the issues of the Spanish Civil War began to be sorted out in the first days after July 18, the paramount question from the Basque nationalist point of view was which side promised them regional autonomy. On that, the Basques already had the commitment of the Republic; the insurgents, in contrast, exalted the centralized state and denounced the fragmentation of Spain. Nevertheless, the issue hung so delicately in the balance that the Basque suppression of the rising in San Sebastián and Bilbao surprised the Republic's leaders almost as much as it did Franco and Mola.[6]

Even after the PNV had declared its support for the Republic, the defeat of the insurgency in Vizcaya and Guipúzcoa still depended on the fortuitous presence of calm and strong nationalist leaders in key places when the rebellion began. Although the PNV was the largest single party in the Basque provinces, they never won a majority of the votes, even in Vizcaya. As the table below indicates, their share of the parliamentary vote had declined between 1933 and 1936, when about 10 percent of their earlier strength had been sapped by joint attacks by left and right parties. In both Vizcaya and in Guipúzcoa, there were risings by insurgent army forces; and in both the major cities, the working classes sought to turn the occasion into an opportunity for a more searching and profound allocation of power and property. The PNV had to contend first with the military threat from the right during the early days of the war, and subsequently with the political challenge from the left, during the seige of Bilbao (see Table 1).

Table 1.
Vote Distribution in Four Basque Provinces in Parliamentary Elections of 1933 and 1936 (percent of total vote).

Province	**Left Wing Parties**		**— PNV —**		**Right Wing Parties**	
	1933	1936	1933	1936	1933	1936
Alava	19.0	22.2	29.0	20.3	52.0	57.5
Guipúzcoa	29.8	30.0	45.5	36.9	24.7	33.1
Vizcaya	34.3	37.2	46.3	37.3	19.4	25.5
Navarra	15.9	21.3	9.3	9.5	70.8	69.2
Four Provinces	28.0	29.8	34.3	28.0	37.7	42.2

Source: Jose Miguel Azaola, *Vasconia y su destino, I: La Regionalización de España* (Madrid: Revista de Occidente, 1972), pp. 544-545.

The first days of the war found San Sebastián in turmoil and confusion. The civilian governor of the province, at first confident of his ability to turn back the insurgency, had grown frightened, and had escaped to the comparative safety of Vizcaya. The streets of the city belonged to the Defense Committee of the Popular Front, an amalgamation of left political parties and labor unions, while the city's military garrison was preparing to defend its barracks and several other key positions throughout the city. Into this power vacuum moved two Basque nationalist deputies, Manuel de Irujo and José María Lasarte, who asserted their right to speak in the name of the Republic in the absence of the governor. They occupied the governor's office, and set about the task of persuading the insurgent troops to surrender. This they succeeded in doing on July 27. The workers mobbed the government building where the commanders of this force were being held; and Irujo tried bravely to dissuade the crowd from executing them summarily. The emotions unleashed by the rebellion were too powerful, however, and the first of several unsavory political killings took place in San Sebastián, where the Defense Committee remained in command.[7]

In Bilbao, the civil governor of Vizcaya, an aging politician named Echeverría, was shaken and confused by the events of July 17 and 18, and was inclined to throw in with the rebels once they proved their power. Afraid of the governor's weakness, one of the leaders of the Basque Republican left, Ramón María de Aldasoro, arranged to have all telephone calls to the Bilbao military garrison routed through Echeverría's office, where he joined the shaking leader. Soon the telephone rang. It was General Mola calling from Pamplona, demanding that the Bilbao garrison rise to join the rebellion. The account of this incident by British journalist George Steer continues:

> Aldasoro seized Echeverría by his telephone shoulder and said much louder, "Cry *Viva la República!*" And then he had an idea. He took the receiver out of the fingers of Echeverría; it was very damp, and he roared down it, "*Viva la República!*" "Now you try," he said, smiling in a fatherly way, handing the machine back.
>
> "*Viva la República,*" came very feebly from the lips of Echeverría. "That's quite enough," said Aldasoro, and took the receiver from Echeverría a second time, and hung it quietly upon the stand.
>
> The die was cast. The Civil Governor looked morosely out of the window and pulled out his pocket handkerchief. Adieu to comfort.[8]

With the preliminary struggles for power out of the way, the four Basque provinces began to settle into their assigned roles for the duration of the Spanish Civil War. In Navarra and Alava, persons suspected of sympathizing with the Republic or with Basque nationalism were ruthlessly sought out and imprisoned or executed without benefit of trial or confession. On the other side of the line, for several weeks after the rising the left-dominated Defense Committees practiced the same kind of arbitrary justice against rebel sympathizers. Thomas estimates that about 500 illegal executions took place on the Republican side of the line before the Basque Nationalist Party could gain control of the situation.[9] In San Sebastián, the PNV never did have a chance to solidify their control, since the war came to Guipúzcoa a month after the rising. But in Bilbao, and the rest of Vizcaya, which enjoyed a brief respite before being assaulted by General Mola's troops, the Basque Nationalists began to assert their authority by September, and were safely in command by the time the Autonomy Statute was passed one month later. Wherever the PNV governed, however, public order was maintained intact, churches functioned openly and freely, priests and nuns were left unmolested, and political prisoners were protected while in prison. A few mild measures were undertaken to introduce a degree of social justice: property belonging to rightist sympathizers was confiscated, rents were reduced, and a public assistance board was created for the needy. Considering the pressures associated with running a society under military attack, the Basque Nationalist Party performed minor miracles in these early days of the war.[10]

Actual military operations began in Guipúzcoa in late July, as General Mola's Carlist troops pushed north from Navarra toward San Sebastián and the French border.[11] Mola's objective was to cut the land communication between the Basque provinces and France, and divide still further the two halves of the country which remained loyal to the Republic. In these early days of the war, military operations still possessed a certain primitive quality: the numbers of troops remained small, weapons were rather crude and old-fashioned, and the threat of aerial bombardment was still completely unknown to either side. Mola's forces advanced slowly against stout resistance; but the rebels' superiority in tanks, armored cars and artillery resulted eventually in the fall of the border city of Irún on September 3.

With the closure of the French border, and the steady rebel advance against the provincial capital of San Sebastián, tens of thousands of civilians began the long trek westward to Bilbao where they were confident the Basque resistance would stiffen and throw back the invaders. Already, the Defense Committees in Vizcaya had confiscated the gold from Basque banks and sent it abroad to buy weapons; and the emerging autonomous Basque government was beginning to fashion a hurried defense of the last remaining sliver of their national territory. On September 13, San Sebastián fell to Mola's forces without a shot; Irún had been almost completely destroyed by the fires set by withdrawing anarchist forces, and the inhabitants of San Sebastián wanted to spare their beautiful city that fate.

As the insurgent army advanced across Guipúzcoa, with escaping civilians fleeing before them, there apparently was no force left to stop them short of Bilbao itself. During the last days of September, however, the Basque government carried out a most remarkable crash military mobilization program. From all over Vizcaya, but especially from Bilbao, young men were mustered into the growing Basque militia, and dispatched to the front by any means of transportation available: bus, private car, or even bicycle. The Basques, not a particularly militaristic people who had not even had an army as late as July, had, by September, thrown into combat nearly forty infantry battalions of 600-750 men each. At first, their arms consisted of whatever they could find for themselves: hunting rifles, pistols, dynamite from the mining regions. The Basque Defense Minister, Telesforo Monzón, had been sent to Barcelona to buy arms, but was told that the Republic had little to spare. From there, he traveled to Paris, only to hear that France was respecting the agreement not to intervene in the Spanish Civil War. Finally, a shipload of weapons was purchased in Germany, of all places, and shipped quickly to Bilbao. The arms finally arrived at the line the Basques had chosen to defend, along the Guipúzcoa-Vizcaya border, near the industrial city of Eibar, in early October. The Carlists attacked the next morning and were repulsed. Vizcaya had been saved, for the time being.[12]

As the war proceeded apace on the military front, the Basques were consolidating their position politically, as well. The unspoken *quid pro quo* for Basque loyalty to the Republic was prompt action on the Basque Statute of Autonomy, consideration of which had been postponed by the military rising in July. In September, the Basque nationalist leaders of the Vizcaya Defense Committee pressed for passage of the statute. On September 26, the Basque nationalist deputy Manuel Irujo accepted a post with the Spanish Republican government of

Francisco Largo Caballero as Minister without Portfolio, to cement the wavering relationships between the Basques and the Republic. Now, on October 1, the Spanish Cortes, meeting in Valencia (Madrid was now beseiged), voted to approve the Autonomy Statute, and, in effect, to cut loose the Basques to fend for themselves. While the Basque nationalists were euphoric over the grant of political autonomy, they were to learn quickly that the Republic likewise felt little obligation to extend aid to the new constituent republic of Euzkadi.[13]

On October 7, the municipal councilors of Vizcaya, and as many of the others as could attend, gathered secretly in the sacred village of Guernica, in the historic Casa de Juntas, to select the first president of Euzkadi. That the meeting would select the prominent Basque nationalist José Antonio de Aguirre was virtually a foregone conclusion. The PNV dominated the meeting, as they dominated most of the municipal governments of Vizcaya; the left was almost completely shut out of the gathering. Following his election, which was nearly unanimous, Aguirre, the new *lendakari* (president) appeared beneath the famous oak tree of Guernica to swear his oath of allegiance to his new position. The act was not without its critics: some felt that Aguirre in so swearing had linked himself to the royal leaders of earlier centuries, rather than to the strictly modern concepts of democracy and nationalism; there were others, more radical than the PNV leadership, who felt that now was the appropriate time to declare their total independence from Spain. But these critics were few, and in later days fell silent. The nationalism of Sabino carried the day.

One last act brought this phase of the war to a close: the naming and installation of a Cabinet, or Council of Ministers. Aguirre claimed for himself the Ministry of Defense; and the PNV were given three other key posts — Interior, Treasury, and Justice. The Agriculture Ministry went to *Acción Nacionalista Vasca;* Aldasoro, the saviour of Bilbao, was given Trade and Supply, as a leading member of the Left Republicans. The Socialists were awarded three posts — Labor, Social Assistance, and Industry — and the Communists, one — Public Works. Thus, an attempt at representation was made in the first government of Euzkadi, but there was no doubt which political force would govern. Importantly, the decision was made to close out the left-oriented labor unions from representation, even though shortly the government would be asking them for aid in forming militia battalions for the defense of Bilbao. At the end of the day, on October 7, the new Cabinet assembled in formal dress for an historic photograph to commemorate the restoration of autonomy to the Basques. On that day, the rebel forces of General Mola (now reinforced with Italian and Moorish troops and German aircraft) were only 40 kilometers from Guernica; less than seven months later, Guernica would lie broken and in flames, almost totally destroyed by the Condor Legion.

The Defense and Fall of Bilbao: October 1936 to June 1937

From October 1936 to March 1937, events in the rest of Spain together with the cloudy weather of winter along the Bay of Biscay served to turn the insurgents' attention away from the Basque front. Franco and Mola threw their main effort into breaking the seige of Madrid, hoping thereby to cut short the war by a year or more. When the Madrid offensive sputtered to a halt, and the oncoming spring caused the clouds to lift along the north coast (making aerial operations possible), the two generals concluded that Bilbao must be taken quickly, not only to restore momentum and prestige to the faltering rebellion, but to secure the city's valuable iron ore and industrial might.

There were, as a consequence, few military operations in Vizcaya through the late fall and winter of 1936-37. In late November, the Basques launched their single offensive of the war, attempting to break out of their encirclement by attacking the town of Villareal, about fifty kilometers south of Bilbao on the road to Vitoria. After several days of seige of the town, reinforcements arrived on the rebel side, and the Basques were driven back, suffering losses of 800 killed and 4,000 wounded.[14] From that point on, all efforts were turned toward strengthening the defense of Bilbao.

The first major issue to be confronted by the new government of Euzkadi was that of feeding and otherwise caring for the tens of thousands of refugees who streamed into Bilbao, not only from the overrun Basque provinces of Guipúzcoa, Alava and Navarra, but also from the non-Basque areas to the west: Galicia and Asturias. At the beginning of the war, the population of Bilbao was slightly more than 175,000; in a matter of months, this figure had grown to more than 400,000. The newcomers arrived with little more than the clothes on their backs, and the government bore the burden of caring for them in the face of severe scarcities.

Until the very end of the seige of Bilbao, fuel, electricity, and water were never in critical supply; but food became seriously scarce almost from the beginning. The Supply Minister, Aldasoro, resolved one crisis after another to provision a major city entirely from imported goods. For long stretches, the city ate almost nothing except chickpeas; and toward the end of the struggle politically reliable functionaries had to be placed in charge of food distribution to avoid black market abuses.

The problem of food shortages was aggravated by the imposition of a naval blockade around the port of Bilbao by the rebel navy, and by the laying of mines in the harbor beginning as early as September. The blockade did not become effective, however, until April 1937, when the British decided to respect it and to deny the protection of their warships to British merchants sailing in Spanish waters. Although some ships continued to penetrate the blockade, the British government's decision was sufficient to cut off Bilbao from the sea, thus sealing the city's fate.[15] In an effort to offset the blockade, the Basques established an armed trawler fleet of slightly more than half a dozen ships, manned entirely by volunteers. Several of the ships of this fleet were responsible for the battle mentioned in the prologue to this volume. Their modest armament was never a match for the powerful rebel cruisers which operated in Basque waters; and the sea voyage from the French ports of St. Jean de Luz and Bayonne to Bilbao was always a hazardous one.

With the question of provisions being dealt with by Aldasoro and the small Basque navy, much of the remainder of the Basque government's attention was focused on the military defense of the city. Although Aguirre set his sights on forming an army of nearly 100,000 men, in the end the Basque infantry never exceeded 35,000 to 45,000. These troops were divided into battalions of 600 to 750 men each. Their strength lay first in the almost fanatic emotional commitment they had to their struggle, and second, in the fact that they were superb physical specimens, many hardened to life in the mountains surrounding the city. These factors allowed them to bear an unusual degree of hardship where other troops would have failed.

Balanced against these strengths, however, were a number of shortcomings which could never be overcome, especially in the short time allotted to Aguirre before the spring offensive. Professional leadership was a crucial problem. Aguirre reports that in the entire Basque army he could find only thirteen officers who had had professional military training, and some of these were of doubtful loyalty.[16] Accordingly, the battalions were led by men from all walks of life, thrust suddenly into a role for which they were ill-prepared. A few failed in their mission; but the majority proved to be resourceful, and able to lead their men in the face of great danger.

Political problems crept into the military structure, however, and caused Aguirre no end of trouble in deploying his forces. Of the 46 or so battalions organized out of the hastily put together Basque militia, 27 were raised by the Basque Nationalist Party, while eight were mobilized by the Socialist Party's labor union, the UGT, and the remainder by mixed groups of Communists, Socialist-Communist Youth, Left Republicans, and Anarchists. In addition, several battalions of non-Basque troops, mostly from neighboring provinces of Asturias and Santander, were sent to the Basque front, and were assigned key places in the defense line. Of the total Basque force, then, no more than about half were ideologically in tune with the Aguirre government; and dissident political leaders exhibited an infuriating tendency to withdraw their battalions from crucial battles to express their discontent with Aguirre's policies. On more than one occasion, Basque Nationalist battalions found themselves in exposed and untenable positions because of the politically motivated withdrawal of battalions drawn from the left, or from non-Basque provinces.

Of greatest importance by far, however, was the deplorable

state of the arms and equipment of the Basque forces. As long as the war remained a struggle between armies indigenous to Spain, the primitive military equipment of the Basques did not constitute a major disadvantage. As the spring offensive neared, however, the insurgents of Mola began to assemble a better equipped fighting force, based on small Italian tanks and artillery and on German bomber and fighter aircraft. In response, to cover a front of nearly 200 kilometers, the Basques deployed an estimated 45,000 men. Twenty of the Basque battalions possessed not so much as a single machine gun. Their air support consisted of six Russian-built fighters (half of the force delivered to them in October 1936), manned by inexperienced Spanish pilots, and seven obsolete French bombers whose slow flying speed made them easy prey for the German fighters and anti-aircraft. (The German Condor Legion had 120 aircraft, both fighters and bombers.) The Basque artillery was half the size of the insurgents'; and their tank support consisted of twelve tiny Spanish models which did not even see service until June 2, 1937, seventeen days before Bilbao fell.[17] The remainder of the Basque armament consisted of a handful of 81mm trench mortars, small arms (always woefully short of ammunition), grenades, home-made explosives, and about two dozen armored cars (also Russian in origin).

The totally inadequate Basque arms situation stemmed from three causes. First, their native arms factories had concentrated almost entirely on small arms and ammunition. Aguirre mobilized in the remainder of Vizcaya all industrial facilities that could be turned to arms fabrication; but they were never able to turn out equipment other than small arms, machine pistols, and the Basque-made mortar mentioned above. Second, the Republic declined to send any arms or equipment to the Basque front, apparently feeling that the Basques were on their own after the passage of the Autonomy Statute. The Basque front was only a portion of the more inclusive Army of the North, stretching from Asturias eastward; and invariably, when materiel reached the north, it was diverted to the non-Basque provinces.[18] Finally, it proved impossible to import more than a few shiploads of arms from abroad. Along with the arms bought in Germany referred to earlier, two shiploads were smuggled in from France bearing small arms and machine guns of Czech manufacture; and one large load of weapons, armored cars and 12 airplanes arrived from Russia near the end of October 1936. But, in sum, the decision of the Western democracies, France and England, to respect the Non-Intervention Agreement meant that the Basques would be closed off from the arms and munitions support of the neighboring industrial powers.

In addition to concentrating on the provisioning of the Basque army in the field, Aguirre launched into the construction of the famous "Belt of Iron" ("Cinturón de Hierro") in order to surround Bilbao completely with a network of fortifications. As planned, the Cinturón would have stretched from the sea on the east, at Sopelana, to the sea on the west, at Somorrostro, 200 kilometers of barbed wire, trenches and concrete machine gun bunkers. To complete the task, Aguirre pressed into service more than 15,000 workers, architects, construction contractors, and engineers, and set them to work in mid-October. Ingeniously planned, the Cinturón (like so many other rigid fortifications such as the Maginot Line) probably lulled the Basques into a false sense of security. For, as they built the line, not only were huge gaps left unfinished or covered by only one thin strand of barbed wire, but the overall conception of the line failed to take into account basic principles of fortifications: defense in depth (the construction of multiple lines offering cover to retreating troops), camouflage, and defense against aerial bombardment. On top of everything else, the engineer officer who designed the Cinturón and supervised its building, a Captain Goicoechea, deserted the Basque cause in March and went over to the rebel side, carrying with him not only plans for the Cinturón and indications of all the weak points in the line, but detailed information on the precise number of artillery pieces, rifles, and ammunition stocks available to the Basque army. His desertion was the last link in the chain of events which brought General Mola's troops into the offensive against Bilbao.

The offensive began on March 31, 1937, with aerial bombardment by the Condor Legion of the key town of Durango, and with the dropping of propaganda leaflets over Bilbao, carrying this message from General Mola:

> I have decided to terminate rapidly the war in the North. Those not guilty of assassinations who surrender their arms will have their lives and property saved. But if submission is not immediate I will raze Vizcaya to the ground, beginning with the industries of war. I have the means to do so.[19]

The bombing of Durango was the first time in the history of warfare that a civilian population had been attacked from the air for other than military reasons. The town had no real strategic significance; it was a small, quiet market village which had the misfortune to be located on a key road leading to Bilbao. In addition to explosive munitions, the German pilots dropped incendiary bombs on the town, setting a large portion of it on fire. In the attack, 127 civilians died, including two priests who died while celebrating Mass, and thirteen nuns.

Durango was the first such episode of the use of strategic bombing against civilian targets; and the Germans continued these tactics throughout this phase of the Spanish Civil War, apparently with the purpose of testing the effects of this entirely new weapon. It was in the Basque sacred city of Guernica, however, that the savagery of aerial bombardment of civilians was raised to its highest level, and the name of Guernica has become virtually synonymous with the atrocities of war since that attack. Guernica, a town of 7,000 population with no major military installations, was holding its normal weekly market gathering on Monday, April 26, 1937, so its population was increased considerably by the farmers who had come to sell their produce in the town. The raid began at 4:40 in the afternoon, and lasted more or less continuously until about 7:45. The attack was carried out by German fighters and bombers, which dropped both explosives and incendiary bombs, and which strafed the fleeing population with machine gun fire. Virtually the entire center of the town was destroyed. Casualties reached 1,654 killed and 889 wounded. Amazingly, the sacred oak tree of Guernica and the historic Casa de Juntas remained unscarred. At first, the insurgent leaders claimed that communists had burned the town to embarrass the retreating army in the eyes of world opinion; but, nine years later, at the Nuremberg war crimes trials, the chief of the German Luftwaffe, Hermann Goering, admitted that Guernica had been a German testing ground for aerial bombardment tactics.

Meanwhile, on the ground, General Mola's troops, consisting of the 61st Navarrese Division, two Italian divisions, and units of Moorish soldiers, began their advance on Bilbao. The campaign began to take on a recognizable pattern: each attack would begin with artillery and aerial bombardment on the Basque positions, followed by an infantry assault which was usually turned back. At that point, the rebels would fall back and continue to hammer the positions from the air until one or more non-Basque or left battalions withdrew, leaving the Basque Nationalists exposed on their flanks. There would then ensue a general withdrawal to new positions, usually anchored on some prominent mountain top or ridge; the Basques would dig in and await the next bombardment; and the whole process would start again. By April 24, most of the forward Basque positions had been reduced to rubble; Guernica and Durango were captured on April 28; and, by early May, the Basques had withdrawn almost entirely within the Cinturón.

At this point, two initiatives were launched from Rome to achieve some kind of peaceful solution to the Basque campaign. The Italian dictator Mussolini sent an emissary to meet with Basque representatives in southern France to offer to receive the surrender of the government of Euzkadi, in return for allowing Italy to establish their protectorate, or puppet government, in Bilbao. Aguirre's cold reply to this offer was that the Basques wanted nothing to do with any peace offer which involved surrender. In a quite unrelated development, the Vatican sent a cable to the Basques offering its good offices to negotiate a peace between Franco and Aguirre, apparently also guaranteeing that there would be no reprisals against Basque leaders. However, the cable was sent by mistake to the Republican government in Valencia, whose leaders immediately concluded that Aguirre was planning to negotiate a separate peace with the insurgents. Without informing Aguirre, the Republicans sabotaged the effort, and relations between the Spanish and the Basques fell to new lows.[20]

The final assault on Bilbao began on June 2. Aided by the information delivered by Goicoechea, the invaders penetrated the Cinturón with ease, and by June 12 they were only 10 kilometers from the center of the city. On June 13, Aguirre met with his cabinet to discuss the crisis, and plans were laid to evacuate the city, to move the government westward into neighboring Santander province, but to defend the city as long as it was feasible to do so. Refugees were already fleeing the city to the west by land or, if they could, by water to friendly countries. The sea evacuation had begun in early May, when the British government agreed to provide escort service to the ships carrying refugees once they had cleared Spanish territorial waters. Now, the pace of evacuation increased. Women, children, the elderly, religious personnel, wounded soldiers, and compromised politicians were given top priority. In many instances, families were split asunder when children and parents were assigned to ships heading in opposite directions. Only four countries agreed to accept the refugees: England, Belgium, France and Russia. The great majority ended up in France; their life in exile will be discussed in the next chapter.[21]

On June 17, the bulk of the Basque leadership withdrew westward, leaving Bilbao in the hands of a three-man Defense Committee to oversee the last stages of the resistance. Even in defeat, the Basques were typically chivalrous and nondestructive. One of the last acts of the Basque Nationalist member of the Committee, Jesús María de Leizaola, was to release the some 2,000 political prisoners being held in Bilbao's prisons, and to have them escorted to the front lines of the invading army. He also intervened to prevent the Anarchists and Communists from blowing up a large part of the city of Bilbao in the wake of their retreat. At dusk, on June 18, the Defense Committee gave the order to the last remaining militia units to evacuate the city. On the 19th, late in the afternoon, the Vth Navarrese Brigade raised the monarchist flag over the Bilbao city hall. Basque self-government and autonomy had come to an end; the life of the Basques in exile had begun.

From Santoña to the End of the Civil War: August 1937 to February 1939

As the remnants of the Basque army retreated westward into Santander province, they still constituted a military force of some significance. In all, about 30,000 troops from the original army were included in the withdrawal. Although they had been beaten in combat, the cause was more logistical than anything else, and could have been remedied by a vigorous program of rearmament by the Republican government. The Basque battalions remained intact; their leadership held together, and the experience gained in the defense of their homeland had toughened them as a fighting force.

With a few exceptions, however, this valuable resource in the struggle against the army rebels would see little action again. Politics and the technical problems involving money and weapons conspired to render the Basque battalions virtually useless for the remainder of the war. Upon their arrival in Santander, the Basques were incorporated into the XVth Republican Army Corps and brought under the overall direction of the Republican army general staff. During the month of July 1937, while General Franco's forces prepared for the final push into Santander, Aguirre flew to Valencia to meet with the Spanish President Azaña. His objective was to secure Republican support to extract the entire Basque army from Santander, to transport it across France, and to bring the troops into the rapidly shrinking front around Barcelona. His proposal was greeted coldly and noncommittally by the Spanish. Aguirre left to fly to Barcelona to discuss the project with the Catalan government, then proceeded to Paris where he began to explore the possibility of obtaining French permission to bring the troops across their territory. In the midst of these discussions, word came from Valencia that the government desired the Basques to remain where they were, and to defend Santander. Aguirre returned to Santander to be with his troops in their final hours.[22]

The campaign against Santander began on August 14. Facing the Republican forces of 50,000 ill-equipped troops were three Italian divisions, six brigades from Navarra, and 30

Spanish battalions, supported by 63 artillery batteries and the now-feared Condor Legion. The campaign lasted less then ten days. The Basques fought well considering that they were defending someone else's territory; but they were simply overwhelmed by the superior fire power of the attackers. Between August 18 and August 22, most of the key figures in the Basque government were evacuated by sea to France, where they began to set up the framework of a government-in-exile and to care for the 150,000 Basque refugees in France. On August 22, the Basques were ordered by the Republicans to retreat still further westward into Asturias province; but they defied the order, and went instead to the port of Santoña, some 30 kilometers east of the city of Santander, there to await their eventual surrender to the Italians and to evacuate as many of their number as possible. On August 23, President Aguirre departed by air for France, leaving behind the various battalion commanders and several leaders of the Basque Nationalist Party to make their way as best they could.

The following day, August 24, all the Basque commanders met in Santoña, and determined to surrender their forces to the Italian commander, on the assumption that they could strike a better bargain with him than with the representatives of General Franco. Later that same day, Basque leaders met with Italian representatives to negotiate their surrender. The agreement, known as the Pact of Santoña, specified that the Basques would surrender their weapons to the Italian occupation troops, maintain public order in their zone, and protect the lives of the political prisoners until they could be freed by the Italians. The Italians, for their part, agreed to protect the lives of all Basque soldiers, to guarantee the departure of all Basque politicians and government officials, to regard the Basque soldiers as free from an obligation to participate further in the Spanish Civil War on the side of the rebels, and to assure that the Basque civilian population that had been loyal to the government of Euzkadi would not be persecuted.

The next morning, August 25, the Basque soldiers and political figures began to gather on the docks of Santoña to be picked up by two British ships, the *Bobie* and the *Seven Seas Spray*. Shortly after boarding began, the order came to halt the evacuation because of the threat of a hostile submarine cruising off shore. Embarkation was renewed on the 26th, and the ships were loaded; but permission to sail never arrived. Instead, on the 27th, the Italians countermanded the agreement, apparently on orders from General Franco, and all passengers already boarded were ordered to disembark. On the morning of the 28th, the Basques were transported in buses and other vehicles to concentration camps and to the local prison, there to await transshipment to other prisons or to forced labor battalions. In the next chapter, we will return to these thousands of men, and follow their paths which led to long prison sentences, concentration camps, torture, and the firing squad.

Not all of the Basque soldiers were captured at Santoña. Some battalions escaped the net and retreated westward, to fight in the next campaign in the north, that for Asturias province. Even after the fall of Asturias, and Franco's complete conquest of the northern provinces, small groups of Basques remained in the mountainous area for years, conducting guerrilla raids and preserving the tenuous network of resistance activities. Other larger groups of Basque troops managed to escape entirely from the northern front, and returned to the struggle against the insurgents in the Aragón region, and around Valencia in September 1937. Basque militia units also played a key role in the later defense of Madrid. But these units constituted by far the smaller portion of the once-proud army of 45,000 formed by the government of Euzkadi.

The government of Euzkadi was reformed in two sections following the evacuation from Santander. President Aguirre returned to establish an office of the Basque government in Barcelona in order to maintain contact with the Republic, and to contribute what he could to the war effort. Aguirre and the remainder of the Basque officials in Barcelona joined the general retreat across the French border in February 1939, as the fall of Barcelona marked the end of the Spanish Civil War. Others of the government went to Paris, where they established the headquarters of the Basque Delegation. This office continued to serve as the home of the government-in-exile until the outbreak of World War II. Throughout the southern part of France, the thousands of Basque refugees quickly set about the business of building their social system anew, complete with schools, hospitals, and the other components of modern society. In the next chapter, we shall return to the life of the Basques in exile.

It would be impossible to exaggerate the importance of the Spanish Civil War for Basque national identity. One old soldier from those days told me that he first felt that he was Basque, and therefore different from the Spanish, on the day he stood with his battalion in the plaza in Bilbao before the Hotel Carlton, where the Basque government had its headquarters, and heard President Aguirre exhort them to the defense of their homeland. What a decade of propaganda by Sabino de Arana y Goiri, and a generation of organization by the Basque Nationalist Party had failed to accomplish, the raising of the Basque national consciousness, Generals Mola and Franco managed to achieve in a matter of months. Younger members of the resistance traced their participation to the wartime activities of a father or older brother in whose footsteps they sought to follow. The focal points of these decisions was usually a complex mixture of revenge and emulation; not only did younger resistance fighters seek vengeance for the damage done to their homeland and their national pride in 1936, but they were also acting out an identity crisis of sorts as they tried to prove themselves worthy of inheriting a proud family name of long standing in resistance circles. For the Basques, the Spanish Civil War was one of those rare psychological moments in history when an entire culture passes through an experience of the deepest significance, and is never quite the same again. Time after time, the leaders of the culture find themselves returning to that experience as they search for ways to make Basques more aware of the meaning of their ethnic heritage and of their existence as human beings.

PART TWO

The Franco Years

Chapter Four

THE EMERGENCE OF THE BASQUE RESISTANCE: FROM 1939 TO 1951

In 1937, when the Basque government went into exile, and the Basque army surrendered at Santoña, there was no "Basque Resistance" to speak of. Few of the then prominent Basque leaders had any experience in clandestine activities; and there existed no organizational framework within which to carry on an underground struggle. Indeed, the only organizational remains of the Basque political order were the shattered government of Euzkadi, in Paris; the Basque Nationalist Party, with most of its leaders either imprisoned or in exile; and several labor organizations, soon to feel the full weight of the oppression of the Spanish state.

Yet within fifteen years, the Basque resistance emerged as a durable and reliable force to be reckoned with by the Franco government. The government of Euzkadi was firmly installed in Paris, watched over by a sympathetic French government, and supported by substantial contributions from exiled Basques in Latin America and Europe. The Basque Nationalist Party had reformed itself on Spanish soil, and its youth branch was busy recruiting new blood into the organization. And the underground Basque labor unions felt themselves strong enough to challenge Franco's authority in the major strike in Bilbao and San Sebastián in April 1951.

In this chapter, we shall follow the transformation of the Basque nationalist cause from a broken and dispersed government to an organized and experienced clandestine insurgency. The resistance movement was woven from many threads. The fierce repression of Basque liberties and culture following the Civil War galvanized anti-Spanish feeling in the Basque country and provided fuel for the fire of the resistance.

The common experiences of the imprisoned Basque political and military leaders forged in them a unity of will and purpose previously unknown. The experiences of the exiled Basques, especially those who fought with the French *maquis* in World War II, laid the groundwork for a resistance underground which could easily be shifted to Spanish territory after the war. Finally, the failure of will of the democracies, especially Great Britain and the United States, between 1945 and 1947 led the Basques to conclude that they could not depend on outside assistance and that they would have to achieve their liberation alone, and even at times in the face of Western aid to Franco.

Repression and Exile: 1937-1940

"These abominable separatists do not deserve to have a homeland," raved the Spanish military governor of Alava, General Gil Yuste, in a newspaper article written during the Civil War. "Basque nationalism must be ruined, trampled underfoot, ripped out by its roots."[1] As if in response to Gil Yuste's call, the occupation forces of General Franco descended upon the Basque country determined to erase forever all signs of a distinctive Basque culture, as well as the remnants of the incipient Basque nationalist political organization.

Beginning in Navarra and Alava, and spreading to Guipúzcoa and Vizcaya as they came under rebel control, there erupted a virulent anti-nationalist purge which extended from businesses and factories to schools and churches. Property of known Basque nationalists was confiscated. Small shops, restaurants and taverns were taken for the rebels, and the major industrial centers in Bilbao were turned immediately to the manufacture of weapons to be used against the Republic. Food distribution was tightly controlled by the occupation authorities, and bread lines became the target of mass arrest raids by rightist vigilante groups.[2] All schoolmasters were fired immediately unless they could prove their political neutrality.[3]

The Francoist occupation landed heavily on those priests and higher Catholic officials who had supported the Basque cause. As long as the Basques continued to fight, the religious aspect of the Civil War was muted and the Vatican could avoid taking sides. After the fall of Bilbao, however, the Civil War became a kind of "holy war," and Franco was able to present himself as the savior of the Catholic religion against the attacks of the atheistic left. This, in turn, meant that the Basque nationalist priesthood had to be chastised severely. Accordingly, on July 1, 1937, the Catholic hierarchy of Spain issued a joint letter to the "Bishops of the Whole World," attacking Basque priests for not having listened to "the voice of the Church." And, on August 28, the Pope formally recognized the Franco government as the legal regime of Spain, thereby removing the last thread of protection from the Basque priests who had sided with the nationalists.

The repression was immediate. Thomas reports that 278 priests and 125 monks suffered imprisonment, or deportation to other parts of Spain. Sixteen were put to death for their role in the defense of their country.[4] In countless cases, parish priests were discharged from their posts and replaced with Spanish priests for "crimes" as petty and insignificant as having failed to ring the church bells to greet the invading army as its troops entered the village. Several elderly parish priests were sentenced to jail terms of more than twenty years each, at hard labor and in solitary confinement. None survived the ordeal.[5]

Of all the acts of suppression, however, symbolically the most damaging was the attempt of the occupation authorities to destroy the Basque language as a functioning communications medium. Almost immediately after the fall of the Basque government, the use of Euskera was prohibited in all public places. Jail sentences were imposed for even casual conversations carried on in the language on public streets. Schools were not allowed to teach the language; and priests were prohibited from sermonizing in Euskera. In civil registries, entries of births, marriages, and deaths which included Basque names were erased, and replaced with their Spanish equivalents. In a few areas, such as around Guernica, Basque inscriptions on tombstones and public buildings were scraped off. Radio broadcasts in Euskera were proscribed. Since Basque nationalism leaned so heavily on the linguistic identification of race, culture, and nation, Madrid placed special emphasis on the destruction of this central pillar of anti-Spanish sentiment.

As is often the case, however, the very act of suppression provoked an attitude of resistance among the people; and Euskera survived clandestinely for over a generation before the Spanish conceded the point that they could not abolish the language, and began to permit certain limited uses of the language once again.[6]

For at least two months after the fall of Bilbao, protection of individual rights was virtually non-existent throughout the Basque provinces. Countless hundreds of innocent civilians were rounded up on the street by day, and in their homes at night, driven to remote country areas, or to deserted graveyards, and executed summarily, without even the benefit of having a priest hear their confession. These free-lance assassinations were carried out by teams of falangists brought in from other Spanish regions to terrorize the Basque civilian population, and to force it into submission. After a time, even Franco's Carlist supporters (who were, after all, Basque also) could not tolerate the breakdown of order in Vizcaya and Guipúzcoa, and intervened to halt the atrocities of the vigilante squads, and to have them recalled by Franco.[7]

The civilians who were dealt with by the Spanish war tribunals fared little better than their comrades who were taken for "rides" gangster-style. Soon after the conclusion of the war, in 1939, Franco promulgated the infamous "Law on Political Responsibilities," which made it a crime for anyone over the age of fourteen (1) to have "helped to undermine public order" at any time since October 1, 1934; (2) "to have impeded the national *Movimiento,*" even by being "grievously passive," at any time after July 18, 1936; or (3) to have belonged at any time to any of the left political parties, or to any regional nationalist organizations, or to the Liberal Party, or to a Masonic lodge. Anyone convicted of any of these crimes was liable to have all his property confiscated, to be deprived of his nationality, to be exiled to Africa, or to be sentenced to a long prison term, sometimes up to life. Trials were conducted by mixed military-Falange tribunals, and there was no appeal. Court procedures only faintly resembled those required of due process; and more than once were confessions extracted by torture.[8]

It is impossible to assess how many Basque civilians were imprisoned under these laws and procedures. Several Basque sources report the Basque population of the Larriñaga prison in Bilbao at about 2,400; of the Penal in Burgos, at over 3,000; of the Dueso prison in Santoña, several thousand; and of the prison in Sevilla, at about 300. Of course, many of these were military prisoners who were subject to their special kind of mistreatment. A reasonable estimate of the total political prisoner population taken from the Basque country would probably range between 4,000 and 7,000 at any given time. Many of these prisoners never saw freedom once they entered captivity.[9]

In the previous chapter, we left the Basque army in Santoña where they had been betrayed by the Italian commander and turned over to the Spanish forces soon after their surrender. In spite of the protections agreed to in the Pact of Santoña, the Basque soldiers were herded into forced labor battalions and sent to work on fortifications along the Pyrenees. In some cases, they were forcibly enlisted in the rebel army and sent to fight for General Franco. In a large number of cases, however, especially for Basque officers, the road led from prison to prison, frequently ending with death by firing squad.

Soon after their surrender in Santoña, most Basque officers were interred in the Dueso prison in that city, where they were transferred to Spanish control on September 8, 1937.[10] Shortly thereafter, all battalion officers and all captured Basque Nationalist Party officials were tried for "armed rebellion." The "trials" were mass affairs, conducted by military tribunals, with virtually no legal defense of the accused and no opportunity for cross-examination of witnesses. Not surprisingly, very few of the accused were acquitted. Large numbers were sentenced to death, condemned to spend up to thirty years in jail.

Conditions in Dueso during this period defy description. Prisoners were put together in groups of forty in cells of not more than thirty square meters with no running water and no toilet facilities. Food consisted of small portions of bread and soup, with sardines on occasion. Prisoners were forced to participate in ceremonial exercises centering on rendering the ritualistic fascist salute, and singing the Spanish national anthem; refusal to do so brought beatings and deprivations.

In October, the tempo of beatings, torture, and forced confessions increased. And then, on October 15, the dreaded executions for rebellion began. Rafael de Gárate kept careful records of the executions in his diary, until he was moved to another prison in mid-November. In the one-month period, 79 men were shot, some for offenses as trivial as crying out "Long Live Euzkadi!" When the executions began, the guards took great delight in threatening prisoners with the firing squad, only to return them to their cells to wait their turn another day.

In the middle of November, many of the *gudari* officers were moved to the Larriñaga prison in Bilbao. Here living conditions were better; food was better; and clothing from home was allowed to pass into the prison. The pace of the executions picked up, however; and the firing squad was augmented by the dreaded *garrote vil* as a technique for carrying out the execution order.[11] In all, from December 1937 to July 1938, 241 men were executed in Larriñaga. In June 1938, Gárate reports that 1,014 of Larriñaga's 2,437 prisoners were condemned to death. In July, 600 of these (including Gárate) were sent to the Penal prison in Burgos, where treatment was much worse. By January 1939, this group had dwindled in size to only 300; and by 1943, when most of the survivors had been released, there were only 200 of the original number who had escaped execution.

For many thousands of Basques, however, escape into exile provided relief from the terror of the Spanish police state. An estimated 100,000-150,000 Basques went into exile between the beginning of the siege of Bilbao and the end of the Civil War. Of these, about 30,000 were children.[12]

For virtually all of these refugees, their first stop was France, where they were received by the well-organized Basque government agencies dispatched in advance to establish the various social institutions needed in a functioning community. Schools were set up at several locations throughout the French Basque region, including one for several hundred children who were housed in an abandoned castle in St. Jean Pied-de-Port. Basque priests made contact with local parish churches and soon began to say Mass in the Basque language for the exiles. Social assistance agencies found homes, clothing and food, and eventually jobs for the thousands of refugees who arrived with little more than the clothes on their backs.

The real pride of the Basque Goverment-in-Exile in southern France was the magnificent 500-bed hospital, La Roseraie, established in a private mansion located near Biarritz. Through this facility passed more than 800 Basque soldiers who had been wounded during the war. In addition, the hospital attended all the refugees for free, and several hundred children were born within its walls.[13]

From France, the wave of Basque refugees spread out to several countries in Europe, and to three in particular in the Western Hemisphere. About a thousand children were sent to Russia, and larger numbers went to Belgium and to England, where they were soon caught up in World War II. Since many of their parents and older brothers and sisters either remained in France, or migrated to Latin America, the effect of this refugee pattern was to split up families, sometimes for years. It was not uncommon for four-member families to find themselves refugees in four different countries by the end of World War II.

Somewhat larger numbers, perhaps as many as 35,000, gradually began to make their way to the Western Hemisphere. Three countries — Mexico, Venezuela, and Argentina — agreed to receive the Basque exiles, so the immigrants soon were clustered in tightly-knit communities, huddled together to protect their cultural unity. The men and women who chose to take this perilous journey did so for one of two reasons: either they feared retribution from the Germans after the war began, or they decided that they had no future left in Europe and wanted to begin anew in a new land. In either case, Latin America attracted much of the intellectual and business elite of the Basques: industrialists, merchants, writers, lawyers, doctors, architects, and so forth. As a consequence, the Basque colonies in Latin America prospered, becoming the source of important financial support for the Government-in-Exile formed in Paris after World War II.

The convergence of all these disparate experiences soon led

to the beginnings of the Basque Resistance. Within the prisons in Spain, wherever Basque political leaders or army officers were jailed together, an underground organization had taken shape to keep alive the spirit of the struggle against fascism. A clandestine newspaper was begun, and copies circulated more or less freely under the eyes of the prison authorities. The underground leaders within the prison organized special ceremonies to celebrate nationalist events, such as Aberri Eguna, the Basque national holiday, and covered the celebrations so well that prison officials never detected their purpose or even their existence. The moving force in the creation of these clandestine organizations was the Basque Nationalist Party through its imprisoned leaders, many of whom had led PNV battalions during the war.[14]

During the first years of the 1940s, as the political prisoners began to emerge from jail, the underground took on a more definite shape and organizational structure. The PNV formed the Resistance Committee (*Junta de Resistencia*) to coordinate the growing number of anti-Franco activities on Basque soil. This group had its counterparts in France and England, and until 1945 it was active in the overall war effort against Nazi Germany. Women began to play a vital role in Resistance activities during the early 1940s, primarily because most politically minded men were in prison. For about five years or so after the fall of Bilbao, the Resistance was held together largely by women, who continued to play an active part in the underground even after 1947.[15]

From 1940 to 1945, the Resistance engaged in activities designed to contribute to the Allied struggle against Germany. The American consulate in Bilbao became a center of Allied intelligence-gathering as Basque couriers delivered information gathered in France about German bases and operations.[16] The network of agents and escape routes across the Pyrenees out of France was placed at the service of the Allies to guide downed American and British pilots to safety. In one of the more remarkable efforts of the underground war, Basque agents cooperated with the French *maquis* to remove bags of sand from various sites on the Normandy beaches and smuggle them across the border to Bilbao, where they could be analyzed for clues as to the best places to land heavy vehicles during the 1944 invasion of France.[17] As far as the struggle against Franco was concerned, however, few measures were taken. Repression was especially severe, and the Resistance was so weak that it could not afford to strike boldly against Madrid. Equally important, however, was the Basques' belief that, once the Second World War ended, the Allies would turn on Franco, drive him from power, and restore freedom to the Basques. In this, the Basques were to be cruelly disappointed.

The Basques in World War II: 1940-1945

The German invasion of France, Belgium and the Low Countries in May 1940 caught most of the Basque nationalist leaders on the European continent. A small delegation led by Manuel de Irujo was in England to settle the Basque refugees there, as well as to persuade the British government to support their return to Spain and to aid in the overthrow of General Franco. A few key leaders, such as Ramón Aldasoro, found themselves in the Western Hemisphere, working to increase support for the Basque cause among second generation Basques in countries like Argentina and Uruguay. The great majority, however, were in France and Belgium.

President Aguirre and his family had just arrived in the Belgian town of La Panne, near the French border, on vacation when hostilities erupted. Gathering together about forty Basques from that region, Aguirre set off on foot for Dunkerque, only fifteen kilometers distant, in hopes of evacuating them to England and safety. In England, Irujo and others worked feverishly to persuade the British to evacuate Aguirre, fearing for his life if he fell into the hands of the Germans. Their efforts were to no avail. No more than 250 refugees from the Spanish Civil War — Basque, or Spanish Republican — actually succeeded in forcing their way aboard one of the vessels at Dunkerque; and most of these were forced to return to France by an unsympathetic British government.[18] Aguirre and his followers were denied passage.

There then ensued one of the most remarkable odysseys of the entire war, as Aguirre journeyed through central Europe to safety.[19] Leaving his family and friends to an uncertain fate in

France, the Basque president made his way back into German-occupied Belgium, where he was allowed to hide in a Jesuit school in Brussels. From there, he went to the Belgian city of Amberes, where, with the help of several courageous Latin American diplomats, he obtained false papers, and a passport identifying him as a Panamanian citizen, one José Andrés Alvarez. In December 1940, disguised with mustache and glasses, the new Sr. Alvarez entered Germany, en route to Berlin, where, he had been told, he could obtain a visa to a neutral country. (Such travel permits were not issued in countries under German occupation.) After several nerve-wracking delays, Alvarez-Aguirre finally received his visa to enter Sweden, where he went in May 1941 (with his wife and children traveling as the widow and family of a deceased Venezuelan). On July 31, the Aguirre family left Sweden by ship bound for Rio de Janeiro, where they arrived on August 27. It was not until October 1941, however, when they had crossed the border into Uruguay, that President Aguirre could resume his real identity. He had spent almost a year in German-occupied territory, half of that period in the heart of the Nazi state itself.

For the thousands of Basques left behind in France, the future held even more suffering. As the government of France passed into the hands of Marshall Pétain, pro-Nazi French officials launched a vicious campaign to punish and discredit the Basques who had been refugees in their country for nearly three years. Even before the armistice with Germany was signed, the French Minister of Interior gave the order to round up all Basque refugees and convey them to the concentration camp at Gurs. With the close of hostilities between France and Germany and the establishment of the Vichy regime, anti-Basque measures became more fierce. The Basque government headquarters building in Paris was confiscated from its owner, a private citizen, and turned over to the Spanish secret police who were operating throughout France to locate Spanish and Basque exiled leaders. The Basque news service was closed permanently. Following the armistice, the Franco government gave German authorities in Paris a list of some 800 important exiles from the Civil War, including many Basques, for apprehension and deportation to Spain. Nearly all the Spanish refugees had fled into the southern zone of France, called the "liberated zone" because French officials still governed there in contrast to the northern zone where the German occupation was complete, so the list was passed on to the French for action. Almost 100 of the persons on the list were caught immediately, and some returned to Spain, including the president of Cataluña, Luis Companys. When Companys' return was followed shortly by a swift "trial" and execution, Marshall Pétain determined not to send any more Spanish refugees back to Spain. Thus the lives of many key Basque leaders were saved as long as they remained in the Vichy-controlled zone of France.

In the meantime, the Basques in London determined to establish themselves as an interim government to maintain continuity until contact could be made with President Aguirre, whose whereabouts remained unknown. Under the leadership of Manuel de Irujo, the senior Basque official still living in a free country, the Basque National Council was created in England in July 1940, in spite of the assurances of British Foreign Minister Anthony Eden to the Franco government that refugees from the Civil War would not be allowed to operate on English soil.[20] Almost immediately, Irujo and the others of the council entered into negotiations with the Free French government of Charles de Gaulle in London with the objective of establishing a Basque military unit with the Free French forces. After lengthy discussions, on May 17, 1941, representatives of the Free French and of the Basque National Council signed the following agreement:

1. That General de Gaulle would take every measure in his power to see to it that Basques then being detained in prisons or concentration camps in French territory would be set free, and helped to return to a normal life;

2. That General de Gaulle would look with favor on the granting of French citizenship to those Basques who had fought in the Free French army, as well as to those Basques who were recommended for such treatment by the Basque National Council;

3. That both parties favored the voluntary enlistment of Basques in the Free French army, and that the Free French

government would undertake to issue passports or safe conduct passes to any Basques desiring to enlist;

4. That the Free French government would grant asylum to Basques desiring same, and recommended by the Basque National Council;

5. That the Basque National Council would use its influence to urge Basques residing in Free French territory to contribute to their utmost to the economic development of the territory; and

6. That the Basque National Council would assist Free French agents in gathering intelligence in France, Spain and certain French territories in Africa.

The one remaining major issue still to be negotiated between the French and the Basques was that of the creation of an autonomous Basque unit within the Free French army. Irujo initiated discussions on this topic in June 1941 but was rebuffed apparently by members of de Gaulle's staff who were fearful of establishing a unit of questionable loyalty within their ranks. Determined not to be denied, Irujo turned to the Free French navy, who proved to be more agreeable to the idea; and on September 10 an all-Basque unit, the Third Marine Battalion, was ordered established. By October 22 the battalion's full complement of officers and men was enrolled and training was begun. The unit was destined never to see battle. The British government, sensitive to the pressures of Spain on their Gibraltar base, made known to de Gaulle their displeasure at the unit's formation, and the latter ordered the battalion dissolved on May 23, 1942. At the battalion's final parade before de Gaulle, the general said that he was not a free agent in the decision, and that, had they been on French soil, the dissolution would never have taken place. The Basque National Council, now acting under the orders of President Aguirre since his escape to Uruguay (and later to the United States), directed the battalion to be dissolved, and those Basques who so wished were enlisted as individuals into the Free French army.[21]

From 1940 to 1945 the many thousands of Basques who had remained in France at the start of the war were dispersed, harassed and persecuted. While each case was unique, in general their paths led in one of five different directions. A relatively small group were captured by the Germans, either as civilians in forced labor companies or as soldiers in the French army, and deported to concentration camps in Germany. Most of these died of the treatment they received in these camps.[22] A comparatively larger group, perhaps numbering in the tens of thousands, were placed in French concentration camps because they constituted a threat to the Vichy regime. Their treatment varied from moderately tolerable to barbaric, depending apparently on the attitudes of those running the camps. Several tens of thousands remained at liberty in the Vichy zone and were "allowed" to work at menial, low-paying jobs in mines and fields. A relative handful, comparatively well off when measured against the misfortunes of their brothers, found their way to ships and managed to escape to neutral countries. Their way was not an easy one, however, for it was hard to find a government that would accept them, and many had no means of earning a livelihood upon their arrival. Many ended up in sympathetic Latin American countries, of which the most helpful were Mexico, Venezuela, Argentina and Uruguay. To its discredit, the government of the United States uniformly refused admission of these groups. A fifth group of Basques fought as members of the French *maquis.*

Many hundreds of Spanish refugees who had migrated to the so-called liberated zone of France after the armistice drifted into anti-German guerrilla groups, from late 1942 until the end of the war in France.[23] The French Resistance fought mainly in built-up urban areas, while the *maquis* operated primarily in one of several mountainous regions along the Spanish, Italian and Swiss borders with France. At the time of the Normandy invasion, there were approximately 14,000 Spanish Civil War refugees serving in the *maquis.* While exact figures are unavailable, we may surmise that at least several hundred Basques were to be counted among the Spanish figure.

The *maquis* were responsible for the hit-and-run kinds of insurgent actions typical of mountain guerrilla forces: ambushes of German convoys, attacks on prisons to secure the release of political prisoners and agents, bombings of German military and political installations, intelligence gathering and transmission, assisting downed Allied pilots and other threatened persons to escape, either by water or across the Pyrennees, and so forth. General Eisenhower remarked that the *maquis* were the equivalent of fifteen Allied divisions in their effects on German installations and morale.

In October 1944, with Paris liberated and the Germans being driven out of France, General de Gaulle ordered that the *maquis* be disbanded as a separate fighting force, and that all *maquisards* who wished to continue to serve in the war be enlisted in the regular French army. His reasoning on this matter betrayed his military suspicion of irregular troops, as well as his political fear of an armed force which responded to political forces beyond his control. At any rate, many Spaniards chose not to enter the new French army units but rather to cross the Pyrenees once again and carry the struggle against fascism back to Spain. Although the Allies tried to block this from happening and interposed their forces between the Spanish and the border, several large groups did manage to infiltrate through the mountains. Thus, in the autumn of 1944 rumors began to circulate of skirmishes between Spanish army units and guerrilla insurgents in the border areas. One such unit, consisting of about 1,500 guerrillas, was engaged at about this time and defeated decisively by regular Spanish troops. One may assume that many such engagements took place which were never picked up by observers and the news media.[24]

In France meanwhile, two battalions — one Spanish and one entirely Basque — were formed within the French army out of the remnants of the *maquis*. The Basque battalion, called "Gernika," entered service in late 1944, and saw fierce action in reducing German pockets of resistance in April 1945. Their service was so distinguished that they were reviewed by General de Gaulle personally. It is indeed ironic that this honor was bestowed on the Basque battalion almost exactly three years after their predecessor unit was disbanded by the same General de Gaulle because of Allied political pressure.

The Democracies Give In: 1945-1951

From the point of view of the United States, World War II was fought in Europe as an ideological war against fascism. Many Americans believed that the struggle should not cease just because Germany and Italy had been defeated militarily. With regard to Spain, the American government's stance was one of sympathy for anti-Franco forces, who, it was felt, were carrying on the logical extension of the fight against the residue of fascism in Western Europe. President Franklin D. Roosevelt expressed these feelings to the newly-named Ambassador to Madrid, Norman Armour, in a letter dated March 10, 1945:

> The fact that our Government maintains formal diplomatic relations with the present Spanish regime should not be interpreted by anyone to imply approval of that regime and its sole party, the Falange, which has been openly hostile to the United States and which has tried to spread its fascist party ideas in the Western Hemisphere. . . .
>
> . . . [I]t is not our practice in normal circumstances to interfere in the internal affairs of other countries unless there exists a threat to international peace. . . . I should be lacking in candor, however, if I did not tell you that I can see no place in the community of nations for governments founded on fascist principles.[25]

From that time on until late 1947, the official American position was that the United States government disapproved of the Franco regime, not only because it had sided with the Axis in World War II, but because it stifled liberties internally. The United States would not intervene directly in Spain's domestic affairs, leaving the form of government of that country in the hands of the Spanish. Nevertheless, the United States would act to see that Spain did not enjoy the privileges of a respected member of the international community. To that end, the American government worked to have Spain excluded from membership in the United Nations Organization and its auxiliary bodies, and denied Madrid the courtesy of naming a representative of ambassadorial rank, after Armour's retirement in late 1945. All of these matters affected the Basque case only incidentally, since from the American point of view the struggle for Basque independence was only one small fragment of the overall confrontation with General Franco. Nevertheless, the Basques in exile, and in the anti-Franco underground in Spain, concluded in mid-1945 that pressure from the Western democracies — the United States, the United Kingdom, and France — would suffice to bring Franco down and to restore the Republic. Regional autonomy via a restoration of the Basque Statute of October 1936 would then follow shortly.

The transformation in the attitude of the major democracies toward Franco did not occur suddenly, or uniformly. Diplomatic correspondence of the United States does not reflect any questioning the wisdom of its original position until early 1946, and the complete reversal of attitude was not evident until late 1947. Further, the three key countries showed varying degrees of belligerency toward Spain. France was most insistent in calling for the breaking of relations from the beginning, and probably was involved in aiding anti-Franco forces to operate unmolested from French soil. Great Britain, on the other hand, urged restraint and caution, lest the three powers appear so aggressive that Spanish public opinion should be mobilized in support of the Franco regime. The United States found itself in a middle position, opposing the breaking of diplomatic relations or the support of anti-Franco guerrillas, but favoring a more assertive policy to encourage Franco to step down from power.

Nineteen-forty-five was marked by distinct hostility between the Spanish and American governments. At the Potsdam Conference of the Big Three, the United States, United Kingdom and the Soviet Union issued a statement to the effect that they could not support Spain's request for admission to the newly-formed United Nations because the Spanish government "having been formed with the support of the Axis powers, in view of its origins, its nature, its record and its close association with the aggressor States, does not possess the necessary qualifications to justify its admission." And, on June 19, 1945, the United Nations Conference in San Francisco voted, with the support of the United States, to exclude Spain from that body. In addition, in several meetings with General Franco, the American ambassador indicated quite directly his government's intense displeasure with the fascist orientation of the Spanish government, and the inability of his government to consider improving relations until steps were taken to liberalize the regime.[26] There were other indicators of the strained relations between Spain and the democracies: France called repeatedly for the breaking of relations; infiltration across the border and terrorist actions in Spain increased; and in Washington, State Department officials met with representatives of the Spanish Republican Government-in-Exile in Mexico City.

During 1946 the United States continued to hew to its hard line: Franco would have to go before Spain could be admitted to the family of nations. In March, the governments of the United States, Great Britain, and France issued a public statement urging

> a peaceful withdrawal of Franco, the abolition of the Falange, and the establishment of an interim or caretaker government under which the Spanish people may have an opportunity freely to determine the type of government they wish to have and to choose their leaders.[27]

Following Charles de Gaulle's resignation as president in January 1946, and the shift of the French government to the left, France was particularly insistent that the three democracies take joint action to oust Franco. The United States usually agreed that strong action was required, but waited to secure joint approval by all three countries. Since Great Britain consistently opposed such a step, the result was inaction both in the embassies in Madrid and in the United Nations, through 1946 and 1947.

Beginning as early as February 1946, however, in a lengthy cable from Moscow, the U.S. charge in the Soviet Union, George Kennan, sought to call attention to the growing interest of Russia in the overthrow of the Franco government.[28] Such an interest, wrote Kennan, stemmed from several sources: the Russian belief that Spain's backward social class structure made them ripe for revolution; Russian hatred of Spanish fascism for the atrocities Spain's Blue Division had committed in Russia during the war; a Russian desire to seek revenge for the Republic's defeat in the Spanish Civil War, and the consequent suppression of the Russian-supported Spanish Communist Party; and, finally, Russia's belief that Spain occupied a key strategic position in the struggle for control of the Mediterranean. "Soviet policy," he continued,

> has thus been (a) to do all in its power to render impossible achievement of any permanent *modus vivendi* between western powers and Franco or any other conservative element in Spain and (b) to utilize every possible channel for mobilizing western opinion against Franco in the hopes that western governments will have to yield to pressure and make strong action to bring about downfall of Franco regime.

In his significant cable, Kennan refrained from drawing any conclusions concerning American policy in Spain. These were supplied in a cable twelve days later from the U.S. charge in Madrid (Mr. Butterworth), who took the opportunity of the Kennan telegram to counsel caution and patience toward Franco. Butterworth's argument was simple and straightforward and, reduced to its essential syllogism, sounded like this: (1) Russia and the United States have contradictory interests in Western Europe, Latin America, the Mediterranean, and in Spain; (2) Russia's objective in Spain is to create such turbulence as would lead to a renewal of the Civil War, in hopes that the Spanish Communists will emerge victorious; therefore (3) the United States objective must seek to counter that of the Soviet Union, and to work for stability in Spain, even if that means relaxing pressures on Franco to liberalize his regime.[29]

The same general theme surfaced again in a cable from Kennan on March 1, 1946, when he urged the United States to stand fast in resisting the pressures of France, and particularly the French Communists, for harsher measures against Spain. In this instance, Kennan argued that America's inability to withstand this pressure would be "carefully noted in Moscow and will be chalked up here . . . as a victory for those indirect methods of diplomacy to which Moscow has recently given such great attention."[30] And in July, Butterworth's replacement in Madrid, Philip W. Bonsal, cabled the Secretary of State to caution that continued agitation "of the Spanish question in the Security Council [of the United Nations] by countries having very definite political objectives in Spain and an unscrupulous attitude regarding the use of misinformation about conditions in Spain for the purpose of attaining those objectives have strengthened the Franco regime by arousing nationalistic sentiments."[31]

Nineteen-forty-seven was the crucial year for United States-Spanish relations, and, consequently, for Basque hopes of seeing Franco brought down by external pressure. As the Cold War escalated, and United States-Russian relations worsened in Europe, American concern over the dictatorial nature of the Spanish regime diminished. On March 12, 1947, President Truman delivered his "Truman Doctrine" speech to the U.S. Congress, asking for aid to the governments of Greece and Turkey to meet insurgencies in those countries, and committing his administration to assist anti-communist regimes to combat externally aided insurrections wherever they might erupt. American public opinion, and government policy, shifted in the space of twelve months from opposition to Franco, to support (if not yet a warm embrace).

The key document in the transformation of American policy toward Spain was a Top Secret memorandum drafted on October 24, 1947, by the State Department's Policy Planning Staff, under the direction of George Kennan, whose opinion of Spanish politics has already been noted in his previously cited cable from Moscow. The memo argued that two and a half years of pressure by the Western democracies on Franco had not caused the dictator to shift his position on internal liberalization, and in fact had solidified Spanish public opinion behind him. While economic recovery in Spain had been delayed because of the U.S.-supported exclusion of Franco from most international bodies, that did not seem to have made much of an impact on national support for his government. On the other side, anti-Franco groups were divided and disorganized, and no clear leader had emerged to define what a post-Franco government might look like. Continued pressure on Franco could only produce disorder and violence, from which only Russia could benefit. Therefore, while perhaps doing so reluctantly, the Policy Planning Staff arrived at the following conclusions: (1) "instead of openly opposing the Franco regime, we should work from now on toward a normalization of United States-Spanish relations, both political and economic;" and (2) this change should be reflected in support by the United States for Spanish entry into the United Nations. The document was initialed for approval by Secretary of State George Marshall, and the changes in American policy were duly transmitted to the Embassy in Madrid in a cable of December 18, 1947.[32]

Pluralistic governments are complex institutions, however; they can rarely change direction and speed in their policies in a brief span of time. Certain circles of influence within the Department of State had, by late 1947, reached the conclusion that the United States must reach an accommodation with General Franco. Yet, as Theodore Lowi points out,[33] President Truman was still adamantly antagonistic toward Franco and refused to extend to the Spanish dictator any gestures of amity until satisfied that there was movement toward liberalization in Spain. Other sectors of the giant American government bureaucracy were preoccupied with more pressing matters, such as the fledgling North Atlantic Treaty Organization (NATO), the development of atomic weapons, and the war in Korea. Segments of the American political community were indeed favorably disposed to the Franco regime, but they had to be pulled together to act in unison, and to exert pressure at the point where Truman was most vulnerable: the United States Congress.

The result was the creation of what Lowi calls "the Spanish Lobby," a coalition of pro-Spain groups put together by special envoy from Madrid, José Felix de Lequerica. Exhibiting impressive insight into the workings of the American political system, Lequerica retained the services of one Charles Patrick Clark to head the lobbying effort to advance through the Congress the cause of rapprochement between the United States and Spain. Clark built a lobbying coalition comprised of five rather disparate but overlapping forces: Catholics who had ties to the Catholic Church in Spain; anti-communists, who viewed Spain as perhaps the only truly reliable ally left to the United States in Europe; a group of admirals and civilians in the Defense Department and in Congress who advocated the establishment of an American naval base in Spain to anchor our position at the western end of the Mediterranean (to complement our emerging Greek-Turkish policy at the eastern end); the anti-Trumanists led in Congress by Ohio Senator Robert Taft, who would never pass up an opportunity to oppose the president; and an economic group, "the vanguard of which," writes Lowi, "was southern cotton."

In Congress, members of both houses, encouraged by the Spanish Lobby, labored to pass legislation authorizing the president to extend to Spain economic assistance of varying amounts. In March 1948, their first such effort concentrated on amending the first Economic Cooperation Act (which was to implement the Marshall Plan) to add Spain as one of the participating nations. To the surprise of many, the amendment passed rather handily, 149 to 52, but it was finally dropped in a House-Senate Conference Committee meeting. A similar effort in July 1949 was likewise defeated by anti-Franco elements in the Congress, with the full support of Truman and Secretary of State Dean Acheson.

By the late summer of 1950, however, events far removed from both Washington and Madrid had changed the balance of power in the Congress. The Korean War had erupted, forcing many otherwise anti-Franco congressmen to reassess their general position on aid to right-wing dictatorships. In August 1950, the Senate approved a measure that would authorize a loan of $100 million for Spain by the decisive vote of 65-15. When the House declined to act on a parallel measure, the issue was attached to the general appropriations bill that was being steered through the Congress, and the Spanish loan (reduced to $62.5 million as part of the compromise) became a quid pro quo for approval of the entire bill. With the Spanish loan still included, the overall bill was approved on August 28, and the president signed the bill into law on September 6. As he did so, however, he declared that he considered the Spanish loan as authorized but "not mandatory"; he would not loan the money to Spain unless "such loans will serve the interest of the United States in the conduct of foreign relations."

The pro-Spanish policy, then, centered on finding a suitable link between Spain and the interest (and the money) of the United States. The eventual answer lay in an arrangement for United States military bases in Spain, and in the increasing reintegration of Spain into the Western alliance structure. Through 1949 and 1950, a growing number of publicists, congressmen, and admirals had traveled to Spain to learn firsthand of the advantages of the country for military purposes, and of the reasonableness of the regime, and of General Franco personally. Within the Truman Administration, the voices in favor of a Spanish bases treaty began to sound louder and more insistently. In November 1950, the United Nations voted 37-1 (with 12 abstentions, the United States voting with the majority) to allow members to send to Madrid envoys of ambassadorial rank. Accordingly, and somewhat against his own will, Truman in December named Stanton Griffis as Ambassador to Spain. American foreign policy was beginning to reflect the basic philosophy of the Kennan memorandum of October 1947.

The final link in the sequence of events that produced the Spanish bases deal was the naming of Admiral Forrest P. Sherman to be Chief of Naval Operations, in the autumn of 1949. The appointment of Sherman (made possible by his pro-unification position during the so-called "revolt of the Navy" during the debate over the creation of the Defense Department) brought to the fore a staunch advocate of closer relations with Spain. Sherman had commanded the Sixth Fleet for two years; and his experiences in the Mediterranean had convinced him that the deployment of American naval power this close to the Russian sphere had had a sobering effect on Moscow. A naval installation in Spain would complement and support this deployment in any future engagement with the USSR. Admiral Sherman, in alliance with the now-Secretary of Defense George Marshall, began to work at the task of changing Truman's mind about the desirability of an American naval base in Spain.

Finally, by July 1951, faced with unrelenting pressure from the Navy and from pro-Spanish forces in the Congress, beleaguered by the war in Korea and by political antagonisms at home, Truman gave Sherman permission to fly to Madrid to begin the long series of negotiations that would lead to an American military presence in Spain. Sherman arrived in Madrid on July 17, less than three months after the Spanish government had successfully suppressed a massive general strike in Vizcaya and Guipúzcoa.

All of these momentous developments in world politics would have been quite irrelevant to the Basque nationalist situation were it not for the faith that the Basque Government-in-Exile and the Basque Nationalist Party had placed in the United States to unseat Franco and pave the way for their return. Given the state of affairs that prevailed in many unsettled parts of the world at the close of World War II, including the inclination of OSS officers to support anti-colonial uprisings and movements in places like Indo-China, it does not seem unreasonable for the Basque nationalists to have expected support from the Western democracies. The fact that they did not receive such aid seems more a consequence of the turn of events I have described than of any mistake of judgment on the part of the Basques.

The open and unabashed alliance between the Basque Government-in-Exile and the United States and the failure of that alliance to produce any favorable results for Basque nationalism have been used repeatedly ever since as part of the argument to show the weakness and timidity of the liberal PNV bourgeoisie, or, what is worse, their willingness to sell out Basque nationalist aims for their middle class interests. Critiques of this period written from a Basque socialist perspective frequently portray the Basque government in Paris as weak and ineffectual, or as agents of the American Central Intelligence Agency, or both.[34] What this argument fails to reckon with is the fact that Basque nationalism was in the late 1940s only an extremely tiny piece of a rapidly shifting mosaic of Great Power interests and ideologies, over which the Basques had absolutely no control. It is most difficult at this historical distance to suggest what a more aggressive Basque government might have done to make any difference, either in the short run or the long.

The Basque Resistance Emerges: 1945-1951

The Spanish Civil War ended officially in 1939, but it was not until 1952 that acts of violence ceased altogether. This so-called "second war" was a guerrilla campaign carried on by the survivors of the Spanish Republican Army in five regions of Spain: Andalucía, Extremadura, Castilla, Aragón, and the "Picos de Europa" area of the Cantabrian mountain range.[35] This rugged country of impenetrable mountains and dense forests became the haven for hundreds of violent men who were drawn to the region for many different reasons. Some were sent under Communist Party orders to lead the insurgency against Franco; some were ordinary deserters from the army, eager to avoid capture; some were bandits who had been serving jail sentences for common crimes at the beginning of the Civil War; and a few were Basque nationalists, bent on preserving the fragile network of political and military ties on which the Basque resistance would rely heavily in the coming years.

Prior to 1945, there was no guerrilla fighting in the Basque provinces, and little resistance activity of any sort that was visible to the outside observer. But within resistance circles, organizational links were being forged, and leaders were emerging. On March 31, 1945, representatives of the most significant political and labor groups in the Basque country met in the French Basque city of Bayonne to form the Basque Consultative Council (*Consejo Consultativo Vasco*), and to pledge their unified support for the struggle for Basque autonomy and against the Franco regime.[36] The Consultative Council, which has remained active through the post-Franco period, contained representatives from the major Basque political parties, the Basque Nationalist Party (PNV), the Basque Republican Left (*Izquierda Republicana Vasca*), Basque Nationalist Action (*Acción Nacionalista Vasca*), and the Basque arm of the Spanish Socialist Workers Party (*Comité Central Socialista de Euzkadi* — PSOE).[37] To insure representation of the Basque working class in their deliberations and activities, the

Council worked closely with representatives of the most important Basque union, *Solidaridad de Trabajadores Vascos* (STV), and the Spanish unions that were active in the Basque provinces, the *Unión General de Trabajadores* (UGT) and the *Confederación Nacional de Trabajo* (CNT). (Formerly known as *Solidaridad de Obreros Vascos,* STV had changed its name in 1933 by dropping *"Obreros"* and replacing it with *"Trabajadores."*) The Consultative Council was responsible for insuring that the Basque Government-in-Exile in Paris remained in close contact with the political forces of significance in the Basque provinces, and for coordinating the strategy of the resistance with the Resistance Committee (*Junta de Resistancia*). This latter group, unlike the Consultative Council, operated primarily on the Spanish side of the border, and so was exposed to much greater personal danger. The role of the Consultative Council was to insure that Resistance Committee activities in Spain coincided with the political strategy that had been fashioned by the Basque Government-in-Exile.

Basque resistance emerged during the period from 1945 to 1947 in the form of acts entirely of a propaganda nature intended to impresss both Basques and the Madrid regime that separatist sentiment had endured the Civil War and the ensuing suppression. Seen today in retrospect, the actions seem timid and insignificant: planting the flag of Euzkadi on inaccessible but highly visible locations, such as atop church steeples; painting revolutionary slogans on walls; and the most daring of all, the detonation of a bomb under the statue of General Mola in one of Bilbao's most public and visible areas. During the clandestine celebration of the Basque national holiday, Aberri Eguna, in 1946, the resistance succeeded in jamming Radio San Sebastián off the air, and broadcasting over that frequency nationalistic slogans and a lengthy speech by President Aguirre. In 1947, Radio Euzkadi was established to broadcast news and encouragement to listeners in the Basque country. At first, the clandestine radio broadcast from France. Later, the transmitter was set up in a remote jungle location some sixty kilometers from Caracas, Venezuela, where it functioned for 13 years with only the *de facto* approval of the Venezuelan government.[38]

In this period there were a few strikes in isolated factories throughout the Basque region; but labor unions remained broken and ineffective. Each time the Resistance Committee organized any activity, hundreds of Basques were swept up in mass arrests, and many were tortured and left in prison for months at a time. The Resistance Committee's organization was jolted repeatedly by these mass detentions; but, the network held together, and key posts were filled by new recruits.[39]

The first major activity launched and coordinated by the Resistance Committee was the strike which began on May 1, 1947, among the miners and metallurgical workers of Vizcaya. In spite of the reaction of Madrid (15,000 workers were dismissed summarily from their jobs; hundreds were arrested in the strike's first days), the action spread to other industries such as the transport workers, and to other areas, particularly the industrial towns of Guipúzcoa, such as Eibar and Pasajes. By the time the strike had run its course, on May 11, nearly 75 percent of the workers in Vizcaya had been idled and the region was placed under a state of siege. The Resistance Committee had shown itself capable of forging an alliance between the workers and the nationalists to challenge the Franco government, but the strike failed to ignite other regions and other socio-economic classes in Spain.[40]

From 1947 to 1951, resistance activities intensified and became more diversified. Propaganda about the Basque nationalist cause remained the foremost objective, however, and the clandestine radio and countless printing presses operated to spread the word throughout the Basque region that the government of Euzkadi survived, and was gaining strength both at home and abroad. At about the same time, the Government-in-Exile undertook several publicity measures to acquaint various international agencies with the state of political freedoms in Spain, with the hope of increasing international pressure on Madrid to speed liberalization. In addition, because of the increase in detention of resistance leaders, the resistance began to organize jail breaks to escort their imprisoned comrades to freedom. In spite of these efforts, in May 1949, there were still eighty-two resistance figures in prison in Bilbao, some of whom had been there since 1941.[41]

Economic recovery from the Civil War had proceeded slowly

in Spain through the 1940s; but by 1951 economic conditions had worsened to such a degree that there were a number of serious strikes throughout the entire country. Spurred on by a message from Pope Pius XII about the workers' struggling for their just rewards, the nation's clandestine unions led their members in a number of work stoppages which were entirely illegal. In March there was a huge transport workers' walkout in Barcelona; and by April the strike fever had spread to the Basque country.

For the Basque resistance, the strike-prone atmosphere presented them with both an opportunity for action and the source of dissent within their own ranks. Acting in accord with the Basque union, STV, the Resistance Committee immediately took steps to halt all economic activity in Vizcaya and Guipúzcoa as a sign of the continued strength and health of the nationalist movement. Internally, however, the Resistance Committee was split by complaints from blue-collar workers that they were always the ones called upon to bear the brunt of Franco repression, and that their professional counterparts (the *trabajadores de corbata*) were not doing their share to advance the nationalist cause. Since this opinion was in the minority, however, and since unions offered the most fertile field for organization activity in 1951, the decision was made to go ahead with the call to strike. In mid-April, Bilbao and San Sebastián were flooded with pamphlets calling for the workers to walk off their jobs on the 23rd. The call to strike was issued jointly by the Basque government, the Resistance Committee, and by all the unions, ranging from STV to the socialists.

On the proposed day, April 23, about 250,000 workers representing nearly all the labor force in Vizcaya and Guipúzcoa began a work stoppage designed to last two days. The government's answer was immediate and harsh: mass detentions (more than 2,000 arrested in the first 24 hours), beatings and dismissals from jobs. Then, to the surprise of the resistance, the strike spread to the previously inert provinces of Alava and Navarra. In Pamplona, 35,000 workers walked off their jobs; housewives marched in protest of food prices, and police resorted to armed force to put down the demonstrations. As in 1947, however, other areas of Spain failed to ignite, and Madrid was able to concentrate its attention on putting down the Basques. Gradually, the strike fever subsided, the workers returned to their jobs, and the Basque provinces became quiet.

Despite the absence of concrete results, the 1951 strike marked a turning point in the Basque resistance. The organization painstakingly put together over the previous decade had held fast under the most brutal repression it had yet seen, and had demonstrated an ability to mobilize a quarter of a million workers on short notice. In addition, the nationalist cause was clearly able to transcend the deep socio-economic splits in Basque society, and unite workers and professionals in common action. Perhaps most important, the strike provided the first opportunity for the younger generation of Basques to assume positions of leadership, and they generally performed well and reliably. Following the 1951 action, the Basque youth would come increasingly to the forefront in the resistance.[42]

During the spring and summer of 1951, however, a new force began to emerge in Spanish politics which would alter the balance of power decisively in Franco's favor. On July 17, Admiral Sherman arrived in Madrid to begin a series of talks on the conclusion of a bilateral U.S.-Spanish military agreement, and the possibility of the United States' using military bases on Spanish territory. On July 26, Secretary of State Dean Acheson added incentive to the negotiations by releasing credits of $100 million to shore up the Spanish economy. Bolstered by American military and economic support, Franco was able to ride out the storm of 1951. The Basques began to realize very uneasily that their long night in exile might prove to be longer than they had ever imagined.

Chapter Five

THE BASQUE NATIONALIST PARTY

The Basque nationalist movement during the Franco years defies easy or straightforward explanations. Open parliamentary competition was of course impossible. Yet within the murky world of the anti-Franco underground one can detect at various times a number of different threads interwoven to produce ultimately the complex tapestry that was the Basque resistance. What a person thought of the resistance depended largely on how he defined the phenomenon. There were those for whom the struggle was principally political and partisan; for them, the Basque Nationalist Party (PNV) was the focal point. Many other Basques saw economic forces as the central issue and joined the struggle through membership in one of the prohibited Basque or Spanish unions. A few defined the resistance in essentially cultural terms, and focused their efforts on preserving the linguistic uniqueness of the Basques. In later years, a number of Basque youths would grow impatient with the slow, plodding style of these incremental approaches and would declare war not only on Spain and on the Spanish language, but on capitalism as well. This chapter, and the four that follow, portray the central events of the quarter century following the 1951 strike by focusing, in succession, on the four principal elements of the Basque resistance: the Basque Nationalist Party, the Basque labor movement, the Basque revolutionary group called *Euzkadi ta Askatasuna* (ETA) and the attempts in an environment of repression to preserve the Basque language.

The Basque Nationalist Party: Organization, Strategy, Tactics[1]

The organizational structure of the Basque Nationalist Party (PNV) has remained remarkably stable since the first provincial Party Council, the *Bizkai Buru Batzar,* was established in Vizcaya by Sabino de Arana y Goiri in July of 1895. The current PNV framework was approved by the Party at its National Assembly held in Tolosa in January of 1933, and remained intact during the forty years that the Party functioned in exile and in the underground.

The PNV was organized both geographically and functionally. Geographically, the Party hierarchy began with the Municipal Councils, or *Uri Buru Batzar,* the local executive bodies that were elected by the Municipal Assemblies. These latter groups, which constituted the legislative authority of the Party at the lowest level, were made up of all the registered members of the Party. These Assemblies gathered periodically, even during the Party's clandestine phase, to select the members of the Municipal Councils, and to give them their charge for the ensuing period. The Councils were responsible for carrying on the daily affairs of the Party at the municipal level, implementing the mandate of the Assembly, and carrying out the instructions of superior bodies within the Party. The Councils were also charged with the responsibility for nominating candidates for municipal office when these were freely elected.

At the next highest level stood the Provincial Assemblies, composed of representatives selected by the Municipal Assemblies of each province. As in the case of the municipal bodies, the Provincial Assemblies named the members of the Provincial Councils, called (according to their respective province) *Bizkai Buru Batzar, Araba Buru Batzar, Guipuzkoa Buru Batzar* and *Napar Buru Batzar.* The Provincial Councils carried out the instructions of the Provincial Assemblies, as well as the directions of higher authorities in the Party. In addition, the Provincial Councils were responsible for adjusting disputes between two or more municipal party organizations, and for nominating candidates for the various provincial offices, including provincial legislature.

The supreme authority of the Party was the National Assembly, made up of fifteen representatives chosen by each Provincial Assembly. In addition, however, whenever the National Assembly met, it was usually joined by the various Provincial Councils, as well as by the National Council and the several Extraterritorial Councils (about which more in a moment). Thus constituted, the National Assembly was responsible for applying and interpreting the doctrinal rules and philosophy of the Party, designing the general political orientation of the nationalist movement, naming the various persons who are authorized to speak in the name of the Party, nominating the candidates for office at the national level (i.e., for the three provinces included under the 1936 Autonomy Statute), and setting the standards that guided the actions of the Party's supreme executive authority, the National Council, called the *Euzkadi Buru Batzar*. The National Council was made up of three councilors from each province who were chosen by their respective Provincial Councils. The National Council met both in this abbreviated version and in plenary session, at which time it was composed of all of the members of the four Provincial Councils.

The Party took great pains to insure that its organization was confederal. That is, each of the four provincial organizations was given rather wide autonomy, and the municipal assemblies and councils were even more autonomous within the loose Party structure. The Party's by-laws specified that the provincial assemblies enjoy only those powers granted to them by the municipal assemblies, and the National Assembly only the powers given it by the lower ranks of the hierarchy. In practice, however, during the Franco era, the pressures of clandestine underground politics frequently dictated more centralization of decision-making power and authority than may be evident from this formal wording.

A number of auxiliary organizations were more or less directly linked to the PNV. Women were admitted to Party membership on an equal basis with men, but they nevertheless had their own constituent organization with a special mission. Called *Emakume Abertzale Batzar,* or Woman's Patriotic Council, this group was especially active in encouraging the cultural and charitable work of the Party faithful, and in assisting the Basque exiles to find homes and work in their new homelands. The youth of the Party was represented by an organization known as *Euzko Gaztedi,* or Basque Youth, founded in 1952 in Bilbao. EGI, as the group is known, has functioned traditionally as a recruiting, selecting and training device for bringing young people into the ranks of the Party. EGI has usually been more aggressive and somewhat more radical than the older Party leaders, and, in 1966, was the first official Party group to call for the use of political violence against Franco. In the latter years of the Franco era, EGI suffered a number of splits as its more radical members began to join ETA out of frustration with the more cautious and conservative PNV. The Party does not have a specific labor organization within it, but for many years has enjoyed a special relationship with the Basque nationalist and Catholic union, *Solidaridad de Trabajadores Vascos* (STV). Finally, the PNV has maintained strong links with the various Basque exile communities abroad, especially in Caracas, Buenos Aires, Montevideo and Mexico City. These communities organized their own executive bodies, called Extraterritorial Councils or *Juntas Extraterritoriales,* which were representated in the National Assembly. These Juntas were of crucial importance to the continued success of the PNV, and of the Basque Government-in-Exile, for the exile communities provided both the Party and government with a sizable share of the funds needed to carry on their business. Abroad, wherever large groups of Basques gathered, a *Centro Vasco* soon appeared. In many instances, these *Centros* became a microcosm of the Basque country and its political divisions. The PNV was represented in most of these *Centros,* as were the other parties farther to the left on the political spectrum. Often, the same conflicts that had divided the Basques in Spain (religion, labor, and so forth) were transplanted to their new homes in exile, and prevented the *Centros Vascos* from playing a unified role in the resistance.

Of major importance, then, was the link between the Basque Nationalist Party and the formal governmental representatives of the Basque people, the Government of Euzkadi in Paris, the Consultative Council, which operated in both France and Spain, and the Resistance Committee, which was located in Spain. Obviously, since the PNV was the foremost power in the Basque political setting, these resistance groups had to be in close touch with the Party without allowing the Party leadership to gain formal control of organizations that were intended to represent all Basques. This problem was usually solved by vesting in one single person the leadership roles of both the Consultative Council and the Resistance Committee, and then naming to this joint position someone who had considerable prestige in the PNV. For many years, until his death in 1974, this dual role was occupied by Teodoro de Aguirre y Lecube, the younger brother of José Antonio de Aguirre.[2]

In addition to these links, however, the PNV also maintained close liaison with many other important groups in Spain, including the two powerful labor unions, CNT and UGT, both of which eventually were brought into an "auxiliary" role in the Consultative Council, and the anti-Franco political parties, the socialist PSOE, and the centrist Christian Democrats. Apparently, the PNV strategy was to remain in close touch with all of the various anti-Franco elements in the Spanish underground (excluding the communists and the anarchists), and prepared the ground for the emergence of a democratic political order in Spain once Franco was dead.

For virtually the entire Franco period, the Basques were torn over the best way to rid themselves of Spanish domination. The PNV approach was to wait for Franco's demise, maintain the strength and vigor of the Basque culture and language, as well as the sense of Basque nationalism, and work for a democratic or parliamentary solution to Spain's problems. The PNV felt that the solution to the Basque problem lay in Madrid. That is, the Basques were most likely to achieve their independence if Spain were governed by a democratic parliamentary regime. This strategy has not gone unopposed by Basque nationalists. Many of these opponents, quite likely more radical or more aggressive than the PNV leaders, believed that the Basques should act to obtain their own independence by themselves, without reference to what was happening in Madrid. These forces and groups have argued that no Spanish government, whether democratic or authoritarian, will willingly release the Basques to form their own nation; participation in post-Franco planning with democratic Spanish parties such as the PSOE was merely deluding the Basques, and lulling them into a false sense of hope.

Beginning in the early 1950s, there appeared two distinct strategic philosophies over the correct way to achieve Basque independence.[3] The more radical approach focused on the creation of a Basque National Front, made up of all Basque nationalist organizations and political forces regardless of their ideological or class orientation, and regardless of whether or not they participated in the Basque Government-in-Exile in Paris. The exile government, argued the advocates of the united front idea, was not the legitimate spokesman for the Basque people, since it had been imposed on them by the Spanish government in the midst of the Civil War and had never been ratified by popular vote. Further, this approach rejected any ties with Spanish political parties, such as the socialists, since they would never be willing to grant full regional autonomy to the Basques no matter how radical they were as far as Spanish national politics was concerned. The opening step in the development of this movement was the resignation of Telesforo Monzón from the Basque government in 1953 in protest against cooperation with various Spanish anti-Franco groups. The strategic philosophy was seen again in the 1960 Caracas Manifesto, issued shortly after the death of José Antonio Aguirre, and the installation of his successor, Leizaola, in the presidency. Until the late 1960s, certain segments of ETA also advocated such a move, but as that organization became more radicalized, they rejected cooperation with the bourgeois PNV as much as with Spanish parties.

The opposite strategy has been fostered by the PNV.[4] The basic elements are simple. First, the Basque government in Paris is the legitimate symbol of Basque self-governance, and it should not be dismantled until such time as the Basque people have had the opportunity to elect a new set of leaders under some sort of new autonomy statute. Second, all forces that wish to fight for Basque nationalism should express that commitment by joining the Basque government's Consultative Council, regardless of whether or not the ideological bent of that government coincided with that of the various leftist Basque nationalist groups. Third, despite the best efforts of Basque nationalists and their political organizations, an appropriate solution to the Basque problem would be found only when a democratic regime was established in Madrid. To that end, the PNV established close ties with Christian Democratic parties in Europe, particularly in Germany, as well as with anti-Franco groups in Spain. Various accords were signed with these groups, including the Pact of Paris in 1956, the Pact of the Union of Democratic Forces in 1961, and the Munich Pact with the PSOE in 1962. In each of these alliances, the *quid pro quo* has been that the PNV would foreswear any move to claim regional autonomy during the period of the Franco dictatorship if, in return, the democratic Spanish parties would agree to grant the Basques their autonomy once Franco was gone.

In September 1955, the Basque Nationalist Party organ, *Alderdi,* editorialized about the duties of the good Basque nationalist.[5] Among these, first and foremost was that of "supporting and pushing" the various nationalist political organizations, of which of course the most important was the PNV. Basques were exhorted to attend PNV meetings, and to participate actively in the gatherings, taking an active interest in the problems faced by the Party, and suggesting solutions to these obstacles. Second, in the home, Basques should be teaching their children more of their culture and their language. Basque parents should learn Euskera themselves if they did not already speak it, and they should endeavor to make their children learn and speak it as well. Third, Basques should be active in the diffusion of nationalist propaganda. They should subscribe to and read nationalist publications like *Alderdi,* they should seek to involve their friends and neighbors in the discussion of nationalist problems, and they should distribute nationalist literature to trusted friends and associates. (These latter activities were, of course, strictly prohibited in Spain, and punishable by jail sentences of several years' duration.) Thus, the support of the resistance would mean to the average Basque citizen not violence and confrontation with the Spanish state, but relatively quiet, inwardly directed tasks aimed at shoring up the cultural and attitudinal structures of the Basque nationalist movement.

As might be expected, the tactical activities of the Basque Nationalist Party reflect this essentially passive form of political struggle. As I have already mentioned, a considerable amount of the Party's energies and resources went to organizational matters, such as the maintenance of lines of communication and authority in the underground; the establishment of links with other anti-Franco parties in Spain, such as the Christian Democrats; and raising money to support both resistance activities in Spain and the Basque Government-in-Exile in Paris. Clearly, it was a major effort merely to survive intact during the generation of harsh repression from Madrid.

Beyond these organizational requirements, however, the bulk of the PNV's efforts went toward activities that were concerned essentially with public relations or propaganda. Some of these activities were designed to preserve and strengthen the various facets of Basque culture, including language, music, art and folklore. In 1956, for example, the PNV and the government of Euzkadi sponsored the First World Basque Congress, bringing together Basque scholars and political activists from all over the world to discuss ways of preserving Basque culture when the core of the Basque elite found itself scattered and disorganized. Among the many outcomes of this Congress was the formation of a coordinating group called the Confederation of Basque Entities in America (*Confederación de Entidades Vascas de America,* or CEVA), which was charged with the task of linking together all of the various Basque Centers in the Western Hemisphere. In recognition of the importance of the Basque exile group in Venezuela, Caracas was named as the seat of CEVA. Another long-term program of the PNV was to support and promote the Basque language schools that operated clandestinely in Spain.

Other propaganda projects of the PNV seemed more closely aimed at making a public statement about the continued health and vigor of the Basque nationalist movement. These statements had two audiences. To neutral or apathetic Basques they relayed the message that they should bestir themselves and join what was a thriving and flourishing movement, even if that entailed some risk. This is what we would today call "consciousness-raising." The other audience, of course, was in Madrid. To Franco and to the Spanish government, these public demonstrations of Basque nationalist solidarity sent the message that the continuation of Spanish domination was futile, for the strength of Basque culture would prevail, just as it had prevailed in earlier, less complicated times.

The most significant examples of these public demonstrations were the annual Easter celebrations of the Basques' national holiday, Aberri Eguna (literally, "Day of the Fatherland"). The matching of political and religious festivals was a long-standing tradition of the Basques, one that was used effectively by the strongly Catholic PNV. The first Aberri Eguna was held in Bilbao in 1932, and the celebration was regularly observed until the Civil War broke out. After the fall of the Basque provinces, the festival was banned. In 1964, however, the Basque government and the PNV began to organize these mass celebrations in the underground, and to hold them in public on an annual basis despite the efforts of the Spanish police to prevent them. The first of this new series of Aberri Eguna was held in Guernica in 1964, followed by Vergara in 1965, Vitoria in 1966, and Pamplona in 1967. On occasion, when the police succeeded in cordoning off an entire city where the celebration had been planned, the PNV was able simply to shift the site and hold the festival elsewhere. The most remarkable Aberri Eguna event was that of 1974, when the president of the Basque government, Jesús María de Leizaola, returned briefly to Spain for the first time since he had gone into exile in 1939. On March 13, 1974, the day before Easter Sunday, Leizaola arrived at 9:00 p.m. in Bilbao where he held a clandestine press conference with representatives of major foreign newspapers. The next morning, he traveled to Guernica, where he presided over an emotional gathering of former *gudaris* and veterans of the Civil War. By 1:00 p.m. that same day, he had clandestinely crossed back to the French side of the Pyrenees.[6] Despite the fact that the trip had been widely advertised on the Basque radio, Leizaola had succeeded in symbolizing the expected return of the Basque government from its days in exile to Basque soil once again. Those watching from Madrid must have had cause to wonder whether such symbolism would prove in the long run to be an empty gesture or an accurate prediction of things to come.

Life in the Basque Resistance: Some Personal Observations

During the 1960s and early 1970s the Basque resistance consisted of two groups. On the Spanish side of the Pyrenees, the Party could count on perhaps as many as 5,000 active supporters, whose activities varied from reading the clandestine literature smuggled across the border to providing food, shelter, transportation and other aid to their more militant comrades. The core of the resistance, however, were the several hundred Party leaders and activists who lived in the small farm and fishing villages clustered against the Spanish border in southern France. From this base, they could cross the mountainous frontier easily to engage in resistance activities and then return to their sanctuary. They had convenient access to Paris and, thence, to other centers of political action in Europe and the Western Hemisphere. Although many of the Basques insisted that they were not in exile (the southern French provinces are referred to as "North Euzkadi," as opposed to "South Euzkadi," the northern Spanish provinces), the atmosphere among resistance circles was highly charged with the energy and devotion of committed political activists engaged in high risk struggle against impossible odds.

One of the key members of the resistance in this region was X, a native of Vizcaya province born in Bilbao in 1931.[7] X's father, originally from a small village in the interior of the Basque country, moved to Bilbao in 1916, attracted by the economic boom of the city's industry during World War I. Although X's father was a supporter of the monarchical Carlist Party in his youth, his move to Bilbao brought about an increase in his nationalist spirit and he became a member of the Basque Nationalist Party. Two years after X was born, in 1933, his father died, leaving the mother to care for X, his older brother, and his three older sisters.

X was five years old when the Spanish Civil War broke out. His older brother, who was eighteen at the time, promptly joined the volunteer Basque army. The brother fought in the single Basque offensive of the war, at Villareal, was wounded in the leg, and subsequently returned to combat in the defense of Bilbao. Captured at the fall of Bilbao, X's brother served five years in a forced labor battalion building fortifications along the Pyrenees border with France, and then was forced to fulfill his regular military commitment with the Spanish Army. Since the brother did not return home until 1946, X was the only male in the household for ten years, until he was fifteen.

During this crucial ten-year period of his life, X became keenly aware of the oppressed conditions of the Basques in Spain. His brother's absence from home was a constant topic of conversation within the family, and X was clearly impressed with the Spanish role in removing from the family what was a father surrogate for him. In addition, the Spanish occupation of Bilbao was especially harsh during this period. Although X's mother and sisters spoke Euskera, he never learned the language, as it was prohibited in Bilbao from 1937 to 1945. One of X's uncles was imprisoned for saying *agur* ("goodby") on the street. Finally, the dificult economic conditions of the times, brought on by World War II and Spanish economic policies, placed X's family in precarious financial circumstances.

When X's brother returned from his military service, he gradually began to introduce X to the world of the resistance. While he never participated in any overt action, the brother contributed money to the PNV. Most important, however, he began to take X with him on frequent mountain climbing adventures, and to introduce him to friends in the PNV. As I have noted, the numerous Basque mountain climbing societies served during this time to shelter the infant resistance movement within Spain. Frequent retreats (*romerías*) offered resistance members the chance to discuss their activities on some remote mountain peak, far from the surveillance of the Spanish police and army. On one of these trips, during Holy Week of 1948 (X was 17 years old), X was approached by several friends about participating in small-scale resistance activities. X needed little convincing; his entire life to that point had given him sufficient reason to join the struggle for the independence of the Basque country. He accepted the offer.

From 1948 to 1951, X took part in marginal or peripheral resistance activities, mostly of a cultural nature. He helped organize dance and folklore groups, he painted slogans on walls, and he distributed propaganda. Further, while he flirted with danger, he lacked direct experience with the Spanish police, since by this time they were beginning to realize that absolute enforcement of cultural restrictions was impossible. Since most resistance work was entrusted to veterans of the War, younger workers were given generally trivial tasks by which they might test their reliability. These marginal responsibilities brought X into contact with resistance circles, however, and so undoubtedly hastened the day when he was to commit himself totally to the Basque cause.

The catalyst for X was the general strike on April 22-23, 1951, of Basque workers in Bilbao and other major cities of the region. The strike, which lasted for forty-eight hours, and which idled almost 250,000 workers, was one of the first direct challenges to General Franco's authority since the Civil War. Spanish reaction was immediate and harsh. More than 2,000 arrests were made, including many key leaders of the PNV. Although the strike was a definite organizational defeat for Basque nationalism, the mere fact that the PNV could organize an activity of such magnitude engendered great enthusiasm for the struggle among younger militants.[8]

For X the 1951 strike was the turning point. The magnitude of the action forced the resistance to turn to younger members for important tasks, and X was given a key part to play in the production and distribution of the pamphlets calling for workers to walk off their jobs. As a result, he was arrested by the Spanish police and held without trial from April to December.

While in jail, X was interrogated, beaten, stripped naked, and kept in solitary confinement. When he was released, he was twenty years old and totally committed to the cause of Basque freedom.

Following the 1951 strike, the youth of the resistance began to take a much more active role in PNV activities. Veterans of the Civil War were growing older, forming families, and generally losing interest in the struggle. The mass arrests in 1951 removed from action large numbers of experienced PNV cadre. As a consequence, in 1952 X joined with perhaps a dozen other young men to form a youth branch of the Basque Nationalist Party, called *Euzko Gaztedi* (EGI). While the older members of the PNV devoted themselves to more general policy matters, the young men of EGI assumed key roles in propaganda distribution, demonstrations, and the general tasks associated with maintaining a visible resistance presence.

In May 1955, X was arrested again for the distribution of illegal propaganda. This time, he spent four months in jail. Along with X, more than thirty key EGI leaders were arrested; and the organization's Bilbao branch was leaderless and in confusion for most of the year. Upon his release, X returned to resistance activity, even though he was awaiting trial for his earlier offenses. X was tried in 1958, and sentenced to 12 years in prison, but was allowed to remain at liberty while his case was being appealed. Finally, in December 1959, X decided that he could no longer remain in Spain but must go into exile. He narrowly escaped capture by jumping out of an upstairs window of his fiancée's house, and made his way to France, one of the first of the "new generation" of exiled resistance workers.

X returned to Spain numerous times, always clandestinely. In 1962, he returned to Bilbao to marry his fiancée of many years. From 1962 to 1975, they lived in France, where were born all four of their children. X occupied a key role in coordinating resistance activities in France and he was especially active as a link between the covert structures of the PNV in Spain, and the more or less open operations in France and the rest of Western Europe. By 1975, he had risen to occupy a high post in the Basque Government-in-Exile.

X's life in exile was sustained by his intense commitment to his family, and the support he derived from the family environment. X said that when a monument is raised in Bilbao to the success of the resistance, it should be to the Basque women who have supported their men in the struggle. Without this support, X believes that neither he nor many of the other PNV leaders would have been able to continue their activities as they did.

I can only sketch briefly what it meant to X's wife to be married to a leader of the resistance. X and his family had few friends beyond resistance circles; and they had little desire to sink any roots in their community, in spite of the fact that they lived more than thirteen years there. Exiles avoided the establishment of long-lasting ties to their host country, feeling that any such emotional attachments might weaken their resolve to return some day to their true homeland. X's children had special difficulties in school, as they were treated as Spanish, and therefore inferior. In self-protection, the children tried to pass as French, even though in so doing they had to de-emphasize their Basque heritage. Economic problems were less important for X and his wife. They lived on a small salary paid by the PNV which provided for a modest standard of living.

In a very real sense, X continued the struggle for Basque independence because there was literally nothing else for him to do. When I met him, he was forty-two years old. He had done little except resistance work since the age of seventeen. He faced more than 100 years of prison sentences in Spain; in France, he neither could, nor wished to, find employment of another sort. In the absence of some sort of general amnesty for all political prisoners and exiles in Spain, X could do little except continue the activity of high risk struggle from his fishing village in southern France.

Yet X did not seem disposed to undertake unlimited guerrilla war in Spain. "When a small man fights a big man," he said, "he should not be surprised at the outcome." He did not want to give the Spanish any reason for increasing their oppression of the Basques. Like so many other Basque exiles, he looked to the future with optimism, and with a confidence based on the historical ability of the Basques to withstand centuries of oppression and still retain their ethnic consciousness. He talked of the increase in *ikastolas* (the Basque language schools) in Spain, of the renaissance in the Basque language, and of Franco's declining health. And he waited for what he believed must be the inevitable establishment of an independent Basque state where the Republic of Euzkadi had struggled, and lost, 36 years earlier.

When we last heard of X, he had returned to Spain, the beneficiary of the general amnesty granted to nearly all who had participated in Basque nationalist politics. When I had said goodby to him in France in 1973, his parting words had been "We'll see each other next in Bilbao." It had seemed dreamlike and unrealistic then. Yet, in only three years, Franco had died, and the historic patience and stoicism of the Basques had gained for them still another victory, even if only a symbolic one.

The Social Setting of the Resistance

One cannot write meaningfully about the Basque resistance without attempting to describe what it meant to the daily family life of the people who devoted their lives to the struggle. During a lengthy visit to the Basque country in 1973, I discovered that one of the key characteristics of the resistance was the determination of the Basques to marry, rear a family, follow a profession, form a home, and generally to carry on as normal a life as possible, in the midst of what for them was undeclared war. The family setting within which resistance workers moved was an important element in sustaining the struggle in the face of impossible odds, frequent failure, and fear for one's personal well being.

For the resistance workers, the family appears to be a true source of emotional strength and shelter. I heard many stories of militants who retreated into the security of their families between risky activities. In most cases, the members of the resistance shared with their wives information about their work, even while withholding details about a particular operation. In all instances, wives gave strong support to their husbands. In a few families, the husband had entered into resistance work without first talking it over with his wife; but, even in these comparatively rare cases, the wives held fast under the great emotional pressures and managed to keep the family together during periods of prolonged absence of the husband and father. In no case did I learn of a family's disruption because of the resistance activities of the father; divorce is as little known among those in the underground as it is in strongly Catholic Basque society generally.

While the family provided great psychological security for Basque resistance fighters, the desire to marry and have children in the middle of a very unorthodox paramilitary life style brought with it certain unusual psychological strains. Many of my informants mentioned economic cramp when I talked of their personal lives. The resistance attempted to maintain a few workers (called *liberados*), like X, who received a salary from the Party and who did not have to take work of an ordinary nature. These were very few, however; the great bulk of the underground workers held regular jobs during the day. I talked, for example, with an electrician, a furniture maker, the manager of a furniture store, an automobile repair shop owner, and several professionals (lawyers, for the most part). The careers of these men were by and large fairly static; progress up the economic ladder was slow and halting. The resistance took so much of their time that they had little to devote to improving their economic status. In addition, the resistance asked that they blend into the environment as much as possible, which meant that they had to appear to be ordinary men in ordinary jobs, attracting as little attention as possible. Overt recognition, even for meritorious service, was avoided. With all these restrictions, then, it is not surprising that economic security was an elusive goal for resistance workers.

Yet insecurity of a psychological nature put great strain on a wife's commitment to her husband's work. One young PNV militant, married and the father of two tiny children, put it this way: "Often, my wife and I lie awake all night and listen to the sound of the elevator in our building as it goes up and down. Every time it stops at our floor, my stomach tightens as I think: 'This is it! They've finally come for me!' " This particular worker, still in his early thirties, had already been involved in the resistance for twelve years and married for five.

Wives of resistance workers were also asked to restrict their social contacts and friendships to the few trusted members of their underground cell. Just a few months in the atmosphere of the resistance were sufficient to instill a powerful sense of caution. Wives were asked to avoid close friendships with other women who were not partisans of the resistance, and underground families quickly found themselves cut off from a normal set of social acquaintances. In a way, this was supportive of the general psychological commitment both husband and wife had made, in that they virtually never came into contact with dissenting voices, or with people who could call into question a central feature of their lives. But when I heard time and time again that a particular worker's wife had no friends or was afraid to talk with other women in her apartment building, I began to form a picture of a group of women who were being asked to bear an enormous burden and to do it in virtual isolation.

The rearing of children in this setting brought its own special kind of psychological problems. Parents were determined that their children should grow up as Basques, speaking the Basque language and relating to the Basque culture and life style. The children, however, had to live in two cultures: Basque in the home and sometimes the school; Spanish (or French) at all other times. There were two languages to be mastered, two sets of mores to be internalized, two sets of friends and companions to adjust to. All this imposed its high price on the development of children in the Basque community, especially of very young children.

Basques of all sorts had to face these stresses and strains. But the returning exile found, in addition, a complex and frustrating set of prejudices against him that made participation in the resistance at times almost intolerable. During the course of the Civil War, an estimated 100,000-150,000 Basques went into exile.[9] Of this number, about 35,000 went to the Western Hemisphere. Some went to the United States; some to Mexico; the largest group eventually ended up in Venezuela (Caracas became the strongest focal point of Basque sentiment outside of Europe). Most of these exiles chose to remain abroad until Euzkadi is freed. The few who elected to return to join the resistance found not a warm welcome but suspicion mixed with envy. Local Basques criticized the returning exiles for having deserted the nation in an hour of crisis, for being naive about the possibilities for direct action in today's Spain, for not understanding what those who remained at home had suffered through the past thirty years, or for having lost their "Basque-ness" while in America.[10] As if that weren't enough, the returning exiles received criticism from those who remained abroad for crawling back to Spain in humiliation without having the courage to wait until the fall of the Franco regime. The exiles, for their part, discovered frequently that the country they had dreamed about for thirty years had changed in culture and life style, perhaps irremediably; that local Basques were prone to be extra cautious rather than willing to run risks; that old friends and favorite landmarks were gone; and that young Basque men generally seemed more interested in making the rounds of the bars drinking "chiquitos" (small glasses of wine) than they were in political action. "Just imagine," complained one exile; "more than 40,000 residents of Bilbao traveled to Madrid to watch Bilbao play in the final match for the national football [soccer] championship. We can't find 40,000 people in the entire Basque country interested in politics at all." It was enough to make the returning exiles wonder if it had been worth all the sacrifice.

The PNV and Basque Political Culture

The role of violence in the struggle for autonomy occupies an ambiguous place in Basque political culture. While some Basques advocated violent action to gain their independence, the Basque Nationalist Party instead chose to rely on the ancient cultural heritage and language of the Basques, and to maintain a stolid patience in the face of the Spanish occupation of their country. They defied the Spaniards' claim on their loyalty by relying on inner strengths of personality, culture, social structure and political organization.

What are we to make of the elusive Basque personality? On

the one hand, one reads these words by an astute observer of the Basques, Rodney Gallop: "In . . . their prehistorical period little is known of them beyond the fact that they had established a reputation for violence and ferocity remarkable even in the Dark Ages. As early as the fourth century A.D. Prudence writes of the 'pagan brutality of the Vascones.' " And, Gallop goes on, the Canon of Compostella wrote of the Basques in 1120: "A race speaking a strange language; real savages as bloodthirsty and ferocious as the wild beasts with whom they live."[11] On the other hand, one can read through virtually the entire library of writings of Sabino de Arana y Goiri and other leaders of Basque nationalism and never find a single call to arms, or even a suggestion that violence was the answer to the Basques' dilemma. As one PNV leader told me in 1973, "As a people, we are much better suited for defensive combat than we are for the offensive." Certainly, the performance of the Basque militia during the Spanish Civil War bears out this observation.

How then can we explain this apparent contradiction in Basque psychology, character and culture? From whence comes this peculiar mixture of adventure, struggle, and desire to avoid violence? Gallop suggests that the well-known Basque penchant for violence disappeared through the civilizing influence of European society. "As the centuries rolled on," he writes, "and the lawless exploits of the Basques came to be viewed with growing displeasure by their neighbors and consequently to be more difficult of accomplishment, they seem to have turned their energies into another channel and to have acquired a reputation for boisterous high spirits. . . ."[12] Whatever the historical forces at work, they seem to have left the Basque culture a mixture of non-violence and the high-risk pursuit of adventure.

Of great importance is the Basque cultural emphasis on non-violence in the resolution of personal conflicts. Basque parents generally take great pains to avoid a suggestion of *machismo* (the Spanish concept of masculinity) in the rearing of young boys. Although Basque males are not taught to be destructively aggressive, they are encouraged to demonstrate their masculinity in physical activities such as vigorous and demanding athletic games, and mountain climbing. Nationalist parents frequently point out to their children that one of the key differences between Basques and Spaniards lies precisely in the peaceful orientation to life of themselves, contrasted with the "bloodthirsty" character of their neighbors to the south.

A second important element of Basque culture that contributes to the nonviolent stance of the PNV has certainly been the dominant role of women in Basque society generally, and the mother in the Basque family in particular. Possibly because of the demands of the mixture of maritime and sheepherding cultures that typifies the Basques, men are seldom around the home for very long, and women bear a heavy responsibility for maintaining the home intact and for rearing the children. It is frequently said by Basques about their family structure that the husband and father holds the authority, but it is the wife and mother who actually administers things, pays the bills, disciplines the children, and conducts the general business of the home.[13] There seems little doubt that this dominance of the female in Basque culture has worked to soften a resort to violence that might otherwise have become much stronger given the provocative and suppressive environment within which Basques have lived for several generations.

Non-violence as a cultural imperative of the Basques has obvious implications for resistance activities. Members of the resistance, especially those in ETA, are severely tested by the internal conflict between the tactical exigencies of a given action, and their deeply entrenched cultural teachings. As we have already noted, a few members of ETA have even found it necessary to hide the details of their involvement from wives and mothers not only for security reasons but because the dominant women in their lives might try to prevent their men from engaging in political violence. ETA members claim that they go to extraordinary lengths to protect uninvolved citizens during their operations; and their record in this respect during the 1960s was quite good when compared with similar groups in Latin America, Northern Ireland, or the Middle East.

Working against these forces for moderation in Basque culture, however, are other influences that stimulate risk-taking in a hostile political environment. Basque child rearing techniques appear to teach mistrust of the environment. Basque children are typically warned from early age that the outside world is capricious if not actually hostile, and that one can survive there only by mistrusting all those who are not of his family or kinship group. Basque parents indoctrinate their children to a wide variety of superstitions involving evil spirits and inexplicable phenomena in a usually malevolent world. In the life of a small Basque child, animals can talk, trees are inhabited by spirits, and evil persons can transmit illness by means of the "evil eye." While such attitudes and beliefs are more common to rural than to urban areas of the Basque country and are no doubt under assault in more modern areas, they die slowly, and it would be quite unusual to find that they have vanished completely from what is passed on from parent to child.[14] Though emphasis on the evil quality of the outside world may be declining, Basques most certainly still tend to regard outside forces as capricious and unpredictable, and beyond their control.

As the mental set described above comes to be translated into the world of politics, Basques have developed two typical political "styles," both well-suited to the clandestine manner in which they must function. On the one hand, some Basques appear to be willing to run exorbitant risks for idealistic political purposes that have little chance of success. These activists are referred to as *conspiradores,* seeming to be most at home in the conspiratorial climate of the long-lived resistance. Other Basques, however, seem disposed to run excessive risks with *no* immediate material end in view. It is said that these Basques possess the "adventurer spirit" (*espíritu aventurero*). The well-known running of the young men before a herd of charging bulls at the annual festival in Pamplona exemplifies that spirit.

In both cases, that of the *conspirador* and of the *espíritu aventurero,* the individual regards the outside world as a direct challenge which he must confront and defeat in combat; it is a direct threat against which he must guard himself at all times. Because of the political and cultural repression of opinion in the Basque country during most of this century, democratic and moderate politicians have not been able to emerge among the Basque. Such political figures as the "ward-heeler," the organization man, or the charismatic leader (with the exception of the first Basque president, José Antonio Aguirre) have simply never developed strong followings among Basques. Under conditions of dictatorship, such political styles would clearly be not only doomed to failure but counterproductive. But the conspiratorial and adventurer modes of political action survive and flourish in the dark and mysterious world of the Spanish underground.

Basque political culture, then, offers the outside observer an unusual mixture of moderation and high risk, of compromise and dedication to struggle. As a result, the Basque Nationalist Party, a clandestine movement that suffered defeat after defeat never embraced violence as the correct strategy to gain its objectives. To explain how Basques were able to sustain their commitment to the resistance under these pressures and constraints, we must go beyond the Basque personality to examine other psycho-cultural factors at work.

For many observers, the key to understanding the Basque character lies in the inclination of the culture to cut itself off from all that is foreign, to turn inward when threatened, and to derive the strength to resist from inner forces that build a wall against all aliens. "There is one word," writes Gallop, "which covers all the qualities that go to make up Basque character; a word which unites the conceptions of independence and 'superiority complex,' of high spirits and deep reserve. That word is 'insularity.' "[15] William Douglass, writing in the early 1960s, noted that Basque rural society is based on one key distinction: that between Basques and non-Basques. Strangers to the village are considered not only as different but as racially inferior. They are excluded from the Basque linguistic community, they are treated with disrespect, and their occupations (almost always of a non-agricultural nature) are regarded as less honorable than the professions of the field. Non-Basques are felt to have no roots in the community, and it is generally believed that they move on after a brief stay in the village.[16] The Basque word for "stranger," *maketo,* carries with it strong connotations of distrust, dislike and suspicion.

Whether the field of battle is military or political, the wise leader is one who selects his strategies on the basis of his forces' strengths. In the case of the Basque nationalists and their primary strategist, Sabino de Arana y Goiri, the insularity of the culture is of paramount importance. The Basques are few in number, not especially given to cooperating among themselves for political reasons, and not particularly adept at the military professions. Their principal weapons have been their supreme self-confidence and belief in the correctness of their cause, their almost sublime faith in ultimate victory against the Spanish, and their reliance on the mystical distinctiveness of the Basque culture and language to set them apart from the rest of the Iberian Penninsula. Insularity in this case becomes the Basque equivalent of the Russian winter faced by Napoleon, or the English Channel that separated Britain from Hitler.

Basque insularity runs deep, profoundly affecting the Basque Nationalist Party. In the face of Spanish occupation, the PNV advocated not the taking up of arms but the maintenance of cultural and linguistic solidarity. They would not attempt to drive out the foreigners, for that would only provoke Madrid to reprisals and repression. Instead, they would turn their backs on the Spaniards, refuse them their allegiance, and deny them their cultural loyalty, until one day the *maketos* would tire of their tedious occupation and leave the Basques in peace.

Such a strategy is demanding in the extreme, for it condemns those who follow it to suffering endless defeats in the short run in exchange for ultimate victory in the long term. Yet, as Lord Keynes put it, in the long run we are all dead. During the long winter of the Basques' exile, even the most dedicated nationalist needed the support of certain crucial psychological and social mechanisms to defend himself against inner doubts. In the midst of the resistance, Basque families clustered together to provide mutual support and to close out those who did not approve of the struggle or who doubted its ultimate triumph. They were compelled to shut out dissonant or divergent ideas.

In the case of the Basque nationalists, the PNV performed

this role of psychological insulation from a challenging reality. As one elderly exiled PNV leader once told me, "For almost forty years now [the year was 1973], the 'Partido' has not been a political party, it has been a civilization, completely self-contained." Young men and women were born into the PNV and into resistance activities. As they grew to maturity, they were confronted almost daily with the exploits of their fathers and older brothers, who presented role models to be emulated. Once arrived at adulthood, they could not avoid the challenge to carry on in the footsteps of the heroes of the resistance. The normal process of emulating and learning from elders in a culture took on clear political overtones and sustained the resistance far beyond the life span of a single generation.[17] The sons of PNV leaders frequently married daughters from other families within the movement, thus insuring continuity in the struggle, and the support of wives who had been socialized from a tender age into the arduous life of resistance society. And we cannot forget the obliging role played by the Spanish in reinforcing the early commitments of the PNV youth. For in attempting to suppress Basque nationalism, Spain has been its own worst enemy. Time and time again, as Basque separatism seemed about to wane and to lose vigor, some especially harsh act of repression would galvanize the nationalist sentiments of Basque youths, and harden them in their dedication to the victory of their cause.

Few outsiders came to know the Basques as well as did Rodney Gallop who, writing in 1930, described them in a passage that sums up qualities that have sustained their struggle for so many years:

> The abiding impression left by the Basques is that of a fine stalwart people . . . who know their own minds and can defend their traditions and convictions with a courage and a spirit of independence amounting almost to fanaticism, and whose hearts are set on one thing, namely, to endure.[18]

Chapter Six

THE BASQUE LANGUAGE

Language serves the purpose of stimulating conflict by sharpening the divisions between the combatants. Language serves to perpetuate struggle by transmitting the conflict from one generation to another. When human beings learn a lesson so well that it becomes an integral part of their personality, we say that they have "internalized" the message. Social groups have their own equivalent of "internalization," in the memories of institutions. Some of these institutionalized memories are informal, such as the folksongs of protest heard so often in Ulster, or the folktales or myths anywhere about ancient heroes who fought against outsiders from barbaric regions to defend the homeland. Other such memories are formal, like the creation of a warrior caste to protect the tribe, or the maintenance of an ousted government-in-exile, even when the source of its legitimate authority has long ceased to be operative. Some institutionalized memories glorify the good qualities of the host culture, its strength, or its love of peace; others may paint in the worst tones the culture of a neighbor, its lust for one's territory, or its deceit and trickery in combat. In many different ways, the oral and written literary traditions of countless cultural groups are used to teach the newly admitted members about the historical reasons for the division of the world into "us" and "them." In these ways, language perpetuates struggle long after the deaths of the people who started it all.

The Basque Language

It is not proposed here to delve into the intricate and complicated debate that has occupied philologists and anthropologists about the real origins of the Basque language,

Euskera. Such an inquiry lies mostly outside the scope of this study of contemporary Basque nationalism.[1]

At one time, according to Rodney Gallop, toward the end of the 18th or the beginning of the 19th century, scholars of the Basque language advanced a number of "theological" notions regarding the origins of Euskera which appear to us today as quite absurd, but which were taken most seriously at the time.[2] Among many of these early investigators of the language, it was commonly believed that Euskera was at least the first human tongue; the Abbé Dominique Lahetjuzan (1766-1818) affirmed that Euskera was the language spoken in the Garden of Eden. The Abbé Diharce de Bidassouet went further, proclaiming that Euskera was the language spoken by the Creator. Others simply held that Basque was the original language spoken before the destruction of the Tower of Babel. During the 19th century, a number of more serious scholars, led by the German William von Humboldt, offered many theories to explain the origins of the Basque tongue. At least twenty other races and languages were suggested as constituting the origin of both the Basque people and their language, including the Finns and Hungarians, the ancient Egyptians, Berber tribes, North and South American Indians, the peoples of the lost island of Atlantis, the Celts and the Caucasians, the Phoenicians and the Eskimo, the Hittites, the Iberians, the Ligurians and others. In the 20th century, theories of Basque origins are of two general kinds. One group has argued that the Basques are remnants of the Iberians, a race from the misty past that must at one time have occupied all of what is now Spain, and left many traces of its existence including cave drawings, and inscriptions. The second group replies that the Basques never lived in any great numbers outside the valleys and coastal areas where they reside today, and were never a great race of dominant peoples. But contemporary interest in the murky past of the Basques seems to have declined; Basque scholars are much more interested in understanding the Basques as they are today.

The distant and poorly understood beginnings of Euskera and the lack of any early works published in the language have hampered scholarly investigators, but have added fuel to the fires of political controversy surrounding the language. The first historians to come into contact with Basques, the Romans, were apparently unconcerned with the language of this strange people, and so kept no records (if indeed they found any) about the language or its history. As far as we know, the first written example of Euskera dates from 980 in a Latin document delimiting the diocese of the French Basque city of Bayonne. In the 12th century, a Norman pilgrim named Picaud composed a record of his pilgrimage to Santiago de Compostella, in the course of which he passed through the Basque region. The document, called the "Codex Compostellanus," contains the first known vocabulary of the Basque language, a list of only 18 words. The first known example of printed Basque is from the vocabulary published by Lucio Marino Siculo in 1530, while the first entire work to be printed in Euskera was a small collection of religious and lyrical poems by a priest named Bernard Dechepare in 1545. Until the end of the 18th century, however, little was written in Euskera except translations of religious works, so that the history of the written language and the literary tradition in Euskera have quite a brief span, especially considering that it is unquestionably one of the oldest languages in Europe.

For reasons that seem both linguistic and social, the Basque language as it was spoken during the 18th and early 19th centuries was apparently ill suited to a modernizing and industrializing region. Whatever the reasons, today the incidence of Euskera-speaking people is relatively much greater in the small still-pastoral villages than it is in the major industrial cities. As the Basque region industrialized through the latter 1700s and the first half of the 1800s, the consequent migration and transformation of the population caused the language to decline in popularity and utility. Map 2, adapted from the pioneering work of Julio Caro Baroja, reveals the steady shrinking of the Euskera-speaking region from the 18th century to today.

Many factors contributed to a decline in the use of Euskera during this period. A lack of a codified and unified grammar, vocabulary, and pronunciation made it difficult for Basques from one region to use the language effectively in another. As

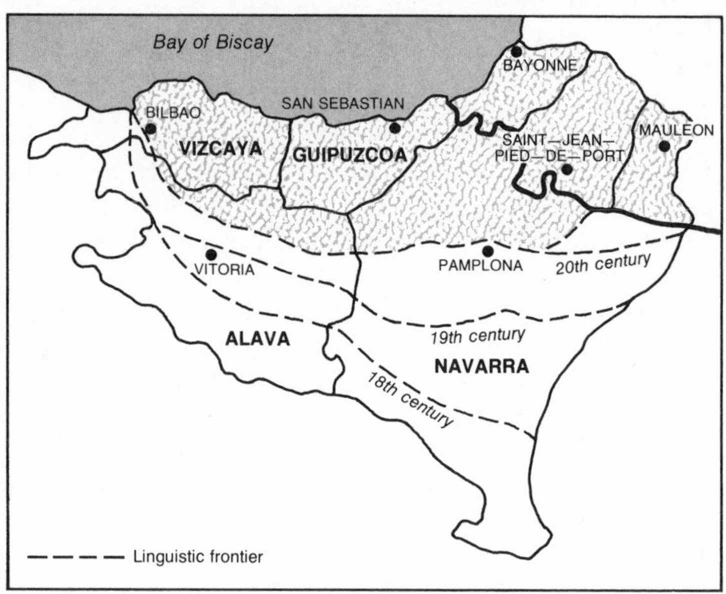

Map 2. Limits of Basque-Speaking Area, 18th Century to Present. Sources: Based on Caro Baroja, as presented by Manuel de Terán Alvarez in "País Vasco," in Manuel Terán, Luis Sole Sabaris, and others, *Geografía Regional de España* (Barcelona: Ediciones Ariel, 1968) Chapter III, Figure 26, p. 85. Also see Meic Stephens, *Linguistic Minorities in Western Europe* (Llandysul, Wales, England: Gomer Press, 1976), p. 634.

migration across province lines increased, the migrant Basques found themselves required to use Spanish in their new environment to make themselves understood. There were no doubt also sociological pressures at work. Use of Euskera came to be regarded as symbolic of one's lower class or peasant origins. Modern, enlightened, middle class, or bourgeois families cast off the primitive tongue of their ancestors and discouraged their children from learning the language even for use in the home. Since Euskera lacked many words necessary to an industrialized society, its native speakers began to absorb more and more of the romance vocabulary, with a consequent deterioration of Euskera.

While the use of Euskera was thus certainly diminishing

during the 19th century for reasons unrelated to state policy, it is also true that Madrid undertook at this time to spread the use of Spanish throughout the region. Many scholars of the period disagree over the extent of Spanish policy in this area, or over the true intent of the policy. Superficially, García Venero is probably correct in his assertion that Madrid never prevented the Basque provinces from teaching their own language in public schools, and even went so far as to decree the protection of the language as one of Spain's legitimate regional tongues.[3] Nevertheless, there is abundant evidence that Madrid at least wanted to convert the Basque region into a bilingual zone, where eventually Spanish would overshadow Euskera as both the political and official language, and as a cultural medium of expression. In 1856, Spain passed a Public Education Law which prescribed that teachers in all regions would be appointed from Madrid by the Ministry of Education, and that, despite Basque protestations, there would be no requirement that they know or teach the regional languages. Given the pronounced shortage of public school teachers in the country at this time, it was highly unlikely that the Spanish government could ever have located enough bilingual teachers to staff Basque schools. Therefore, while the Basque provincial governments were at liberty to create programs of study in Euskera, they were not free to hire teachers to administer them, and the net result was a steady erosion of the study of Euskera in schools. Further, while such a policy may not have been dictated formally from Madrid, the local school teachers in the Basque region certainly did systematically discourage Basque children from using their native language in the classroom. Thus, in both the home and in the school, there was little interest in, and much opposition to, the preservation of Euskera as anything more than a museum curiosity.[4]

While the causes of the change in attitude remain controversial, there is no doubt that there was a major resurgence in the use of Euskera from the latter decades of the 19th century to the period of the Second Republic. There was, for example, a flourishing of periodicals and literary magazines in the language, much of which was fostered by such learned societies as the Academy of the Basque Language (*Eusko Ikas-*

kuntza) of San Sebastián, or by the societies for the preservation of Basque culture, such as the *Euskalzaleen Biltzarra* of Bayonne, in France. The International Review of Basque Studies began to appear regularly, as well as a number of well written magazines, including *Gure Herria* in Bayonne, *Argia* in San Sebastián, and *Euskadi* in Bilbao.[5] According to Beltza, there were by the 1930s more than forty regular periodical publications in Euskera, including both newspapers and magazines.[6] The arts, literature, and science all flourished in the Basque language, giving evidence that the tongue was beginning to be adapted successfully to the requirements of modern industrial society. By 1931 there were an estimated 400,000 Basque-speaking people spread throughout the seven provinces (including those in France), while by 1934 the number had risen to an estimated 570,000. Thus, we can assume that by the time of the outbreak of the Spanish Civil War approximately half of the population of the Basque provinces spoke, understood, or used regularly Euskera in one form or another. In addition, the Autonomy Statute of 1936 gave to the Basque provincial assemblies the authority to promote the use of Euskera as a co-official language with Spanish in any zone where they determined that Euskera was still a viable means of communication. Given these advances, it seems that Euskera would have grown in strength and popularity even more had the Civil War and the Franco era not intervened.[7]

The policies of the Franco government toward the Basque language can be divided into three historical periods. From the fall of Bilbao, in 1937, until the middle 1950s, the policy in effect was one of nearly complete suppression of the language. For those of us far removed in time and space from these events it is difficult to grasp the extent of Madrid's efforts to eradicate Euskera as a functioning language. Perhaps the best we can do to illustrate the degree of suppression is to cite a message written by the Basque President José Antonio Aguirre to the United Nations Educational, Scientific, and Cultural Organization (UNESCO) in 1952 at the time of Franco's request for admission to the international body. Aguirre's note of protest summarizes the steps taken to curb free expression of Basque culture:

Closure of the Basque university created by the government of Euzkadi in 1936 under the terms of the Autonomy Statute of that same year.

Occupation by armed force of the libraries of social and cultural associations, and the mass burning of books in Euskera.

Elimination of all use of Euskera in schools, whether public or private. Prohibition of use of Euskera in all public gatherings and in all publications. Prohibition of use of Euskera on radio. Of special importance was the measure to eliminate the teaching of Euskera in all rural schools, since in most rural areas the children did not speak or understand Spanish.

Suppression of Basque cultural societies, including the International Society for Basque Studies, its magazine, and the Academy of the Basque Language. Prohibition of the publication of all magazines, periodicals and reviews in Euskera, including those of a purely cultural nature with no ties to political organizations at all. Prohibition of use of Euskera in all religious publications, as well as in the celebration of the Mass and in other religious ceremonies.

Decree requiring the translation into Spanish of all Basque names in civil registries and other official documents, the prohibition of the use of all Basque proper names in baptismal and in other official documents, and the official directive to remove all inscriptions in Euskera from tombstones and funeral markers.[8]

But already by the early 1950s the ability of Madrid to suppress the use of Euskera was beginning to erode. In 1949, the first book since the Civil War was published in Euskera, followed in 1950 by the first magazine to be issued in the language, *Anaitasuna-Guipúzcoa.* More importantly, the first Basque schools, the *ikastolas,* were beginning to operate clandestinely, even though they continued to be prohibited by law. Studies at the university level began to reflect a slightly looser grip over regional languages. In 1954, chairs of Galician and Catalan studies were established at the University of Madrid, and in 1955 a chair of Basque studies was initiated at the University of Salamanca. Basque language academies were allowed to reopen at about this same time, and the strict limits on the use of Basque and Catalan in sermons were loosened somewhat.[9] By the early 1960s, the Spanish government had clearly begun to realize the impossibility or the inadvisability of trying to eliminate the language and concentrated instead on regulating its use. Sermons were now routinely given in Euskera, and after Vatican II permitted the use of vernacular languages in the celebration of the Mass, Euskera was used for this ceremony as well.[10] The language could be used for religious purposes on certain radio stations that were owned or used by the Church. Dance groups and musical ensembles were permitted to return to the performance of folkloric themes that had previously been thought inflammatory of nationalist or separatist in tendency. The most important step of this period was the 1968 Law of General Education, which authorized (but did not encourage in any way) the teaching of regional languages at the primary level, thus legalizing the *ikastolas*.

The third phase of Spanish policy toward Euskera dates from 1975. Even before Franco's death, there appeared the first signs of a genuine reconciliation toward the Basques and their language, no matter how timid the first steps might be. In May 1975, the government issued a decree which brought up to date the regulation of instruction in regional languages. The teaching of Euskera would henceforth be allowed in state-supported primary schools on an optional basis, after regular school hours, and at the full discretion of the school principal. The decree made no provision for the training or the recruitment of teachers for these classes, set no requirements for their qualifications, and made no allowance for their pay. In October 1975, a second decree provided for the protection of the regional languages, although it was made clear that Spanish would continue to be the only official language permitted in government offices, courts, and legislative assemblies. Nevertheless, these two decrees represent a remarkable slackening of the grip of Madrid over the language practices of the Basques. In sum, the failure of the Spanish government to eliminate one of the most hated symbols of the disintegration of the Spanish state reveals not only the essential strength of Euskera and the other regional languages, but also says something about the inability of even dictatorial governments to coerce human behavior in certain intensely private realms.

During the latter half of the 1970s, Spain's newly established constitutional democracy was increasingly supportive of the preservation and even expansion of the Basque language. The new Spanish Constitution in Article Three specifies that while Spanish is the official language of the state and all Spanish citizens are obligated to know and use it, the regional languages are "co-official" in their respective autonomous regions in accord with the Autonomy Statutes. In the section of the Constitution that deals with the powers of the Autonomous Communities, it is clear that each region will have authority over the teaching and use of its respective regional language, so long as those residents of the region who speak only Spanish will not be discriminated against as a consequence of regional policy. Significantly, once the Spanish Constitution was approved by the country's voters in December 1978, it was promulgated in an official version in each of the country's several regional languages, including Euskera, as if to certify the official nature of each regional tongue.

Following the promulgation of the new Constitution, the Basques moved swiftly to draft their own Autonomy Statute, and to submit it to ratification by the Spanish parliament. This process is described in detail in Chapter Twelve. At this writing, March 1979, the fate of the draft Statute is uncertain. I can only report how the draft treats the question of regional language.[11] Article 6 of the draft Statute specifies that Euskera will be "co-official" with Spanish in the Basque region, and all the region's inhabitants will have the right to know and use both languages. The institutions of the Basque Autonomous Community will guarantee the official use of both languages, and will insure that no one will be discriminated against on account of his language. It is made clear that the Autonomous Community will assert its right to support the teaching of Euskera, although exactly what that means is left to subsequent interpretation. Through 1978 and 1979, there were a number of discussions between Basque linguists and Spanish and Basque political leaders about what a regional language policy would entail. One plan would begin essentially at the university level, creating within each post-secondary school in the region a Basque Language Center whose purpose would be to teach teachers (university as well as elementary and secondary) at least enough Euskera to be able to converse with their students.[12] A second approach, contained in an agreement reached between the Basque interim regional government and the Spanish Ministry of Education, would begin the obligatory teaching of Euskera at the elementary level in those areas where the language is still a functioning medium of expression, and optional Euskera classes, where parents request, in zones where the language has ceased to be used, such as southern Alava province.[13] Thus, while the general environment for the preservation of Euskera seems slightly more favorable now than in the mid-1970s, there remain a number of issues that must be confronted if an effective regional language policy is to be developed and implemented in the Basque provinces.

Recent Developments in the Use of the Basque Language

While Franco's policies fell short of driving Euskera out of existence, it also seems apparent that such coercive efforts must have had some effect. Although it would be reasonable to assume that use of Euskera must have declined during the Franco era, until recently experts could only estimate roughly the number of native language speakers remaining in the Basque provinces. During the 1960s, scholars generally followed the 1964 approximation made by Manuel de Lecuona that about 600,000 Spanish Basques and about 90,000 French Basques then spoke Euskera sufficiently well to be classified as ethnic Basque.[14] Somewhat later, but still without supporting evidence, Meic Stephens asserted that "By [1976] out of a total population of 2,100,000, about 500,000 are believed to be able to speak [Basque] in the four southern [Spanish] provinces."[15] Still other observers have relied on surveys of regional language usage conducted by the Spanish sociological research organization Fundación FOESSA. These survey data, which are reproduced here in Tables 2 and 3, taken from the 1969-1970 period, generally show that fewer Basque housewives were familiar with their regional language than their Galician or

Table 2.
Housewives Having Specified Degree of Familiarity with the Regional Language, 1970 (percent).

Region	Understand	Speak	Read	Write
Galicia	96	92	42	24
Balearic Islands	94	91	51	10
Cataluña	90	77	62	38
Valencia	88	69	46	16
Basque Provinces	50	46	25	12

Source: Fundación FOESSA, *Informe sociológico sobre la situación social de España, 1970* (Madrid: Euroamerica, 1970), pp. 1264-1304.

Table 3.
Attitudes of Housewives Toward Having Their Children Speak the Regional Language, 1970 (percent).

Region	Would Like it Very Much or Fairly Much	Believe it Necessary (Very Much or Fairly Much)
Cataluña	97	87
Balearic Islands	91	75
Valencia	78	50
Galicia	73	49
Basque Provinces	69	31

Source: Fundación FOESSA, *Informe sociológico sobre la situación social de España, 1970* (Madrid: Euroamerica, 1970), p. 1306.

Catalan counterparts were with their languages, and further that these women felt much less pressure to have their children learn the regional language than did the mothers from other regions of Spain. Some authors suggested that fewer children would be learning the language, and that eventually it would probably die out. Since Basque nationalists had themselves made so much of the identity of ethnicity and language, critics of nationalism could begin to argue that the decline in Euskera speaking meant that the ethnic basis of Basque distinctiveness was also eroding. Presumably, this trend, if carried to its logical conclusion, would have meant that Euzkadi had no ethnic or "national" *raison d'être.*[16]

As scholars in recent years began to gain greater access to the Basque population, more extensive efforts have been made to determine the actual degree of Euskera use in the Spanish Basque provinces. The Basque historian Beltza, for example, cites surveys conducted by Basque cultural societies that indicate that the number of Euskera-speaking people is on the order of 750,000, or about one-third of the 1970 population (estimated 2.3 million). These surveys conclude that about one million persons at least understand Euskera, about 510,000 read easily in the language, and 300,000 can write it effectively.[17]

These findings are disputed by the study by Pedro de Yrizar made in the early 1970s. Yrizar surveyed parish priests, town mayors and other knowledgeable persons in an attempt to verify how many residents of the Basque provinces spoke Euskera, as well as how these individuals were distributed geographically and which dialects they spoke. His survey covered about 650 population units, representing 395 townships or cities on both the Spanish and French sides of the border.[18] Based on these data, Yrizar estimated that there were in the world approximately 613,000 Euskera-speaking persons, of whom about 80,000 lived somewhere other than France and Spain (other European countries, North and South America), about 77,850 lived in France, and slightly more than 455,000 lived in the four Basque provinces of Spain. Yrizar found that the Euskera-speaking population was distributed highly unevenly, with heaviest concentrations in Guipúzcoa, somewhat less in Vizcaya and Navarra, and very small numbers in Alava (see Table 4).

In terms of percentages, and at least as far as Alava, Guipúzcoa and Vizcaya provinces are concerned, Yrizar's findings are supported by an extensive 1975 survey conducted by Salustiano del Campo and his colleagues.[19] According to the del Campo study, 19.1 percent of the residents of the three provinces surveyed said they can speak Euskera, 5.8 percent said they can write it with ease, 7.9 percent said they could write it with difficulty, and 26.2 percent said they could understand it when spoken. Understanding that non-Basque immigrants to the Basque region usually have great difficulty learning Euskera, del Campo and his associates went further to probe the extent to which ethnic Basques spoke, wrote, or read the

Table 4.
Basque-Speaking Persons in Total Population of Four Basque Provinces, 1970.

Province	1970 Population (in thousands)	Estimated Numbers of Basque Speakers	Percent
Alava	204	1,863	0.91
Guipúzcoa	631	276,843	43.87
Navarra	465	36,143	7.77
Vizcaya	1,043	140,229	13.44
Total	2,343	455,078	19.42

Sources: (a) Population: Amando de Miguel, *Manual de Estructura Social de España* (Madrid: Editorial Tecnos, 1974), Table 3, pp. 64-65. (b) Basque-speaking Population: Pedro de Yrizar, "Los dialectos y variedades de la Lengua Vasca: Estudio Linguístico-Demográfico," *Separata del Boletin de la Real Sociedad Vascongada de los Amigos del Pais,* 29, 1/2/3 (1973), pp. 74-76.

language. The results of this questioning are presented in Table 5. (For the purposes of the del Campo study, "native-born Basques" were any of his respondents who reported their province of birth as one of the three surveyed provinces, regardless of the province of their then-current residence. This usage differs somewhat from the concept of "indigenous Bas-

Table 5.
Use of Basque Language Among Native-Born Basques and the General Population in Three Basque Provinces, 1975. N = 350 (percent).

Response	Understand		Speak		Write	
	Native-Born	Gen'l Pop'n	Native-Born	Gen'l Pop'n	Native-Born	Gen'l Pop'n
Yes	39.3	26.2	30.4	19.1	8.9	5.8
Yes, with difficulty	12.4	12.2	13.3	*	12.9	7.9
A few things	—	*	—	*	6.6	*
Nothing	45.6	54.3	53.7	61.3	62.4	*
No answer	2.7	*	2.7	*	9.3	*

Notes: "*" indicates data not reported in source. Survey deals only with Alava, Guipúzcoa and Vizcaya provinces. "Native-born Basques" are those respondents who reported their province of birth as one of the three surveyed provinces, regardless of province of then-current residence.

Source: Salustiano del Campo, Manuel Navarro and Felix Tezanos, *La cuestión regional española* (Madrid: EDICUSA, 1977), p. 212.

ques," who are defined by the Spanish census criteria as those persons born in one of the Basque provinces and still residing in that same province. See Table 12, below.) Of the native-born Basques who responded to the del Campo survey, 51.7 percent could understand Euskera, 43.7 percent could speak the language, and 21.8 percent could write it. On the basis of the data del Campo and his colleagues present, we cannot calculate the approximate numbers of Basque-speaking persons in the Basque region of Spain. However, since the del Campo study supports in broad measure the Yrizar findings, we may reasonably conclude that the latter's survey is accurate, and that the Basque-speaking population amounts to about 455,000 persons, or about 19 percent of the total population of the region.

The implications of these findings are stark. In 1934, out of a total population slightly larger than 1.2 million, about 570,000 were judged capable of speaking Euskera. In the early 1970s, although the population had nearly doubled to 2.3 million, the number of Basque-speaking persons had declined to slightly more than 450,000. It would clearly be conjectural for me to assess precisely the reasons for this decline, and the degree to which an influx of non-Basques into the region was causing the use of Euskera to diminish. But on the basis of the above findings, it seems incontrovertible that use of the language among ethnic Basques has declined during the Franco years from causes quite apart from whatever impact there may have been from immigration from the rest of Spain.

Before we leave the del Campo study, we should consider a number of other findings that show how and under what conditions Basques use their regional language. Del Campo found that only 36.1 percent of the Basque-speaking people in the survey use Euskera more than they do Spanish when speaking, only 9 percent read in Euskera more than they do in Spanish, and only 6.2 percent write the majority of their correspondence in Euskera. These data reflect the exigencies of their situation more than personal preference, however, for in each instance higher percentages said they would prefer to use Euskera most of the time: 59 percent said they preferred to speak Basque; 28.9 percent said they preferred to read it; and 27.9 percent reported a preference for writing it.

The center of Euskera usage continues to be the home and family. About 50 percent of the Basque speakers reported that they always or almost always use the language in the home, only 21 percent reported doing so with neighbors, 19 percent in the work place, 15 percent in commercial establishments, and 18 percent "on the street." Of course, no one was asked about use of Euskera in official settings such as courts or government offices, since in 1975 such usage was still prohibited.

Other data from the del Campo study reveal a growing interest in the study of Euskera, an interest which one might presume would be reflected in increased use in a decade or so. For example, 47 percent of the non-Basque-speaking native-born Basques reported an interest in learning Euskera, while only 39 percent said they were not interested in studying the language. Among the native-born Basque population, 66.9 percent said that all people who lived in the Basque region should learn to speak Euskera, while only 25 percent disagreed.

If the Basque nationalist position has been to encourage the use of Euskera, they have not advocated eliminating Spanish as a co-equal language. Indeed, what the great majority of the population seem to want is a truly bilingual state. For example, del Campo asked the Euskera-speaking respondents in his survey which languages should be used in various settings, such as advertisements, public documents, street names or business names. Small percentages ranging from eight to sixteen percent advocated use of Euskera only in these settings, while large proportions from 45 to 60 percent favored using both Spanish and Euskera for these purposes. Similarly, in the area of language education, only 2.7 percent of the Basque-speaking population favored education solely in Euskera, 10.8 percent favored it only in Spanish, and the remainder (nearly 84 percent) favored some blend or mixture of the two languages.

Finally, del Campo gives us some data on the age and social

class distribution of Euskera usage as derived from his study. Unsurprisingly, the proportion of Euskera-speaking population is relatively high among older persons (29.6 percent for those 56 years of age or older), declines markedly for the middle aged (14.3 percent for those between 36 and 55), and rises again slightly for the younger group (18.6 percent for those between 18 and 35). The social class distribution in usage of the language shows some marked changes from the beginning of the century. In the del Campo study, the social group most able to speak Euskera was that consisting of business managers, small shop owners, professionals and independent workers (28.9 percent). Skilled laborers showed 19.2 percent, and unskilled or manual workers, 14.4 percent.

One of the most crucial developments of the post-Franco period in the Basque country has been the resurgence of interest in the Basque language in both official and informal circles. There has been a renaissance of publications in Euskera. About 200 books are published in Basque each year, covering subjects as wide ranging as religion, sociology, philology, economics, poetry, novels, and art. These books are issued by ten publishing houses, which are also responsible for publishing some twenty magazines that appear on a regular basis. There are six newspapers that publish on a daily basis, and several weekly and monthly papers as well. None of these publications receive any assistance from Spanish funds (though they are all subject to the still watchful Spanish censor).

Although other aspects of Basque culture, including dance, music and song-writing have flourished once again,[20] the inability of Basques to gain access to radio and television communications is a significant obstacle to mass usage of Euskera. Of the sixteen radio stations that broadcast in the Basque region, only two or three carry programs in Euskera, and these are spaced sporadically throughout the day at times when the audience is apt to be rather low.[21] In the field of television there are no programs in Euskera, and throughout northern Spain only half an hour daily is dedicated to regional programming. From December 1975 to August 1977, Spanish national television did permit one half hour per week in regional programming to be used for broadcasting in Euskera. This program, called "Euskalleria," failed after a year and a half according to its producers because of intermittent exposure to its potential audience, and because scarce financial resources meant that its staff was unable to hire the kind of personnel needed to produce a high quality program that would attract a supportive audience.[22]

Whatever the reason, despite clear evidence that Basque-speaking people want a portion of their television programming to be in Euskera, there does not seem to be at this writing any inclination on the part of the Spanish government to change its policies on the question.

Probably of greatest impact for Basque-language use has been the increase in public support for, and interest in the Basque schools known as *ikastolas*. Outlawed for many years, the *ikastolas* began in clandestine settings in private homes or churches in the early 1950s. Until 1968, instruction in Euskera remained illegal, but the *ikastolas* were known to Spanish authorities and generally tolerated as long as they did not become a center of political propaganda or nationalist incitement. Until the early 1970s, however, very few parents sent their children to the *ikastolas,* not only out of fear of reprisals, but because of the relatively high cost. During the 1970s, the number of schools and enrollment have risen steadily. In the 1971-72 school year, there were an estimated 18,500 children registered in 67 *ikastolas* in the Spanish Basque provinces. These schools offered courses of study from pre-school (age four) to the end of the primary grades (age 11). There were sufficient teachers to provide a student-teacher ratio of 25-30:1. In the next several years, enrollment increased markedly. Articles from 1974 and 1975 report about 25,000 children enrolled in about 138 Basque schools, while a 1977 study revealed more than 40,600 students registered. The majority of the 1977 enrollees were registered in Guipúzcoa (about 24,000), while Vizcaya had 8,000, Navarra, 5,000, and Alava, 3,000. Thus, out of an estimated 450,000 school age children in the Basque provinces, about nine percent attend *ikastolas.*[23] Despite the increase in attendance figures, this hardly constitutes the kind of mass language training that will have to occur for Euskera to become a co-equal tongue with Spanish in all fields of life. Nevertheless, the *ikastola* movement does constitute an important attempt to make Euskera a living language that can adapt itself to modern society, and play an effective role in education.

Despite the Spanish government's commitment to protect the country's regional languages, *ikastolas* are subject to considerable harassment from police and educational authorities. The schools are often placed under surveillance on the grounds that they are the centers of subversion or anti-Spanish propaganda. Lists of teachers, pupils and the sources of income must be submitted to Spanish authorities. Licensing of the *ikastolas* is made particularly difficult through administrative restrictions, building codes, and so forth. The schools are supported entirely by the parents of the students, and by Basque cultural societies; and the small amount of grant-in-aid that is available from Madrid comes with such bureaucratic interference and surveillance that most Basque parents reject the assistance.[24] In 1973, Spain began to organize in Guipúzcoa a number of nursery schools where the students would receive an occasional lesson in Euskera. The purpose of these nursery schools, according to some observers, is to lure Basques away from the still struggling *ikastola* movement.

The obvious intention of the Madrid government is to keep the Basque language subordinate to Spanish in all official matters (no matter how much it might be used in homes and neighborhoods). And there are two other serious obstacles to the spread of Euskera usage: the problems presented by the language itself, and the sociological context within which the language must be learned and spoken.[25]

Basques love to relate to the foreign visitor the tale of how the Devil himself came to their country to learn their language, but after seven years he had progressed no further than *bai* (yes) and *ez* (no). In disgust, he left the country, but as he passed through Bayonne on his way out he forgot even these two words. One medieval scholar of European languages is said to have remarked about the Basques: "They say that they understand one another, but I don't believe it."

Gallop has highlighted four major obstacles to the learning of Euskera by non-Basques. First, there is the enormous difficulty presented by the complicated syntax and morphology, which are completely unlike those of any Indo-European language. Without plunging into the technicalities of these difficulties, I shall simply present the illustration used by Gallop: the sentence "I give the book to the boy" is rendered in Basque (roughly) as "Book-the boy-the-to in-the-act-of-giving I-have-it-to-him." The verb in particular gives problems for the speakers of European languages. Gallop's second obstacle — the lack of facilities for study, such as grammars, and dictionaries — is much less of a problem now than when he wrote almost fifty years ago. The flourishing of education and publishing in Euskera since the 1960s has produced a strong outpouring of such media for instruction; and the *ikastolas* have had published a series of 28 textbooks covering the basic elementary subjects (religion, mathematics, and so forth) in Basque. Likewise, the third problem mentioned by Gallop, the rather wide gap between the spoken and the written versions of Euskera, seems to be diminishing in importance as the rejuvenated Basque literary societies struggle to codify and systematize the language and its instruction.

The fourth obstacle, however, remains serious. According to Gallop, there are eight quite different dialects into which Euskera is divided. These dialects are to a large degree mutually unintelligible. They are divided along regional or geographical lines. García Venero tells us that earlier Basque scholars identified four literary dialects, spoken in Vizcaya, Guipúzcoa, and the two French provinces, Labourd and Soule, and four "rustic" or more primitive dialects, spoken in northern and southern Navarra and eastern and western Basse Navarre, in France. In addition, these eight principal dialects are divided into about 25 sub-dialects, and, to quote Gallop, "The truth is that the language varies from village to village, from house to house, and indeed one might say from one individual to another."[26]

The *ikastolas* are attempting to employ a unified form of Euskera called Euskera *batua*, which is a modernized form developed by the Basque language academy Euskaltzaindia. Nevertheless, there is considerable opposition to Euskera *batua* both in Vizcaya, where the provincial dialect differs greatly from the new unified form, and among conservatives who regard *batua* as a maneuver of communists to attack the earlier codification attempts of Sabino de Arana and the Basque Nationalist Party. Because of this stout opposition, the success of a unified Basque dialect seems quite in doubt at this time.

But two important social trends — urbanization and migration — also seem to present significant threats to the survival of Euskera as a viable language. The greatest concentrations of Euskera-speaking persons remain in rural districts and the small villages of 5,000 to 20,000 in population. In the town of Hernani in Guipúzcoa, for example, more than 80 percent of the population speaks Basque, and in the farming zones around Hernani, the percentage soars to more than 95 percent. In Guipúzcoa in 1967, when only 34 percent of the total provincial population spoke Basque, in the towns of less than 2,000 population the figure was about 75 percent, and in those towns that were consistently losing population to the cities the percentage reached 88 percent.[27]

In Vizcaya province one sees much the same situation. In the Greater Bilbao area, according to a 1976 survey of school children, more than 88 percent neither spoke nor understood Euskera, while in the smaller towns and villages in the interior of the province, percentages go the other way. In Marquina, for example, about 71 percent speak Basque; in the Guernica-Bermeo area, the proportion is about 57.5 percent; and in the Plencia-Munguia region, about 54.7 percent of the children speak and understand the language.[28] Apparently, as people move from small town to large industrial city, they have a tendency to abandon the local dialect of their origins in favor of the more modern and utilitarian language of their new surroundings. Even if the original migrants attempt to retain Euskera in the home, the pressures on the second generation are so strong that Euskera tends to die out almost completely among the youth of the major cities. As I have noted before, there are some signs that Euskera is beginning to adapt itself to the conditions of modern life, and that young people and those from upper and middle social strata are beginning to see renewed value in learning the language. Perhaps, if these developments continue, the trend toward erosion of Euskera in large cities can be reversed. Certainly, there are a number of dedicated Basque nationalist scholars, teachers and parents who are trying to make this happen. Whether they will be successful or not is a question that cannot yet be answered. Indeed, we may not know for certain for about another generation whether the Basques can repair the damage of forty years of decline of their language.

The second trend that threatens Euskera is the large scale migration of non-Basque workers into the Basque region in search of jobs and a more comfortable standard of living. In a number of conversations I had with Basque leaders in 1973, I received the impression that they felt that the wave of Spanish migrants into their area could be absorbed into the Basque culture, taught to speak Euskera, and, eventually they (or their children) would come to feel a real identification with the region and its peculiar qualities. This latter development has taken place only to a very slight degree. In the provinces of Alava, Guipúzcoa and Vizcaya, about 38 percent of the residents are not indigenous Basques. Yet, in the 1975 del Campo survey, 29 percent of the residents of these provinces claimed to feel no sense of identification with their region. Further, while about 40 percent said they were happy to be living in the Basque region, nearly that many (39.8 percent) said that they would prefer to return to their home region. More than 40 percent said they *would* return home if the Basques achieved regional autonomy.[29]

It seems likely that one of the chief reasons for this low rate of absorption of Spaniards into Basque culture is their inability or unwillingness to learn Euskera. In his study of Basque nationalism and social classes, Beltza cites surveys of a number of Basque industrial cities and towns that reflect very low percentages of immigrants who have learned Euskera. In Mondragon, for example, 93.3 percent of the immigrants know nothing of Euskera, and only 2.7 percent speak it to any degree. In Hernani, only 3.6 percent of the non-Basques speak the language, and 94.2 percent cannot speak effectively. In Elgoíbar, 93.9 percent are ignorant of Euskera, and 0.5 percent speak the language on a regular basis. In Pasajes, near San Sebastián, only 1.3 percent of the children of immigrants have learned Basque. In the larger cities, the percentages would reflect even lower levels of Euskera usage among non-Basques.[30]

The conclusions drawn from these figures, and others presented above, can only be tentative and suggestive at this juncture in Basque cultural and political history. While there are many talented and dedicated people working very hard to restore Euskera to the status it once enjoyed in the Basque region, there are many others, including some Basques, who would oppose such a trend. In truth, one must observe that the impersonal social forces accompanying industrialization — urbanization and mass migration into the Basque region — are working against those who would save Euskera. Yet it seems hard to believe that a people who could resist forty years of Francisco Franco could not find a satisfactory solution to the problem of their linguistic identity. One thing is certain: if Basque nationalism depends solely on its linguistic distinctiveness to draw the social fault line between Basques and Spaniards, its political future remains hostage to the fate of Euskera. If the language perishes, or becomes simply a museum piece, Basque nationalism will have to discover another rationale for its existence, or suffer the same fate.

Chapter Seven

ETA AND THE CHALLENGE OF "DIRECT ACTION"

The weather in Madrid was cold and wet as the Premier of Spain, Admiral Luis Carrero Blanco, emerged from the morning Mass at the Church of San Francisco de Borja early on the morning of Thursday, December 20, 1973. A staunch Catholic who attended Mass each day before going to work, Carrero Blanco was accompanied by a small entourage of aides and bodyguards. As his automobile convoy pulled away from the Church, and turned onto Claudio Coello Street, an explosion was detonated in a tunnel beneath the street. The bomb was timed precisely to destroy the car in which the Admiral was riding. The force of the explosion lifted the car five stories into the air, over the roof of the church, and deposited it onto a high patio wall. Carrero Blanco was killed, along with his driver and a police guard.

Eight days later, at a press conference held just south of the French city of Bayonne, four hooded men confessed to assassinating Carrero Blanco and asserted that the work was that of the Basque separatist organization ETA (*Euzkadi ta Askatasuna*, or Basque Nation and Freedom). Moderate Basque nationalist leaders had insisted for the preceding week that Basques were not responsible. But the four men revealed knowledge of such detail about the killing that Spanish police were convinced that their confession was legitimate.[1] At about the same time, the Spanish government officially charged six ETA militants with the murders, and closed the Spanish-French border to Basque travelers.[2]

ETA: Origins, Structure and Development

ETA's struggle against Spanish rule in the Basque country was not without Spanish precedents. In the 19th century, irregular insurgents and guerrillas had appeared during the war against Napoleon, and again during both of the Carlist wars. In the 1920s, during the Primo de Rivera dictatorship, Basque mountain climbing clubs, called *mendigoitzales,* were turned into paramilitary organizations to keep alive the fire of Basque separatism. In the years immediately preceding the fall of the Second Spanish Republic and the onset of the Civil War, a few of the more left-oriented Basque nationalist organizations, such as *Acción Nacional Vasca,* began to stockpile weapons and to drill in their use, to guard against the growing threat of illegal violence from the right.[3] Following the Second World War, the remnants of the Basque contingent in the French Resistance crossed the Pyrenees to apply to the struggle against Madrid the lessons they had learned against the Germans.

Drawing on these precedents, ETA has always exhibited an interesting mixture of industrial and pre-industrial characteristics. Nevertheless, it seems to me that ETA was, and is, basically a product of industrial society. Its members are predominantly either workers themselves, or students or priests who grew up in working class families. For example, the fifteen ETA members tried and convicted in the famous Burgos trial of 1970 held the following occupations: chemical analyst, piano teacher, construction worker, priest (2), agricultural technician, mechanic, industrial arts teacher, printer, student (3), and bank employee. Two were unemployed.[4] The six ETA members accused of killing Premier Carrero Blanco included five students and one factory worker.[5]

Both strategically and tactically, ETA has focused its attention on Basque industry and its symbols. Most of ETA's efforts have been concentrated on the two industrial provinces of Vizcaya and Guipúzcoa, while Navarra and Alava have been almost ignored. The densely populated urban areas of Bilbao and San Sebastián, and the industrial towns of Eibar, Irún, and others in the two coastal provinces, have sheltered ETA members, as well as provided the settings for some of the group's most striking actions. ETA's targets, when not actually officials of the Spanish state, have been symbolic representatives of Basque industry, either objects (radio towers, trains, automobiles, factories, banks), or people (noted Basque industrialists or financiers, like Felipe Huarte or Javier de Ybarra).

The technological base of industrial society has also provided a supportive logistical setting for ETA's activities. The organization has apparently never had difficulty acquiring the most sophisticated small arms, automatic weapons, or explosives available. They seem to show a special liking for the 7.65 mm pistol manufactured in Czechoslovakia; but the automatic and semi-automatic rifles and submachine guns they use come from a variety of sources: from Great Britain, the famous Sten gun, Mark V; from Belgium, the Vigneron M2 (9 mm); and from the United States, the favorite weapon of all insurgents, the Ingram submachine gun, called the "marietta."[6] This latter weapon, manufactured by the Military Armaments Corporation of Marietta, Georgia, weighs only seven pounds and is only about 11.5 inches long, yet it fires a standard .45 cal. or 9 mm bullet at the rate of 900 rounds per minute. Many of these weapons are bought freely in the clandestine arms market in Western Europe and smuggled across the Pyrenees in sizable quantities.[7] ETA has apparently never felt the need to assault Guardia Civil posts or barracks in order to obtain arms and ammunition, although there have been a few instances of thefts of weapons from the important armaments factories in Eibar, and officials usually blame ETA for these. Likewise, the acquisition of explosives has never been much of a problem for ETA. There are about 270 major deposits of explosives and blasting agents in Spain, and ETA has successfully assaulted several of these that are located in the Basque provinces.[8] It is hard to conceive of ETA apart from the urban industrial setting within which it operates, and which continues to support it.

It is more than coincidence, then, that ETA was born not in the comparatively pastoral calm of the small village of Guernica under the shadow of the Basques' historic oak tree, but rather in the University of Deusto, in the heart of industrial Bilbao. The year was 1952. The collapse of the Bilbao strike the preceding year had symbolized the continuing failure of the Basque Nationalist Party to ignite the Basque people and to unify them in their hatred of the Spanish. A small group of only seven college students began to meet to discuss possible political action and to raise their political consciousness. The members of this group realized their lack of experience with political action. But they were deeply frustrated by the inability of the PNV to direct the resistance in a more positive style. The first several years of their existence were directed more at mutual education than at taking steps to achieve independence.

In the summer of 1953 the original group of students was able to recruit two more small groups of young people, and the enlarged circle began to meet regularly to listen to presentations on the need for action to gain Basque autonomy. At about this time, the group began to publish a typewritten and mimeographed newsletter titled "Ekin," from which they subsequently took the name for the group itself. As the group gained strength and adherents, it was inevitable that they were approached by the Basque Nationalist Party and invited to merge their organization into the older and more established movement. Negotiations between the two groups lasted from 1954 to 1957, when Ekin agreed to dissolve itself and join the youth section of the PNV, called EGI (for *Euzko Gaztedi,* for Basque Youth). But the rapprochement lasted only two years. The more moderate PNV felt the Ekin group lacked patience and discipline. The Ekin youth became more and more restive under the restraining hand of the PNV leadership, whom they accused of immobilism and even cowardice. The definitive break occurred in 1959, the same year that the letters "ETA" began to appear spray-painted on walls and at the top of pamphlets. As is often the case in Basque politics, the founding was set for a date with symbolic religious significance: July 31, the feast day of Saint Ignacio de Loyola, the patron saint of Guipúzcoa and Vizcaya provinces.

ETA was not at the outset either committed to violence or particularly revolutionary. In 1959, its leaders described the organization as a "patriotic, democratic and nonconfessional movement," not unlike the older and more established *Acción Nacional Vasca*. It was not engaged in any violent actions, and restricted itself almost entirely to the printing and distribution of pamphlets and occasionally to displaying the prohibited Basque flag. In 1960, at the World Basque Congress held in Paris, one Federico Kruttwig Sagredo, the son of a German industrialist living in Bilbao, stunned the more sedate Basque nationalist movement by arguing for the launching of guerrilla war in Spain to free Euzkadi. He was, as might be expected, regarded as a lunatic.

However, as events unfolded in Spain, ETA was not allowed the luxury of anonymity or of advocating revolution in writing while pursuing peaceful change in practice. Twice in 1960, in March and again in August, raids on EGI cells produced information that brought ETA and its activities to the attention of the Spanish government. The violence of the suppression of the fledgling organization drove the group further underground and hardened its leaders. It also pushed ETA closer and closer to an ideology of revolutionary violence.

On July 18, 1961, ETA attempted to carry out its first act of sabotage. A number of trains were en route to San Sebastián on that date, carrying large numbers of Franco supporters to festivals to celebrate the 25th anniversary of the military uprising that began the Civil War. ETA's plan was to derail the trains without harming any of the passengers. Their plans were laid so delicately that none of the trains left the track. The Spanish government reaction was fierce: more than 100 were arrested and tortured; about 30 of these were taken to the infamous Carabanchel prison in Madrid for more interrogation and torture. Most of those arrested were either sent into exile or sentenced to jail terms of fifteen to twenty years. ETA's leaders now moved more swiftly toward their eventual commitment to revolution. From their exile in 1962, the group's major founders issued a statement redefining ETA as "a clandestine revolutionary organization with three fronts: cultural, political and military."

ETA's first general meeting, called the *Primera Asamblea*, or (in Euskera) *Biltzar Nagusia*, was held in May 1962. Now, the social revolutionary tendencies of the organization began to emerge in its propaganda. The Assembly defined the organization as a "Basque revolutionary movement for national liberation." Revolutionary socialism became an important segment of the group's ideology. The vocabulary of the meeting reflected these changes. Members were referred to as "comrades" or "militants." The struggles in Algeria, Cuba and Vietnam were studied for lessons that the Basques could apply to their circumstances; and while rural guerrilla warfare seemed inappropriate to the Basque case, ETA found in revolutionary socialism the justification they had sought for violence.

The second general assembly, the *Segunda Asamblea,* took place in March 1963, and attracted delegations from various European and Latin American countries. In the autumn of that same year, the Spanish authorities launched a campaign to crush ETA once and for all, and nearly succeeded. The counterattack by ETA's committee of leaders had significant impact on the shape of the struggle for several years thereafter. A number of members were given full time jobs and responsibilities in the organization and were told to resign or relinquish their regular employment permanently. They were henceforth to be supported by the treasury of the organization. They became known as *liberados* because they were freed of any need to hold a normal job, or to try to blend in with the surrounding society. The Basque provinces were formally divided into zones of operations and of responsibilities. These zones were called *herrialdes.* Finally, ETA decided to publish and disseminate the 45-page pamphlet called *Insurrección en Euzkadi,* written by an ETA leader known only by the cover name "Goiztiri."

The pamphlet by Goiztiri was adopted as official ideology and policy by the third general meeting, the *Tercera Asamblea,* which was held in 1964. It merits considerable interest as the earliest statement of ETA's revolutionary strategy. Goiztiri criticized the organization for having tried to skip over the required stages for the making of revolutionary war. The 1961 train-derailing episode, he argued, was a grave error, because it reflected a mistaken belief that ETA would be able to wage war against Franco and the Spanish army without proper preparation. Revolutionary war, he asserted, advanced in stages. To move beyond the stage that was correct for any given revolutionary group was not only incorrect but criminally negligent, for it risked human life needlessly. Thus, the Basque revolutionaries would be forced to move cautiously and slowly until such time as they could afford to strike at Spain directly. In the short run, their efforts would have to be devoted to consolidating their position, to recruiting trusted members, to flushing out the spies and informers that had infiltrated the movement,[9] and to acquiring weapons and training members in their use. At the appropriate time and place, ETA would attack, but it would be ready and not make the mistakes of 1961.

Two resources would be needed to bring the organization up to attack strength: money and propaganda. ETA leaders quickly learned that contributions by members alone would be totally inadequate to finance their operations and preparations. Thus, they decided to initiate a series of activities to obtain large amounts of funds: bank robberies, kidnappings of wealthy persons, and the exaction of a "revolutionary tax" from well-to-do industrialists and bankers. Their first bank robbery took place on April 21, 1967, when they struck the Banco Guipúzcoano, in the town of Villabona. They obtained more than one million pesetas in that operation. According to one source, up to mid-1977, ETA had obtained more than sixty million pesetas (or about one million dollars) from its bank robberies.

Money, weapons, training, organization: all of these elements of revolutionary war were worthless unless the organization were able to affect the state of mind of both the Basque noncombatants and the Spanish authorities. This task is essential to all revolutionary struggle and is more psychological than anything else. All revolutionary violence is launched by groups that suffer from noted discrepancies in power and military resources. In Spain, ETA had to contend with a military force that in the middle 1960s numbered about one-third of a million troops supporting the feared Guardia Civil, which consisted of about 60,000 to 80,000 paramilitary effectives. Confrontation of these forces by the weak and outnumbered ETA commando units would have been catastrophic. Instead, war would be waged not against the military units of the Spanish but against the minds of the Spanish. Instead of military confrontation, ETA would seek ways of forcing the Spanish out of the Basque country by psychological war. The objective was not to defeat the Spanish forces on the field of battle, but to raise the cost of occupying the Basque country to the point where the Spanish would tire of the effort and relinquish their grip on the rebellious provinces. To accomplish this goal, targets would be selected that were poorly defended but which had great symbolic importance for Spain. Objectively speaking, the impact of ETA's military operations would be no greater than a pin prick to the Spanish. If the targets were correctly chosen, however, the importance of their loss or destruction would be far greater in the minds of Madrid than merited by their intrinsic effect. This was "the propaganda of the deed" in the truest sense of the word.

In the middle 1960s, then, money and psychological impact became the central features of ETA's strategy. They have remained central up to the present time, even if achieved at a steadily increasing level of violence and shock. In the early 1960s, ETA's tactics were intended to avoid provoking excessive and disastrous countermeasures by the Spanish government. Events with special psychological shock value, *acciones cruentas* in the vocabulary of ETA, would have to await the later stages of revolutionary war. Whether by strategy or out of desperation, as the years wore on ETA's strategy did indeed create ever higher levels of public outrage and disapproval, even from some of the more progressive forces within Basque nationalist circles.

As ETA gained strength during the first half of the 1960s, and as the organization's ideology inclined toward the left, the agents of Spanish socialism in the Basque country began to infiltrate the organization and try to use it to advance their own cause. Prior to the Civil War, the Spanish left parties in the Basque cities, especially in Bilbao, had flourished primarily by their ability to recruit new members from among the non-Basque working population. As we have already seen, a significant split developed between the PNV and the Spanish socialists, communists and anarchists, and their affiliated unions. The Basque nationalists regarded the Spanish left as a threat to them both as Spanish domination, and as advocates of class struggle. The Spanish left, in turn, hated the Basque nationalists both as bourgeois and as a separatist element that would weaken Spain. The emergence of ETA gave the Spanish left an opportunity to appeal to the sentiments of Basque workers by taking over the organization and using it to advance the cause of socialism in the guise of Basque nationalism. These groups argued that a strictly ethnic struggle for Basque nationalism was undermining the much more important struggle for the liberation of the working classes everywhere on the peninsula. Basque separatism had to be subordinated to this broader fight. The proponents of this position called themselves ETA-*BERRI* (New ETA). Their opponents were ETA-*ZARRA* (Old ETA).

Apparently, the leaders of ETA-*BERRI* were taken aback by the violently negative reaction of the Old ETA to their proposals. The turning point in this internal dispute was the organization's Fifth Assembly, the *Quinta Asamblea,* held in two phases, in December 1966 and in March 1967. At the close of the December meeting, the representatives of ETA-*BERRI* were expelled from the organization, and eventually formed the Spanish Communist Movement (MCE, or *Movimiento Comunista de España*). From this episode, two concepts began to take on special meaning in Basque politics. Groups that advocated cooperation with, or subordination to, some Spanish party or movement that shared a similar social or economic position were called *sucursalista,* from the Spanish word *sucursal,* meaning "branch office." These groups were treated with derision and scorn by those who condemned any cooperation with Spanish parties no matter what their point of view. This latter position arose from the premise that Euzkadi had to gain its independence first before radical social change could take place in the Basque provinces. No Spanish party, it was believed, no matter how radical, would assist the Basques in gaining their autonomy, because they needed the support of the Basque working class and the Basque unions to offset the power of the Spanish right-wing parties. Thus, these latter groups, like the original ETA-*ZARRA*, came to refer to themselves as *abertzale* parties, from the Basque word for "patriotic." For years thereafter, and even up to the 1977 elections and beyond, the clash between *sucursalistas* and *abertzales* would continue to dominate the rhetoric and the symbols of Basque politics.

The other divisive issue in ETA was over the role of violence in revolutionary war. For nearly ten years, from 1966 to 1975, ETA was plagued by repeated internal splits over this issue. The Fifth Assembly reaffirmed the traditional ETA position of non-cooperation with Spanish parties, of commitment to revolutionary war within the framework of Marxism-Leninism. Violence was sure to come, but it had to await the correct moment and come only after careful preparation, both militarily and technologically. The Basque people, and especially the Basque working class, were not particularly avid proponents of armed struggle, and they had to be prepared by careful psychological reorientation before an all-out war would be productive for ETA. The first split came in 1967, when a group known as Aintzina broke away to form a radical party that condemned the resort to violence of ETA. A second group, called Saioak, left ETA in 1968, to end up eventually as the Basque section of the Spanish Communist Party (PCE, or *Partido Comunista de España*). In 1970, the most significant division since the Fifth Assembly nearly destroyed ETA: a sizable portion of ETA split off to become ETA-*Sexta*, named for the Sixth Assembly, or *Sexta Asamblea*, where the dispute broke out. Eventually, ETA-*Quinta* (the group that had remained after the expulsion of ETA-*BERRI* at the Fifth Assembly, or *Quinta Asamblea*) won back some of the adherents of the more radical ETA-*Sexta*. What was left of ETA-*Sexta* further subdivided into the Basque branch of the Revolutionary Communist League (LCR, or *Liga Comunista Revolucionaria*), and a tiny *abertzale* group that refused to rejoin ETA. From this point, until 1972, ETA languished somewhat as it tried to infuse its doctrine of *abertzale* revolutionary war with new meaning and fervor. The addition of new members from EGI in 1972 helped bring the organization to life once again, and it was during this period that ETA planned and carried out the assassination of Carrero Blanco. Nevertheless, the problem of ideology would not go away. In 1974, the organization split again, into a branch that advocated armed conflict in lieu of organization work with the working classes (called ETA-m, meaning ETA-*militar*, or military ETA), and a branch that argued for simultaneous efforts in both the military and the political spheres (ETA-pm, for ETA-*político-militar*).

At about this same time, a number of small parties were developing on the left in the Basque political spectrum. These parties were nearly as radical and as *abertzale* as ETA, but they looked forward to the day when Franco's death would make it possible for non-violent electoral politics to be carried on in Spain. These parties usually had close relations with a parallel workers' organization or labor union. In Chapters 10 and 11, I shall discuss the emergence of these groups as important factors in electoral politics in the post-Franco era, groups that helped to smooth the return of former ETA members to non-revolutionary and non-violent political action.

Let us return now, however, to 1966-1967 and the crucial Fifth Assembly. In addition to expelling the dissident leaders of ETA-*BERRI*, and solidifying the organization's ideology and operating principles, the *Quinta Asamblea* took some important steps to strengthen ETA's internal structure, to make it more efficient, and to harden it against pressures from Spanish counter-violence.

To begin with, the Fifth Assembly established the annual *Asamblea* as ETA's supreme authority. The powers of the Assembly were delegated to an Executive Committee, which was responsible for controlling the day-to-day activities of the organization. In turn, the political orthodoxy of the Executive Committee was monitored by the Little Assembly, or, in Euskera, *Biltzar Txikia*. The BT met in exile and had little direct authority over the Executive Committee. However, the Little Assembly could convene the General Assembly whenever it felt that the Executive Committee had violated the organization's ideological or strategic guidelines. While the Executive

Committee operated on the Spanish side of the border, in France there were also established an office of ideology and theory, called the Political Office, and an agency that controlled the especially difficult projects or operations, called the Strategic Command. At the operational level, ETA's structure was divided into four "fronts": worker organization, cultural, political, and military. Most of the acts of violence directed by the organization were carried out by the military front. After the Fifth Assembly, ETA emerged as a major force in Basque resistance politics. It had an ideology that was distinctive and that sustained its particular brand of action; it had an organizational structure that was resilient under the pressure of the Franco regime; and it had dedicated members and money sufficient to make an impact on Spanish and world opinion. Followers of the organization that emerged from the 1966-1967 period were known as adherents of ETA-*Quinta,* to distinguish themselves from various splinter groups that purported to speak for the organization in other periods and for other interests.

Observers and analysts of the ETA phenomenon have some obligation to dig beneath the labels and epithets of revolutionary insurgency and to examine the empirical record in an effort to establish in clear outline the real nature of ETA's actions and the impact they had on Basque and Spanish society. For obvious reasons, it is impossible to compile for analysis a complete and authoritative list of ETA's insurgent activities. Doubtless there have been incidents attributed to ETA that were in fact ordinary crimes committed by persons with no political motivation or institutional backing. It is also highly likely that some of ETA's actions went undetected by the news media or by law enforcement agencies. Our analysis, then, must be based on potentially flawed secondary sources and can be only suggestive of the range and direction of ETA insurgent actions during the decade from 1966 to 1976.

Data on ETA killings are drawn from an article written in 1977 by Bilbao journalist José María Portel who was said to have very close contacts within ETA.[10] (In 1978, Sr. Portel was assassinated by unknown assailants, allegedly because of his role in trying to negotiate a truce between ETA and Spanish authorities.) The first death connected with ETA was that of ETA member Javier Echebarrieta, a 23-year-old economist who was killed in June 1968 at a Guardia Civil roadblock. From 1968 to 1973, according to Portel, there were nineteen deaths associated with ETA, including eleven ETA members and eight non-members. (It should not be assumed automatically that all ETA deaths were inflicted by police; some were the result of internecine quarrels between or among ETA members themselves. Likewise, the reader should not assume that all non-ETA deaths were caused by ETA; some were persons caught in police-ETA crossfire or otherwise killed accidentally. Exact details of this sort are exceedingly difficult to come by.) During the two-year period from 1974 through 1975, the number of dead grew to 55 additional: 19 from ETA; 36 non-members. In 1976, there were 29 killings: 19 non-members; ten from ETA. During the first six months of 1977, there were 16 ETA-related deaths: 12 were members of ETA or closely associated with the organization; four were not members (three police, and the Bilbao industrialist Javier de Ybarra). Thus, during the nine-year period from mid-1968 to mid-1977, 119 people lost their lives in ETA-connected events. Of these, 52 were ETA members, 67 were non-members.

More information on ETA actions can be derived from material contained in a critique of ETA written by Federico de Arteaga (a pseudonym), *ETA y el Proceso de Burgos,* published in 1971.[11] This material is summarized in Table 6. It seems to this author that this listing of alleged ETA incidents and activities suggests a conscious effort to avoid harming bystanders or inflicting needless casualties. Nearly three-fourths of all incidents were apparently designed for propaganda effect. About 20 percent of the incidents, including thefts and burglaries, were intended to obtain the resources — weapons, explosives, vehicles, and money — needed to engage in propaganda efforts.

Students of insurgent warfare have concluded that dissident groups that focus most of their attention on bombings and arson are in fact interested neither in inflicting large numbers of casualties, nor in risking any themselves.[12] ETA's chosen activities seem to fit this pattern rather clearly.

Table 6.
Pattern of Alleged ETA Activities, 1967-1970.

Nature of Incident		Nature of Target	
Bombings	30	Government agencies: Police, government offices, schools, etc.	32
Armed assault, robbery	18	Transportation: cars, trains	16
Harassment of individuals	12	Monuments, flags	16
Sabotage	12	Financial institutions: banks, stock exchange	9
Arson	11	Communications: newspapers, TV transmitters, telephone relays	8
Destruction of symbolic objects	10	Industrial, construction sites	8
Theft, burglary	6	Miscellaneous individuals	8
Propaganda	4	Unclear, other	7
Assassination	3	Electric power supply	3
Other	2	Church	1
Total	108	**Total**	108

Source: Federico de Arteaga, *ETA y el Proceso de Burgos* (Madrid: Editorial E. Aguado, 1971), pp. 345-350.

In their choice of targets, ETA also appears to have tried to avoid causing the mass casualties associated with indiscriminate terrorism. About one-third of its targets were government agencies, including police stations, Guardia Civil barracks, civil government headquarters, schools, and the private dwellings of government officials. Most of the remainder of the target list were either monuments or other symbolic devices, such as flags; financial institutions, including banks;

symbols of capitalism, such as industrial installations; the media of mass communications, including television and telephone relay stations and newspapers; and electric power supplies. Only eight cases involved attacks on specific individuals aside from government officials. The only case which involved an attack on a large number of noncombatants was the 1961 train derailment attempt already discussed above. Significantly, such care was taken to avoid injuring the passengers that no practical effect was achieved. At no time during this period did ETA attack sites where large numbers of persons were known to gather, such as sports arenas, airports, bars or restaurants, churches, etc. This helps explain why, in the early years of revolutionary struggle and violent insurgency, from 1968 to 1973, only one bystander died as the result of ETA-related incidents. All of the remaining ETA victims during that period were law enforcement authorities, or specific intended targets such as Premier Carrero Blanco.

Although I do not have access to systematic data to cover the more recent period, it is obvious that ETA's activities between 1973 and Franco's death in 1975 became more violent, and produced many more casualties. The data I have been able to gather covering this more recent period, primarily from newspaper articles and other similarly unsystematic sources, confirm this impression. Again, many of the reports allege ETA participation in certain events without presenting supporting evidence to confirm such participation. Nonetheless, the following are some of the typical events reported during the period that purportedly involved ETA members:

April-May 1973: A series of shootings and arrests in the Bilbao area resulted in two deaths, one each for the police and ETA, and eight ETA members arrested.

June 1973: Three ETA members allegedly robbed a bank in Santurce of 1.5 million pesetas.

June 1973: A shooting between ETA and Guardia Civil members took place in Santuchu. No casualties on either side.

July 1973: Three ETA members apprehended in the process of planning an attack against the Guardia Civil barracks in Lequeitio.

June 1974: Four or five ETA members allegedly participated in the robbery of a factory payroll in Irún. Fourteen million pesetas were stolen. One Guardia Civil killed.

September 1974: Four ETA members took part in the robbery of a factory in Llodio. Ten million pesetas were stolen.

September 1974: An explosion in the Rolando Restaurant in Madrid killed 12, wounded 68. ETA was implicated in the incident. However, an ETA communiqué from France a month after the event disclaimed responsibility for the bombing.

September 1974: A shooting in Bilbao resulted in one ETA member killed.

October 1974: A shooting between the Guardia Civil and ETA members resulted in one killed on each side.

December 1974: A series of shootings and robberies in Mondragón and Urduliz resulted in one ETA member killed, two Guardia Civil killed.

December 1974: A bank robbery in Vitoria was carried out by three members of ETA. One Guardia Civil was wounded. Six million pesetas stolen.

February 1975: 550 kgs of dynamite stolen from a construction site near Deva. The police presumed that it was the work of ETA.

August 1975: A series of shootings resulted in the death of seven policemen over a several week period.

October 1975: A bombing attributed to ETA killed three Guardia Civil and wounded two. This was part of the violence and turmoil that accompanied the execution of five terrorists by General Franco in September and October 1975. Franco's death the following month initiated a series of momentous changes in Spanish and Basque politics, and ETA was affected significantly by these changes.

We do not, of course, have access to any psychological data that would reveal the levels of fear or social paralysis in the Basque provinces, nor do we know the origins of such fear if indeed we were able to observe it to an abnormal degree. As a visitor to the Basque country in 1973, I observed no situations that seemed to equal the social disorientation of Ulster as a result of the violence between northern Irish Catholics and Protestants, or of Uruguay after the struggle against the

Tupamaros. Certainly, the casualty levels of the ETA insurgency are quite small compared with more brutal guerrilla wars in other countries. In Argentina, for example, more than 2,300 persons were killed between July 1974 and August 1976; in northern Ireland, more than 1,600 were killed in the seven-year period that ended in 1976. Furthermore, ETA-inflicted casualties were not indiscriminate. The victims were not randomly killed but were either officials of the Spanish state (police or Guardia Civil troops), or were important figures in Basque capitalist circles. ETA did not attack large crowds of persons randomly, but rather was quite selective, and careful to avoid large-scale death or destruction.* Before 1968, virtually all ETA actions were purely symbolic: distribution of leaflets, hanging of Basque flags, and the like. Even for several years after 1968, the higher levels of violence, including bombings and bank robberies, were still employed primarily not to instill fear, but to communicate messages to a watching public.

If there was terrorism in the Basque country during the 1960s and early 1970s, it was practiced by the Spanish state. The first death in the struggle between ETA and the Guardia Civil was that of the ETA activist, Javier Echebarrieta. After his death, in June 1968, ETA retaliated with the assassination of Meliton Manzanas, the action that led to the controversial trial of Burgos in 1970. The violence escalated from that point onward, with each side attempting to wreak vengeance for the other's actions. But the first step in the terrorist spiral was taken by the Guardia Civil. If I observed any genuine fear among Basques

---

**Author's Note:* The lines above were written early in 1979. On July 29, 1979, three bomb blasts ripped through two Madrid railroad stations and the Madrid airport, killing 4 and wounding at least 113. About half an hour before the blast, a person claiming to be a member of ETA telephoned the Spanish National News Agency (EFE) to warn them of the impending explosion. If it turns out that ETA was indeed responsible for this attack, it is the first such indiscriminate attack on civilians launched by the group, at least to my knowledge. If such attacks continue, they would definitely mark a new and more desperate phase in the history of the organization.

during my visit to the Basque country in 1973, it was fear of the Guardia Civil, not of ETA.

The Spanish Government Response to ETA: The "State of Exception"

One of the enduring tests of a political regime is how well it continues to protect fundamental human rights under conditions of stress, disorder, and crisis. In Spain, the official violence of the police and the Guardia Civil were unleashed during times of special stress by means of a juridical device known as the "state of exception." The state of exception is one step short of martial law. It is a temporary abrogation by the government of six rights theoretically preserved and guaranteed by the *Fuero de los Españoles:* freedom of expression, privacy of the mail, assembly and association, habeas corpus, freedom of movement and residence, and freedom from arbitrary house arrest.

In moving from a regime of law to one of arbitrary coercion, the most significant abrogation was that affecting the right of habeas corpus. In Spain, when the right is in effect, persons detained by the police must be brought before a court for arraignment within 72 hours of the arrest. There are ample provisions for securing legal counsel, and for informing family or friends of the whereabouts of the detainee. However, when a state of exception is in effect, the right of habeas corpus is suspended. Persons can be arrested and held at any location for any length of time without informing anyone of their whereabouts, or even of the fact that they have been arrested. The courts, lawyers, and family are completely helpless to come to the aid of the detainee. Under these conditions, police brutality is encouraged and even protected. Confessions extracted under torture are particularly common during states of exception. Persons have been imprisoned and tortured more or less continuously for weeks on end without any charge being brought against them, without ever having been seen by a judge or having consulted with an attorney.

States of exception also lead to extra-legal violence by right-wing vigilante groups. Freed from government restraint, these groups have assaulted both political activists and ordinary citizens in the street and in their homes, and have created their own "reign of terror" quite apart from what the police and the Guardia Civil were accomplishing with their official state-sanctioned violence. There are a number of these right-wing groups, but the most active in the Basque country has been the organization known as the *Guerrilleros de Cristo-Rey* (Warriors for Christ the King). *Guerrilleros* combine Catholicism with a self-appointed mission to carry on the nationalist-Francoist crusade even after Franco himself is gone. They operate typically by attacking persons and other targets that support the political opposition in Spain. They have been especially virulent in their attacks on separatism, both in the Basque provinces and in Cataluña. Because these rightist groups have operated with impunity during states of exception, there is no way of knowing how much damage they have done, or how many people have fled into exile to avoid their assaults. One account asserts that right-wing groups operating in the Basque provinces committed 85 "actions" (including two that resulted in deaths of the victims) in the Basque country during the 18-month period following the state of exception declared in the spring of 1975.[13]

It is impossible to calculate the impact of the state of exception on Basque life. From 1960 to 1977, the state of exception was declared in effect six times in the Basque provinces. Constitutional rights were suspended for periods ranging from two to six months. José María Portel estimates that during these six states of exception, more than 8,500 Basques were in some way directly affected, either through arrest, imprisonment and torture, or by fleeing into exile to avoid the police or vigilante groups.[14]

During the late 1960s and early 1970s, the number of Basques in prison for political crimes varied between 100 and 200.[15] At the time of Franco's death, in November 1975, there were approximately 1,250 persons in Spanish jails for political crimes, mostly "illicit association," propaganda, and other crimes of conscience. Thus, Basques constituted about fifteen to twenty percent of all Spanish political prisoners. However, about 250 of the political prisoners had been convicted for more serious crimes, such as assassination, bank robbery, or terrorism. I estimate that between 40 and 50 percent of these persons were Basque.[16] Yet, over the past two decades, residents of the Basque provinces (including, of course, many non-Basques) have accounted for only seven to nine percent of all crimes in Spain,[17] both political and nonpolitical, a percentage much more nearly in accord with the proportion of Basques in the total Spanish population (6.9 percent in 1970).

During 1975, two states of exception were declared. The first, which lasted from April 25 to July 25, affected only the four Basque provinces. The second, which lasted from August 22 to Franco's death, on November 20, covered Spain in its entirety. This entire period was especially noteworthy for the level of violence, both official and that emanating from extralegal vigilante groups. In a rather sad way, the spasm of violence during 1975 symbolized the agonizing end of the Franco period in Spanish history.

The first state of exception stemmed from a wave of bank robberies, street shootings and assassinations in the Basque provinces during early spring. The police and the Guardia Civil, now unfettered by the state of exception declaration, sought to suppress not only the violence but all popular support for expressions of Basque separatism. During the first month of the exception decree, 198 persons were arrested in Vizcaya province alone, not counting an unknown number of individuals who had been taken to police headquarters or Guardia Civil barracks for interrogation and eventual release without charges.[18] Police roamed at will throughout the major cities in the Basque provinces, stopping ordinary citizens in public places to request documentation about place of residence or work location. Young people gathered in bars or restaurants were singled out for special attention, and police frequently raided these sites to seek out ETA members or other political activists. According to one source, more than 150 Basques fled into France to avoid these searches and arrests.[19]

A number of priests with alleged ties to ETA were arrested and detained for long periods without charges. Six priests were arrested near Bilbao in May and tortured savagely to extract confessions that they had sheltered ETA militants in their churches or homes. One priest, Father Eustaquio

Eriquicia, was later admitted to a hospital on May 10, 1975, with a skull fracture, almost total kidney malfunction, and other serious injuries, after interrogation by the secret police.[20]

Right-wing Spanish forces lost no opportunity to contribute to the rising level of tension and violence in the Basque country. Rightist crowds held officially sanctioned demonstrations in Madrid, Barcelona and other Spanish cities to urge the police, the Guardia Civil, and the armed forces to take whatever steps necessary to suppress not only ETA but Basque nationalism in general. In early June, the commanding general of Spain's VI Military Region (which includes the Basque provinces) toured the Guardia Civil posts in the Basque country, and was quoted as telling the Guardia Civil that "although the mission of the Army is not to maintain public order, I want you to know that we are behind you."[21]

The most complete coverage of the effects of the state of exception was provided by a team sent by the human rights organization Amnesty International, to investigate charges of police brutality.[22] The findings of the Amnesty International investigation included the following observations:

1. Although the exact number of detainees remains unknown, AI found conclusive evidence that massive detentions took place in Vizcaya and Guipúzcoa provinces at levels far higher than the official statistics claimed (as of May 27, 1975, the Spanish government claimed that 189 people had been detained, of whom 90 had been subsequently released). AI discovered evidence that more than a thousand persons had been detained in each of the two provinces, and that more than five hundred of these detainees were held by security or law enforcement forces for more than 72 hours without notification of family, without consultation with an attorney, and without formal charges being made.

2. While the state of exception was in effect, the civil governors of the two provinces ordered the rearrest of a number of detainees after their release by a judge. In addition, the governors also ordered the removal of detainees from police stations or Guardia Civil barracks and their transportation directly to prison, thereby circumventing the judicial process.

3. The AI mission received "personal and direct evidence"

of the torture of 45 detainees during the state of exception. In addition, the investigation revealed "credible and convincing evidence that torture was systematically used against a *minimum* of 250 Basque detainees . . ." in the two most seriously affected provinces. Torture was used against many more people, AI affirmed, in all four Basque provinces; but the evidence was somewhat more circumstantial and not as directly convincing. Every victim interviewed by the mission had been tortured at least once a day during his period of imprisonment. Some had been tortured as many as five times a day. Sessions lasted from half an hour to six hours. One victim reported 30 sessions of torture in 21 continuous days. Five of the torture victims interviewed had been illegally transferred from one province to another to circumvent the rule prohibiting detention for more than 72 hours without charges or notification of legal counsel.

The nature of the torture indicates that it was used as a systematic technique to punish and suppress Basque nationalists and was not a series of isolated and irregular violations of law by a few police. All three major law enforcement authorities in the Basque provinces, the Policia Armada, the Guardia Civil, and the Brigada Político-Social, participated in the beatings and torture. The methods of torture included (to quote the AI report),

> severe and systematic beatings with a variety of contusive weapons, falanga (beating on the soles of the feet), burning with cigarettes, near drownings by being submerged in water while suspended upside-down, enforced sleeplessness, and forms of psychological stress, including mock executions, sexual threats, threats to relatives and the technique known as *el cerrojo* (the frequent fastening and unfastening of bolts on the cell doors in order to keep prisoners in perpetual fear that the torturers have returned).

4. AI found that torture was used for two reasons. In some instances, torture was employed to obtain information or confessions that would enable the security forces to combat the ETA challenge. In addition, however, AI found that torture was used to intimidate the Basque population into submission, and to frighten them into abandoning support for the Basque

nationalist cause. Even when detainees had no knowledge to reveal, torture was employed in order to intimidate the general Basque population, and to seek revenge for the assassination of two policemen during the month of May.

The violence of the spring and summer of 1975 entered its second phase in late August. As a result of the arrests made during the first state of exception, a number of detainees were brought to trial and convicted by a summary court martial. (The nature of justice meted out by the summary courts martial in Spain is the subject of the following section of this chapter.) During the first three weeks of September, ten political activists were sentenced to death in connection with the slaying of several policemen. Two of the ten were young women who claimed to be pregnant. In addition, an eleventh suspect was sentenced to 20 years in prison for aiding the assassins. Still another suspected Basque separatist was under arrest in Barcelona and faced trial by court martial for murdering a policeman. Two terrorist suspects had died in gun fights with police, a third was wounded, and fifteen had been detained.

In late September, five of the convicted terrorists were executed by firing squad. Two of the five were members of ETA, while the others were from the radical Spanish group called the Patriotic Revolutionary Anti-Fascist Front (FRAP). Six other convicted activists, including the two women, and one Basque who suffered from a serious brain injury, were granted reprieves by General Franco in an attempt to lessen public criticism of the executions. Nevertheless, a wave of protests swept across the Basque country and throughout Western Europe. In San Sebastián, more than 30,000 workers walked off the job to protest the executions. Pope Paul VI revealed that he had made three separate appeals to Franco for clemency for all the prisoners, but was rebuffed by Madrid. There were demonstrations against the executions in Lisbon, Paris, Brussels, Copenhagen, Athens, Rome, and Frankfort. The European Common Market issued a strong official condemnation; and the governments of West and East Germany and Holland recalled their ambassadors to Madrid.

Despite these pressures and mounting unrest within the Basque country, the Spanish government moved forward in its plans to place on trial two more ETA militants. ETA military chief José Múgica Arregui and strategist Ignacio Pérez ("Wilson") Beotagui were accused of participating in the 1973 assassination of Admiral Carrero Blanco. At the time of the 1975 unrest, the two men faced almost certain conviction at the hands of a military court. Conviction would almost certainly be followed by execution. Mass demonstrations began to mount in the Basque provinces to persuade the regime to back away from such harsh measures for the two. Nevertheless, on September 29, sources in Madrid revealed the government's plans to bring to trial fifteen accused ETA members, including Múgica and Pérez Beotagui and five women. ETA responded to the news by assaulting a government social security office in Barcelona, making off with $600,000, and wounding two police officers during their escape. It was the largest robbery in Barcelona in forty years.

On the following day, Spanish Premier Carlos Arias Navarro spoke to the nation on television, urging Spaniards to remain calm during the crisis, and to show their support for General Franco. The same day, one of the policemen wounded in the Barcelona robbery died of his wounds. The following day, only hours before a mass demonstration in Madrid to support the Franco regime, gunmen attacked police in three separate areas of the Spanish capital. Three policemen died in the attacks and a fourth was seriously wounded. From January 1974 to October 1975, 22 police and fourteen civilians had been killed in insurgent violence in Spain. On October 5, three Guardia Civil troops were killed and two were injured in an explosion that destroyed their jeep on patrol about 60 miles west of San Sebastián. The next day, extreme rightists machine-gunned to death a Basque bar owner in reprisal for the ETA killings. The upward spiral of violence and reprisal seemed to be headed out of control when news of General Franco's collapse and impending death in November brought to a close one of Spain's most agonizing moments since the Civil War.

The Spanish Government Response to ETA: The "Sumarísimo"

The legal relationships between ETA and the Franco government were contained largely in the Decree-Law on Military Rebellion, Banditry and Terrorism, promulgated by General Franco in 1960. By making a wide variety of insurgent activities subject to military court martial, the Decree-Law of 1960 effectively denied the accused ETA members the protection of due process of law. I can find not a single instance in which a member of ETA was found guilty of terrorist activities in a civilian court, where evidence was presented in an adversarial proceeding, and where the legal rights of the accused were protected adequately. In most of the ETA trials, the accused either denied their guilt, or repudiated the confessions attributed to them as having been extracted under torture. The Decree-Law, and the resultant court martial, were two more weapons that the Franco regime employed to suppress Basque separatism in general, and ETA in particular.

The historical path to the 1960 Decree-Law leads back to July 18, 1936. In the proclamation accompanying the military rebellion of Generals Franco, Sanjurjo and Mola, one finds the following statement: "Spain is a unity. All conspiracy against this unity is repulsive. All separatism is a crime that we will not pardon."[23] This proclamation was followed ten days later by one of the first decrees issued by the Committee of National Defense (the rebels' governing body), which extended the declaration of war to the entire Spanish territory, and which made it a military offense to bear arms, to possess flammable or explosive substances, or to oppose in any other way the course of the military uprising. The same Committee, on June 23, 1937, formally declared the provinces of Vizcaya and Guipúzcoa to be traitorous and disloyal, thereby depriving them of their special economic privileges (still enjoyed by Alava and Navarra).

Although the Civil War ended officially in April 1939, insurgent pressures did not. Thus, on March 2, 1943, the earlier proclamations concerning armed opposition to the Franco regime were codified, and made a part of Spain's peacetime judicial system. This was followed four years later by the Decree-Law for Repression of Banditry and Terrorism, the so-called "law against the *maquis.*" These two decrees, plus the Code of Military Justice, promulgated in July 1945, constituted, until 1960, the Spanish government's legal approach to problems of insurgency.

The upsurge in violence and political disorder, most apparent in the Basque country in the late 1950s and early 1960s, made it clear to Madrid that new measures would have to be taken to meet this challenge. The result was the Decree-Law on Military Rebellion, Banditry and Terrorism, issued on September 21, 1960. This decree covered the following offenses:

"Crimes of military rebellion": the dissemination of false or tendentious information in order to cause disturbances in public order, international conflicts, or a decline in the prestige of the State, its institutions, the government, the army, or the authorities;

the joining, conspiring or taking part in meetings, conferences, or demonstrations, intended to accomplish any of the above goals;

strikes, sabotage, or any analogous act which has a political objective, or which causes serious disturbance of public order.

"Terrorism": attacks against public security, terrorizing the inhabitants of a particular location, revenge or reprisals of a political or social character, or disturbing tranquility, order, or public services; causing explosions, fires, sinking of naval vessels, derailment of trains, interruption of communications, landslides, floods, or the employment of any other means or artefacts that can cause great damage;

the deposit of arms and munitions, the possession of explosive apparatuses or substances, flammable items, or other lethal devices; the manufacture, transport, or supply of any such items; the mere placing of any such substances or artefacts (even if they fail to explode or otherwise malfunction).

"Armed attack and kidnapping": armed robbery, with or

without any intention to employ the weapons to threaten or to harm the victims;

the assault of any industrial or commercial establishment, or any person charged with the custody or transportation of any valuable items, or the holding captive of any such person;

kidnapping.

"Banditry": living in, or otherwise forming, groups of armed persons whose intent is to engage in banditry or social subversion;

any act of assistance given to such groups, even though such assistance may not in itself constitute complicity with the act;

any act designed to take advantage of the fear or the disorder caused by any of the above proscribed acts, by threatening harm, or by exacting retribution in the form of money, jewels, or any other kind of goods, or by compelling any person to engage in any activity or to desist from any activity.

The penalties called for in the Decree-Law of 1960 were severe. The death penalty was required for any of the punishable offenses if the act resulted in the death of any person, whether or not that person was the intended victim of the act. If the death penalty was required by the law, no extenuating circumstances were allowed to intrude into the court's assessment of punishment. Life imprisonment was required for armed attack, kidnapping or terrorism. Lesser jail sentences were envisioned for certain crimes under the categories of military rebellion and banditry.

The most significant feature of the 1960 Decree-Law was its assigning of jurisdiction over the punishable offenses. Persons accused of having violated the law were to be judged not by a civilian court but a military tribunal. In a subsequent modifying decree of December 2, 1963, this provision of the 1960 Decree-Law was suspended, and the punishable offenses were transferred to a new set of courts, called Tribunals of Public Order. While this measure was hailed as a liberalizing step, in fact the change was made because the military courts found themselves unable to keep up with the case load caused by the law. However, with the upsurge of violence after 1967, the Spanish government decided to reinstate the original provisions of the 1960 law. The offenses of banditry, military rebellion, and terrorism were returned by the Decree-Law of August 18, 1968, to the jurisdiction of military courts, where they remained until the entire law was revoked following Franco's death.

Placing the trials for terrorism and related offenses in a military context altered substantially the protection of the human and civil rights of the accused. The defense of the accused was hampered significantly by the military surroundings. Trials were customarily carried out in secret, with the press and family denied access to the courtroom. Until 1963, the defense attorneys had to be active-duty military officers, but that provision was not reinstated in the 1968 decree. Even so, defense lawyers were often given only a brief time to prepare the defense of their clients. Appeals were processed literally in a matter of hours. Defense attorneys were not allowed to cross examine adverse witnesses, or to question the validity of evidence presented by the state. Accused persons were frequently brought into court in handcuffs or chains, and the courtroom was under heavy armed guard. Members of the military court were frequently armed during the process of the trial. Testimony of the accused was restricted entirely to matters directly related to the crimes alleged. No evidence was permitted to be introduced concerning the use of torture or coercion in the extraction of the confessions. No extenuating circumstances could be adduced to explain the behavior of the accused. On the other hand, the trial attorney representing the state was given a free hand to develop evidence to attain conviction of the accused. Finally, there could never be any appeal as to the jurisdiction of the military tribunal. In cases where there was dispute over whether or not the military court had jurisdiction, the military panel itself was the final arbiter of its own jurisdiction, and there was no higher court to which this question could be carried.

Spain was divided into military regions, and the boundaries of these regions were used to determine the jurisdiction of the courts martial. The four Basque provinces were located in the Sixth Military Region, of which the headquarters was the city of Burgos. Thus, all of the alleged violations of the laws on terrorism were tried in the Burgos court. An example of the case load and sentence record is provided by this sample of cases, drawn at random by Salaberri, from the period June-October 1969:

June 11, 1969: five Basque priests sentenced to jail terms of ten to twelve years apiece for writing rebellious letters to the Spanish Minister of Justice, the United Nations, and the bishop of the diocese.

July 15, 1969: Basque male sentenced to seven years in prison for making speeches of a clearly subversive and Marxist character.

July 16, 1969: Basque male sentenced to four years in prison for making mimeograph copies of ETA propaganda and distributing same.

July 16, 1969: Basque male sentenced to two years in prison for distributing ETA propaganda.

July 15, 1969: Basque male sentenced to five years in prison for attending illegal meetings and distributing ETA propaganda.

August 6, 1969: two Basque priests and two other Basques sentenced to prison terms ranging from four to ten years for reproducing and distributing separatist propaganda.

August 20, 1969: Basque priest sentenced to eight years in prison for distributing 200 sheets of separatist propaganda.

August 20-21, 1969: four Basque males sentenced to prison terms ranging from six to 16 years, for participating in illegal study groups and distribution of illegal propaganda.

October 20-21, 1969: four Basque priests and three other Basque males sentenced to prison terms ranging from four to ten years for aiding the escape from prison of ETA member Miguel Echeverria Iztueta.

October 27, 1969: one Basque sentenced to death and two others sentenced to 25 years in prison for placing a bomb in a shop in a small town in Guipúzcoa. The device exploded, but no one was injured, and the only damage was some broken glass.

The most famous trial held in Burgos, however, was that of the fifteen men and women accused of aiding or participating in the killing of a police commissioner named Meliton Manzanas.[24] Manzanas was returning to his home in the town of Irún, in the province of Guipúzcoa, at about 3:15 in the afternoon of August 2, 1968, when he was shot several times at close range by a single assailant. The attack took place as Manzanas was about to enter the front door of his apartment. His wife, who was opening the door to greet him, and his daughter, who was inside the apartment, were the only two witnesses. Apparently, at least one other person saw the murderer flee the scene of the crime, but a heavy rain prevented him from making a positive identification.

There seemed little doubt that ETA was involved in the killing. Manzanas had acquired a reputation as a sadistic and brutal police official who delighted in torturing Basque nationalists. He had been marked for assassination for some time, but it was not until ETA had its first casualty, in June 1968, that the struggle between ETA and the police spiraled upward in open bloodshed.

Following the assassination of Manzanas, Madrid declared a state of exception in the Basque provinces, and began to round up suspects for questioning. In the course of these arrests, and several that followed indirectly from the state of exception, 16 members of ETA were eventually charged with the crime. The chain of events began with the arrest of Gregorio Lopez Irasuegui and his wife, Arantxa Arruti, on the streets of Pamplona, November 7, 1968. Lacking evidence, the police released Lopez Irasuegui, but kept his wife in jail. After being subjected to considerable torture, his wife suffered a miscarriage. Eventually, she was absolved of all guilt in connection with the Manzanas killing.

Meanwhile, however, Lopez Irasuegui made plans to enter the prison in Pamplona and free his wife. His attempt was carried out on January 5, 1969, in the company of Francisco Javier Izco de la Iglesia. The attempt failed, and both men were captured. The weapon carried by Izco, a 7.65 mm Czech machine-pistol, was confiscated, and subjected to ballistics tests, which showed that it was the weapon used to kill Manzanas. Izco was immediately charged with murder.

Others on the accused list were captured during the ensuing

year. José María Dorronsoro was caught in the town of Mondragón, December 11, 1968. Xabier Larena was captured in Eibar on March 6, 1969. Jokin Gorostidi and his wife, Iciar Aizpurua, were captured in the home of her parents in Deva, March 8, 1969. Jose Antonio Carrera was arrested on March 15, 1969. Victor Arana, Mario Onaindia and Jesús Abrisqueta, were all captured in one of ETA's "safe houses" in Bilbao on April 9, 1969. One of the priests in the group, Jon Echave, was caught along with three other members, Eduardo Uriarte, Jone Dorronsoro, and Enrique Guesalaga, at a camp grounds in Santander, April 11, 1969. The final arrest was that of the second priest, Julen Kalzada, on June 4, 1969, as he participated in a fast in the offices of the bishop of Bilbao.

In all, five of the ETA members arrested in connection with the Manzanas killing were wounded during their arrest, and nearly every one of them claimed that he had been tortured during the first days of his imprisonment, either to make him sign a confession, or simply to intimidate him. Each of the accused repudiated his confession when he had the opportunity to do so in open court.

The summary court martial of the "Burgos 16" featured many of the characteristics of military trials of political prisoners that I have already mentioned. Access of the defense attorneys to their clients was sharply restricted. Cross examination of adverse witnesses was not permitted. The accused were not allowed to testify regarding the brutal methods that were used to extract their confessions. While the prosecution was allowed to introduce general information about ETA, and its revolutionary intent, to brand the defendants as terrorists, the accused were not permitted to introduce testimony about extenuating circumstances that might soften the weight of the court's verdict. The trial was conducted in a military setting, with the court room ringed by armed troops and the members of the tribunal appearing armed most of the time. At first, it was the court's intention to hold the trial in secret, a decision based, they said, on the 1953 Concordat with the Vatican which assures priests of secret trials when accused of civil crimes. Some observers went so far as to charge that the two priests — Echave and Kalzada — were arrested in the Manzanas group in order to justify the invocation of this rule. As it turned out, the Vatican waived its right to this kind of protection. Madrid vacillated on the issue and finally decided to permit the trial to be conducted in open session. Nevertheless, access of family and press representatives to the courtroom was curtailed. At least one foreign press representative, Gisele Halimi of France, was expelled from Spain because of adverse treatment of the trial in the French press.

The defense of Javier Izco de la Iglesia became the focal point of the trial. We can do no more here than highlight the major issues brought to the surface by the defense by Izco's lawyer, Sr. Echebarrieta. One major flaw in the state's case lay in the ballistics evidence. The bullets taken from Manzanas' body had disappeared shortly after the killing, and had never been delivered to the proper authorities for safekeeping. They were not seen again until after Izco had been captured in the attempt to free Arantxa Arruti and had had his machine pistol confiscated in the arrest. It was after this time that the bullets that had allegedly been removed from Manzanas were compared with those from Izco's pistol and found to match exactly. Even if the weapon had been the one used to kill Manzanas, Izco's mere possession of it four months later could not constitute circumstantial evidence, since one of Izco's jobs in ETA was smuggling weapons into Spain from France, and he could have acquired the pistol in any one of a number of ways without being aware of its history. Indeed, as Echebarrieta explained, Izco had access to a large number of similar weapons, and common sense would have made him dispose of the pistol in question if he had been aware that it was the Manzanas murder weapon.

The testimony of the witnesses was another weak point in the prosecution's case. Although given several opportunities to do so, Manzanas' widow and daughter never did officially point out Izco as the assailant. His photograph was not among those identified as being most like the killer during the first identification session. Later, when Izco was already under arrest, the two witnesses identified him as he sat between two uniformed policemen; but the women later failed to sign the official statement identifying Izco. Although this point was brought up during the trial, Manzanas' widow was not brought to the trial to be cross examined about her reluctance to identify Izco. Indeed, the description she had given of the assailant at the time of the killing described someone quite different from Izco in height, age, skin color, length of hair, and so forth. Thus, it is unlikely that she could have legitimately pointed out Izco as the author of the crime, even after all the prodding by the police. The victim's daughter told police that she was unable to see the assassin's face because she was in an inner room at the time of the killing. Nevertheless, her identification of Izco was accepted as valid by the court.

In sum, it appears that the Burgos court regarded the 16 accused ETA members not as the true authors of the crime, but rather as the symbols of revolutionary Basque separatism. Each of the 16 admitted in open court that he was a member of ETA, and most of them admitted being revolutionary socialists as well. None of them admitted having anything to do with the Manzanas killing, however; and the confessions that had been given under torture were repudiated by the accused. Nevertheless, their convictions were almost a foregone conclusion.

The trial lasted one week, from December 3 to December 9, 1970. Although a verdict was expected shortly after the testimony and arguments were completed, the Burgos trial quickly became one of the hottest political issues in Spain. General Franco was being subjected to very strong pressures on all sides to adopt a particular stance either for or against the "Burgos 16." On the side of a hard line were arrayed the leaders of the armed forces, who wanted the trial to be a sharp rebuff to separatist sentiments not only in the Basque country but elsewhere in Spain. In addition, the hard liners wanted to use the trial as a weapon against the more moderate Opus Dei faction within the government. If the Opus Dei approach were allowed to persist, they argued, Spain could expect more such upheavals as the Manzanas killing, and more ETA violence. Thus, Franco was being pushed from the Spanish right to crush the ETA threat by means of a harsh verdict in Burgos.

The "Burgos 16" were not without their defenders.

Thousands of Basque workers went out on strike repeatedly during the period of the trial. Street demonstrations in the Basque country resulted in bloody confrontations between the police and the demonstrators. In other Western European countries, mobs attacked Spanish embassies and called upon their own governments to cut off relations with Madrid. A number of European governments recalled their ambassadors for consultations, although the United States held to its position that the issue was a domestic question for Spaniards to resolve without foreign intervention.

The matter of the trial was complicated greatly by the kidnapping on December 2 of the Honorary West German Consul in San Sebastián, Eugen Biehl, by an ETA group.[25] An ETA communique asserted that Biehl would be released in exchange for more lenient treatment of the Burgos prisoners. On December 22, after the trial was completed, but before the announcement of the court's verdicts, Basque representatives issued a statement claiming that Spanish government officials had been in contact with them to secure Biehl's release. The official Spanish government news agency would only confirm that meetings had taken place between ETA members and "parties interested in securing the release of Biehl." The Basques claimed that a three-step arrangement was worked out: Biehl would be released, the court would then announce its verdicts and sentences, and any death sentences would subsequently be commuted by Franco. Thus, Spain would be spared the appearance of having given in to terrorist demands.

The exact details of the agreement have never been published. However, on Christmas Eve, Biehl was released unharmed. On December 28, the court met to hand down its verdicts and sentences. All of the accused except Arruti were found guilty. The sentences were as follows:

José Mari Dorronsoro: death
Gregorio Lopez Irasuegui: 30 years
Francisco Javier Izco: two death sentences, plus 27 years
Xavier Larena: death, plus 30 years
Jokin Gorostidi: two death sentences, plus 30 years
Iciar Aizpurua: 15 years
José Antonio Carrera: 12 years

Victor Arana: 60 years
Mario Onaindia: death, plus 51 years
Jesús Abrisqueta: 62 years
Jon Echave: 50 years
Eduardo Uriarte: two death sentences, plus 30 years
Jone Dorronsoro: 50 years
Enrique Guesalaga: 50 years
Julen Kalzada: 12 years

On December 30, General Franco commuted all of the death sentences to 30 years in prison. The details of the Biehl agreement had been fulfilled. Franco had been able to satisfy his hard line critics, while at the same time offering a slight sign of generosity during Spain's holiday season.

If Madrid thought that Burgos would mark the end of ETA they erred. Only three years after Burgos, an ETA commando unit carried out the assassination of Premier Carrero Blanco, and Spain was plunged once again into an endless round of violence and counter-violence that would not end even after Franco's death. Seven years after Burgos, the convicted members of the "Burgos 16" would be back on the streets, either in their homeland or in exile in Europe. If there was a key to the problem of violence in the Basque country, it was not to be found in the state of exception, police brutality, or military justice.

Chapter Eight

THE ECONOMICS OF BASQUE-SPANISH RELATIONS

In an earlier part of this book, I argued the point that during the 1930s, Basque nationalism was caught between the two extremes of Spanish politics: an anti-Catholic left that wanted to deny autonomy to the Basque region because of the Basques' close ties to the Church; and an intransigent right that feared the growing power of the labor movement in Bilbao and San Sebastián. Prior to 1936, the Basque region was the victim of the inability of the rest of Spain to work out some sort of solution to its festering class struggle.

Since World War II, or more precisely since the early 1950s, Basque-Spanish relations have turned on a second set of economic considerations. The relatively higher level of industrial development of the Basque region has meant that Basque industry, especially the Basque working class, has played a crucial role in Spanish economic modernization. It is not unusual for the social and economic systems of less-developed countries to be sharply divided between the wealthy few and the poorer masses. What makes the Spanish case so challenging is the degree to which economic, geographic, social, linguistic and ethnic fault lines coincide and reinforce one another. If one draws an imaginary line from Oviedo through Madrid to Valencia, he has done more than separate wealthy Spain from poor Spain. He has also divided progressive Spain from traditional Spain, bourgeois Spain from gentry Spain, industrial Spain from agricultural Spain, and (of greatest significance for our story) ethnic Spain from ethnic groups that have little identification with the Spanish nation.[1] The struggle for Basque autonomy has sharpened all of these conflicts, and given them special intensity. The Basque-Spanish conflict has its roots in ancient history. But the struggle owes its special passion to the peculiar social and economic forces of the past three decades.

Economic Modernization and the Franco Coalition

In 1939, at the close of the Civil War, General Franco faced three serious economic problems. Two of these were immediate threats to the stability of his regime: the enormous devastation wrought by the war, and the growing clouds of a general war in Europe that would menace but not directly involve Spain. The third economic problem was one of much longer standing that would require, accordingly, much more time to eradicate. Put very simply, the Spain of the 1940s was still a poor country.

A few numerical indicators from this period show the dimensions of Spain's economic backwardness. In 1942, for example, the nation's per capita Gross National Product had reached only about $340 (in 1969 pesetas, converted at the rate of 60 pesetas to $1).[2] A slow rate of economic growth meant that a per capita GNP of $500 could not be reached until 1955. The structure of Spain's economically active population also revealed its heavy reliance on agriculture and the relatively low level of industrialization, except for Madrid, Barcelona and the Basque country. Table 7 shows the relative percentages of the working population in each of the three principal sectors of the economy in 1940 and 1950.

Table 7.
Structure of Spain's Economically Active Population, 1940 and 1950 (percent of total dedicated to each sector).

Sector	Madrid, Barcelona, and Basque Country		Rest of Spain		Total of all Spain	
	1940	1950	1940	1950	1940	1950
Agriculture	16	12	61	59	52	50
Industry	43	46	19	19	24	25
Services	41	41	20	21	24	25

Source: Amando de Miguel, *Manual de Estructura Social de España* (Madrid: Editorial Tecnos, 1974), p. 398, Table 30.

The traditional, anti-modern structure of the country's agrarian sector was an additional burden for Spain after the Civil War. The failure of political reform and the slowness of economic change prior to 1960 caused the rural structures of the post-War period to resemble closely those of the Second Republic. In general terms, in Spain in the 1950s, half of the farm land was concentrated in one percent of the holdings, the average size of which was about 50 hectares, while the other half was held in 99 percent of the holdings, the average size of which was less than half a hectare, or one percent of the size of the larger holdings.[3] Although the larger landed estates were farmed, they were exploited very inefficiently with an owner class that was absent from its property more often than not, and a peasant work force that was still only slightly removed from the living conditions of serfdom.

The peculiar approach of General Franco to the challenging tasks of economic modernization was much influenced by the nature of the governing coalition he headed. If the old adage about politics making strange bedfellows is true, it has no clearer application than in the Spain of the 1950s and 1960s. Francisco Franco governed Spain through a coalition of interests, institutions, and individuals that agreed on little save their common fear of what Spain would be like if Franco were removed from power.[4] By astutely playing upon that fear and by balancing one group or interest against another, Franco was able for nearly forty years to perpetuate his personal rule and to restrict the play of politics to an arena where he alone set the boundaries of the acceptable.

Franco's major coalition partners can be divided into at least three categories, according to the degree to which they advocated or opposed modernization of the country's political, economic, and social structures. Radical modernizers favored revolutionary changes in Spanish social and economic structure; moderate modernizers favored industrial development within the framework of a basically liberal, capitalist political and economic order; and the opponents of modernization argued against making such changes, no matter what kind of environment they would be made in. (The members of

Franco's governing coalition are grouped in Table 8 according to how they stood on this issue.)

While they were careful to disguise their policy proposals with labels that avoided Marxist cliches or rhetoric, the *falangistas* were a source of truly radical ideas, especially during the first two decades of Franco's regime.[5] They argued for the commitment of the entire state apparatus to mobilize the nation's resources for economic and social modernization. Spanish society, and especially its productive sectors, should be organized into gigantic, state-run syndicates that would include both workers and managers in each industry. State direction would insure that all sectors would be managed in the interests of the corporate entity, and class struggle and conflict would be avoided. The big structures of capitalism — industrial combines and banks — would be nationalized. The huge landed estates would be broken up and their lands given to the peasants who work on them. The state would endeavor to regulate or actually control every significant center of economic decision-making, especially those affecting prices, wages, and the interconnections between the national and the international economies (exchange rates, foreign investment, etc.), in order to harmonize diverse interests without conflict. Perhaps most significantly, the Falange advocated a vigorous program of heavy industrialization, stimulated by state investment if needed, in order to insulate Spain from the pernicious effects of an international economy dominated by the industrial giants of Western Europe and North America.

In the opinion of many influential Spaniards, including General Franco, though the *falangistas'* policy proposals tended to sweep people up in heady enthusiasm, they failed when exposed to the cold dawn of reality to meet the day-to-day needs of Spanish life. Yet few could deny Spain's need to change some of its ways in order to fit into the emerging Western European order. For those who wished to modernize Spain but also wanted to avoid the apparent excesses of the Falange, a more moderate kind of development recommended itself.

Moderate modernization received the support of those forces in Spanish politics and economics that wanted to

Table 8.
Franco's Coalition and Supporting Groups and Institutions.

Radical Modernizers	Moderate Modernizers	Traditionalists	Other*
Falange	Opus Dei	Carlists	Armed Forces
	Bourgeois middle class (Madrid only)	Rural oligarchy	Monarchists
	Industrialists, Bankers	Traditional middle class	Church hierarchy
		Landed gentry	

*Groups in this category either were of various opinions regarding the desirability of modernization, or did not consider *economic* modernization to be a central issue for them.

"liberalize" the nation's resources by subjecting the country to the discipline of a market economy. In other words, they advocated the introduction of a typical twentieth century industrial state on the basis of a modified *laissez-faire* system, in which the private sector would bear the burden of developing the country, while the state would restrict itself to providing the correct set of incentives to further this process: establishing a rational, predictable, and stable environment within which private business could operate, and (not insignificantly) restraining the country's increasingly restive labor movement.

The advocates of modernization with moderation emerged during the 1950s from Spain's new generation of economists, business leaders and bankers. They came from varying walks of life and from different ranges of ideological persuasion, but they had in common one important characteristic: they were closely connected both personally and professionally with key business, intellectual, and financial circles in North America and Western Europe. They had had important educational and professional experiences in Geneva, London, Paris, and New York; and they were convinced of the power of the capitalist model to speed the pace of Spanish industrialization. While they were definitely of the entrepreneurial class, they were modern capitalists in that they believed in the imperatives of Keynesian economics, the role of the state in regulating the private sector, and the need for public policies that would redistribute income slightly and gradually and would soften the ill effects of "robber baron" capitalism.

The most significant group to support moderate modernization was a cluster of economists and technocrats who had been recruited from a Catholic lay organization called the Priestly Society of the Holy Cross and God's Work, but better known by its brief name, Opus Dei. Opus Dei was founded in 1928 by an Aragonese priest named Josemaría Escrivá de Balaguer y Albas, and rose during the 1940s and 1950s to become one of the most potent political forces in post-Civil War Spain. While the society has only about 25,000 full members plus perhaps another 100,000 associate members or sympathizers (the exact membership figures are kept secret and Opus members are usually reluctant to admit their affiliation), it includes not only many key individuals in the Franco regime but also a solid cadre of well trained and ambitious intellectuals and technocrats, men whose skills will be needed in a modern, industrialized Spain. The organization exists to encourage Catholic laymen to work for their personal sanctification by excelling in their chosen secular professions. The society's members are taught to seek the highest posts in their particular areas in fulfillment of their Catholic duty to their social community. Perhaps because of the society's secretiveness, or perhaps because of the ambition and personal advancement of its members, Opus Dei became the focal point of much antagonism and even hatred among the Franco coalition. Spokesmen for Opus contend that the organization has no political perspectives on any issue and does not impose any kind of ideological uniformity on its members. Nevertheless, many groups in Spanish politics opposed the growing role of Opus Dei in Franco's ruling elite. More traditional Catholics, such as the Christian Democrats, felt that Opus Dei was using its religious affiliation for the personal advancement of its members. The Falange opposed Opus, for they saw it as a means for businessmen and industrialists to gain the liberalization of the economic system, a move which would thwart their plans for the radical remaking of Spain. Monarchists simply regarded Opus as a major rival.[6]

Despite the growing opposition, Opus Dei prospered, and during the 1950s experienced a meteoric rise to power. By 1957, Opus members had been appointed to key posts in the Franco administration: the Ministries of Industry, Agriculture, Public Works, and Finance, as well as in the technical secretariat of the Ministry of the Presidency, headed by Admiral Carrero Blanco, long-time supporter and (some said) *éminence gris* of Franco, and a strong friend of Opus Dei (although not a full member). In the economic changes that took place from 1959 through the early 1960s, Opus Dei members led the way in both the liberalization measures and the drafting of Spain's first development plan. Throughout the decade of the 1960s, Opus Dei ministers and technocrats enjoyed wide ranging power to restructure Spain's economic system and to impose on the country their ideas of moderate modernization. No group has dominated Spanish politics for long, however, and even Opus Dei's star began to decline by the late 1960s. The Matesa scandal, which involved the granting of export credits to a Catalan textile firm which falsified the export records, was laid at the door step of the Opus Dei technocrats, apparently because the company's president had been close to Opus members prior to the deal. In 1973, the number of Opus members in the Cabinet was reduced; and after the assassination of Carrero Blanco, in December 1973, the group was driven entirely from power. Nonetheless, they had left their distinctive mark on Spanish politics and economics for nearly two decades. When Opus Dei began its move to gain power, Spain was dominated by the advocates of radical change, state-run capitalism, and autarky. When they left power in 1974, Spain was a classic case of modern liberal capitalism, modernizing, but at a moderate pace and with many traditional structures left intact and undisturbed.

The representatives of these traditional structures and institutions constituted the third pillar upon which Franco rested his regime. Their defense of the privilege and position of traditional Spain no doubt helped Franco to the realization that radical change would be too unsettling to his country and to his regime. Thus the moderate pace of change proposed by Opus Dei satisfied his need for a suitable compromise between the traditionalists and the Falange.

Two of the most important opponents of modernization that participated in the Franco coalition were the Carlists and the rural oligarchy.

The Carlists, from their base of support in Navarra province, had been among the first to announce their support for the rebellion of 1936. The red-bereted *requetés,* or Carlist militia, had formed one of the key elements in the military operations on the northern front until the fall of Bilbao in 1937. For Franco, however, perhaps their greatest contribution came after 1937, when he was able to use them as a counterweight to the more radical and aggressive Falange.[7] In 1937, the Falange and the Carlists had been forcibly united by Franco into an organization called the *Falange Española Tradicionalista y de las Juntas de Ofensivas Nacional-Sindicalistas,* a name whose awkwardness reflected Franco's attempt to bring under one roof two diametrically opposed political forces. Thereafter, the Carlists (who were also known as the Traditionalists) were only lukewarm in their support of Franco; and, toward the end of his regime, even this mild degree of support eroded and became open hostility (but never to the point of advocating a revolutionary change).

The conflict between Franco and the Carlists involved two separate issues. The first was primarily symbolic, having to do principally with the restoration of the monarchy and the identity of the person who should occupy the throne after Franco's death. The second issue was more substantial, and involved the opposition of the Carlists to modernization of Spain's economy and social structure.

To characterize the ideological positions of the Carlist movement has always been rather challenging, since they are derived from philosophical assumptions that reject the role of the modern nation-state. Perhaps the phrase "medieval socialism" comes closest to describing the Traditionalist perspective. In their scheme of things, Spain would be carved up again into sovereign (or nearly sovereign) regions, each of which would be in some vague way linked to Madrid and to the ruling Carlist monarch, but which would also be free to develop their own economic programs as they saw fit. To this point, there appears to be a superficial similarity between Carlism and Basque nationalism. Carlism, however, refutes such institutions as nation-states and the governments that rule them. Society in the Carlist view is best organized when it is structured hierarchically and organically, with religious and monarchical institutions responsible for the welfare of the unorganized and quiescent masses of peasants (there would be little industrial proletariat, since industrialization would not be supported or, indeed, necessary). National governments only confuse and bewilder the citizens by subjecting them to a barrage of propaganda, and demands that they vote on matters they cannot understand. The traditionalist view avoided all that by limiting sharply what the national government can do, and in fact what is done in general by society. Clearly, Franco could not accept this point of view since to do so would have meant turning his back on modernization, industrialization, and the attendant requirements for political and social change.

From the south of Spain, however, came a force opposed to modernization that Franco had to respect: the rural oligarchy that had dominated the land and the politics of conservative Spain for at least two centuries. This was the second major anti-modern element in the Franco coalition.

The problem of the under-utilization of Spain's scarce arable land has been a chronic one for the country for the past several hundred years. The concentration of land in the hands of a small number of aristocrats who felt little incentive to turn their property into active farm land, combined with the plight of great masses of landless (or nearly landless) peasants, had deprived Spain of that crucial link in economic development and modernization, the rise of rural capitalism.

At the end of the eighteenth century, the landed nobility may have numbered as many as 400,000 out of a population of about ten million. These aristocrats enjoyed near-feudal rights over enormous stretches of land which belonged to them through the ownership device called entail. The practice of entailing large landed estates began with the decline of feudalism and was intended to protect the property of a noble family from being wasted away by careless heirs. Because the practice of entail encouraged the conservative management of the large estates, the ultimate effect was to perpetuate the uneconomic holding of land out of production, contributing thereby not only to the maintenance of a large idle class but to low agricultural production as well.[8]

There were other groups that favored conservative practices like holding land in entail. Quasi-commercial societies, like the Mesta, were made up of the owners of herds of migrant sheep which were pastured across the open lands of central Spain with little regard for property boundaries. These groups were protected by royal decree, and their right to use the land thus was guaranteed in perpetuity, despite the introduction of new and competitive means of employing the country's agricultural resources. Communities and small villages held the land surrounding them in commune, and private farmers were prevented from gaining access to them to fence them off (what in England was called the enclosure movement) and turn them to their personal profit. Countless thousands of small privately owned plots were too tiny to permit the application of modern farming techniques; but the owners, who lived perpetually on the edge of economic disaster, opposed any attempts to alter their misfortune. Last, but certainly not least, the Church was one of the biggest holders of entailed land. According to the farm census of 1797, the Church exercised jurisdiction over one-twelfth of Spain's total land area.[9]

During the nineteenth century, certainly one of the most turbulent in Spanish history, the issue of disentailment of entailed lands lay at the heart of much political and economic controversy. While noted economists had pointed as early as 1800 to the need to eliminate entail and to bring these unproductive lands into production, the process of disentailment did not begin in earnest until the period of the First Carlist War. In July 1837, the government, in an effort to draw a clear line between the traditional views of the Carlists and their own modernizing views, decreed the disentailment and sale of the feudal estates, the communal lands, and the Church's huge acreage. Such a revolutionary step did not come easily or quickly. Until the end of the Second Carlist War, the traditionalists managed to stave off disentailment completely. By about 1876, however, the process was essentially terminated.

To the surprise of economists and government officials, the breaking of entail did not produce any major change in the agrarian structures of the Spanish countryside. As the Church, the feudal estates, and the communities began to sell their lands, they were purchased not by modernizing, commerce-oriented capitalistic farm businesses but by a new oligarchy that sought property not for production and enterprise, but for prestige and symbolic status. The landless peasants continued as before, ground down by their inability to produce enough for a small margin of surplus for reinvestment and advancement. As Tamames put it, "Disentailment did nothing more than make our countryside pass from a feudal structure to a capitalist structure with important feudal vestiges."[10]

The upshot of this was that upon the creation of the Second Republic in 1931, Spanish farm land was as unequally distributed and as poorly utilized as it had been prior to disentailment. The intervening governments, whether monarchical or liberal or military dictatorships, had chosen to attack the problem of agarian underproduction through massive irrigation projects or through the resettlement of peasants on unowned (and, thus, undesirable) land with only slight technical assistance. The fundamental issue — one of land ownership and utilization — lay unresolved, primarily because of the enormous power of the landed gentry. Even during the radical years of the Second Republic, aggressive agarian reform measures failed to accomplish much in the way of redistribution of land to the landless peasant. Part of the reason for failure lay in the intransigence and ideological myopia of the radical left; part lay in technical flaws, either in surveying or in production or in crop storage, or in any one of a dozen areas where farm output depends greatly on technology. But agrarian reform was blocked during the Second Republic at least partly by an obstacle that existed before and after the experiment: the power of the landed gentry.[11] After more than one hundred and thirty years of disentailment, agrarian reform, irrigation projects, colonization of distant lands, technical assistance, improved roads, land expropriation, and other policies designed to alter Spain's rural structure, the land was still distributed in a grossly unequal manner: 3.5 percent of the owners possessed nearly 61 percent of the arable land; 96.5 percent of the owners possessed the remainder. And further, in the latter part of the 1960s, Spain, which should be largely self-sufficient in food staples, imported more than half a billion dollars in agricultural products each year.[12]

These observations bring us to the perspective of the Caudillo on economic issues. According to most observers, Franco, in addition to being a crafty and pragmatic leader, was also relatively uninterested in most economic and development-related matters. Gunther tells us, for instance, that Franco's main interests were four: church-state relations, military affairs, problems of public order, and the basic character of the regime's institutions.[13] As far as most economic questions were concerned, he was inclined to let his Cabinet ministers make most important decisions, and he rarely intervened even to set priorities or to make resource-allocation decisions. It may be that Franco was, as Vincente Pilapil says, a man who "lacked strong ideological convictions," who "despised politics and politicians," and who wanted mainly to preserve the unity and the order of Spain, its Church, and its armed forces.[14] It may also be accurate to argue, following Charles Anderson, that Franco was the ultimate political and economic pragmatist, who sought modernization for his country not because he was a modernizer himself but simply because he saw that option as the best one for achieving his other goals, primary of which was the preservation of a non-radicalized Spain in the wake of a disastrous Civil War.

Whatever the explanation, Franco seemed to weary easily of economic matters, and was inclined to let his ministers take the lead in fashioning national economic policy. Benjamin Welles relates the now well-known outburst of a tired and frustrated Franco in the midst of the stabilization-liberalization crisis of 1959; turning angrily to the waiting Opus Dei ministers, he cried, "Hagan lo que les da la gana!" ("Do what you want!")[15] At least in this area Franco was not the leader of the Spanish state, but merely provided the institutional matrix within which Opus Dei, the Falange, the industrialists and bankers, the military, the Carlists, and the landed gentry debated economic issues. If this portrayal is accurate, then the Spanish miracle of economic development during the 1960s was due first to the technocratic and political abilities of the Opus Dei liberals and their industrialist supporters on the one hand, and to the ideological vacuum that was Francisco Franco on the other. The interplay of the two produced a policy of moderate modernization, with profound effects for Spain and for the Basque provinces.

Spanish Industrial Development: Strategy and Achievements

The policies and practices of the Franco regime in the field of industrial development and economic modernization fall into three fairly clear periods. From 1939 to the late 1950s, the emphasis was on autarky, on rebuilding the war-ravaged nation, and on surviving in a world hostile to the aims of Francoism. From 1959 to 1963, the stress was on stabilization and liberalization, as well as on gradually linking Spain's economy with that of Western Europe. From 1963 to Franco's death, Spanish economic policy consisted of planned development and rapid industrialization, and took advantage of two key factors that had been largely unforeseen: the tourism boom, and the remission of foreign exchange from Spanish workers in other European countries.

Spanish industrial-development policy from the early 1960s onward was contained essentially in the first three Development Plans issued by the government's Planning Commission, which covered four-year periods (1964-1967, 1968-1971, 1972-1975). This policy consisted of four basic programs: incentives designed to stimulate the spread of industrial plants to depressed or backward areas of the country; joint action measures that involved public-private cooperation to revitalize and restructure individual industrial sectors; tariff and nontariff measures to protect national industry; and export-promotion programs.[16]

The program to encourage the spread of industry to Spain's depressed provinces consisted of a set of special benefits for manufacturing firms that located within specific geographic areas. Such incentives were designated in each of the first two Development Plans. These areas were called either industrial development poles (*polos de desarrollo*), if a manufacturing base already existed, or industrial promotion poles (*polos de promoción*) if there was little existing industry in the area. It was assumed that industrial development in the latter areas would require substantially greater effort and incentive than would the more highly industrialized development poles. Manufacturers who built their plants in one of the designated areas were eligible for benefits ranging from exemption from import duties and certain corporate taxes, to cash grants and five years' free depreciation on plant and equipment.

The First Development Plan also created a program of industrial incentives called *acción concertada,* or joint action. Through this program, government joined with the members of a particular sector to modernize production facilities, merge firms, provide for common services, create larger-scale production units, improve product quality, and raise working standards, including wages and professional training. Private firms that joined in the *acción concertada* received benefits that included special treatment on taxes, credit, and tariffs. In return, the private enterprises accepted contractual obligations to modernize their plants, merge with other firms in the same sector, and aim at production targets set by the Ministry of Industry. By 1972, some 200 firms had become associated with these programs, the most important of which included iron and steel production, shipbuilding, and coal mining.

Spain's import-protection and export-promotion efforts have been much more conventional than the programs aimed at dispersing the nation's industry and modernizing its outdated plants and equipment. The nominal protection afforded to Spanish industry by tariffs was in the range of about 30 percent during the 1960s, rather high for industrialized countries, but not so high when compared with developing countries in Latin America or Asia. (The nominal rate of protection is the percentage by which domestic prices exceed world prices as a result of protective measures.) The effective rate of protection (defined as the percentage by which domestic value added exceeds foreign value added as a consequence of tariffs and other devices) declined during the 1960s to about 50 percent lower than comparable developing countries such as Mexico, but still quite high compared with EEC countries. In addition, Spain imposed other kinds of protective instruments such as border taxes and preferential interest rates on domestic manufacturing for export, which made Spanish industry not only more competitive at home, but more aggressive in gaining sales abroad.

From the standpoint of social classes, Franco's industrialization policies were definitely regressive, favoring the banking and industrial elite at the expense of the country's industrial working class.

The industrialists were favored by a series of measures aimed at protecting them from competition, both foreign and domestic. High tariffs and other devices made Spanish industry the most protected in Europe. Special credits, tax advantages, and import privileges for industrial raw materials helped fuel the industrial boom. A highly regressive tax structure worked against the low-income, salaried employee or hourly wage earner. Spain's concentration on indirect taxes, and especially on the sales tax, bore heaviest on the poor and middle-income consumer, and least on those who earned their living from returns on investments or on real estate. Table 9 indicates the relative importance as revenue for the Spanish state of each source of income. Finally, the weak antimonopoly laws of the Franco regime were so filled with exemptions and special cases that they constituted no more than a "symbolic gesture toward the commitment to antimonopoly legislation," according to Charles Anderson.[17]

Table 9.
Structure of Tax System in Spain, 1970.

Category of Taxed Sources	Percent of Total Taxes Derived From Source
Direct Taxes	32.1
Property taxes	2.3
Personal income	9.7
Capital gains	3.4
Corporate licenses	3.8
Corporate income	9.1
Inheritance	1.5
Other	2.3
Indirect Taxes	68.0
Transfer of stock, property	9.0
Sales tax	30.1
Special taxes	8.6
Monopolies (tobacco, petroleum)	9.0
Customs duties	11.3

Source: Ramon Tamames, *Introducción a la Economía Española* (Madrid: Editorial Alianza, 1972), Table 14.2, p. 474.

The working classes, on the other hand, were being asked to bear most of the burden of Spain's industrialization effort. Free labor organizations were prohibited. All workers were represented by the state-run syndicates, which in theory were supposed to reflect the interests and attitudes of both the workers and the managers/owners in a conflict-free environment. The right to strike was strictly prohibited. It is true that in late 1965 a revision in the Penal Code distinguished between work stoppages for purely economic motives (higher wages), which were tolerated, and those that sought to disrupt public order, which were suppressed even more than before. In practice, however, that distinction proved difficult to make, and police broke up many strikes after that date despite the changes in the law. Not surprisingly, the workers went underground to form *Comisiones Obreras,* or Workers' Commissions. Caught between inflation and rising unemployment on the one hand, and a suppressive anti-labor regime and controlled wages on the other, Spain's working class endured a greater share of the disadvantages of Francoism than did any other social group, except the regional separatists.

The second prong of Franco's economic modernization strategy lay in his treatment of Spain's rural areas. Almost immediately after the Civil War began, in late August of 1936, the military-rebel government issued a decree suspending the land reform measures that had been legislated by the Second Republic. In addition, it was decreed that a study be made of the adverse effects of the land expropriation and redistribution program of the Republic, and steps were soon taken to return the large estates to their original owners. With the war over, Franco set into motion a much more conservative form of agrarian reform that emphasized colonization of unused lands, the concentration of small parcels into larger and more easily worked units, and irrigation and technical assistance to improve the productivity of Spain's agricultural resources.

The government's colonization program was contained in a series of decrees, the most important of which was that of April 1949. This law aimed at encouraging the colonization of lands that were located in an unirrigated zone but for which dams and reservoirs had already been constructed. For many years, going back to the early part of the twentieth century, the Spanish government had discovered that it was not sufficient for it to build water reservoirs if the land owners would not spend their money to build the canals or pipelines necessary to carry the water to the fields. The 1949 colonization law was intended to open up such lands to colonizers who would work the land under contract to the land reform agency called INC (National Institute of Colonization). The state in turn would pay for the irrigation of the specific fields. The land was expropriated from its original owners, but the state remained in possession of the property until the colonizers had paid for the land at its original market value, plus interest. The INC continued to exercise supervision over the use of the land even after that, and its subdivision and sale was prohibited. Since the original owners were compensated for their seized property in cash, and since the new owners had to pay for the land in full, it is obvious that this aspect of the land reform program was completely conservative in its social impact. There was no transfer of wealth, either in theory or in practice. In addition, there was little transfer of actual land, since the financial and administrative burdens of the program were more than the INC could bear. By 1962, when the program shifted its emphasis to irrigation and away from colonization, only about 45,000 families had been resettled on new lands, compared with the nearly two million farmers who worked plots of less than five hectares and who could have made good use of the newly irrigated land. Even for those who received land, their good fortune soon dimmed; they came under the influence of the large agribusinesses in cotton, rice, and sugar that were coming to dominate the colonized lands, and which were the real beneficiaries of the colonization policy.

The other half of Spain's land reform program was aimed not at the large estates at all, but at the incredibly small *minifundia* of the country's north and northwest regions. Since the latter part of the nineteenth century, Spanish economists and agricultural experts had realized that a major obstacle to utilizing the agrarian wealth of the country was the inefficiency caused by the fragmentation of parcels into sizes that were uneconomical. In some areas, the size of the average parcel was measured in meters instead of hectares; and a typical owner might have to walk considerable distances between his various plots of land to work them all in a single day. Machinery and irrigation were out of the question as long as the separated parcels remained so tiny and inefficient. The reaction of the Franco government was to enact a program called *concentración parcelaria* by a law of October 1952, subsequently expanded by a number of similar decrees. Through these laws, the National Service for Parcel Concentration and Rural Management (SNCPOR) initiated a series of incentives to encourage the owners of *minifundia* to merge their properties into larger and more efficient units. Such merged units received benefits in the form of credit, technical assistance, and machinery to aid in their exploitation of their new lands. By all indications the program of parcel concentration has been a success where it has been carried through to completion, as in some of the fragmented areas of Galicia. The rural campesino class has been reduced sharply in these areas, either through migration to the cities, or by absorption into a small but growing rural *petit bourgeoisie.* By 1971, more than three million hectares had been affected by the parcel concentration program, about one-half of the amount believed to be required. Nevertheless, since this policy operated on the farm units at the opposite end of the spectrum from the *latifundia,* and at the opposite end of the country as well, it had little impact on Spain's real agricultural problem, the under-utilization of its large estates.

Franco's approach to these large estates is best seen in the 1953 decree on the improvement of unused land found in the *latifundia.* The law provided for studies to determine where the large estates could be put to some productive use. If, after study, such a zone was discovered on a given estate, the owner was given a certain period of time in which to make improvements. If he refused to institute these measures, his land taxes automatically doubled. This law has remained almost as under-utilized as the land it promises to improve. By 1960, the studies it provides for covered only 216,000 hectares out of the 23,000,000 hectares contained within the large estates. The investments induced by this gentle prodding had reached 43,000,000 pesetas, or an average of about $3 per hectare. The law now seems to be regarded as a curiosity rather than a sharp tool to attack the problem of misuse of Spain's agrarian lands.

What have been the results of Spain's long struggle to industrialize? Without doubt the record of Spanish industrial growth since the early 1950s has been an impressive one. During the decade from 1951 to 1960, Spain's GNP grew from 722 billion pesetas (in 1969 terms) to 1,052 billion pesetas, while population increased only slightly, from 28 million to about 30.4 million. As a result, the per capita GNP of the country grew from 25,600 pesetas to 34,600, an increase of about 35 percent in ten years, or an average annual increase of 3.5 percent. At that rate, per capita GNP would double in about a generation, a not unimpressive performance. Nevertheless, the really salient growth rates were yet to come. Manufacturing industry grew during the decade of the 1960s at the rate of 10 percent annually. Industrial product increased from about 178 billion pesetas in 1960 to 461 billion pesetas in 1970, a rate that made Spain the fastest growing economy in Europe, and second only to Japan among the OECD countries. It is true that industrial growth tended to slow down during the last half of the decade to an annual rate of about 5.7 percent; but the astonishing increases of the 1960s (annual rates of over 11 percent) were sufficient to put the country's industrial sector solidly on the road to developed status. Primarily as a consequence of such industrial records, the overall economic growth of Spain was more than satisfactory. By 1975, per capita GNP had reached approximately 76,300 pesetas (in 1969 terms), or nearly $1,300. In the generation from 1950 to 1975, the average Spaniard saw his share of the national wealth rise from less than 23,000 pesetas to more than 76,000 pesetas, an increase of about 230 percent for the period, or about 10 percent per yer. Consumption levels of the urban industrial and middle classes grew accordingly, despite serious problems with inflation, and the government's regressive wage control policies. By the late 1960s, Spain produced about 400,000 cars a year, and one out of every twenty-five Spaniards owned an automobile. Fifty-three percent of Spanish families owned their own apartments, 39 percent had washing machines, and one-third had television sets in their homes. Little wonder that the new urban bourgeoisie in Madrid offered no threat to the Franco regime; they had too much at stake in their newly increased standard of living to rebel against the political system that had made it possible.[18]

Beneath the surface of Spain's industrial transformation a second set of radical changes was taking place. Spain's social structure, virtually unchanged in some areas since the eighteenth century, was experiencing wrenching dislocations that required that Spaniards learn new roles and new social and political attitudes. Industry was coming to be the foremost source of wealth in the country, and industrial workers the most important sector of the labor force. In 1950, the industrial sector accounted for about one-fourth of the total national work force; by 1970, the percentage had reached 27 percent; and by 1980, it was expected to increase to nearly one-half. The share of industry in the total wealth of the nation increased along roughly similar lines. In the historical industrial centers of Spain, Madrid, Barcelona, and the Basque Provinces, the increase was noticeable (from 46 percent in 1950 to 51 percent in 1970); but in the rest of Spain, where industry had more difficulty gaining a foothold, the increase was even more impressive (from 19 percent in 1950 to 31 percent in 1970).[19]

With the rise of the industrial worker class in Spain there came the inevitable changes in social structure, life style, and attitudes. The percentage of women employed grew to nearly one-fourth of the working population. The population density of the large Spanish cities rose sharply, creating new problems in housing, pollution, education, recreation, sanitation, and other aspects of urban congestion. Great waves of migrants poured out of the countryside toward the centers of economic attraction, principally the three major industrial areas of the north. Consumption rose, but so did social problems, such as delinquency, family disruption, and symptoms of social pathology such as suicide. In brief, Spain was leaving the ranks of the world's traditionally agrarian countries, and was entering the realm of industrial (and in some regions even post-industrial) society. Like every industrial society before them, Spaniards now found that they had more to consume but were uncertain about how to translate their newly found affluence into greater contentment or personal satisfaction.

While undeniably successful, the Franco strategy appears so manifestly unstable and so negatory of social justice that one wonders how he was able to achieve his goal of industrialization without more social upheaval than there was in Spain from 1950 to 1975. The answer lies, I think, beyond the quiescent attitude of the urban middle class, who supported Franco out of a desire to maintain their economic status quo and who were willing to look the other way on issues like freedom of the press, or denial of human rights. Rather, the key to Franco's economic success lay in two factors that were peculiar to Spain: an extraordinarily high receipt of foreign exchange that entered the country in response not to economic changes domestically but for reasons that were external to Spain; and the physical separation of Spain into two societies or communities, the rich and the poor, the progressive and the traditional, the North and the South.

I shall treat only in summary fashion the first of these two factors, the essentially unearned flow of foreign exchange, not because it was unimportant, for it was most significant for Spain's overall development, but because it has less meaning for my discussion of Basque-Spanish relations. In brief, what was involved were large foreign exchange earnings that, unrelated to any economic development in Spain, made possible substantial purchases abroad without requiring any major changes at home, other than rationalizing the exchange rate and liberalizing the peseta trading regulations. The unexpected windfall in foreign exchange came from the two sources already mentioned: tourism, and remittances from Spanish workers living in other Western European countries.

The combination of the Civil War and the devastation of World War II had just about destroyed Spain's tourist appeal, but the inherent attractiveness of the country for other Europeans was so great that it was not long before German, French, and British tourists began to find their way back to "sunny Spain." It was not until 1949 that the number of tourists reached the pre-Civil War level; by 1951, the figure was slightly more than one million. In the early and mid 1960s, however, the tourist flood began in earnest: ten million by 1964; more than twenty million by 1969; and in 1973 the number of tourists visiting Spain exceeded the population of the country itself (34 million). Tourists brought badly needed foreign exchange; more than one billion dollars annually between 1965 and 1970, more than two billion dollars annually thereafter. During the decade from 1961 to 1970, tourists brought into Spain more than $10 billion; and if one could overlook the usual complaints a country's natives have about rude and boisterous tourists, it was, as the saying had it, "an industry without smokestacks."

The second big source of foreign exchange came from the earnings of Spaniards working abroad, principally in Germany. The flow of Spanish workers abroad rose or fell according to the conditions of the Spanish economy and the availability of jobs. During the lean years of the early 1960s, when the stabilization plan made jobs scarce and prices high, more than 100,000 Spaniards left annually to work in the EEC countries and send their earnings home. As economic conditions grew better at home, they returned; and in one year, 1967, there was even a net influx of migrants to Spain. Yet as the economy turned downward again, in the late 1960s the flow reversed itself once again. In all, from 1960 to 1970, a cumulative total of over 600,000 Spaniards migrated to countries where economic conditions were better. During the same period, their remittances totaled more than $3.2 billion. In addition their emigration relieved a serious social problem at home, for without the safety valve of work in foreign countries, the unemployed workers would have been a major threat to Spain's precarious social order during the latter years of the Franco era.

We come, finally, to what is the central concern of Spanish industrial development and of Basque-Spanish relationships. I am referring to the gulf that separates Spain into two nations. "The Two Spains" is a concept one meets frequently in reading what Spaniards write about their own country; it is not an invention of this study or a contrivance used to explain the peculiar Basque role in Spanish modernization. To the south and west lies poor Spain, traditional, agricultural (but inefficiently so), struggling to catch up. In stark contrast are the three focal points of rich Spain, industrial, bourgeois, progressive. These three centers are (and have been historically) Madrid, Bilbao, and Barcelona. To modernize all of Spain, to draw poor Spain up to the level of the remainder, Franco called upon the financial, material, and human resources of the

Basques and the Catalans. The challenge raised by regional separatism in these two areas threatened not only Spanish unity, which was, after all, only a psychological factor; it also threatened the carefully balanced strategy which enabled Franco to industrialize and modernize his country without invading the sphere of influence of some of his most powerful supporters. What we call the "Spanish economic miracle" could not have been accomplished in a Spain minus the Basque and Catalan provinces without a social revolution in the rest of the country. Since Franco was not a social revolutionary, he achieved his goal of industrial growth by suppressing separatist sentiments in the two rich northern zones of Euzkadi and Cataluña.

The Franco Coalition and Regional Separatism

While the major members of the Franco governing coalition may have differed on the correct direction or pace of economic change, or even on its desirability, on one thing they agreed. Regional separatism was bad, both for their interests and for Spain, and had to be blunted at any cost. In this, they coincided with the thoughts of Franco himself, who held national unity as one of the highest goals to which his regime could aspire. This combination of interests and ideology produced a policy of fierce suppression of regional separatism, both in the Basque country and in Cataluña.

Of all the Franco-supporting groups, none opposed regional separatism more ardently than the Falange. The radical modernization aims of the *falangistas* meant that national unity must be preserved at all costs. All obstacles to national development must be overcome. The symbols of national unity would be used to persuade citizens to accept the sacrifices imposed upon them by the push for development. The internal barriers to national development, class as well as regional, were to come down. In addition, Falange ideology demanded that Spain take its place among the major powers of Western Europe, at least, and assume its role as leader of the Hispanic world. The prestige afforded by these leadership roles would make it possible for the uprooted Spanish lower classes to retain some pride and self-respect by identifying with a nation that others respected.

The special Falange approach to class conflict and public policy also dictated the suppression of regional separatism. As a general philosophy, the Falange called for the dismantling of all voluntary associations, and all intermediate institutions that stood between the individual and the state. The *falangista* emphasis on the corporative nature of the state meant that the regime would bind all of the citizens together through state-directed associations such as the *sindicatos.* All state-citizen relations would be channeled through these official organizations. Other institutions that might compete with the state for the loyalty and allegiance of the individual were proscribed. Thus, all political parties were outlawed. In fact, the very concept of the party as a voluntary association that provides an alternate route for the citizen to approach the government was decried as degenerate and corrupt liberalism. Likewise, voluntary labor unions and regional institutions must be suppressed and replaced with organizations run from Madrid.

We have already noted the stress placed by the Falange on radical change. In Spain, however, it was unacceptable to couch these proposals in terms of class struggle. In a corporative state, social and economic classes were not supposed to be locked in struggle; rather, a hierarchically structured society worked harmoniously in unison to achieve higher things for the national entity. In this context, the Falange had to present its policy prescriptions as attacking the evil of regional disequilibria. Radical reforms would serve the aim of reducing the level of economic imbalance between Spain's very wealthy provinces (the Basque country and Cataluña) and its poorest ones. Thus, national unity and regional development were linked to further suppress regional separatism in the Basque and Catalan areas.[20]

If the Falange was especially virulent toward regional separatists, other members of the Franco coalition shared their dislike for Basque and Catalan nationalism, although perhaps not with the special passion exhibited by the *falangistas.* The Carlists, for example, opposed Basque nationalism for several reasons. First, the very notion of "nationalism" was mistaken because it was a pernicious modern idea that drained a person's loyalty away from the true and right sources of authority, the monarchy and the Church. Since Basque nationalism was a product of the liberal and modernizing elites from the coastal provinces of Vizcaya and Guipúzcoa, it was an idea that would divert the "real" Basques — the tradition-minded Navarrese — from their objective: a return to the Spain of the conservative monarchy and the *fueros*. Perhaps worst of all, the Carlists feared that any separate or autonomous Basque political entity, whether it was called a "nation" or not, would be dominated by the liberals of Vizcaya, or (what would be even worse) by the workers of Bilbao and San Sebastián. In that event, the privileges and ideology of the traditionalists of Navarra would most definitely be under attack, and they would not be able to rely on any alliance with a conservative regime in Madrid to stave off such an assault.

The Church likewise opposed Basque (and especially Catalan) separatism out of their fear that the liberals and left parties would come to dominate such a unit, with consequent damage to the spiritual interests of the Church. Despite the strong Catholic convictions of the Basque people in general, the Church had reason to believe that the leaders of Basque nationalism would be unable to protect Church privileges in the circumscribed realm of the four Basque provinces. Increasingly, during the 1950s and 1960s, developments in Basque nationalism made it seem as if the links between the movement and the Church were breaking down. The private Basque language schools were less interested in religious education than were their public Spanish counterparts. The Basque Nationalist Party began to move away from its status as a confessional party (one with ideological ties to the Catholic Church), even though the break was not ratified until 1977. Perhaps most importantly, however, the Church simply supported Francisco Franco as the man who defended the Church during the Civil War and who would continue to do so against the forces of radicalism during the 1950s and 1960s. Anything that weakened the Franco regime, including regional separatism, was bad. Anything that strengthened Franco, such as stress on national unity, was good. Quite apart from the specific merits of the issue or the interests at stake, the Church was led to oppose regional separatism because of what separation would do to the Franco government and thus to their interests in the rest of Spain.

In the immediate context of political power, however, the most significant opposition to regional separatism came from Spain's armed forces. The senior officer corps of the Spanish armed forces set their faces sternly against expressions of regional sentiment, a feeling that Franco both supported and encouraged. As Stanley Payne puts it, "To the military, the menace of the twentieth century has seemed to be national division, as represented by violent class struggle, liberal-oriented regional separatism, national impotence, dishonor in the face of new challenges that parliamentary politicians could not or would not face, and international leftist conspiracy."[21]

There had been a time, admittedly, when Spain's military commanders had been willing to use Basque separatism as a weapon against the emerging Second Republic — in 1931. In those days, however, Basque nationalism, because of its strong pro-clerical stance, was seen by many Spaniards as more conservative than most of the leaders of the Republic. Any source of disorder that weakened the Republic and advanced the cause of a military takeover was welcomed, even if it lay in the rebellious Basque region — another case of politics making strange bedfellows. Whatever the source of this rather unusual alliance, it faded away into nothing as the 1930s passed and Spain neared its tragic Civil War. In the end, the Civil War was to harden Spain's victorious military against regional separatism, just as it stimulated regional loyalties where none had existed before.

The northern campaign, which included the struggle to reduce the Basque provinces of Vizcaya and Guipúzcoa, and which ended for the Basques with the surrender of their forces at Santoña, was a symbol of pride and of military effectiveness for the Spanish commanders who conducted the war on this front. One may question their right to remember this campaign with pride: the Basques had been outmanned and outgunned from the beginning; the Spanish rebels had enjoyed air superiority, supplied by Germany; and the war had been the scene of some major atrocities of modern combat, including the use of strategic bombing against undefended civilian populations. Moreover, the Spanish had needed the help of two Italian divisions to crush the Basque defenses, and it was an Italian commander who received the Basque surrender at Santoña. Nevertheless, the war had been costly for the Spanish military: about 10,000 dead, and 100,000 wounded. The camaraderie of fighting in a winning battle led to the forging of many close friendships among the Spanish officer corps, and as Payne says, "In later years, this northern campaign would be remembered with nostalgia by some senior officers."[22]

There were other sources of opposition to Basque regionalism in the background of Spain's military commanders. The army contained many officers (Franco himself was one) who had served in Africa to suppress rebellion in Spain's colonies there, and their experiences had made them oppose any threats to national unity. The army was loyal first and foremost to the nation, as defined by the phrase "national unity and integrity," and their loyalty was closely linked to the sanctity of the national boundaries. There were tangible reasons as well for the military to oppose regional separatism. The armed forces favored a strong military establishment, and they needed the industrial capability of the Basque country to support that need. The Basque industrial centers in Vizcaya and Guipúzcoa, such as the city of Eibar, are among Spain's principal weapons manufacturing regions, which the Spanish army could ill afford to lose. Finally, the Spanish military depended greatly on American assistance which, in turn, was conditioned on the reliability of Spain in the Western alliance, and on Madrid's ability to suppress disturbances that threatened to unseat the Franco government.

After Franco's death, the armed forces began to speak out forcefully against the progressive liberalization of the regime, and its "softer" measures in the Basque provinces. One of the central features of the proposed military reorganization plan of August 1977 was the curbing of the power of the commanders of the country's military districts, which give them correspondingly less influence over the course of events in the Basque provinces and Cataluña. A month later, in September, a resurgence of disorders and attacks against policemen in Madrid and the Basque area prompted a meeting of a large group of military officers in the Army Ministry in Madrid to discuss the "rapid deterioration of public order," and to urge the government to use a strong hand to maintain public order. Also in September, reported Miguel Acoca of the Washington *Post,* a group of powerful, conservative generals met in the Valencian town of Jativa to discuss "how to save Spain from chaos, a leftist takeover and fragmentation of the nation by Basque and Catalan nationalists." To cite Acoca's dispatch at length:

> the generals expressed deep concern over the expressions of nationalism in the Basque and Catalan regions. They were especially angered by Basque youths appearing in the uniform of the Basque Republic's army, which was defeated by Franco. . . . Military unrest in the Basque country is so widespread that two weeks ago Lt. Gen. José Vega Rodriguez, army chief of staff, toured the region to speak to officers who wanted to take action against Basques demonstrating not only for self-rule but for "independence." Several officers . . . complained to him that the Basque demonstrators were threatening "a new civil war" that would endanger national unity.[23]

The opposition of the armed forces affected the political status of Basque nationalism. In the context of economic and social change, however, the key opponents of regionalism proved to be the advocates of moderate modernization, Opus Dei and their allies, the industrialists and bankers (many of whom were, of course, Basque). Spain's economic liberals influenced not only the country's direction in development during the 1960s, but were also extremely influential in shaping Madrid's policies toward the restive Basque and Catalan regions. Franco's hatred of regional separatism was a visceral reaction; that of the liberals was more strongly motivated by economic interests. Opus Dei did not hate the Basques and Catalans. Rather, the reverse seems true. The moderate modernizers needed to integrate the Basques and Catalans into a unified Spanish economic system in order to achieve their development goals of national industrialization, and the spreading of capitalism throughout the country.

Perhaps the Basques should have felt proud and important that they had the wealth and industry needed to achieve such goals for the rest of Spain. Yet, as José Ortega y Gasset wisely remarked in his book *Invertebrate Spain,* written before the Civil War:

> There are few things so indicative of the present state of affairs as the contention of Basques and Catalans that they are peoples "oppressed" by the rest of Spain. The privileged place which they enjoy is so evident as to make this complaint seem grotesque. But anyone more interested in understanding men than in judging them will do well to note that this feeling is sincere. It is all a matter of relativity. A man condemned to live with a woman he does not love will find her caresses as irritating as the rub of chains.[24]

The Basque Role in Spanish Industrial Development

Of Spain's fifty provinces, nine are usually treated apart because of their relatively more advanced state of industrial development: the four Basque provinces (Alava, Guipúzcoa, Navarra and Vizcaya), the four Catalan provinces (Barcelona, Tarragona, Gerona and Lérida), and the national capital, Madrid.[25] Together, these nine provinces account for only 11.4 percent of the national territory, but, as of 1970, for nearly one-third of its population (33.2 percent). As one might expect, then, the population density of the industrial areas exceeds that of the national average by a considerable degree: in 1970, the density of Madrid was 474 persons per square kilometer; of the other eight provinces, slightly more than 150 persons per square kilometer; and of all of Spain, only 67 persons per km^2. Further, the gap is widening rapidly, due not only to natural birth rate differences, but to significant migration trends.

A number of economic and industrial indicators illustrate the concentration of Spain's productive capacity in only a little more than 10 percent of its territory. The nine industrialized provinces account for nearly one-third of the total national wealth of Spain (as of 1965), more than 47 percent of the nation's industrial work force (as of 1969), more than half of the country's industrial production, as measured by value (in 1969), and 44.9 percent of the nation's income (also in 1969). The nine modernized provinces are largely organized for industrial production, in contrast with the remainder of Spain, where traditional economic modes of organization prevail. Thus, while in Spain as a whole only about one-third of the total work force is found in industry, in the Basque and Catalan provinces, the figure exceeds 50 percent, and in Madrid, it is 40 percent. The industrial workers in the more progressive regions of Spain are more productive than their industrial counterparts in the more backward areas. In 1969, the average industrial worker in the Catalan and Basque regions accounted for about 160,000 pesetas of production, while Spain's national average was only 145,900. In the late 1960s, the nine industrialized provinces contained 85 of the country's 100 largest industrial corporations. The industrial work force of Spain tends to be clustered to the north and to the east of Madrid, along the Bay of Biscay and Mediterranean coasts, and in the Ebro River basin, although some development is beginning to take place to the south, in the Valencia-Alicante area, and in the Cadiz-Sevilla region. Per capita income figures indicate no movement of wealth to the south, however. From 1955 to 1969, no southern province rose above the mean in per capita income, although three northern provinces did so (Huesca, Lérida and Castellón).

Basque industry weighs heavily in the context of overall Spanish development. The four Basque provinces account for only 3.5 percent of Spain's territory, and about 7 percent of its population. Nevertheless, the Basque region contains between ten and fifteen percent of the nation's energy capability (in oil refining and nuclear energy), between one quarter and one third of its weapons manufacturing capacity, 17 percent of the nation's bank assets, about one-third of its shipyards and shipping lines, and two-thirds of its integrated steel mill capacity. In 1969, the provinces of Guipúzcoa, Vizcaya and Alava ranked one-two-three in terms of per capita income in Spain; and Navarra ranked seventh. As a region, the four

Basque provinces rank first in per capita income among Spain's fourteen economic regions.

Basque industrial power and wealth have benefited Spain and facilitated its development in many different ways. Basque entrepreneurs have provided the leadership so necessary to a modern and technological society. Technological innovations of great value have been introduced from abroad through foreign investments in Basque industries. Basque industry has been responsible for the manufacture of significant export lines, not the least important of which has been in the area of shipbuilding. The transportation and communication infrastructure of the Basque area will be of great value in linking the Spanish economy to that of France, and, thereby, to the European Economic Community when and if Spain becomes a member.[26] Perhaps equally important, the concentration of heavy polluting industry in the Basque region has allowed Spain to become an industrial nation while preserving for tourists the sunny skies and clean beaches and waters of the country's Mediterranean coast.

The four Basque provinces as a unit contribute about 13 percent of Spain's taxes, a figure that indicates that their per capita tax burden is about twice what the Spanish national average is. The figures from 1970 illustrate the nature of the tax burden on residents of the Basque provinces.[27]

In 1970, the Spanish treasury received slightly more than 30,000 million pesetas (or approximately $500 million) from the Basque provinces. The income was accounted for by revenue payments from each province as follows:

Alava	631.2	million	pesetas
Guipúzcoa	12,375.3	"	"
Navarra	1,070.1	"	"
Vizcaya	16,044.9	"	"
Total	30,121.5	"	"

The data from Guipúzcoa illustrate the different sources of national revenue from that province.[28] Of the 12,375 million pesetas collected by the Spanish treasury in Guipúzcoa, 7,008.3 million pesetas (or about 56.6 percent) came from customs duties on items imported through ports in the province.

(It will be recalled that prior to the Carlist Wars, and the reduction in provincial powers and privileges, customs duties collected in the Basque provinces remained in the province of entry.) Of the remainder, 1,840 million pesetas (14.9 percent) came from business and commerce taxes, 1,124 million pesetas (9.1 percent) from luxury taxes, 845 million pesetas (6.8 percent) from personal income taxes, and 766.5 million pesetas (6.2 percent) from licenses and other "association" levies. The remaining revenue was derived from smaller miscellaneous taxes. It appears, then, that the Spanish government employed a tax system in the Basque provinces that was as regressive as that which prevailed nationally.

It is important to note that Alava and Navarra have enjoyed a special economic relationship with Madrid since the Civil War, due primarily to the support for the military rebellion in those provinces. While Vizcaya and Guipúzcoa were punished by the removal of the last vestiges of their special economic privileges after 1939, Alava and Navarra continued operating under the terms of the *Conciertos Económicos* of the previous century. In the case of Navarra, for example, the economic agreement stems from an 1841 accord between the province and the central government. In essence, Navarra is taxed at special rates and is given much more local autonomy to gather the taxes and to levy their own provincial and municipal taxes than are the other provinces of Spain (including Vizcaya and Guipúzcoa). The tax categories and rates are established by negotiation between Madrid and Pamplona, and are not imposed directly on the Navarra provincial government without the latter's approval. Until 1969, the tax burden on Navarra had been quite small. In 1969, however, the overall rates were increased substantially to attempt to bring the Navarra burden more into line with that of other provinces. The 1969 tax bill to Navarra province included 230 million pesetas as a fixed tax on the provincial government, 390 million pesetas as a variable indirect tax on the provincial government that would be increased automatically each year, 80 million pesetas derived from taxes on exports, and 365 million pesetas from taxes on gasoline and fuel oil (collected by the provincial government and passed on to Madrid). Thus, Navarra's tax burden rose to 1,065 million pesetas, still less than 10 percent of what it was in Vizcaya and Guipúzcoa.[29]

The pattern of Spanish government expenditures in the Basque provinces offers an interesting contrast to the sources of revenues. While Madrid took out of the Basque provinces in 1970 more than 30,000 million pesetas, it returned to those provinces slightly more than 8,500 million pesetas, distributed as follows:

Alava	823.9	million	pesetas
Guipúzcoa	2,465.9	"	"
Navarra	1,403.0	"	"
Vizcaya	3,905.3	"	"
Total	8,598.1	"	"

It will be observed by comparing this table with the preceding one that Alava and Navarra both received in return from Madrid more than each paid out in provincial taxes. In Alava's case, the return revenues were 30 percent more than those paid initially. In the case of Navarra, the percentage was slightly higher: 31.1 percent. Guipúzcoa and Vizcaya, however, received from Madrid much *lower* amounts than were paid out in taxes. Vizcaya received only 24 percent of what it paid to the Spanish government; Guipúzcoa, only 19.9 percent.[30] Further, what funds Madrid did expend in these provinces went primarily for the maintenance of order, and the support of the Spanish central administrative bureaucracy, and relatively little went to finance needed social-infrastructure improvements. Of the 2,465 million pesetas spent in Guipúzcoa in 1970, 577 million went to the Ministry of Interior, which is responsible for the Guardia Civil and the provincial police; 172 million pesetas were expended on the armed forces; and 93.3 million pesetas were devoted to the Ministry of Justice, which included prisons. Thus, more than one-third of Spanish expenditures in Guipúzcoa went for the maintenance of order. About 400 million pesetas were spent on education, which for Basque nationalists is merely an arm of the indoctrination effort by Spain to dilute the ethnic awareness of Basque children. In contrast, only about 5 million pesetas were spent on housing, 9 million pesetas on improving industrial working conditions, 9.5 million pesetas on labor needs, and 175 million pesetas on public works.

If the Basque provinces are an important source of public revenues for Madrid, they constitute an even more significant source of private investment capital for the rest of Spain, although here at least certain sectors of the Basque economy seem to derive important advantages from this relationship.

Because of the weakness of the other alternative methods of industrial financing, such as stock markets, the private banking system has a special role to play in the industrialization process in Spain. According to Ramón Tamames, private banks account for more than 60 percent of all investment capital available normally in the Spanish economy.[31] Further, Spain's private banking resources are as concentrated as its industrial sites and its manufacturing power.

As of the early 1970s, there were 119 private banks in Spain, of which only thirteen were banks of truly national scope. These thirteen national banks accounted for 80 percent of the deposits made to Spanish banks, and for more than 80 percent of the investment credits issued by the private banking network. Within this list of thirteen, five stand out as the dominant banking institutions of the country. Of these, two are domiciled in the Basque country: Banco de Bilbao, which accounts for nearly 10 percent of Spain's entire volume of bank-issued credit, and Banco de Vizcaya, which is responsible for more than seven percent. In all of Spain, only three banks are larger than these two Basque financial giants; and only Madrid domiciles as many powerful banks as does Vizcaya province.

Basque capital finds its way to other Spanish provinces through a second important route: the self-financing of Basque corporations that invest in branch factories outside the Basque country.[32] While comprehensive data are not available, the case of the Altos Hornos investment in the important steel mill in Valencia illustrates the influence of Basque-based capital on Spanish industrial development. In 1971, the Spanish government decided to locate the nation's next major steel mill in Sagunto, in Valencia. The intent of this decision was not only to reduce the concentration of Spain's iron and steel capacity in Vizcaya, but to bring the benefits of industrialization to Valencia. Nevertheless, Valencia-based capital was unable to finance more than a small fraction of the cost of the mill. The outcome of negotiations was that the mill would be paid for by the following combination of financial sources: Valencia capital, 8 percent; Altos Hornos (of Vizcaya), 46.2 percent; United States Steel Co., 15 percent; and 30 percent to be divided among three Basque banks (Bilbao, Vizcaya, and Urquijo). In addition, U. S. Steel is an important participant in the Altos Hornos operations in Vizcaya. Thus, even though Valencia had the steel mill, more than 90 percent of the capital to build it came from Basque industrial and financial circles and their foreign partners.

Of course, when one considers the net movement of private capital between Spanish provinces, the Basque region is an important beneficiary of such transfers. As the original investments of Basque industry and banking begin to mature, the flow of profits from such investment exceeds new investment to such a degree that Vizcaya and Guipúzcoa receive more funds transferred from other provinces than they send out to these provinces. In the late 1960s, according to the findings of José de Azaola, the four most industrialized Spanish provinces (Madrid, Barcelona, Vizcaya, and Guipúzcoa) received net inflows of funds from the rest of Spain of 19 to 22 thousand million pesetas annually. (The net losers of funds were, of course, the poor provinces, such as Jaén, Almeria, Cáceres, and Orense.) Of this amount, Vizcaya province received about 16 percent to 17 percent, or about three to four billion pesetas. Guipúzcoa province received about 9 percent of the total, or between 1.7 and 2.0 billion pesetas. Thus, the two most heavily industrialized Basque provinces received about one-quarter of all the funds transferred from poor to rich provinces during this period. From the point of view of income, one can also conclude that between four and five percent of the total income of Vizcaya and Guipúzcoa provinces was derived from funds transferred from other provinces, after subtracting new outgoing private investment.[33]

The inflow of funds from other Spanish provinces does not benefit all Basques equally, however; and again we can note the degree to which the Basque urban working class bears the burden of the loss of Basque autonomy. Short of being distributed evenly throughout the Basque population, these funds are concentrated in the well-to-do Basque industrial entrepreneurial class and the professional sectors, including bankers and attorneys. This Basque elite opposes Basque nationalism because it enjoys significant benefits from being a part of Spain. In addition to their fruitful investments in Spain, which return nice profits to them, they also benefit from having access to the Spanish market for the sale of their products, and from the protection of Spain's tariffs and other trade barriers, which enable them to sell to Spaniards unmolested by external competition. Finally, Spanish labor policy has also benefited Basque industrialists. Under Franco, unions were outlawed, and strikes prohibited; and even today the competition from Spanish migrants forces Basque workers to accept lower wages and poorer working and living conditions. If Euzkadi were one day to achieve true separation from Spain, or even a diluted form of autonomy that included economic matters, the Basque industrial and banking elite would not continue to enjoy these benefits, which may explain why so few of them have supported Basque nationalism.

Chapter Nine

THE BASQUE LABOR MOVEMENT

The economic aspects of Basque regional sentiment have perplexed several generations of outside observers. Given the relative prosperity and high level of industrialization in the Basque provinces, one is led to wonder why Basques should resent being integrated within the broader Spanish economic system. More readily explained are those instances of regional separatism in which the restive areas are relatively worse off than the remainder of the nation.

If outsiders have been confused about the role of economic issues in Basque separatism, so, it must be admitted, have the Basques themselves often quarreled with each other regarding the importance that should be given to economic matters as against questions of culture, ethnicity or political power. In Chapters Five and Six, for example, I sought to locate the sources of Basque nationalist political strategies in certain dimensions of the society and the culture that are more or less common to all Basques, regardless of the economic class to which they belong. That these strategies have failed to generate substantial support among the majority of the members of the Basque working class illustrates the growing significance of economic issues in defining Basque nationalism. In this chapter, I shall treat some of the more salient economic questions that bear on the life of Basque workers by describing the role of the Basque labor movement in the resistance, both during the Franco years and in the post-Franco period.

"Globalism" and "Regionalism": Two Approaches to National Development

Since the end of World War II, Spain has been confronted with two serious economic problems which are in fact two sides of the same coin. One problem is the relatively backward state of the national economy generally; the other is the high degree of concentration of industrial wealth in a comparatively small fraction of the nation's territory. Over the long run, Spanish leaders have known that both problems must be solved more or less concurrently if either is to be solved satisfactorily. Wealth will not be distributed more nearly equally until there is more of it to be distributed; and the overall level of economic production will not increase until all of Spain is sharing in the prosperity of Madrid, Bilbao, and Barcelona.

Since the 1950s, two general policies have been debated as offering the best solution to Spain's dual economic worries. The *globalista* approach concentrates on trying to increase the country's Gross National Product, wherever and however that may be accomplished, without much concern for the short-run spatial distribution of that product. Anything that stands in the way of economic growth must be pushed aside, including demands for improvement of the poor provinces. In other words, this policy aims at stimulating more economic growth in the already wealthy and industrial regions.

There are both economic and political reasons behind the globalist position. Economically, globalism makes sense if one adopts the "trickle-down" theory of economic progress. The growth of the industrial areas will eventually reach the less well endowed regions in one of several ways. Some growth will extend out from the industrial centers such as Bilbao to the nearby provinces, such as Alava, Santander, Burgos, and Logroño. This growth, which resembles the spread of an oil blot, will benefit the poor provinces in the long run, as they will receive the advantages of industrialization (increased jobs, better living conditions, improved infrastructure) as the basic industries (iron and steel, construction, chemicals, etc.) create a growing demand for secondary and tertiary industries and services. In addition, the overall standard of living in poor provinces will be raised as the wealthy provinces attract migrants from their poor neighbors. As the migrants move to the industrial cities in search of jobs, they relieve the pressure on the resources of the poor provinces as well as provide low-cost labor for the booming industries to the north.

Politically, the globalist approach also had much to recommend it to the Franco regime. The movement of agricultural workers from Spain's south and west provinces to such cities as Bilbao and Barcelona weakened the rural workers' organizations by siphoning off discontented workers and providing alternative ways of remedying their unsatisfactory working conditions. (Migration to other European countries such as West Germany and Switzerland fulfilled the same need.) Their arrival in the new industrial centers also served to weaken the urban workers' organizations since they would be more difficult to mobilize, and they would work for lower wages, thereby making it more difficult for the more skilled Basque and Catalan workers to remain off the job for long. In simple terms, they would serve as strike-breakers when needed. Finally, the influx of new migrant workers from southern and western Spain would dilute the ethnic composition of the Basque and Catalan regions. Since it was reasoned that these workers would not trouble themselves to learn the difficult Basque and Catalan languages, and did not share many of the cultural values and attitudes of the separatist regions, they would not be assimilated into their host cultures. After a generation or so, they would bring up families that would be more Spanish than Basque or Catalan, and that would weaken local support for regional separatist movements.

If globalism serves economic and political goals that are primarily of a short run character, the regionalist policy aims at remedying ills of a much more fundamental and structural nature. Thus, its results are seen more in the long run than in the near. In essence, the regionalist approach concentrates on the redistribution of wealth from the rich provinces to the poor, and the implantation of industry in areas that previously lacked it. Regionalism implies that the needs of the wealthy provinces (especially in such areas as social infrastructure: schools, hospitals, roads, sewage treatment facilities, housing, and so forth) will not be met completely. Instead, through taxation and public spending, funds will be transferred from rich provinces to poor to build the infrastructure needed to encourage industrial construction in the latter zones. The aim here is not to encourage worker migration from south to north, but rather to keep the workers in their home regions by increasing job opportunities and improving the standard of living. In theory at least, since the waves of migrants do not arrive in the industrial provinces, the absence of infrastructural improvements there is not critical, as purely local population growth is not sufficient to overwhelm already existing facilities.

The regionalist approach led to the so-called "growth poles" policy of the development plans of the 1960s. Although the overall aim of these plans was to increase the GNP in absolute terms, the Spanish government also sought to distribute the nation's industry somewhat more evenly by means of favoring certain key provinces and cities with preferential policies and spending programs.[1] In the 1964 Development Plan, two categories of geographic zones were established in order to attract industrial development to previously nonindustrial areas. Industrial development poles were areas in which manufacturing already existed but was judged to be inadequate. Industrial promotion poles were zones that had little or no existing industry. In the latter case, it was presumed that special incentives would be required to attract industrial investment. Eligible firms that located in the zones of one of the development or promotion poles were to be given significant financial incentives. From 1964 to 1971, the government issued over 7 billion pesetas' worth of special credits, and 2 billion pesetas in cash grants, to industries located in the poles.

Nevertheless, the actual accomplishments of the industrial pole policy were mixed. By 1971, about 350 firms were in actual operation in the designated zones, with another 237 under construction. The 350 operating units accounted for fixed investment of some 41 billion pesetas, and provided about 41,000 new jobs. Yet the Vigo pole was the only one that actually achieved goals approximately what the planners had set for it. The investment levels of the other poles ranged from 46 percent to 58 percent of that planned. Further, as de Miguel has noted, the development rates of the seven original poles have only roughly matched those of the historical industrial areas. From 1960 to 1970, while the percentage of work force dedicated to industry grew by about 29.8 percent in the seven development poles, it grew by 34.9 percent in Madrid, the Basque country and Barcelona. The development pole policy apparently did not stem the flow of out-migration from the favored provinces. During the 1960s, the net labor force gain for the industrial provinces was 29.7 percent, while the favored work force declined slightly (minus 2.9 percent).[2]

Not surprisingly, with two competing policies and two sets of social goals to choose from, the Franco regime chose to avoid the dilemma by using both policy alternatives and by pursuing both objectives more or less simultaneously, although not with equal fervor or equal resources. The *globalista* approach was followed in order to achieve the relatively short run goals of social peace, political stability and dilution of the separatist threat, at least among the working classes. The *regionalista* policy, as embodied in the "development poles" program, was adopted to achieve the long run goal of redistribution of national wealth across regions (although not across classes).

The result of these combined policies has been to squeeze the Basque working class from two directions at once. On the one hand, Basque workers faced competition for their jobs from migrant workers from southern and western Spain. These workers were competitive in the sense that they were willing to work for lower wages and in poorer conditions, and they resisted organization. They were also threatening in that they did not share the Basque cultural orientations, attitudes, or (most important) language, so they could not be assimilated easily into Basque culture or Basque nationalist political organizations. The workers' organizations were suppressed by the Franco regime, and the nationalist inclination of the region's industrial workers was neither shared nor supported by Basque industrialists, bankers or corporate executives.

Before the Civil War, to cite Edward Malefakis, the oppressed agricultural laborers of southern and western Spain did not migrate in large numbers to the industrial cities of Bilbao and Barcelona, apparently because they chose to stay and fight for an improvement of their condition, rather than use the safety valve of migration, as their counterparts did in other European countries.[3] After the war, however, as Franco

Map 3. Migration and population changes in Spain, 1961-1970. Source: John Naylon, *Andalusia* (London: Oxford University Press, 1975), p. 22.

used the power of the state to suppress the rural proletariat in the south and west, the rate of migration northward began to grow, until in the 1960s it reached flood proportions.

Net in-migration has tended to be concentrated in relatively few Spanish provinces, and they are predominantly the industrialized areas in the Basque and Catalan regions. During the 1950-1960 decade, only six peninsular provinces received more migrants than they lost, and they were all from the industrialized zone of Spain. In the following decade, thirteen provinces had net in-migration flows, including eight of the nine industrialized provinces. Map 3 portrays the relationship between in-migration and population growth in Spain from 1961 to 1970. With this map, we can see the four Basque provinces gained a total of 202,580 new residents over the decade, the Catalan provinces gained 684,436 also through migration, and Madrid gained 280,831. The only other peninsular provinces gaining migrant population through the decade were Castellón, Valencia, Alicante, Valladolid and Zaragoza.

To understand the political impact of migration into the Basque provinces, we must examine in detail the patterns of migration. Tables 10 and 11 show us these patterns with data drawn from the *Anuario Estadístico de España* for 1970 and 1973.[4] These data reveal first that net in-migration to the four Basque provinces amounts to between 24,000 and 27,000 persons annually. Vizcaya accounts for 10,000 to 13,000 of the total, or about 40 percent to 50 percent. Guipúzcoa receives about 5,000 migrants annually, or about 20 percent of the total. And Alava and Navarra divide the remainder, about 4,000 to 5,000 apiece. Migration from one Basque province to another constitutes a noticeable portion of the total flow. In 1970, about 15 percent of all net in-migration to the Basque provinces came from one of the other Basque provinces; in 1973, the figure was slightly higher than 16 percent.

Unlike Madrid and Barcelona, the Basque provinces do not attract migrants uniformly from across all of Spain. Using the average figures from 1970 and 1973 as our base, we find that fifteen Spanish provinces sent more than 500 migrants annually to the four Basque provinces. Of these fifteen, five were from Old Castilla (Logroño, Santander, Burgos, Palencia and Valladolid), three were from León (León, Zamora and Salamanca), two were from both Galicia (La Coruña and Lugo) and Extremadura (Badajoz and Cáceres), and one province was from each of three regions: New Castilla (Madrid), Andalucía (Jaén) and Aragon (Zaragoza). Four of the fifteen (San-

Table 10.
Migration Patterns to Basque Provinces, 1970 and 1973.

	Destination									
	Alava		Guipúzcoa		Navarra		Vizcaya		Total	
Origin	1970	1973	1970	1973	1970	1973	1970	1973	1970	1973
Basque Provinces										
Alava	—	—	84	98	53	79	330	423	467	600
Guipúzcoa	369	555	—	—	533	684	574	726	1,476	1,965
Navarra	203	217	366	308	—	—	135	201	704	726
Vizcaya	573	627	262	360	200	263	—	—	1,035	1,250
Total	1,145	1,399	712	766	786	1,026	1,039	1,350	3,682	4,541
Remaining Spanish Provinces	2,805	3,717	4,746	4,311	3,109	2,407	9,762	12,193	20,422	22,628
Total	3,950	5,116	5,458	5,077	3,895	3,433	10,801	13,543	24,104	27,169

Source: Instituto Nacional de Estadística, *Anuario Estadístico de España* (Madrid: INE, 1971 and 1974).

Table 11.
Most Important Sources of Migration to Basque Provinces, 1970 and 1973.

Province*	Alava		Guipúzcoa		Navarra		Vizcaya		Total		Average
	1970	1973	1970	1973	1970	1973	1970	1973	1970	1973	
Cáceres	587	404	1,077	773	174	96	703	698	2,541	1,971	2,256
Burgos	394	587	176	159	90	48	811	1,172	1,471	1,966	1,718.5
Salamanca	174	260	527	547	82	102	641	881	1,424	1,790	1,607
Badajoz	45	108	509	346	214	88	823	676	1,591	1,218	1,404.5
León	114	339	142	241	83	51	599	857	938	1,488	1,213
Palencia	170	261	180	137	34	35	619	796	1,003	1,229	1,116
Zamora	132	174	153	102	54	56	609	732	948	1,064	1,006
Logroño	256	254	110	131	399	293	193	256	958	934	946
Santander	87	122	53	86	21	19	506	747	667	974	820.5
Madrid	22	140	117	185	105	182	254	533	498	1,040	769
Jaén	59	89	103	77	484	182	142	143	78	491	639.5
Coruña (La)	30	53	148	115	16	31	422	454	616	653	634.5
Valladolid	98	107	144	156	29	39	243	417	514	719	616.5
Zaragoza	36	30	89	49	301	285	102	151	528	515	521.5
Lugo	8	33	43	52	18	8	438	420	507	513	510

*Arranged in descending order of importance, as measured by the average number of migrants sent to Basque provinces in 1970 and 1973.

Source: Instituto Nacional de Estadística, *Anuario Estadístico de España* (Madrid: INE, 1971 and 1974).

tander, Burgos, Logroño and Zaragoza) are contiguous to at least one Basque province; and two more (Palencia and Valladolid) are at least partially within the economic market influence of Vizcaya and Alava. Madrid is on the list because, as the focal point of Spanish economics and politics, its residents interact at a high level with every Spanish province. The national capital both sent and received large numbers of migrants to and from nearly every province in Spain. The only southern province, Jaén, was eleventh on the list, mainly it seems on the strength of an unusually large wave of migrants to Navarra in 1970, which may be a unique event. Thus, the most significant distant sources of migrants to the Basque country are Galicia (La Coruña and Lugo), and the western provinces that border or lie near to Portugal (Léon, Zamora, Salamanca, Cáceres and Badajoz).

Madrid authorities regularly called for an increase of migration from Spain's poorer provinces to such flourishing industrial areas as Alava both in order to relieve the industrial congestion of Vizcaya and Guipúzcoa, to ease the burden of rural unemployment in the south and west, and to fill the growing number of industrial jobs in Vitoria and Pamplona. In the summer of 1973, for example, at the request of the provincial authorities of Alava, and of Vitoria's business leadership, the Deputy Director of Planning and Employment and the Deputy Director of the Syndicates' Placement Service traveled to Alava to examine the serious need for more workers to fill the gaps in the province's industrial work force. The growing shortage of workers, announced these two men, would soon be a grave obstacle to the continued industrial development of the province.[5]

As a consequence of these migration trends, the Basque provinces' population is only about 65 percent indigenous to their province of residence. Table 12 shows Spanish census data from 1970 that indicate the percentage of each province's population that was born in that province. Because inmigration to Alava, Guipúzcoa and Vizcaya has been greater than that into Navarra, the latter is still about 80 percent indigenous Navarrese. It must be pointed out here that migrants from one Basque province to another are not counted as indigenous to the receiving province, even though they continue to be indigenous to the Basque region. As Table 10 shows, however, this figure amounts to only about 15 percent of the total in-migration to the Basque provinces.

Table 12.
Population Indigenous to Spanish Provinces, 1970.

Province	**Total Population of Province***	**Indigenous Population**	**Indigenous as Percent of Total Population**
Alava	199,296	117,547	58.98
Guipúzcoa	623,015	406,500	65.25
Vizcaya	1,037,345	628,682	60.60
Total 3 Provinces	1,859,656	1,152,729	61.99
Navarra	465,149	379,756	81.64
Total 4 Provinces	2,324,805	1,532,485	65.92
Average of 46 Other Spanish Provinces			86.26

*Includes only persons of Spanish nationality.

Source: Instituto Nacional de Estadística, *España: Panorámica Social, 1974* (Madrid: INE, 1975), Table 1.12, p. 60.

The policy of regionalism, on the other hand, meant that the rapidly growing Basque industrial region would not have access to the resources necessary to cope with the tensions of modern industrial life. In Vizcaya and Guipúzcoa, more taxes flowed out to Madrid than were returned, and those that did return came to finance the Spanish law enforcement system that maintained order in the rebellious Basque provinces. Local provincial and municipal authorities lacked the necessary power to tax and spend to remedy the dislocations caused by the industrialization process. And there was no mechanism available to plan for the development of the four Basque provinces as a unit, which led to misallocations of resources and to duplications or scarcities in many important public services. Thus, the Basque working class has felt the full brunt of a rampant industrialization process. Air and water pollution, scarce and expensive housing, inadequate schools and hospitals, too many cars and not enough parks or other means of recreation: these are just some of the tangible disadvantages that have been experienced by Basque workers since the early 1950s. While the Basque professional classes and middle strata could be preoccupied with such symbolic issues as language, flag, and political expression, the working class came increasingly to define the issue of Basque autonomy in concrete economic and "quality of life" terms.

The most immediate and visible consequence of Spanish policies in the Basque provinces was the increased pressure on jobs, wages, and unionization in the industrial sector.

The central issue in the struggle over increasingly scarce industrial employment lies in the growth in productivity of the individual Basque or Spanish worker precisely in those industries that dominate the Basque economy. As a result of the liberalizing measures taken by the Spanish government in the late 1950s and early 1960s, and the steps taken to industrialize the Spanish economy, many Basque factories developed new production techniques or installed new equipment to permit radical increases in production with little or no increase in employment. Amando de Miguel cites data from several industries that experienced great productivity increases throughout the 1960s. The consumption of iron and steel products rose in Spain by 299 percent between 1961 and 1969; but the productivity of each individual worker in the industry grew accordingly, from 74 metric tons per worker in 1967, to nearly 120 metric tons per worker in 1970. Thus, as de Miguel writes, "In recent years, increases in production of steel have taken place without a corresponding rise in employment."[6] Construction of ship tonnage increased similarly, from about 234,000 metric tons in 1964 to 1,125,000 metric tons in 1972; but employment rose only slightly, from 42,000 to 47,000. Worker productivity rose from 5.5 metric tons to 24.7 metric tons per worker during the same period. Likewise in the sector of machinery and capital equipment, while production rose from about 153 billion pesetas in 1966 to 213 billion pesetas in 1969 (in current pesetas), employment declined from 346,120 in 1966 to 342,371 in 1969. Thus, while thousands of Spaniards flocked to the Basque country to what they thought was a flourishing industrial market, reforms in manufacturing techniques and equipment were eliminating the need for more employees. Basque workers were caught in the squeeze between the Spanish migrants and their own industrial elite.[7]

In another way, the increase in population brought about by the waves of migration caused its own special kind of problems. As Figure 1 shows, the population of the four Basque provincial capitals began to rise sharply in the late 1950s, at about the time that Spain's economic boom was beginning. In San Sebastián, the growth was more subdued; but in Pamplona and Bilbao, population growth rates averaged 5.25 percent and 4.25 percent annually between 1957 and 1970. Growth was sharpest of all in Vitoria, which grew an average of 9.37 percent each year during the same period. While the population of Spain increased at a very slow rate of about 30.7 percent in the thirty-year period from 1940 to 1970, that of the three most dynamic Basque provinces (Alava, Guipúzcoa and Vizcaya) rose during the same time by 96.4 percent, or doubling in a little more than a generation. Only Navarra failed to achieve similarly high growth rates, a condition likely to change as industrialization spreads to Pamplona and its suburbs.

The immediate consequences of such rapid population

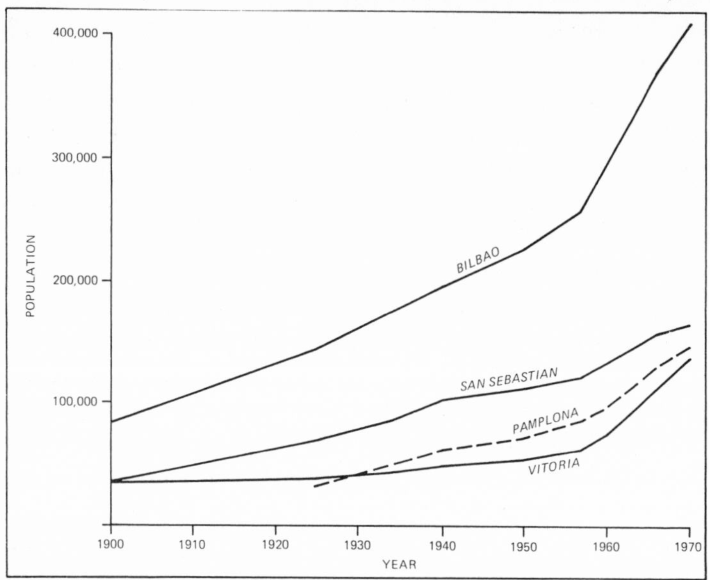

Figure 1. Population Growth in Basque Provincial Capitals, 1900-1970.

growth have been a sharp increase in population density, and a similar rise in the burden created by the economically nonactive portion of the population. Between 1940 and 1970, population density (as measured in terms of habitants per square kilometer) grew quite slowly in Spain as a whole, from 53 persons per km^2 to 67, an increase of only slightly more than 26 percent in 30 years. In Vizcaya, in contrast, during the same period population density increased from 232 persons per km^2 to 471, a rise of 103 percent; in Alava, from 37 to 67, or 81 percent; in Guipúzcoa, from 166 to 316, or more than 90 percent; and in Navarra, from 35 to 45, or 28.5 percent.

The problems of population growth and density are worst in the Greater Bilbao metropolitan area. This area is composed of twenty-eight separate *municipios.* During the period from 1951 to 1960, two of these townships had population increases of more than 100 percent; that is, they doubled in only ten years or less. Five had growth rates of between 40 percent and 100 percent during the period, seven grew at rates of between 20 percent and 40 percent (which would still yield a doubling time of about a generation); and ten increased at a lower rate of between zero and 20 percent. Only four townships actually lost population during the decade. As a result, Greater Bilbao exhibits some of the highest population densities in Europe. Bilbao itself has more than 5,000 habitants per km^2; and the heavily industrialized *municipios* of Sestao and Portugalete have densities of 6,828 and 8,719 persons per km^2, respectively.[8]

This dramatic increase in population has been accompanied by an influx of large numbers of economically nonactive persons (mostly young children) who place a heavy burden on infrastructure and social services, and who must be supported by the smaller percentages who work. The migrant data from 1973 illustrate this phenomenon. In that year, *two-thirds* of all migrants to the four Basque provinces were classified as economically nonactive. In the same group, only 2.3 percent were classified as professional or technical personnel, and 25.6 percent were listed as industrial workers.[9]

One of the principal consequences of this rapid population growth has been an acute shortage of essential social services, such as hospitals, schools, and parks and other recreation facilities.

The four Basque provinces suffer from a marked scarcity of psychiatric hospital facilities. To serve a population of more than two and a half million, there are only about 4,000 beds available in a dozen clinics and hospitals throughout the four provinces. Many of these are maintained by religious orders, and there are few trained medical or nursing personnel assigned to these hospitals. The psychiatric hospital for the city of San Sebastián, with a population of nearly 200,000, has only 107 beds and can handle only the most severe and aggressive patients. The hospital serves about 1,250 patients annually, and about 4,500 cases are attended on an outpatient basis. Vizcaya province suffers from an even worse situation. For a population that nears a million and a quarter, the province has only three clinics or hospitals for psychiatric patients, with a combined total of less than 900 beds. In the worst of these, in Bermeo, there are so few staff personnel to attend the 350 patients that many of the elderly and children spend the entire day either drugged to sleep or tied to chairs to prevent them from injuring themselves or others. In the winter, lack of adequate heating causes the interior temperatures to drop to near freezing; in the summer, water shortages force the hospital to limit baths to one per week. Treatment consists of drugs and electric shock. Of the 350 patients at Bermeo, more than 300 have spent decades in the hospital.[10]

Schools and child care are another source of concern for the citizens of the more industrialized Basque regions. To begin with, day care centers are virtually nonexistent in most areas. In Vitoria, for example, there are day care centers for only about 2,000 children, and at least 5,000 additional spaces are needed to meet the demand from working mothers. More and more families are being disrupted by the necessity for both parents to work where the cost of living makes it difficult to maintain a family on one income. The shortage of community-based child care facilities is eroding the strength of the Basque family structure, for centuries one of the distinguishing features of their culture. According to a recent educational survey of Vizcaya province, 19,000 students graduated from the eighth grade in the province's public schools, but there were only slightly more than 10,000 seats available in the ninth grade to accommodate these pupils. Of these 10,000 places, only about 6,000 were maintained and paid for by the government's Ministery of Education; 4,000 were in private schools. Thus, nearly half of the eligible fourteen-year-olds in Vizcaya would be without space to continue their education in the absence of emergency measures. According to Spain's primary education law, school attendance is obligatory and free from ages six to thirteen. Yet for the 211,000 children in this age group in Vizcaya in 1977, there is space for only 147,756, unless classrooms are overcrowded and teachers pressured to accept more students in their classes.[11]

Anyone who knows the Basque people is well aware of their love of nature, and of their almost mystical regard for conserving the beauties of the surrounding environment. Yet as urbanization and industrialization have caused the progressive crowding of people together in less and less space, the great cities such as Bilbao have not been able to dedicate sufficient space for parks and other outdoor recreation purposes. The original urban land use plan for Bilbao, set down in 1961, specifies a minimum of 28 square meters of "green space" per habitant of the city. As of 1975, however, the actual figures fell far short of the prescribed goal: in park space, there was about three quarters of a square meter per person; in other green areas, such as public gardens, about four tenths of a square meter. As a result, in the city of Bilbao, each citizen has access to an average of about 1.19 square meters of parks and gardens for recreation and relief from the congestion and pollution of industry and urban living. Some of the more densely populated areas of the city, such as Sestao and Portugalete suffer even worse. There, the averages run more on the order of .2 to .44 square meters of park per person. The social consequences are noticeable: mothers and children no longer meet in neighborhood parks to play and exchange local news; children must play in unhealthy and dangerous settings; and the tensions of urban family living are compressed into a confined residential area, with little opportunity for the relief of an outdoors stroll or weekend picnic.[12]

But of all the consequences of unrelieved industrialization, the one that is most noticeable to the visitor to the Basque country is the pollution of its formerly clean air and water. A French journalist traveling along the picturesque Basque coast to Bilbao reported, for example, that the beaches and the rivers flowing to the Bay of Biscay were awash with garbage, bottles and cans, plastic and other discarded construction materials. The rivers that crossed the industrial districts around San Sebastián, such as Rentería, varied in color from pale yellow to brown, and their odor was a sickening stench. Factories located along these rivers discharged their waste products without regard to the environment or the quality of life of those who lived near the plants.[13] The thriving industry and the coastal location of Vizcaya and Guipúzcoa provinces have made them attractive spots for building nuclear power reactors and oil refineries. There is already a major refinery in Guipúzcoa, and two nuclear reactors are under construction in the Bilbao region, with a third planned for the small coastal village of Deva. Without proper precautions, these installations will soon be adding their share to the water pollution that plagues the Basque coastal provinces.

Air pollution is also a severe problem, and getting worse by the year. A 1975 *Business Week* article calls Bilbao "a warren of smelly, smoky plants cheek-by-jowl with housing," and says the city's air "is perhaps the foulest in Europe."[14] From 1970 to 1976, Bilbao succeeded in passing Madrid and Barcelona to achieve the dubious distinction of having the most contaminated air in Spain. While the SO_2 content in the air of Madrid was being reduced during this period from 150 micrograms per cubic meter of air to 114, and that of Barcelona from 154 to 86, the air worsened in Bilbao; concentrations of SO_2 increased from 142 to 173 micrograms per cubic meter of air.[15]

The increasingly severe environmental pollution of the area's major cities has prompted protests and demonstrations from workers' groups and from citizens' associations. In 1976, local citizens' groups in the Vizcayan town of Lejona put such pressure on their municipal government that permits were denied to Dow Chemical Company to construct a new insecticide plant until the company agreed to close down its sulfuric acid and titanium oxide factories in the same area and to cut back on the high sulfuric acid emissions from the remaining plants. In October 1969, the workers of the industrial area of Erandio, near Bilbao, demonstrated against air pollution from the area's factories. The demonstration was broken up by police firing live ammunition into the crowd, killing two and wounding four more of the workers.[16] More recently, the workers for a chemical company called Sefanitro protested the planned construction of a new ammonia factory in Baracaldo, and were successful in forcing the company to introduce pollution control devices to reduce hazardous emissions.[17] Even the less industrial areas of the Basque region, such as Navarra, are beginning to organize their citizens against possible future threats to their environment. In Navarra, a group called Estudios Belagua has been formed to block damage to the Belagua River valley and its surrounding hillsides and drainage basin. For the time being, the group has confined itself to studies and public meetings on the subject; but there is no doubt that were industrial development ever to threaten this wild and unspoiled part of Navarra, the group would be mobilized to prevent it from happening.[18]

Basque Labor and Nationalist Politics

In recent years, there has emerged a new school of revisionist Basque historians who have sought to explain Basque nationalism by means of a theory based on economic class struggle. The foremost of these new historians writes under the pen name of "Beltza," and it is on his major works that the following paragraphs are based.[19]

According to Beltza, the PNV and the Basque Government-in-Exile in Paris conducted a very vigorous resistance campaign during what he calls "The Golden Years," from 1945 to 1947. Commando training units were established along the French-Spanish border employing former American military officers as instructors and (some said) paid for with American funds. Inside Spain, the Resistance Council was urged to take a very active role in organizing strikes and in building and maintaining an underground organization that could be responsive to political strategies crafted in France.

These resistance activities were brought to an end about 1947, according to Beltza, in response to conservative pressure from two quite different fronts. The first was the government of the United States. The reader will recall that the Basque government had placed great emphasis on the pressure that the Americans could bring to bear on Franco either to force him to democratize his regime, or in the last analysis to overthrow him in favor of a more liberal government. As American policy became more and more interested in stopping communism in Western Europe, the Basques turned increasingly to a resistance without communist participation. The communists were ejected from the Basque Government-in-Exile, and resistance activities were steered away from Spanish communist organizations on the other side of the Pyrenees. In addition, as we have seen, after 1947 the United States had decided that their best strategy was not to pressure Franco but to try to placate him, and purchase his cooperation through military and economic aid. One important consequence of this shift in Washington was the Basques' decision to disband their commando training units and to abandon the tactic of "direct action" against Madrid. Thus the overall effect of the onset of the Cold War after 1947 was to steer the Basque resistance toward less violent means of political struggle.

But the Americans were not the only source of counter-revolutionary pressure on the Basque government and the PNV. From within Spain itself, claims Beltza, former members of the PNV urged restraint on the Basques in exile. These men formed a part of what Beltza calls the "national bourgeoisie," upper middle class professionals and business men who advocated Basque autonomy but who also wanted a certain amount of social peace to go along with the region's liberty. In working with the region's labor movement to foment strikes and other acts of disruption, the PNV was making it difficult for the Basque business and commercial class to continue to earn comfortable incomes, especially given the economic hardships through which Spain had passed and continued to experience even after World War II. If the customary Basque standard of living was to be maintained, the workers would have to be restrained, not mobilized and provoked. While the PNV and the government wanted worker support for purely nationalist political activities, they found that once they had mobilized the unions it was difficult to turn off their emotion and commitment and make them return to low paying jobs and steadily rising prices. Thus, the stimulus of Basque nationalist political struggle was beginning to make itself felt in labor unrest as well, and the national bourgeoisie could not countenance the latter in order to enjoy the benefits of the former.

The result of these pressures and of the Basque government's shift in strategies was the emergence of a major rift between the government and the Basque labor movement. The last real cooperation between the PNV and the unions was in the major strike of 1947. Eventually the strike spread from a small beginning in Vizcaya to include most of the workers in that province and in Guipúzcoa. The repression was brutal and swift. More than 15,000 workers lost their jobs, and many hundreds were arrested for their role in the work stoppage. After about two weeks, the Basque government issued a call to the workers to end the strike and return to their jobs. Many workers felt betrayed by this failure of the government in Paris to support them, especially since it was the workers who were bearing the brunt of the suppression of the nationalist movement by Franco. In the 1951 strike, as I have already noted, the unions participated only grudgingly with the PNV. But by 1956 the Basque labor movement had reached the point where it could organize the workers by itself without the help or the cooperation of the Basque government or the PNV. In the mid-1950s, then, we began to see signs of other dimensions of non-violent political struggle as the Basque working class began to assert itself.

The Basques are a classic case of conflict between class and ethnicity. Many Basques of the national bourgeoisie see the basic social fault line as separating ethnic Basques from Spaniards. For them, metaphorically speaking, the important frontier is the Ebro River. Others, who are members of the working class, think of political struggle in terms of social and economic class, and perceive the world as divided between those who own property and buy labor, and those who own no property and who sell their labor to others. For them, again thinking metaphorically, perhaps the appropriate dividing line is the Nervion River as it flows to the Bay of Biscay through Bilbao, separating the working class neighborhoods on one side from the bourgeois suburbs on the other. A major flaw in the Basque struggle has been their inability to forge a movement that could reconcile the contradictions inherent in these two perceptions and weave the two strands into a coherent ideology and political force that would define Basque nationalism in terms of *both* class and ethnicity.

The origins of the Basque labor movement in the first several decades of this century affected markedly the differing Basque perceptions of the "we" and the "they" of politics. As the working class emerged from the booming industrialization of Bilbao and other cities in Vizcaya and Guipúzcoa, the unions that sought to enlist their support and to mobilize them in strikes and other united actions were either branches of Spanish unions or tied so closely to the middle class Basque Nationalist Party that they were unable to represent vigorously the needs of the industrial proletariat.

The growth of the urban industrial work force after the turn of the century made inevitable the organization of the proletariat. The only real questions would be who would lead the organizational work and what kind of perspective would be applied to the workers' struggle. As Beltza points out, the significant increases in the population of Bilbao during the industrialization boom were taking place in the working class neighborhoods. Between 1901 and 1910, Bilbao increased in population by only slightly more than 6,000. Between 1910 and 1920, the city grew by more than 32,000 persons. Meanwhile, the bourgeois middle class towns around Bilbao were growing more slowly, and merging into the expanding central city to form suburbs. The small villages of the interior of Vizcaya, however, were losing population at the rate of about 500 persons each year for the twenty-year period at the beginning of the century.[20]

The growth of the industrial working class was even more dramatic. In 1903, there were an estimated 30,000 to 40,000 industrial workers in Vizcaya, and few in the other Basque provinces. A major strike was one that idled 15,000 workers. The socialist UGT could count no more than about 1,700 members in Vizcaya in 1910 after more than 20 years of organizational effort. Other unions were even more feeble. By 1921, the UGT had grown in Vizcaya to represent more than 21,000 workers. In 1930, there were 80,000 industrial workers in Vizcaya, of whom about 30,000 worked in the steel industry; 47,000 industrial workers in Guipúzcoa; 20,000 in Navarra; and 8,000 in Alava. Thus, there were about 155,000 industrial workers in the four provinces in the early 1930s, of whom more than 80 percent lived and worked in Vizcaya and Guipúzcoa.

The increase in the urban, industrial sector brought not only an increase in the industrial proletariat, and in their representative unions, but in incidents of labor unrest as well. Throughout the period from 1900 to 1930, northern Spain was wracked periodically by strikes, lock-outs, and considerable violence as police and Guardia Civil attempted to suppress the striking workers. Major strikes were called in 1903, 1906, 1910, 1917, and 1923. The usual reasons were the rapid increase in the cost of living that could not be matched by the workers' slowly rising wages, unsafe working conditions, unsanitary and crowded living conditions, abuse of the "company store" concept to keep workers tied to the industrial management, and finally the brutal treatment of workers by the police.

The first labor unions to be formed in the Basque region were not Basque at all but branches of Spanish unions.[21] The socialist union, the UGT (*Unión General de Trabajadores*) was founded in 1882 and established in the Basque region before 1890. The anarchists' counterpart, the CNT (*Confederación Nacional de Trabajo*), was founded in 1910. Both of these organizations were Spanish in scope, and regarded the Basque workers' struggles as simply another phase of the overall fight between capitalism and the working class. They had no sympathy for the regional aspirations of the Basques, and little understanding of their special cultural and ethnic outlook.

The first ethnic Basque union was founded in 1911, and it has continued to dominate the ethnic side of organized labor in the region ever since, despite numerous splits and internal conflicts. The union was called *Eusko Langileen Alkartasuna* in Euskera, or *Solidaridad de Trabajadores Vascos* (Solidarity of Basque Workers). Even today, the union is frequently referred to by its combined letters, ELA-STV, although with the increased emphasis on Euskera, the Basque title and letters seem to predominate.

The new Basque union began slowly. At its founding meeting, there were only 178 members in attendance. By 1916, its membership had risen to only 3,750. According to Beltza, the union attempted to organize not the workers of heavy industry, such as steel or shipbuilding, but rather skilled workers, small shopkeepers, and even peasants still working in the fields. For this reason, ELA had great difficulty in making common cause with the majority of Basque labor, especially that portion that experienced the most contaminated and unsafe working conditions, and the lowest wages, and which was therefore the most radicalized. Of great significance, however, were the union's initial religious and political inclinations. In contrast to the socialist and anarchist unions, ELA was ardently pro-Catholic, a fact that helped them with Basque society generally but which marked them as tainted by the anti-Church socialists. Most important, ELA established and maintained close links with the bourgeois Basque Nationalist Party, since the other unions were affiliated with parties whose ideologies matched their own. Beltza argues that the ELA and the PNV formed an alliance of the Basque center, that is, those social groups and forces that opposed both the big capitalists of the so-called "oligarchy" of Basque industry, as well as the anti-religious leanings of the socialist and communist proletariat. The ELA-PNV collaboration brought together skilled workers, small farmers, peasants, artisans and small businessmen and middle and upper-middle class professionals (lawyers, journalists, doctors, and so forth) into one single force which had as its rationale opposition to "Big Capitalism" without following the ideologies and parties of the left.

A number of observers assert that the clash between Basque nationalist unions and Spanish socialists began to be a problem as early as the first decades of the twentieth century. According to some reports of the period, employers tried to magnify the differences between Basque and non-Basque workers in order to exacerbate intra-working class strife and divert workers' attention away from the miserable conditions under which they lived and worked.[22] Beltza argues that in a number of cases, workers' housing was arranged in such a way as to separate Basques from non-Basques to perpetuate their ethnic suspicion and hostility.[23] In any event, as Larranga reports, almost from the very beginning, the Basque nationalist union, ELA, drew as many criticisms from the Spanish socialists as it did from the business and industrial elite.[24]

For the first two decades of its life, ELA experienced only slight popularity and growth; but following the establishment of the Second Republic in 1931, the fortunes of both ELA and Basque nationalism generally began to soar. In 1931, ELA could count on about 21,000 members (14,000 in Vizcaya, 5,000 in Guipúzcoa, 1,200 in Alava and 800 in Navarra), or about 14 percent of the total industrial work force of the four provinces. By 1935, ELA's membership had grown to 42,000 (20,000 in Vizcaya, 17,000 in Guipúzcoa, 3,500 in Alava and 1,500 in

Navarra). Still, though doubled in strength, the union contained only about one worker in four; by 1936 its position was analogous to that of the PNV in politics: a minority union but still the largest single labor organization in the Basque provinces.

Following the Civil War, ELA was closely linked to the Basque resistance and to the Basque government for a number of years. The formal mechanism by which this linkage was effected was the *Alianza Sindical de Euzkadi* (ASE), or the Basque Labor Alliance. The ASE was supposed to be the counterpart in the field of organized labor to the Basque Consultative Council. As such, the ASE was intended to bring together the union equivalents of the political forces that supported the Basque government. Thus the ASE included representatives of the ELA, the socialist UGT and the anarchist CNT. Communist unions were not included.

For many years, the Basque government and the PNV used the ASE as a device to control the workers' organizations, and to insure that the unions' activities coincided with the broader political strategies of the Government-in-Exile. For example, it was in the interest of the Basque government that strikes for political reasons and those for economic causes coincide, to insure maximum impact on the street. At times, workers were asked to go out on strike for a particular political cause or motive, or conversely, to eschew work stoppage for more directly related economic reasons. As time wore on, the workers began to complain that their cooperation with the resistance's political forces was not resulting in any economic benefits for themselves. Another inflammatory issue had to do with the role of the UGT in the alliance. After the early 1960s, the Spanish Socialist Party, the PSOE, pressured the PNV into abandoning its idea of announcing immediate autonomy for Euzkadi following Franco's otherthrow or death. When the PNV agreed to this policy, and accepted the need to work for autonomy through the democratically elected parliament (which the PSOE hoped to control), they used their control over the ASE to restrain ELA and to insure that the Spanish union, UGT, would be able to direct the Basque labor movement on political issues.

This condition worsened through the late 1950s and early 1960s, until it exploded into open conflict in 1964. At that time, ELA lost a very large number of its more restless and activist members, who left the parent organization to form ELA-*BERRI* (New ELA). ELA-*BERRI* quickly asserted itself as a mixed political party-labor union that attacked the PNV vigorously for its policy of cooperation with the PSOE, and the older ELA (now know as ELA-*oficial*) for failing to represent the interests of the Basque working class.

At about this same time, the leaders of the remnants of ELA, ELA-*oficial,* began to explore the possibility of achieving their goals by working within the growing, illegal Spanish workers' movement, known as the *Comisiones Obreras* (Workers' Commissions). Throughout the Franco period, the only labor organizations that were permitted by law were the official state-run syndicates, whose purpose, many observers felt, was to restrain the workers' demands and maintain social peace in the industrial sector. The *Comisiones Obreras* derived their name from an *ad hoc* illegal strike committee that was established during a miners' strike in Asturias in 1956.[25] Similar committees emerged from a wave of strikes in other parts of Spain in the period from 1962 to 1964. By the latter 1960s, the Spanish Communist Party had fairly effectively established its control over the workers' commissions; but in the middle part of the decade, they were regarded as the vanguard of the illegal Spanish labor movement.

Thus, in 1966 a number of ELA-*oficial* leaders formed a special negotiating committee, called the *Comisiíon Obrera Profesional de Guipúczoa,* or COPG, to open talks with the *Comisiones Obreras.* The COPG drafted a series of principles which they thought should govern relations between the Basque ELA and the Spanish *Comisiones.* Central to these principles was the declaration that ELA would participate in a Spanish labor movement only if the Spanish workers accepted the legitimate demands of the Basques for regional autonomy and agreed to let ELA join the *Comisiones* as a confederal partner rather than a subservient branch of the Spanish organization. Not surprisingly, at the *Comisiones Obreras* meeting in Madrid in 1967, the ELA principles were rejected as threatening to weaken the

Spanish labor movement, whereupon ELA decided not to participate in the *Comisiones Obreras*. As far as is generally known, it was the last time that Basque working class organizations attempted to join any Spanish labor front.

The decade from 1967 to 1977 was marked by a bewildering series of schisms and consolidations in the Basque labor movement. New splinter groups formed, joined with others, split anew, and faded out, leaving a proliferation of organization titles and initials, but little in the way of solid institutions. In 1968, ELA-*BERRI* was weakened by the departure of a group of leaders who advocated more direct political action and less emphasis on the strictly economic front. This latter group, called ELA-MSE (*Movimiento Socialista de Euzkadi*), was to suffer a number of schisms itself before dying out in 1976. In 1969, ELA-MSE began to debate the wisdom of a strategy of direct confrontation of Madrid just when Franco's regime appeared to be achieving near invulnerability. Five years later, in 1974, one of the groups that advocated a more cautious, less risky approach to the struggle split off to become virtually the labor arm of the PNV. This group was called ELADIOS and supported a more technocratic and less disruptive road to regional freedom. In 1976, ELA-MSE split again, with the more radical and activist members fusing with one of the new *abertzale* (patriotic in Basque) socialist parties, *Euzkadi Sozialista Biltzarrea*. The more cautious members joined forces with a splinter group that had broken away from ELA-*oficial* in 1975 to form ELA-*AUTOGESTIONARIA* (roughly, ELA-Selfgoverning), now known simply as ELA-A. Meanwhile, what was left of ELA-*BERRI* after the departure of ELA-MSE split again, with the more economically oriented leaders rejoining ELA-*oficial*, and the more radicalized members joining a new socialist political party, EZKER BERRI.

Depending upon how one chooses to define the boundaries of the category, there were about 650,000 in the working class population of the Basque provinces in 1976, of whom about 300,000 were in the industrial sector, 100,000 in agriculture and fishing, and 250,000 in services.[26] Only a relatively small percentage of these workers are represented by the various Basque unions: ELA-*oficial*, ELA-A and ELADIOS. ELA-*oficial* is by far the largest of these three, claiming about 40,000 members.[27] Neither of the other two organizations could claim a membership even remotely approaching this figure. The Basque labor movement is weakened further by the more or less constant struggle that goes on among these three unions to exert paramount control over Basque workers. In November 1976, for example, the Spanish unions issued a call for a massive general strike across the entire country to protest wage freeze plans and the increase in unemployment in Spain, as well as the right of employers to fire striking workers. ELADIOS condemned the strike and refused to call out their members; ELA-*oficial* supported the strike "with reservations" because it failed to address the issue of regional rights; and ELA-A took no stand on the strike.[28] Further, the unions have fought one another bitterly on the issue of which should be legally recognized by the Spanish Labor Ministry as having the authority to negotiate in the name of the Basque workers.[29] Finally, the Spanish unions that have particular strength in the Basque region have since Franco's death begun to pay more attention to the ethnic dimension of the Basque workers' situation. For example, in late 1976 the Basque branch of a Spanish union named USO (*Unión Sindical Obrera*) held its first assembly in Pamplona, and came down squarely on the side of Basque ethnicity, calling for amnesty for Basque political prisoners, increased respect and protection for Euskera, and even urging that its members (Basque and Spanish) begin to use Basque names.[30] If these trends continue, the legitimate right of ELA-*oficial* to represent and speak for ethnic Basque workers will become even more in doubt.

Table 13 portrays the results of the election of union representatives in more than 1,400 industries, firms, shops, and offices across the four Basque provinces in 1978. At stake was not only the competition over key leadership roles in each organized industry or firm, but the symbolic leadership of the Basque labor movement as well. It is interesting to note that the nationalist union, ELA-STV, won slightly less than one-quarter of the overall vote, followed closely by the *Comisiones Obreras,* and at a slightly greater distance by the socialist UGT. ELA won the most votes in Vizcaya and Guipúzcoa, but trailed

Table 13.
Results of Labor Union Elections in Basque Provinces, 1978.

	Vizcaya		Guipúzcoa		Alava		Navarra		Total	
Union	**No.**	%	**No.**	%	**No.**	%	**No.**	%	**No.**	%
ELA-STV	745	24.4	782	29.2	155	22.5	44	8.7	1,726	24.9
CC. OO.	700	22.9	677	25.3	149	21.7	91	18.0	1,617	23.3
UGT	708	23.2	480	17.9	187	27.2	75	14.8	1,450	20.9
None	338	11.1	327	12.2	100	14.5	96	19.0	861	12.4
Others	565	18.5	412	15.4	97	14.1	199	39.4	1,273	18.4
Total	3,056		2,678		688		505		6,927	

Source: *Deia* (Bilbao), February 11, 1978.

behind the UGT in Alava, and did very poorly in Navarra. Thus the position of ELA in the Basque labor movement is closely analogous to the position of the PNV in Basque politics generally: while it is one of the two or three most important unions in the region, it is not even close to representing a majority force, even in Vizcaya and Guipúzcoa, where most of its strength is concentrated.

Labor Unrest in the Basque Provinces

According to almost any measure one can choose, industrial labor in the Basque provinces is a major source of conflict and unrest in Spain. With about ten percent of the nation's industrial labor force, the Basque provinces have customarily accounted for more than 30 percent of all labor conflicts in the country, and nearly one-third of all man-hours lost due to strikes and other work stoppages. Table 14, based on the work of sociologist Luis C.-Nuñez Astrain, shows the relative importance of the Basque provinces in Spanish labor conflicts between 1963 and 1974. On the average over the twelve-year period, the Basque provinces as a whole accounted for 37 percent of all labor conflicts in Spain, and in 1969 the figure rose to more than half! Vizcaya and Guipúzcoa, with their more radicalized working class organizations, account for the bulk of the conflicts, but the incidence of labor strife is beginning to increase in Navarra as well. Another important dimension of labor unrest is the relative significance of the political motivation of a given strike. In 1967, according to Kepa Salaberri, nearly 39 percent of all strikes in Spain were initiated to protest political or social problems or questions, while only a little more than 9 percent were launched to gain improvement in workers' salaries, and about 6 percent were called to demonstrate solidarity with other striking workers.[31]

Faced with such a large diversity of events to describe, I can do no more than paint the highlights of several of the more important and widely reported strikes in the Basque country, with emphasis on those that have taken place in recent years.

April, 1956. In response to the slow rise in wages and the rapid price inflation throughout Spain, workers in the four Basque provinces walked off the job. The government had just

Table 14.
Labor Conflicts in Basque Provinces, 1963-1974, as Percentage of Conflicts in Spain.

Year	Number of Conflicts in Spain	Percentage of Conflicts in Basque Provinces				
		Alava	Guipúzcoa	Navarra	Vizcaya	Total
1963	640	0.0	3.1	0.0	12.5	15.6
1964	384	0.0	19.8	0.0	18.2	38.0
1965	164	0.0	9.8	0.0	26.8	36.6
1966	179	0.0	13.4	1.1	15.6	30.1
1967	567	0.0	6.9	0.2	25.4	32.5
1968	351	0.0	5.4	2.0	14.2	21.6
1969	491	0.4	27.1	1.8	23.0	52.3
1970	1,595	0.4	31.4	1.8	8.2	41.8
1971	616	0.6	11.0	5.4	11.2	28.2
1972	853	1.9	11.5	4.2	15.2	32.8
1973	931	0.4	11.7	11.3	11.6	35.0
1974	2,290	0.5	22.8	4.2	17.3	44.8

Source: Luis C.-Nuñez Astrain, *Clases sociales en Euskadi* (San Sebastián: Editorial Txertoa, 1977), Table 53, p. 202.

a short time before decreed a 20 percent increase in wages, but there had been a 50 percent rise in prices since the last wage increase in 1953. The strike spread to other regions of Spain, including Barcelona and Asturias province. In the Basque region, the cities of Bilbao and Pamplona were especially involved in the strike. In Pamplona, workers congregated in the main square and knelt saying the rosary. Police were thus prevented from breaking up the demonstration. In Vizcaya, where the primary targets were foreign firms such as Babcock and Wilcox, and General Electric, the Civil Governor responded to the strike by locking out the striking workers. Eventually, 40,000 workers were affected. In the end, the workers went back to work, and the Spanish government decreed an increase of 25 percent in their wages. Since business could pass these costs on to the consumer, the inflationary spiral was simply heightened.[32]

Spring, 1958. On this occasion, the strike received its impetus from another restive sector of Spain, the miners of Asturias, who walked out of the mines in March to protest the inability of wages to keep up with inflating prices. In 1957, the cost of living had risen 16 percent, and in the first quarter of 1958 by another 10 percent. Wage increases were simply not sufficient to keep pace with such a boiling inflation. As the Asturian miners walked off the job, sympathy strikes erupted throughout Spain's industrial regions. At least 25,000 workers joined the strike in Barcelona. In the Basque region, the areas most significantly affected were the steel mills of Vizcaya and Guipúzcoa. This time, police succeeded in breaking up the gatherings, and the workers eventually returned to their jobs without receiving any wage increases.[33]

Winter, 1962. These important strikes were the first instances of unrest organized by *Comisiones Obreras* in the Basque region. After their formation in 1956, the *Comisiones* had played only an occasional and sporadic role in organizing labor activity in the Basque work force; after 1961-1962, they were permanently organized, and played a regular role in the Basque labor movement until later in the 1960s, when they were taken over by the communists. In January 1962, the Basconia iron and steel works in Vizcaya was struck by about

3,000 workers, who were promptly locked out by provincial authorities. In February, the workers of Guipúzcoa began to demonstrate in the street; and the men in the steel mills and arms factories in Eibar and Irún walked off the job. There were renewed street demonstrations and some sit-ins in Guipúzcoan industries, and the Guardia Civil had to be called in to drive the workers out of the buildings they were occupying. Marching workers chanted their demands for a minimum wage of 100 pesetas a day (about $2.00). The Spanish government responded with suppression, while the Basque government, seeing the workers' movement slip out of their grasp, reacted by forming the *Alianza Sindical de Euzkadi.* Otherwise, the workers' standard of living showed little noticeable improvement.[34]

Spring, 1962. The failure of Madrid to respond to the strikes of earlier in the year brought the workers back onto the streets only a few months later. Again, the strikes began in Asturias and spread quickly to the Basque and Catalan regions. Especially affected in the Basque country were the industrial cities of Beasaín and Bilbao. On May 4, Franco decreed a state of emergency in Asturias, Vizcaya and Guipúzcoa. Despite this measure, the strikes spread to other factories, the workers in Madrid began to join their comrades to the north, and the students began a series of demonstrations showing their solidarity with the miners. By May 9, at least 100,000 workers were off the job throughout Spain, and the number rose to 300,000 in a week. Virtually all of the nation's miners had walked out of the pits, and many other important sectors were crippled badly. Shaken by the confrontation, the Spanish government lifted the wage freeze that had been in effect since 1957. Effective in January 1963, the minimum daily wage would rise to 60 pesetas (about $1.00).[35]

November-December, 1966. This strike affected primarily the workers of only one plant: Echevarri steel works in the Bilbao suburb of Basauri. On November 30, the men had walked off the job to protest a reduction in wages made necessary, said the company, by a restriction in government credits. The strikers had occupied the factory, and were driven out on December 2 by Guardia Civil troops armed with submachine guns. The owners of the works had then locked out the strikers, dismissed 564 of their number, and charged fifteen with the crime of leading an illegal strike. A Spanish court subsequently found the workers guilty and declared that the owners had the right to dismiss them permanently. Sympathy strikes in Vizcaya were suppressed by the Guardia Civil. Despite the fact that changes in the Penal Code had in theory made economic strikes legal, these workers were still held legally liable for their actions. The Penal Code was altered by court action a year later to make all strikes illegal, regardless of their purpose.[36]

May-June, 1973. One of the most significant developments in the Basque labor movement in recent years has been the growing radicalization of the workers in the traditionally conservative province of Navarra, and most especially in the provincial capital of Pamplona. In the spring of 1973, a general strike in Pamplona demonstrated the impressive strength and militancy of the *Comisiones Obreras* of that city's new industries. The strike began on May 9 in the Motor Ibérica plant, where workers were demanding higher wages. Several neighboring plants were struck the following day. On May 24, the provincial *Comisiones Obreras* called for a province-wide strike in support of the Motor Ibérica workers. The Authi automobile plant was struck even though the plant's owners threatened the workers with the loss of pay if they walked out. On June 9, a protest march of about 2,000 workers was broken up by police using tear gas and rubber bullets. From this point on until June 23, the violence and disruption escalated markedly. The *Comisiones Obreras* claimed that they had succeeded in closing down all businesses with more than 50 employees. Many churches began to side with the workers, providing them with food and shelter during the disturbances. Schools were closed, shops had to be locked up, and the city's food supply began to dwindle. Police and Guardia Civil were brought in from neighboring provinces. At its height, the strike affected about 50,000 workers. By late June, however, the plant owners began to accede to some of the strikers' demands. It was agreed that the leaders of the strike would not be punished for their role in the unrest, and that they would regain their former employment. By June 27, many of the workers were back at their jobs. Wage problems remained an irritant; but the *Comisiones Obreras* had demonstrated an unsuspected ability to shut down an entire city given the necessary provocation.[37]

Summer, 1974. The labor unrest in Pamplona did not subside after the 1973 disorders. In the summer of 1974, workers at the Authi plant returned to the street to demand wage increases, and were met with police suppression, arrests and numerous dismissals from their jobs. Again the Church supported the striking workers as it had in 1973, allowing them to use church buildings for meetings and refuge from police attacks. At least two priests were arrested in the course of the disorders. After 37 days of work stoppage, the plant owners granted an increase in wages of about 4,000 pesetas per month, and arranged to find work for the three strike leaders who had been fired from their jobs. Once again, the unity of the Pamplona labor organizations was a key element in their victory over the target firm.[38]

December, 1974. As we have seen, strikes for purely economic motives attracted the participation of workers measured in tens of thousands. When a particular strike combined both political *and* economic protests, as in December 1974, the participation became much more massive. In this specific case, when the issues were both economic (inflation) and political (to show support for about 140 Basque political prisoners who had just begun a hunger strike), reports of the numbers of participants ranged from 150,000 to 200,000, depending on the bias of the observer. In Bilbao's industrial district alone, more than 50,000 workers stopped work, and the total reached 90,000 in Vizcaya province as a whole. More than 150 major enterprises in Bilbao closed completely, as well as most of the schools. Many of the most important industrial plants in the Basque region, such as General Electric, Babcock and Wilcox, Firestone, and Westinghouse, were paralyzed. Throughout the smaller industrial towns of Vizcaya and Guipúzcoa, such as Eibar and Durango, all business and commerce came to a halt, schools closed, and demonstrators marched the streets shouting slogans and carrying placards. In Guipúzcoa province, an estimated 80 percent of the industrial work force walked off their jobs. In Navarra, about 10,000 stopped work on the first day of the strike, and the number doubled the following day. There was little strike activity in Alava, however. Certainly one of the major reasons for the success of this strike was the combined effort of the labor unions and the still clandestine left political parties and insurgent groups, including ETA. The socialist party, PSOE, and its union, UGT, were active supporters of the strike, as were the communists and the Trotskyites. Interestingly, the PNV and ELA were not conspicuous in the pre-strike activity, although their absence did not seem to diminish the ardor of the Basque working class to join in the manifestations of their grievances against Madrid.[39] In all, most observers regarded the 1974 strike as the most significant challenge to Madrid since the unrest of 1962, and some even likened it to the miners' strikes in Asturias in 1934.

It would take me beyond the scope of this chapter to relate in great detail the story of labor unrest in the Basque region after Franco's death. For information about the political strikes during this period, the reader can turn to Chapter Ten. Work stoppages for economic reasons certainly have not declined in post-Franco Spain. From October 1976, until the middle of 1977, for example, a construction workers' strike in Vizcaya idled more than 30,000 workers and closed more than 370 of the largest building firms in the province. At stake were worker demands for an increase in wages of 8,000 pesetas per month (about $115), the establishment of a forty-hour week as the norm, payment of Social Security levies by the industry, 100 percent salary guarantee in case of accident, running water and sanitary services at all the construction sites, and others.[40] In March 1977, more than 70,000 Bilbao workers downed tools in support of 1,400 of their comrades who had been dismissed from their jobs by a radiator factory for striking to gain an increase in wages. The workers also took this opportunity to criticize the Suárez government for its decree-law on labor relations which apparently facilitated the firing of striking workers by the affected plant or business enterprise.[41]

For a number of years after Franco's death, as Spain groped for a new structure within which to organize its social and economic relationships, the Basque working class found itself torn between its class consciousness and its ethnic ties. The national bourgeoisie, represented through the PNV, argued that the best way to free Euzkadi from Spanish domination was through a united Basque front. After that occurred, socially progressive democratic forces within the Basque region could work out class conflicts. Others, such as the historian Beltza, asserted that the Basque working class must aid the forces of social revolution within Spain in order to democratize and socialize Spain first. Then, and only then, would Madrid be willing to free the Basque provinces. There are some political leaders who are struggling to find a way to combine these two approaches, to build institutions and social forces that will secure autonomy from Spain *and* a social revolution in Euzkadi, more or less simultaneously. Merely to articulate this goal is to recognize its formidable character; in Chapter Eleven, I discuss the new left *abertzale* parties that have emerged to fight for this objective. Increasingly, however, the fate of Basque nationalism became inextricably linked with the direction and the strength of the ethnic consciousness of the Basque working class.

PART THREE

Basque Nationalism after Franco

Chapter Ten

ETA AND AMNESTY: TWO CONTINUING PROBLEMS

General Franco, according to an old Spanish political joke, had on his desk two boxes for official papers and documents. One was labeled "Problems that Time Will Solve," and the other, "Problems that Time Has Solved." The Generalissimo's unusual approach to governance lay in shifting papers from the first box to the second.

Whatever truth there may be in this story, it certainly had no applicability to the two persistent and interlocked problems involved in Basque-Spanish relations in the two years following Franco's death. One of these issues was the role of ETA in post-Franco politics. While some members of ETA did attempt to return to non-violent political action, many others remained committed to violent struggle and began to resort to increasingly dramatic acts of disruption. The other issue concerned the promised amnesty for Basque political prisoners. Many Basque nationalists had hoped that Juan Carlos would pardon all their imprisoned colleagues immediately following Franco's death, thus clearing the slate of old grudges and hatreds and beginning to forge new relationships between Madrid and Euzkadi. While a large number of Basques were released in the first months after Juan Carlos' coronation, a significant group of ETA insurgents remained in prison through the period of the June 1977 elections. Their continued presence in jail increased the friction between Madrid and the Basque provinces despite genuine efforts at reconciliation on both sides.

One Year without Franco: November 1975 - November 1976

All during Franco's five-week illness, ETA had remained mysteriously quiet, as Spain waited anxiously for the end of an era. As soon as the dictator had passed away, however, ETA did not delay in throwing down the gauntlet to the new regime. Franco died on November 20, 1975, and Juan Carlos was crowned King of Spain on November 22. Two days later, on November 24, two gunmen armed with submachine guns shot to death Antonio Echeverría, the mayor of the Basque town of Oyarzún, 12 miles from San Sebastián. The mayor had been unpopular with Basque nationalists since the preceding September, when he had fired two city councilmen for participating in the protests against the execution of the five alleged terrorists, including two Basques, that was discussed in Chapter Seven. Police in San Sebastián asserted that ETA was responsible for the killing, but the identity of the gunmen was not immediately verified. Several days later, however, an ETA spokesman said in a Paris radio interview that his organization had killed Echeverría because "he was a police informer."

King Juan Carlos would not let himself be thrown off course by this provocative attack. The next day, November 25, he proclaimed a general amnesty for nearly all of Spain's political prisoners, a reduction of prison terms for many of the remainder, and a revocation of stiff fines levied against 30 Roman Catholic priests for criticizing the Franco regime. About 15,000 common criminals and political prisoners were expected to benefit from the terms of the king's amnesty. About 4,000 would be freed at once, and sentences reduced by twenty to thirty percent for the remainder, depending on their crimes. A government spokesman announced that about 1,000 political prisoners would be among those given immediate freedom. About 700 political prisoners would have their terms reduced significantly. However, about 250 to 350 persons being held for suspected terrorism would not be affected by the amnesty. Instead, the pardon would affect primarily those who had been arrested and tried for lesser crimes, such as distribution of illegal propaganda, or for "illicit association," i.e., belonging to separatist organizations or Basque nationalist political parties. Once announced, the amnesty program began to work almost immediately. By November 28, about 250 prisoners were already freed.

But the new year was welcomed by a series of fresh incidents linked to ETA insurgents. On January 15, 1976, four masked gunmen invaded the home of a Basque industrialist named Arrasate in the town of Berriz and kidnapped his twenty-six-year-old son, José Luis. After leaving a note demanding the payment of a ransom of $1.6 million, they fled in a hijacked taxi. However, the foundry of the senior Arrasate was too modest an industry to provide the capital for such a demand, and eventually ETA released the young man unharmed without payment of the ransom. The release came on February 17, only one week after ETA insurgents had shot and killed the mayor of the Vizcayan town of Galdácano.

Despite these incidents, the amnesty program moved ahead. By February 1, 1976, the government had released about 6,500 prisoners, including some 500 who had been convicted of political crimes. Thus, there remained in Spanish prisons about 8,500 prisoners, of whom an estimated 500 were there for political reasons; of these latter about 250 would still be unaffected by the amnesty. In addition, on February 6, the regime issued a decree abrogating fourteen articles of the August 28, 1975, Law on the Prevention of Terrorism, returning jurisdiction of terrorist crimes to civil courts and eliminating mandatory death sentences.

In March, however, the tenuous peace that had settled over the Basque provinces exploded in unrestrained street fighting between police and demonstrating workers and students. The violence began in Vitoria, the capital of Alava province, on March 3, a day proclaimed as a "day of struggle" by the city's work force. An estimated 80 percent of the city's workers participated in the mass demonstrations that had been called to support about 6,000 workers from seven firms that had been on strike for two months demanding pay increases. Even as the workers marched and demonstrated, the Spanish government was sending to the Cortes a bill to legalize such demonstrations. Nevertheless, police charged the striking workers with clubs, tear gas, and rubber bullets, finally firing live ammunition into the crowd. At least two people were killed and a dozen others wounded, according to early reports. In retaliation, the streets were barricaded, and demonstrators continued the fight against police after nightfall.

As so often happens in situations like this one, the violence not only continued but escalated during the following several days, as crowds flooded the Vitoria streets to protest the first killings, and were met with renewed police suppression. By the end of the fourth day, the death toll stood at five, and the Basque country prepared to mount a general strike to protest the killings and police beatings. On March 8, in what observers called the biggest general strike in Spain since the Civil War, thousands of workers marched through a number of Basque cities to manifest their discontent with the regime's handling of the Vitoria strike. Another demonstrator was killed by police in Bilbao, and workers began to erect barricades in the city's industrial suburbs to confront strike-breaking police and special urban violence units. According to Washington *Post* correspondent Miguel Acoca, the strikers numbered "about half a million,"[1] and at one point controlled most of Bilbao's industrial complex, including steel mills, chemical works, and a major shipyard. Eventually, the striking workers were dislodged by police firing live ammunition overhead. The city was reported to be like an armed camp, with police helicopters hovering overhead to monitor the movements of the strikers and demonstrators.[2] Typically, however, the strike slowly dwindled away, leaving little except animosities and renewed distrust on both sides of the Ebro River.

As the Basque country simmered in the aftermath of the March strikes and demonstrations, ETA continued to attract attention with its exploits and attacks. On April 4, a group of 29 prisoners, including 24 from ETA, escaped from the Segovia prison by digging a tunnel into the city sewer system. The mass escape came almost simultaneously with a government announcement of the arrest of some 50 members of ETA in a move intended to break the central cells of the organization and disrupt its activities. Of the Segovia escapees, only five managed to reach the safety of the French border. One was killed, another wounded, and the remaining 22 were captured as they tried to cross the Pyrenees. They were sent back to jail, mostly to punishment in solitary confinement; but a number were released during the following months as a part of the regime's amnesty program.[3]

The remainder of the spring was marked by several acts of bloodshed, as ETA and rightist vigilante groups traded attacks and reprisals. On April 7, an ETA insurgent group assassinated a conservative Basque industrialist politician named Angel Berazadi, and on May 3 a bomb explosion claimed the life of a member of the Guardia Civil. ETA again claimed responsibility for the attack. On May 9, right-wing terrorists fired on a Carlist rally near Pamplona, killing one and wounding three. The most provocative attack came in early June, as the Spanish parliament was considering two regime-sponsored bills to authorize the formation of political parties and to remove penalties for illegal political activities. On June 9, a group alleged to belong to ETA assassinated the leader of the Francoist "Movimiento" in the Basque town of Basauri, a suburb of Bilbao. The resultant uproar was enough to block approval in the Cortes of the penal reform bill, but the law permitting political parties was approved, albeit with language that effectively barred communist groups and separatist associations like ETA.[4]

By the summer of 1976, the reform program of King Juan Carlos had progressed to the point where he felt the freedom, and the necessity, to appoint a new government, headed by a premier who would be more cooperative and more effective in advancing the king's proposals against determined opposition in the Cortes and the armed forces. On July 3, Adolfo Suárez was named new premier and given a new Cabinet with which to work. While the Basque conservatives Areilza and Fraga Iribarne declined to serve in the new government, the Cabinet contained a number of younger and more liberal political figures, and so earned the Basque nationalists' support, at least for the near term. Suárez lost no time in proposing a far-reaching extension of the king's original amnesty decree. On July 17, Suárez asked the king to grant amnesty for all political and ideological crimes. As part of a much broader program aimed at reconciling all of the opposition groups in Spain, the Suárez proposal was intended to affect the fate of 334 of Spain's remaining 636 political prisoners. As before, those accused of terrorism or guerrilla activities (called *delitos de sangre,* or blood crimes, in the Spanish parlance) were not eligible for amnesty under the terms of the Suárez proposal. Coming symbolically on the eve of the fortieth anniversary of the outbreak of the Spanish Civil War, the reconciliation program and the pardon seemed crafted by the young, predominantly Christian Democrat Cabinet with the express purpose of eliminating the last vestiges of Francoism, less than one year after the dictator's death. So certain was the government of Juan Carlos' acceptance of its proposal that many of the concerned prisoners were released before the king's decision was formally announced. While few Basques were expected to be affected by the amnesty decree, the government took pains to point out that at least 500 former and current members of ETA had been allowed to return home from exile since the Cortes had approved the penal code reforms which in effect eliminated punishments for political crimes.[5]

Taking his time in the matter, the king nevertheless confirmed his acceptance of the Suárez proposition before the government left for Spain's customary August vacation. On July 30, King Juan Carlos granted amnesty to all political prisoners except those sentenced for terrorist acts. The regime's spokesman said that between 400 and 500 persons of the 650 political prisoners would be freed immediately. Predictably, the amnesty decision angered both right and left political forces. Rightists criticized the decision as reflecting softness on regional separatists. Basque nationalists, on the other hand, were dismayed at the king's continued unwillingness to pardon those who had been convicted of taking part in any acts that "caused death or endangered the life of any person." Many of them felt that the first such criminal act had been Francisco Franco's military uprising against the constitutional regime of the Second Republic in 1936, and that all alleged crimes since that date should be pardoned and forgotten. It was obvious, however, that the growing restiveness of Spain's political right constituted real limits to how far and how fast Suárez and the king could go in their steps toward reconciliation with the Basques.[6]

August and September are traditionally the months for festivals and merrymaking in the Basque provinces. One of the centers of such festivities is the beautiful city of Fuenterrabía, on the Bidasoa River just across from France. On the evening of September 8, at about 9:30 pm, groups of youths were marching and chanting patriotic Basque songs when the demonstration began to take a more intensely political turn. Shouts of *"Presoak Kalera"* ("Prisoners on the street") and *"Amnistía"* were heard. At once, police began to arrive in large numbers to disperse the crowd. In the commotion, rubber bullets and tear gas were used, and shots were heard in the crowd. In a narrow blind alley where he had been pursued by the police, a young twenty-four-year-old Basque named Jésus Zabala was shot dead. Eye witnesses claimed that he had been killed by a police officer who was hurried away from the scene by his fellow policemen.

Almost instantly, the dry tinder that was Guipúzcoa threatened to go up in flames over the Zabala incident. By midnight of the 8th, nearly the entire city of Fuenterrabía knew of the incident and extra police had to be brought in to suppress new demonstrations. The following day, September 9, the town council of Fuenterrabía met in extraordinary session to condemn the killing and the other acts of violence by the police, and to hand in their resignations unanimously. All over the city, shops and factories began to close in a spontaneous show of protest. Attempts were made to hold protest demonstrations in Fuenterrabía, but permission was denied by the provincial governor. The strike began to spread to other towns in Guipúzcoa. On the 10th, the socialist *Koordinadora Abertzale Sozialista* (KAS) and the Basque union ELA proclaimed a general strike that began slowly, but gathered momentum as it moved through the other Basque provinces. On the 11th, ceremonies were held in Fuenterrabía and Zabala's home town, Irún, to commemorate the man's death, although the police authorities would not allow Zabala's body to be removed from their jurisdiction to the family's home for burial. Police were called in to disperse these demonstrations and ceremonies. Throughout Guipúzcoa, town councils passed resolutions of solidarity with the position taken by their colleagues in Fuenterrabía, and several mayors and other officials resigned their posts in protest.

On September 11, strikes erupted all over the Basque provinces, in protest not only against the Zabala killing but against Suárez' decision to postpone further consideration of plans for regional autonomy until after the provinces had settled down politically. In Bilbao the strike paralyzed the major factories and shipyards; six people were injured by police fire. On the 13th, 300,000 workers joined the strike, and were suppressed by police with tear gas and rubber bullets. A few workers returned to work the next day, but at least 75,000 remained on strike in Bilbao. On the 19th, ten Basque prisoners in the Burgos prison began a hunger strike against the oppressive conditions of the prison, as well as against the suppression of Basque rights of dissent and expression in the current disorders. It was at this time that Spanish Interior Minister Martín Villa ordered police to tolerate the public display of the Basque flag, the *ikurriña,* and to show restraint in their use of firearms in the Basque provinces. These decisions, however well intentioned, were too little and too late. On September 27, another general strike was called for the Basque provinces, and this "day of struggle" brought more than 700,000 people out on the streets across the Basque provinces. Basque relations with Madrid had not been worse since Franco's death.[7]

If the source of upheaval in September was police suppression of nationalist demonstrators, in October violence took an even uglier turn, as a sensational ETA assassination was answered by rightist mob disorders, angry demonstrations from neo-Francoists, and calls for military seizure of power. On October 4, the President of the Provincial Assembly of Guipúzcoa and member of the Council of the Realm, Juan de Araluce, was machinegunned to death on the streets of San Sebastián in the middle of crowded mid-day traffic. Four bodyguards were also killed, and ten by-standers were wounded by the automatic weapons fire. The assassins escaped in an automobile. San Sebastián police officials blamed ETA for the crime.

The Araluce assassination was the most sensational since the Basque separatist group murdered Prime Minister Carrero Blanco in December 1973. Araluce was not only a senior political official of Guipúzcoa province but also a member of the Cortes and a trusted advisor of King Juan Carlos. Premier Suárez met with his Cabinet in an emergency afternoon session following the killings to consider measures to deal with this latest incident of presumed ETA violence. Later, Interior Minister Martín Villa appeared on nationwide television to assure the people that military units would be deployed to the Basque region to search for the Araluce killers. He stressed, however, that the government would not yet declare a "state of exception" or martial law in Guipúzcoa, even though there was considerable unrest in the province. He also emphasized that the reform program of the king and Suárez would go ahead on schedule despite the ETA assault.

Significantly, no one in a responsible position in Spanish or Basque politics attempted to justify or rationalize the Araluce assassination. The Spanish right wing said it was an example of the "accelerating social deterioration" since Franco's death. Basque moderates condemned the act as unnecessary in the reform atmosphere of post-Franco Spain. Even the Basque left criticized the attack as "adventurous," and said that it risked provoking Madrid into even harsher countermeasures. From about this date on, one can begin to sense a decline in public support for ETA among even the more radical Basque socialist forces, a trend that was to be completed some eight months later with the kidnapping and assassination of Javier de Ybarra.

The day following the killing of Araluce, October 5, bands of rightist demonstrators went on a rampage in San Sebastián following the emotional funeral of the five victims of the attack. Demonstrators fired shots into the air, smashed shop windows, stopped buses and dragged passengers to the street where they were beaten severely, entered movie houses and forced patrons to leave, and caused a great deal of destruction to bars and coffee houses. One report said that at least ten persons were injured in this rightist reprisal. The violence began as a crowd of more than 1,000 rightists marched through San Sebastián streets shouting "The Army to power," and "Assassins to the wall." The crowd also demonstrated against amnesty for Basque political prisoners. Police reportedly made no effort to control the violence of the neo-Francoists. One week later, the right-wing vigilante violence spread to the small festival town of Durango in Vizcaya, where angry bands set upon groups of citizens celebrating the local fiesta and beat them with clubs and other weapons. Beating incidents went on throughout the week of October 11, and caused the municipal government of Durango to call on police to bring the rightist violence under control immediately.

Meanwhile, in Madrid, political pressure from the right mounted as the Suárez regime seemed unable to meet the challenge of the Araluce killing with assurance and firmness. On October 5, a coalition of six right-wing political parties, all headed by former Franco ministers (including Fraga Iribarne) issued a statement warning of the "progressive crumbling of authority" in the country. On October 7, a group of ultraright civilians called on the armed forces to seize power in a coup against the Suárez government. On October 13, a ceremony to mourn Araluce's death was held in Madrid. One of those in attendance was Lt. Gen. Carlos Iniesta, a former head of the Guardia Civil and a Civil War hero, who, at age 68, was putting up a stout resistance to the Suárez attempt to retire all Army officers at 70. As he emerged from the church, Iniesta was cheered by a large crowd, which chanted slogans urging him to seize power. The press of the crowd was so great that Iniesta had to be protected on his way to his waiting car.[8]

The first phase of the post-Franco era came to an end almost one year to the day after the dictator's death. On November 18, the Cortes approved the Suárez plan for constitutional reform to return Spain to parliamentary democracy. The following day, Suárez issued a decree convoking the national referendum that would allow the Spanish people to vote for or against the proposed reform plan. The date for the referendum was set for December 15, less than a month away. After some

37 years in power, Franco had built so little of lasting strength that it was all swept away in little less than a year, with surprisingly little opposition from hard-line conservatives or neo-Francoists.

At the end of the first year without Franco, it was possible to strike something of a balance sheet on the fate of the Basque political prisoners and exiles. As of November 1976, a total of 848 passports had been issued to Basques living in exile, and most of those who could return had already crossed the border into Euzkadi-Sur. Even a relatively large number of former ETA militants (the government claimed nearly 500) had been allowed to return to Spain. Nevertheless, the Basque government remained in exile in Paris, from which President Leizaola declared that he would not return until the Basque provinces had been allowed to select his replacement in a free election. According to one report, there remained at least 500 Basques living in exile who would return if allowed to by Madrid.[9]

Of far greater significance, however, than the Basques still in exile were the some 150 Basques who remained in Spanish prisons for political crimes. In late November 1976, a number of Basque nationalists formed provincial Pro-Amnesty Associations in each of the four Basque provinces in order to bring pressure to bear on the Suárez regime to free the remaining prisoners. Their slogan was *"Etxera Gobonetarako,"* or "Home for Christmas." In addition to carrying their message to Madrid, the Pro-Amnesty Associations toured major western European capitals such as Paris and Brussels to conduct public hearings and press conferences to publicize their grievances. At home, rallies were held to drive home the public's support for a prompt and total amnesty, as well as to raise money to aid families of those still in prison. Finally, as their comrades emerged from prison, the Pro-Amnesty Associations provided them with medical aid to help correct some of the conditions that they suffered after so many years of harsh prison life. These Pro-Amnesty Associations soon became important actors in the drama of the Basque political prisoners.

The Development of ETA: 1976-1977

About one year before Franco's death, in October of 1974, ETA had gone through still another ideological and tactical split. One branch of ETA remained fully committed to armed struggle and argued that a single organization could not undertake political violence and mobilization of the masses simultaneously. Thus, this wing became known as ETA-*militar,* or simply ETA-m, for short. This group, which of necessity remained quite small, became a self-styled revolutionary vanguard force whose mission it was to carry out the more daring and risky attacks against the symbols of Spain and of capitalist exploitation. The leaders of ETA-m realized, however, that once they began this new series of *acciónes cruentas,* or especially violent incidents, they and their associates would become the targets of renewed repression by Madrid. They wished to isolate themselves from the mass mobilization efforts of their less radical comrades, so they determined to form two entirely separate organizations to carry on what should be two separate functions. After some months, ETA-m had grown to about twenty well-trained insurgents, many of whom had been instructed in the art of revolutionary warfare in Algeria. They had established ties with the more radical insurgent groups in Europe and Latin America, including the Provisional wing of the Irish Republican Army, the Bader-Meinhof Gang in West Germany, and the Tupamaros in Uruguay. Their leader was José María Beñarán Ordeñana, whose military pseudonym was "Argala." The "Argala" group was reputed to have been responsible for the 1973 kidnapping of Pamplona industrialist Felipe Huarte, the assassination of Carrero Blanco, also in 1973, and the October 1976 killings of Araluce and his bodyguards in San Sebastián. In November 1976, members of "Argala" were believed to be in Madrid to join forces with the famous international terrorist "Carlos," whose presence in Spain was confirmed by Interpol and by French security agencies. Thus, ETA-m, or the "Argala" group, belonged to the trans-national network of insurgent groups that spans the world from Latin America and Europe to the Middle East, Africa and East Asia.[10]

The other wing of ETA adopted quite a different style of revolutionary struggle. This group, which became known as ETA-*político-militar,* or simply ETA-pm, felt that there was a need for an organization that devoted itself to building support for social revolution among the working masses but which could also resort to armed action if the need arose. In fact, such an organization was not one single group, but two, each of which attended to its specific functions within a single ideological and strategic framework. ETA-pm needed the support and active membership of two groups of activists. One group, called *"legales,"* were members who continued in their chosen professions and who carried out organizing tasks on a sporadic basis so long as they did not become known to the police (*fichados* in ETA terminology). The second group, much smaller and more clandestine, consisted of those ETA members who were already known to the police and thus unable to lead relatively normal lives. This latter group carried out armed actions as necessary. Originally, ETA-pm developed under the leadership of Eduardo Moreno Bergareche, known as "Pertur." When Pertur was kidnapped and presumed killed in July 1976, allegedly by a Spanish neo-fascist group operating in France, leadership of ETA-pm fell to Miguel Angel Apalategui Ayerbe, whose political pseudonym was "Apala." The Apala group was reputed to be responsible for the assassination of industrialist Angel Berazadi, but the group has denied the accusation.[11] It is also believed that ETA-pm organized the Segovia jail escape, in which about two dozen ETA comrades tried to achieve their freedom.

The death of Franco and the progressive democratization of the Spanish political arena opened wider the breach between ETA-m and ETA-pm. Increasingly, the groups disagreed not only on the necessity for armed struggle and the need to organize the working masses, but also on the role of the party in the fledgling Spanish electoral process and on the acceptability of forming alliances with other parties. In June 1976, ETA-pm issued a pamphlet stating their belief that it was acceptable for them to establish ties with political groups that had revolutionary strategies that were nation-wide, that is, that spanned all the Spanish provinces, and that were not restricted to only Euzkadi. The group apparently had in mind such *sucursalista* organizations as the *Movimiento Comunista de Euzkadi,* or the Carlist EKA. Anything that contributed to the eventual success of a socialist revolution in an independent Euzkadi was acceptable to them, even if it meant collaboration in the near term with parties that also operated in Spain. ETA-m naturally disagreed sharply with this position.

In the summer of 1976, ETA-pm held the Seventh Assembly of the organization in Biarritz, France. The outcome of the meeting was that ETA-pm moved closer to the formation of a conventional political party directed at organizing the working masses, while increasingly ETA-m would be left to carry out the armed actions against police and capitalism. As published subsequently in the group's magazine *Berriak,* in September, the new workers' revolutionary organization would be based on four cardinal points:

1. ETA defined itself as an organization dedicated to the independence of Euzkadi, which would be formed in the framework of a Reunified Basque State.

2. ETA defined itself as a revolutionary organization at the service of the working class. It proposed the conquest of power of the popular classes led by the workers, the destruction of the oligarchy as a class, and the installation of a socialist state, including the socialization of all means of production.

3. ETA-pm proposed further a strategy to be worked out within bourgeois democracy, but which would base its power on the development of the potential of the "autonomous organisms" of the Basque popular classes. (What this means apparently is that ETA-pm would depend not just on a conventional political party structure, but would attempt to involve workers, students, intellectuals, and other groups that perceived a need to achieve independence for Euzkadi.)

4. At the organizational level, ETA-pm assumed the principles of democratic centralism guaranteed by a permanent internal debate on ideological and political questions.

Through the last months of 1976 and the first three or four months of 1977, there was considerable movement within the Basque left, as its leaders worked to bring about a unified and coherent socialist and working class political party. The core of this effort was in the Basque Socialist Coordinating Group, known as KAS (*Koordinadora Abertzale Sozialista*), which was founded principally by Paco Letamendía, who had been one of the defense lawyers for the Burgos trial. The KAS consisted of both labor unions and political parties and advocated independence for Euzkadi, socialism within the region, and a reunification of the French and Spanish zones of the Basque nation. In addition, of course, KAS also demanded immediate and total amnesty for all political prisoners and free and open elections in Spain. The relationship between KAS and the various branches of ETA remains unclear. ETA-*militar* was never a member of KAS, although its members maintained a liaison with the socialist party, and often sent observers to its meetings. ETA-pm was officially a member at least until the late winter or early spring of 1977, when apparently its place was taken by a conventional electorally oriented party known as EIA (*Euskal Iraultzarako Alderdia,* or Basque Revolutionary Party). Some observers felt that EIA was merely ETA-pm transformed into a political party; others thought that it was the political wing of ETA-pm that had split off and renamed itself in an effort to achieve legitimacy. Letamendía discounted all of these rumors and declared that EIA was a completely different organization whose membership was drawn from both the old ETA ranks and totally new groups.[12]

There was no doubt that some former members of ETA-pm wanted very much to leave their clandestine and dangerous life and join the legitimate political arena.[13] The diehards in ETA-*militar,* however, were determined to continue their commitment to revolutionary armed struggle as long as they could physically do so. And there were instances in which key members of ETA-pm wanted to leave the armed struggle but found they could not because the police arrested and charged them as soon as they dared to reappear in normal political settings. These complicated personal and organizational issues converged in the summer and fall of 1977 to make much more difficult the search for an acceptable middle ground between Basques and Spaniards.

The Pro-Amnesty Campaign and Assassination: November 1976 - November 1977

On December 11, a group of four to six gunmen (witnesses' versions differed on this point) armed with small submachineguns entered the office of Antonio María Oriol y Urquijo in Madrid and forced him into a waiting car. Thus began one of the most dramatic kidnappings in recent Spanish history. Oriol, president of the prestigious Council of State and a top advisor to the king, remained a prisoner until February 11, 1977, two months later, when he was rescued in a police assault of the Madrid apartment where he was being held.[14] A few hours before Oriol was rescued, the Spanish government also rescued a senior military official, Lt. Gen. Emilio Villaescusa, president of the Supreme Military Tribunal, who had been kidnapped on January 24.

Although early reports indicated that Oriol had been kidnapped by members of ETA, these were incorrect, and it was soon learned that he had been seized by a mysterious Spanish leftist group known as GRAPO (*Grupos de Resistencia Antifascista Primero de Octubre,* or Antifascist Resistance Groups of the First of October), so-called because of their origins in an October 1, 1975, shooting that left dead four police officers in Madrid. Little was known of GRAPO except that it was a clandestine revolutionary force on the far left of the spectrum.[15] Rumor had it that foreign subversive agencies, either the Russian KGB or the American CIA, were actively supporting the group. In any case, these events would have had little to do with Basque nationalism except for one thing: they tended to harden Spanish public opinion and the Suárez government in their resistance to further concessions in the amnesty program and the early release of convicted Basque terrorists.

At first, the kidnappers of Oriol had demanded the release of fifteen political prisoners as the quid pro quo for the return of their victim. (This demand was subsequently raised to 200 terrorists, or virtually all of the prisoners then in Spanish jails for politically related crimes. Not surprisingly, the Spanish government never really considered meeting this later demand.) Among the list of fifteen prisoners were eight who had either been members of ETA or were somehow connected with one of ETA's alleged crimes. Three of the prisoners had been among those convicted at the Burgos trial for the assassination of police official Manzanas: Francisco Javier Izco, José Mari Dorronsoro, and Mario Onaindia. Four of the prisoners had been associated in some way with the assassination of Carrero Blanco in 1973: Eva Forrest, Iñáki Múgica, Jose Pérez Beotegui, and Antonio Durán. The eighth prisoner, José Antonio Garmendía Artola, was serving a lengthy sentence for killing a member of the Guardia Civil. Thus, all eight Basques on the GRAPO list had been convicted of the so-called "blood crimes," and thereby would not be included in the Suárez amnesty proposal of the preceding July.[16]

The combination of the Guipúzcoa riots of September, the Araluce killings in October and the Oriol and Villaescusa kidnappings in December and January meant that the Suárez government had been under severe pressure from the left almost constantly for nearly six months. In addition, the Spanish political right, particularly the neo-Francoist forces and the older military officers, were clearly pressing on the government to toughen up its stance on Basque nationalists, as well as other sources of civil disorder. The effect of these cross pressures was to complicate considerably the progress of the amnesty program. On the one hand, Suárez was becoming less and less interested in conceding any more to moderate Basque nationalists. Contrary to the requests of the Basque Pro-Amnesty Committees, there was no amnesty by Christmas of 1976. In fact, from the Oriol kidnapping until the following March, there would be no general extension of the July amnesty decree, and only the slightest official inclination to broaden the effects of the decree: prisoners were released on a case by case basis. This policy caused the amnesty program to move with glacial slowness. The Basques became very frustrated and even more disillusioned by Madrid's approach to settling their grievances. Under these conditions, relations between the two contending parties could only worsen.[17]

It is worth considering at this point the various measures that the Basques invoked to put pressure on Suárez to move more quickly toward total amnesty. These measures involved a combination of public demonstrations that tended at times to become rather disorderly and even violent, some conventional pressure group activities that depended on propaganda and "consciousness raising," and private discussions in which the Basque representatives attempted in effect to hold hostage the coming elections if their prisoners were not released promptly.

According to some observers, the Spanish government was shaken by the low degree of support in the Basque country for the December referendum. In Vizcaya and Guipúzcoa provinces, about half of the eligible voters abstained from voting in the December 15 referendum. No doubt the reasons for such opposition were varied. Some conservatives probably opposed the proposal because of its radical nature; others, because it did not go far enough. The Pro-Amnesty Associations in the four provinces campaigned hard against the referendum, on the grounds that a large abstention would send a message to Madrid that the Basques wanted their prisoners freed down to the last remaining man or woman, and they wanted them home by Christmas. The Associations advocated abstention rather than a "No" vote for two reasons: "No" votes are customarily very rare in Spanish referenda, and the large number of apathetic or passive abstentions could be added to the protest or active abstentions to make a stronger argument in Madrid.

The Pro-Amnesty Associations also tried to influence informed public opinion in the more liberal countries in Western Europe. In December about a dozen well known Basque political figures, intellectuals and artists visited Brussels and Amberes, in Belgium, to meet with individuals and groups that were influential in international human rights activities. There were major meetings with the League of Human Rights, with Amnesty International, and with the League of Oppressed Peoples. Interspersed with these meetings were a number of public expositions or "teach-ins," marked by scholarly discussions of the special nature of the Basque problem in Spain, as well as by films that dealt with pertinent topics. At the end of the marathon of meetings and conferences, however, the Basque delegation returned to their homes with little to show for their efforts except a resolution introduced in the Belgian parliament expressing Belgium's support for the cause of human rights in Spain.[18]

As Christmas neared, the efforts and activities of the Pro-Amnesty Associations intensified. An attempt was made to convene a "Congress of Families of Prisoners, Ex-Prisoners and Political Exiles of the Peoples and Nationalities of the Spanish State" in San Sebastián, but the provincial governor denied the request to meet, giving as his reason the upheaval surrounding the Oriol kidnapping. (The Congress was to request permission to meet at least twice more in the following months, but these requests were also denied.) On December 23, about twenty persons took over the cathedral of Bayonne, in the French Basque region, to express their discontent with the slow progress of amnesty in Spain. At 9:00 that evening, police finally persuaded them to leave, and they were removed to the Bayonne police station, warned, and released. The strikers spent that evening in another church, and returned to Bayonne the following morning to attend Mass and to continue their vigil for amnesty. The leader of the group, the former Basque Cabinet minister Telesforo Monzón, had cabled Basque President-in-Exile Leizaola to ask him to join the sit-in, but the latter, finding himself in Bayonne that day, declared that he would go to church to confess but not to see the strikers.

In Bilbao, about fifty demonstrators took over the office of the Bishop of the Diocese and engaged in a hunger strike until December 23. At that time, they were dislodged by local police, and had to move to another location, where they continued their protest through Christmas Eve. On December 23, the Pro-Amnesty Association of Bilbao sent a letter to the French government protesting the miserable living conditions suffered by the Basque prisoners who were at that time under imprisonment on the French prison island of Yeu. There were a number of demonstrations across Vizcaya province during the day and early evening of December 24, but local police or Guardia Civil succeeded in dispersing the demonstrators without major incident. In San Sebastián, however, the smaller demonstrations of December 23 were broken up by considerable police violence, and true to form, the following day there were even larger marches to protest the police tactics of the previous evening. The worst incidents took place in Pamplona, where the Christmas Eve celebrations turned into massive political demonstrations, with the celebrants shouting patriotic, pro-amnesty slogans during the march. This demonstration was broken up by police with tear gas and rubber bullets, producing at least one seriously wounded demonstrator who suffered a fractured skull from the rubber projectiles.[19] On January 6, the demonstrations spread to Madrid, where a number of pro-amnesty demonstrators locked themselves inside churches to express their solidarity with the Basque protestors. That same day, the church sit-in tactic was used again in Bilbao, Pamplona, and several other Basque cities. Foreign observers saw a gathering momentum in the pro-amnesty movement, and there began to be fears that the amnesty issue would spoil Suárez' bid for elections in mid-year.

Sensing the government's desire to avoid making amnesty an issue in the coming elections, the negotiating committee of the opposition parties, the *Comisión de los Nueve,* began to press Suárez to declare total amnesty. If there were no amnesty, they said, the opposition parties would boycott the elections and deprive them of any legitimacy they might enjoy. One of the most important meetings between the four-man amnesty sub-committee of the commission and Suárez took place on January 11. According to the report published later in *La Actualidad Española,* the Basque representative on the commission, Julio Jaúregui, made an emphatic plea that the amnesty problem be definitely resolved before the elections. Implicit in his remarks was the suggestion that the PNV would find it most difficult to participate in the elections if the amnesty matter had not been cleared up by June. Once the PNV had agreed to participate in the activities and negotiations of the

Comisión de los Nueve, it had compromised itself in the eyes of many of its adherents, and it could not leave the negotiations now without a major concession from Suárez, namely, an amnesty program that freed each and every Basque political prisoner without regard to the nature of his alleged crime.

Suárez for his part proposed a solution to the amnesty issue that involved a complicated two-step formula, made necessary by Suárez' decision not to seek any new and broader amnesty decree similar to but more extensive than that of the previous July. Suárez based his proposal on the recent dissolution of Franco's political crimes court, the Tribunal of Public Order, which had been approved in a meeting of the Cabinet on December 30.[20] Since the decision to dissolve the Tribunal had also transferred all of its cases to ordinary civilian jurisdiction, Suárez proposed a re-hearing of each case in which the Tribunal had sent to jail a prisoner still behind bars. In the course of these re-hearings, the new court would be advised of the Crown's desire to amplify its July decree without actually issuing a new amnesty announcement. It would be hoped, then, that the prisoners who had been jailed by the Tribunal would be released by the more lenient civilian court, and the objective of total amnesty would be achieved without actually proclaiming a new amnesty program.

This policy would leave unaffected a still large number of prisoners awaiting trial who would have to be tried by the ordinary courts that had replaced the Tribunal of Public Order. But Suárez hoped that he could grant to these men and women some sort of temporary or provisional freedom which would permit them to walk the streets freely by the time of the elections. They would still have to return to be tried by the new court system, but again a more lenient outcome was to be expected. There thus arose a new element in the amnesty issue, a distinction between the "old" prisoners, those whose cases had been tried by the Tribunal of Public Order and who could be freed under the terms of a more liberal adjudication process, and the "new" prisoners, whose cases had not come up before the Tribunal had been abolished and who would still have to stand trial under the Tribunal's replacement court.[21]

A few days after the Suárez meeting with the amnesty

sub-committee of the *Comisión de los Nueve,* other elements of the compromise proposal began to appear. The government now affirmed its intention to have fully 95 percent of the "old" cases judged and pardoned by the time of the Basque national holiday Aberri Eguna, which was to fall on April 10. Nevertheless, there still remained about a dozen prisoners whose cases were so inflammatory to Spanish public opinion that the government simply could not tolerate the idea of allowing these people back on the streets as free men and women. The solution for this tiny handful of political prisoners was to grant them freedom only on the assumption that they would go into exile, strictly prohibited from ever returning to Spanish territory. In greater or lesser degree, then, this was the compromise amnesty program that Suárez proposed, and which would constitute the government's attempt to placate Basque opinion and secure PNV participation in the June elections.[22]

As winter turned to spring, there were renewed rumblings from the Basque provinces. A year earlier, in March 1976, there had been several days of violence in the workers' strike in Vitoria. In 1977, memories of the strike would return in various ways to continue to plague the efforts to improve Basque-Spanish relations. In Vitoria itself, thousands of persons marched on the first anniversary of the strike to commemorate the deaths of their five comrades under police fire. Hardly had the marchers begun to assemble than army and police jeeps and trucks began to appear to surround the demonstrators and to impede their progress. Through numerous loudspeaker messages, the marchers were advised to leave the area and to discontinue the demonstration. One of the leaders of the march addressed the crowd and urged them to follow the police instructions, and to leave quietly now that they had demonstrated to the watching public their concern for the state of the workers' rights in Alava. No sooner had he finished his request than the police attacked with tear gas and rubber bullets, dispersing the crowd in a matter of minutes. Several score of the marchers succeeded in escaping only by seeking refuge in the cathedral. The next day, there was a ceremonial funeral for the five fallen strikers from the previous year's march. Again, thousands of demonstrators appeared and the streets of Vitoria were filled to overflowing. The cathedral was the scene of a maximum audience. Fifty-seven priests participated in the Mass. That evening, a number of union leaders were arrested, and the crowds again jammed the streets in protest. Late into the evening, police roamed the city to close off any attempt at renewed demonstrations; isolated shots were heard throughout the city. Despite the tense and at times violent circumstances of the demonstrations, no one was killed and there were only about two dozen reported wounds connected with the incident.[23]

Events of the next several days occurred with such speed that they tended to pile one upon another in the public consciousness. On Saturday, March 5, the Spanish government announced that henceforth the workers would enjoy the right to strike, a freedom they had been denied throughout the entire Franco period. In the same announcement, the Suárez government also affirmed its promise to develop a third amnesty decree over the next few weeks. The next day, Sunday, March 6, thousands of persons turned out in Pamplona and San Sebastián to demand amnesty for all political prisoners. In Pamplona, police fired rubber bullets and tear gas at the demonstrators, who responded with rocks, and smashed windows and disrupted traffic.[24]

On the following Tuesday, March 8, in mid-afternoon, a Guardia Civil truck patrolling the streets of San Sebastián stopped for a routine search a Renault carrying three Basque youths. As the Guardia Civil troops were examining the youths' documentation, they noticed a suspicious package inside the car and demanded to see its contents. One of the youths produced from the package a 9 mm Browning automatic pistol. At this point, according to the Guardia Civil, the youth began to fire at them, an act denied by the accused. In any case, the police opened fire, killing the two other occupants of the car. As it turned out, all three were convicted members of ETA, one of whom had just recently been released from jail on the condition that he go into exile in France.

By late afternoon, the rumors began to fly through San Sebastián, and nearly five thousand persons joined a march to protest the police action in killing the two ETA members. On Thursday, March 10, the city of San Sebastián went on a general strike. Not a single shop or store could be found open in the entire city. More than 34,000 businesses closed their doors. The government estimated that about 85,000 workers had joined the strike; the Pro-Amnesty Association of San Sebastián estimated the figure at 120,000. By mid-day, the crowd had been swelled by workers from nearby cities who had walked off the job to join the demonstration. Barricades were erected, and the protestors made ready to confront the police. Despite the repeated police charges with tear gas and rubber bullets, the workers and students controlled the streets throughout the afternoon. Amazingly, there were no deaths and few major injuries, although there were scores of minor wounds from the day-long skirmishes. The civil governor of Guipúzcoa appealed to the people to remain calm, and the province's Pro-Amnesty Association condemned the Guardia Civil and called for the Spanish government to withdraw the Guardia from the Basque provinces to restore calm to the region.[25]

The next day, March 11, the Spanish government announced that it would soon be issuing a new amnesty proclamation that would either free completely or shorten the sentences of all of the country's remaining political prisoners. According to the announcement, there were still about 170 persons in Spanish jails for political crimes. Under the terms of the decree, all would be released except those convicted of having killed, injured, or kidnapped for political motives. The sentences of these remaining few would be reduced by one-fourth. Predictably, the response of the Pro-Amnesty Associations was profoundly negative. Total amnesty was what they had requested; anything less was completely unacceptable. All Basques would have to be released for them to abandon their demands and actions. The Pro-Amnesty movement also began to criticize the Basque Nationalist Party for its participation in the negotiations of the *Comisión de los Nueve* with Suárez, and by implication for accepting the Suárez compromise position. At the PNV Assembly meeting in Pamplona on March 28, the speech by Julio Jaúregui, the party's representative on the commission, was met with boos and a generally hostile attitude, and several delegates to the Assembly walked out during the address. Jaúregui did not make things any better when he defended his actions by pointing out that of the 103 Basques still in prison (49 awaiting trial and 54 already convicted), none was an affiliate of the PNV. These remarks were taken by non-PNV members as confirmation that the party was interested only in seeking the release of their own members, while more radical ETA prisoners could remain in jail.[26]

There was yet more blood to be spilled in the Basque country before the March political violence had run its course. On March 13, a group of ETA militants attacked a Guardia Civil patrol, killing one and wounding two others. "Our action," read an ETA communiqué, "is an act of response" made necessary by the Spanish government, "which does nothing but make promises and half way concessions, such as the pardon decrees of this most recent Council of Ministers [the Cabinet], but which refuses to suppress the fascist institutions and promulgate the measures necessary to reach a true democratization. . . . It is first of all a response, but also a warning. We have said that we do not wish violence, but we see ourselves forced to use it. If the total amnesty is conceded immediately, this response will be stopped, as we have already announced." With these words, ETA put the Suárez government on notice of its intent to join the amnesty struggle with the weapons at its disposal: kidnapping and assassination. The full impact of that threat was soon to be felt.

On March 14, the fourth death in the recent wave of killings occurred in San Sebastián, when a young Basque named Luis Aristizabal was hit in the head by a rubber bullet while he was inside a moving automobile. Aristizabal was in no way connected with the demonstrations that were going on about him, and his death was clearly an accident. Yet the reaction of Guipúzcoa was strongly negative. Again, the Pro-Amnesty Associations called for the removal of the Guardia Civil from the Basque country. In the resort town of Zarauz, a demonstrating crowd of more than one thousand was blocked and dispersed by a force of Guardia Civil troops firing rubber bullets into the midst of the demonstrators. In the town of Mondragón there was a funeral service for the dead Guardia Civil member, and the rightist crowd that gathered outside the cathedral chanted "Franco, Franco, Franco" and "Death to ETA." Finally, following the funeral in San Sebastián for Aristizabal, a crowd of more than 6,000 marched silently through the city until they were blocked by the police and dispersed once again with rubber bullets and tear gas.[27]

While the violence in San Sebastián drew considerable attention and caused much turmoil, what could have been an even more dramatic rupture of the social order was narrowly missed when, on March 6, the rightist former Minister of Interior Manuel Fraga Iribarne altered his usual Sunday schedule and thus avoided an ambush that had been set for him by persons alleged to be ETA militants. Apparently, ETA had chosen that particular day to assassinate Fraga because of the conservative political figure's role in suppressing the Vitoria strike of a year earlier. A speech at a political luncheon lasted longer than he had planned, however, and Fraga was unable to return to his apartment for his mid-day meal and stroll through a near-by park where the assassins allegedly were expecting him. The incident only came to light a week later when several bags filled with dynamite were discovered on a station platform near Pamplona. Together with the explosives were a series of papers describing how the Fraga assassination was to take place. The papers allegedly named as the leader of the group an ETA figure whose military pseudonym was "Andoni." Police alleged that the papers identified as Andoni's chief in France the leader of ETA-pm, Apala. More than two weeks later, in late March, a squad of four persons carried out a series of bank robberies in Madrid which netted them nearly $50,000. The fingerprints left by one of the members of the group tied them closely to former ETA-pm members. Some observers felt that these clues indicated that either ETA-pm had been dissolved, with the politically inclined members tending toward the *abertzale* socialist parties, and the military figures remaining to carry on armed struggle; or, that ETA-pm had decided to go on the offensive once again, and to abandon parliamentary means of gaining Basque autonomy. In either instance, the developments indicated that the next several months would be difficult ones indeed.[28]

Meanwhile, through the last weeks of March and the first ten days of April, the amnesty program worked its way slowly through the remaining Basque prisoners. Although the Suárez proposal had seemed simple and efficient in principle, in practice there remained many steps that had to be completed before the prisoners actually saw the light of day as free men and women. In some cases, the prisoners had been convicted by military courts, and they theoretically were not affected by the amnesty, since it dealt only with the now defunct Tribunal of Public Order. The military courts were extremely reluctant to turn over their records to the ordinary courts to permit the re-hearing of the cases, so the prisoners remained behind bars until the bureaucrats had decided how to handle their cases. In several instances, the prisoners were pardoned of one crime and about to leave the prison, when it was discovered that they had another crime charged against them for which they had not yet been pardoned, so they were returned to their cells for the second amnesty. Outside the infamous Carabanchel prison in Madrid a crowd of about two hundred Basques gathered every day to wait for more of their comrades to emerge from the jail. Regardless of the weather or the time of day (many Basques were released at midnight of the day ordered for their freedom, in order to make them wait until the last possible moment in prison), these people waited patiently to cheer for the prisoners who emerged and to chant and shout slogans to reassure those who remained inside the prison's walls. Yet at the rate of only two or three per day, it was impossible for the Spanish government to release virtually all of the Basques by the time of Aberri Eguna, on April 10.[29] Perhaps because of this failure, Madrid declined to give the Basques permission to celebrate their national holiday. Despite the government's warnings, many thousands of Basques converged on Vitoria on April 10, where they were met by numerous roadblocks, contingents of the Guardia Civil, and more than 5,000 riot policemen. The police used smoke grenades and tear gas to keep the demonstrators dispersed, and charged the crowds repeatedly with riot sticks, driving the Basques to seek shelter in churches. Many were dragged from their refuges and beaten in the street. A heavy snow storm contributed to the Basques' discomfort, and they had to cancel the Aberri Eguna celebration for the first time since 1966.[30]

During the first week of March, the various Pro-Amnesty Associations had celebrated a week-long series of meetings, demonstrations, sit-ins, and other gestures designed to focus public opinion on the amnesty question. This First Pro-Amnesty Week, held in San Sebastián, had been a peaceful gathering, unmarked by violence and left more or less unmolested by the police and the Guardia Civil. Thus, when the March amnesty decree fell short of total freedom for all Basque prisoners, the Pro-Amnesty Associations naturally decided to repeat their earlier efforts. The results were tragically different.

The Second Pro-Amnesty Week, also planned for San Sebastián, was scheduled to begin during the week of May 10. Almost immediately, the demonstrations began to take an ugly turn, and the police responses became increasingly violent. On Thursday, May 12, at about 8:00 pm, a large crowd gathered around the Guardia Civil headquarters in San Sebastián. According to Guardia officials, the crowd began throwing rocks and Molotov cocktails at the building, and those inside felt assaulted and menaced. The Pro-Amnesty Associations replied that they were doing nothing more than peacefully demonstrating. Whichever the case, the Guardia began to fire live ammunition into the crowd. There was one death, of a 78-year-old man named Rafael Gómez Jáuregui, and many were wounded in this first encounter. At about the same time, there were two more deaths in Pamplona, of a 15-year-old boy who was hit in the head by a rubber bullet and a 28-year-old Madrid man who had gone to Pamplona to visit relatives. In addition, a highway toll collector was struck and killed by a car as he tried to remove one of the traffic barricades erected by the demonstrators. The civil governor of Guipúzcoa immediately banned all types of public meetings in an effort to bring the escalating violence under control. A general strike affecting nearly 150,000 workers idled much of Basque industry, and traffic in San Sebastián was halted for hours by barricades and burning buses.[31] The upheaval was so extensive now that even the moderates began to talk of joining the demonstrations. A number of influential political figures demanded that the Basque political prisoners be released by May 24 (the day when the electoral campaign was slated to begin) or the Basque parties would boycott the elections.

The violence continued unabated into the following week. There were clashes between police and demonstrators all over the region and a general strike involving nearly half a million workers. As of May 16, there had been six deaths connected with the violence, five of them of Basques. At least 57 persons, including 24 police officers, were seriously wounded. Premier Suárez, expecting a visit to Madrid by American Vice President Walter Mondale, flooded the Basque region with armed police and Guardia Civil troops to suppress the violence. On May 15, a spokesman of ETA-pm issued a communiqué declaring that his group was abandoning its tentative parliamentary experiment and was going over to unrestrained insurgent violence. The statement was followed shortly on May 18 by the assassination of a policeman near the San Sebastián railroad station, and attacks on two other policemen in San Sebastián and in Pamplona. A large group of mayors representing 65 towns in Guipúzcoa met with representatives of other Basque political forces in the French city of Biarritz to seek a solution to the mounting violence. Aside from sending a delegation to talk with Suárez and threatening to resign *en masse,* however, there was not much they could do to stem the tide of disorder. The Basque Nationalist Party issued a statement that in effect criticized not only the police and Guardia Civil for their unrestrained violence, but also the small leftist groups that sought to take advantage of the turmoil to advance their own revolutionary causes. The statement contained these passages: "The use of the amnesty issue by anti-Basque and anti-democratic groups has brought us to a situation parallel to that of the Franco epoch, in which coercion has returned to reign. A Red Euzkadi is not our objective, neither is the general strike the adequate remedy at this time for the grave economic problem through which our country is passing. We denounce the physical and psychological violence to which we are induced by the law enforcement authorities and by the perfectly complementary groups of social-fascists (communists)." With this statement, the PNV seemed to break with the Pro-Amnesty Associations, a fact that no doubt hurt the party with some Basque voters in the June elections.[32]

There were at this time 23 Basques still in Spanish prisons. Fifteen of these were still waiting trial or sentencing. Eight had been convicted of *delitos de sangre,* and thus were not eligible for release. The Suárez response to the May violence was to offer amnesty to this group if they would leave Spain and never return. The Spanish government would undertake the legal requirements, as well as negotiate their entry into their chosen host state.

The most dramatic blow in the amnesty struggle was yet to be felt. On May 20, a group of masked men disguised as hospital orderlies entered the home of Javier de Ybarra in Bilbao, tied and gagged the other members of his family, and kidnapped Sr. Ybarra in a stolen ambulance. Ybarra, a very prominent conservative political figure, industrialist and banker, was known to have been on ETA's "death list" since the beginning of the year. He was related on his wife's side to the Oriol family, which had also been singled out by ETA for reprisals. According to other members of Ybarra's family, the kidnappers said that they demanded total amnesty for the remaining 23 Basque prisoners in return for Ybarra's release.

The Spanish government met immediately after the kidnapping to determine its response. At first it was believed by some observers that the Suárez Cabinet would be set more firmly than ever against early release of the eight terrorists still in jail. Nevertheless, late in the night of May 20 the government announced that it would permit all 23 prisoners to leave the country and go into exile. This move was regarded as the first time the government had ever given in to kidnappers' demands, although Franco's response to the kidnappers of the German Counsul Biehl had been ambiguous and could have been interpreted as a concession to their requests.[33] By May 23, five of the remaining 23 Basque prisoners had chosen this method of obtaining their freedom and were flown into exile in Belgium.[34] Over the course of the next three weeks, thirteen more of the original 23 had been released: on June 1, one to Norway; on June 4, one to provisional freedom but allowed to remain in Bilbao; on June 6, two more to Norway; and on June 9, again two to Norway, two to Austria and five to Denmark. Thus, as of June 10, only five of the 23 remained in prison: two "historical" prisoners, that is ones that had been convicted before December 15, 1976; and three "new" prisoners convicted after that date.[35] Thus, although Madrid had made substantial progress toward releasing all Basque prisoners, there were still several awaiting amnesty as the June elections neared. The Pro-Amnesty Associations celebrated a Third Pro-Amnesty Week in San Sebastián timed to end on the day before the elections. Several splinter parties on the extreme left of the spectrum declared that they were going to boycott the elections, but groups as far to the left as EIA (Basque Revolutionary Party, the offshoot of ETA-pm) retained their role in the campaign. The central problem remained the safety of Ybarra.

The fate of the kidnapping victim was complicated considerably when, on June 2, French police arrested Miguel Angel Apalategui, "Apala," the leader of ETA-pm. Since it was believed that ETA-pm was responsible for the kidnapping of Ybarra, Madrid requested that Apala be held for eventual extradition to Spain. On June 5, Apala was transferred to the French prison island of Porquerolle, where he was held along with an undisclosed number of other Basques, most of whom were members of ETA.[36] Most of the remaining Basques were released after the June 15 elections; but Apala remained in French custody. On June 21, Madrid officially requested that Apala be returned to Spain to stand trial for the assassination of Angel Berazadi, whereupon the French authorities changed their prisoner's status to "preventive detention," and transferred him to the Baumettes prison in Marseilles.

The response of the Ybarra kidnappers was to raise the price for their hostage's release. Angered by the arrest of Apalategui, ETA-pm replied by means of a communiqué that the French decision had been made to turn Apala into a counter-hostage with which Madrid could bargain for Ybarra's freedom. For reasons that are difficult to discern, ETA-pm now demanded not only the release of the remaining Basque prisoners, but the payment of a ransom of one billion pesetas, the equivalent of about $14 million. Despite the Ybarra family's great wealth, they could not reach that much ready cash in a short period and so sought to postpone the deadline set by the kidnappers for payment: June 18. All their efforts to delay the deadline went unanswered. The deadline of June 18 passed without news. On June 20, a message was sent to the family announcing Ybarra's "execution," with a map of the location of the body. Attempts by the Guardia Civil to locate the body were in vain, and a telephone message from ETA disclaimed knowledge of the first note. On June 22, however, a second note was received which corrected an error that the Guardia Civil had made, and new efforts to locate the body were successful. Ybarra's corpse was discovered about 25 yards from an old farmhouse in Navarra province. It was wrapped in a plastic sheet. The victim had been shot once in the head and probably was killed on June 18, the deadline set by his abductors.[37] Virtually every significant political voice in the Basque community spoke out against the barbarism of the act, but the damage was done, and the goal of smooth Basque-Spanish relations receded even further.

With the Ybarra case brought to its tragic conclusion, and the June elections behind, Basque public opinion turned once again to the few remaining political prisoners, whose number was growing with additional arrests, and above all, with Miguel Angel Apalategui still fighting extradition in France. On July 10, more than 2,000 Basques took the first steps on a "Freedom March" designed to focus opinion once again on the Basque prisoners. Beginning at separate points in each of the four provinces, the marchers would come together near Pamplona on August 28, after having walked more than 450 kilometers in each column. The colorful march began and ended without major incident and attracted much news media coverage. Nevertheless, at its conclusion, the marchers could find little evidence that their labors had moved Madrid any closer to full and complete amnesty for their comrades.

The Apala case was more inflammatory of Basque public opinion. On July 19, the French court in Aix-en-Provence had heard the Spanish petition for return of Apala to stand trial for the murder of Berazadi, and had rejected the petition because Madrid had failed to provide the court with the correct kind of information and documentation. Nevertheless, Apala was not freed. On July 23, Spain requested again that he be extradited, this time to be tried for the murder of Javier de Ybarra. On August 2 and again on August 9, the court met to hear this later request. Across the Basque country, there were demonstrations in support of Apala. For nearly a week, more than 20,000 turned out daily in San Sebastián to shout their demand that he be set free. As was customary, the marchers were dispersed by the police with tear gas and rubber bullets. More than 500 Basques journeyed to France to demonstrate outside the court room where his case was being heard. On August 9, the court recessed and announced that it would not decide the case until October 14. At this point, Apala began a hunger strike to prevent France from sending him back to Spain for trial. "If France delivers me up to Spain," he told attending physicians, "they will deliver a corpse." His health declined steadily; he lost more than fifty pounds during the first month of the strike. Then, several days before his case was to be heard and decided in France, the famous subject escaped to join the increasingly radicalized ETA insurgent forces.

At last, after what seemed an eternity of clamor and bloodshed, the newly elected Spanish parliament approved a total amnesty for all political prisoners on October 14, 1977. It was the first law approved by the new Cortes, a fact full of significance for those who had waited so long for democracy to come to Spain. The lower house, the Congress, passed the bill by a vote of 296 in favor, two against, and 18 abstentions. The only real opposition came from the rightist Popular Alliance, which in the end could only bring themselves to abstain to register their disapproval. The Senate passed the same bill later in the day, this time by a vote of 196 in favor, none against, and six abstentions. For the first time since July 18, 1936, Spaniards were not at war with one another. The new amnesty law seemed to bode well for the future of Basque nationalism as well as for the future of Spanish democracy.[38]

Yet dark storm clouds remained over the Basque country.

On October 8, the day after the Suárez government and the opposition parties had agreed on a draft of the amnesty bill, ETA gunmen shot and killed the president of the Provincial Assembly of Vizcaya, Augusto Unceta Barrenechea, and his two bodyguards. It seemed clear that the killing had been timed to wreck the impending accord between Suárez and the opposition. But the Unceta assassination had an even greater and more chilling meaning for the long-term future of peace and social change in the Basque region. For the evidence showed that the killing had been carried out by an entirely new ETA group, one formed out of a union between the still intransigent ETA-*militar* and the now disillusioned members of the former ETA-*politico-militar*. Apparently, ETA-pm, having tried electoral politics and found it inadequate to their purposes, had returned to armed struggle with renewed ferocity. At their head was Apala, recently escaped from the French prison, radicalized far beyond where ETA had been before, and made a kind of folkhero by his hunger strike and intransigence in France. It was this kind of combination — of personality, organization and support among a significant minority of the general population — that had kept ETA alive for nearly twenty years. This same kind of mixture threatened to keep Euzkadi wracked by violence for many weeks and months, and maybe years, to come.

Chapter Eleven

POLITICAL PARTIES AND VOTING PATTERNS: TO THE 1977 ELECTIONS

Until the long-awaited event actually occurred, most observers of Spanish politics felt that Franco's death would be followed by considerable upheaval and instability leading eventually either to a military coup or a resumption of the Civil War after a forty-year hiatus. Many Basques shared these apprehensions. The Basque Nationalist Party, mindful of the vigilante violence of the Civil War period, even went so far as to train small commando units whose mission consisted of breaking into Spanish prisons to rescue Basque political prisoners from the reprisals of unleashed falangist assassination squads.

With the advantage of hindsight, we now know that these fears proved groundless. There was violence in the Basque country to be sure. Large crowds of demonstrators were met by police charges, tear gas, and rubber bullets. ETA escalated its challenge to the Spanish state with acts of increased violence and drama. Yet the large-scale disorder and the vigilantism that were so much feared by both Spanish and Basque moderates simply did not materialize. Instead, Spain moved to dismantle the Francoist legacy and to reinstitute an Iberian version of parliamentary democracy. The process began in June 1976, when the Spanish Cortes approved a law authorizing political parties for the first time in more than thirty years. It continued through December, when the Spanish people, voting in plebiscite, approved the proposed democratization plan for the country. And it came to a close in June 1977, with the election of Spain's first democratically chosen parliament since the Civil War.

The period from November 1975 to June 1977 definitely marks a turning point in both Spanish and Basque history. Yet, that Spain had abandoned Francoism and had embraced (however tentatively) the norms and institutions of parliamentary democracy did not mean that Basque nationalism had thereby achieved its goals or that there would henceforth be no cause for friction between Madrid and the Basques. It simply meant that Basque nationalists had to shift their attention to a new arena, one characterized by the open competition for votes and by bargaining with other political forces. The Basques would have to leave behind institutions, programs, and strategies better suited for the underground and exile and focus their efforts on the open political style of parliamentary contest and electoral mobilization. How they did this in Spain's first days as a restored democracy is the subject of this chapter and the one that follows.

Political Parties: The New Basque Political Spectrum

As these lines are written, we are still too close to the beginning of Spain's new experiment with democracy to know for certain whether or not the post-Franco reforms will be ephemeral or long-lasting. One thing is certain: they were numerous. In one decision after another, the liberalizing regime of the new king, Juan Carlos, as interpreted through his premier, Adolfo Suárez, decreed the dismantling of the structure of the Franco dictatorship. At first, there was merely tacit acceptance of open political activity by non-communist parties or groups; but soon the organization of parties, including the Spanish Communist Party (PCE), was made legal, and authorized parties began to blossom where only one had existed for nearly four decades. Many municipal government officials, including mayors and town councilors, had their terms of office shortened so they could be replaced by freely elected leaders. In most areas of Spain, the police were ordered to discontinue the arbitrary mass arrests of citizens, and there were attempts to curb police brutality and right wing vigilantism. The popular press began to function in a less censored environment, although some publications, such as *Cambio 16*, were closed on occasion for revealing details about police torture, or for ridiculing the king. Labor unions were permi- ted to conduct non-political strikes; but the governme not hesitate to intervene to block the work stop sector of the economy affected was espec Passports were issued to a large numb including important leaders of a number o cal movements. A number of important reforms mnesty for political prisoners or the abrogation of o ionable features of the anti-terrorism law, were brought into effect especially to placate opposition groups in the separatist regions, including the Basques and the Catalans.

The reform work of the Suárez government was formidable. In all, from July 3, 1976, when Suárez took office as premier, to June 15, 1977, when the process reached its first milestone with the election of the first democratic parliament, Suárez pushed through a reluctant Cortes 56 major laws affecting the structure of the Spanish state. He issued more than 3,000 official decrees that had the force of law; and he authored or sponsored more than 9,500 government directives. About 400 former Franco officials lost their posts, and more than 550 new senior political leaders were brought into the Suárez administration during the first year.[1]

One of the most significant areas of political reform was that affecting the establishment of legal political parties. The Spanish government approached this subject gingerly. At first, only political "associations" were permitted. In March 1976, the government sent to the Cortes the draft of a bill that would guarantee the freedoms of assembly and political association. On June 9, the parliament approved the law, authorizing parties for the first time since the Civil War. The law continued to prohibit communist and separatist parties, however. Suárez had to intervene personally to legalize the Communist Party, and "separatist parties" was defined strictly to apply only to revolutionary groups such as ETA. Between June 1976 and May 1977, when the period for party registration officially ended, at least 162 separate political organizations had become legalized. However, by the time of the June 1977 elections, these parties had clustered into a much smaller number of coalitions that spanned the entire range of ideologies and regional interests.[2]

On the right side of the spectrum, two groups competed for the honor of representing the "true" neo-Francoist position. The more intransigent of these two coalitions was composed of several extreme right-wing parties, including *Fuerza Nueva, Falange Española de las JONS,* and the *Comunión Tradicionalista.* The less strident neo-Francoist group was called *Alianza Popular* (AP), and was led by former Franco minister Manuel Fraga Iribarne, who, despite the fact that his mother was French Basque, was vehemently opposed to regional autonomy for the Basques. The center and center-right of the spectrum belonged to the political creation of Adolfo Suárez, called the *Unión de Centro Democrático* (UCD), a coalition of more than a dozen smaller parties that shared little except a desire to gain power by following the popular Suárez.

The remainder of the center, which proved in the final analysis to be little indeed, was occupied by the Christian Democrats, whose coalition was called the *Equipo Democrático Cristiano del Estado Español,* or the Christian Democratic "Team" of the Spanish State. The core of the *Equipo* was in the *Federación de la Democracia Cristiana* (FDC) which had debated seriously the idea of joining the Suárez centrist party but rejected the proposition for fear of being dominated by the UCD. The *Equipo* also included a number of regional parties that had been associated historically with the Christian Democratic position, and among these was the Basque Nationalist Party.[3] Nevertheless, when the June elections forced the parties to determine their true allegiances, the *Equipo* presented a separate slate of candidates in the Basque provinces under the name of *Democracia Cristiana Vasca* (DCV). This slate was advanced in direct competition with the PNV, but since it was tarred with the brush of collaboration with Madrid it made little impact on voting patterns.

On the non-communist left of the party spectrum, the socialist vote was divided among several splinter parties, including the *Partido Socialista Popular* and the *Alianza Socialista Democrática,* and one major group, the historically powerful and well organized *Partido Socialista Obrero Español,* or

Spanish Socialist Workers' Party (PSOE). Many of these parties would present slates of candidates in the Basque provinces in the 1977 elections; but only the PSOE succeeded in winning impressively across the region. Indeed, under the aggressive leadership of the populist-styled Felipe Gonzalez, the PSOE was soon to emerge as Spain's largest single party, if one discounts the UCD as merely a coalition of convenience with little ideological cohesion.

On the extreme left of the party system, but before the limits of illegality were reached, stood in splendid isolation the Spanish Communist Party (PCE), under the leadership of Santiago Carrillo. Ardent spokesmen of the new wave of "Eurocommunism," the PCE counted on the vigorous support of its sister parties in France and Italy for money and organizational support. In addition, it inherited the mantle of anti-Franco opposition, since, as is so often the case, the communists had spearheaded the Spanish underground during the difficult years of the dictatorship, while many other anti-Franco leaders had remained in exile. Nevertheless, the exact range of support for communism in Spain's working classes remained unknown until the 1977 elections.

Spain's variegated parties differed on many key social and economic issues, but their stance on what was called during the election "the regional problem" fell into a fairly narrow range of choices. As one analysis put it, party positions ". . . oscillated from a regionalist decentralization in a diffuse autonomist framework, to a system of autonomy statutes that might lead to self-government, as a step to federalism."[4]

On the right, *Alianza Popular* defended the "recognition of regional autonomies in a united solidary Spain, with collective support for the deprived regions." However, AP pronounced itself firmly against any kind of separatism or regional nationalism, and condemned federalism as too "inadequate, expensive and complex" for Spain. The center-right coalition of Premier Suárez, the UCD, called for the structuring of the State by means of an autonomy-statute framework that would permit the self-government of the peoples or regions that "constitute the unitary historical reality that is Spain." The UCD also envisioned the free election of popular legislative assemblies at the regional level, something opposed by more conservative parties that supported the continuation of the Franco practice of naming regional authorities from Madrid. But the UCD opposed placing the issue of regional autonomy in the new constitution, favoring instead the drafting of a separate autonomy law that would permit the regions to request autonomy (in practice, a more restrictive and conservative provision than that of the Second Republic).

The centrist Christian Democrats, recognizing the important support they were receiving from the major regional parties such as the PNV, were more decidedly pro-region than were the more conservative groups. The FDC, for example, advocated including the regional autonomy provision within the new constitution, where it could not be tampered with or blocked so easily as if it were merely another law. The FDC called for a constitutional provison that would "establish a distribution of competence between the State and the regions that compose it, in accord with the principles of autonomy, solidarity and regional participation in the organs of government of the State." Again, however, the specific autonomy statutes would have to go through an approval process much like that of the Second Republic, wherein the regions would have to request special treatment, the law would have to be drafted by the Cortes, and then approved by a referendum of the affected region. Some observers felt that the FDC was in fact advocating a "Federal" solution to the regional problem, but the party declined to use this word because of its historically negative connotations in Spanish politics.

The leftist PSOE program was actually quite similar to that of the Christian Democrats, which may help to explain why the electoral battle of 1977 was fought out in the Basque provinces between the left and the center not solely on the regional issue, but rather on social and economic questions as well. The PSOE advocated the creation of a constitutional framework that would grant full powers of self-government to the "nationalities and regions of the State, as well as to the municipalities." The PSOE proposal was flexible, in that it would permit different kinds of autonomy statutes to be drafted according to the needs of each region. But, reflecting the redistributive inclination of the left, the PSOE felt that any one region's autonomy would have to be developed in accord with a nation-wide economic development plan that would meet the needs of Spain's poorer regions. While the PSOE defended stoutly the "unity of the Spanish state," it also admitted freely that what it had in mind was a federal system.

The Communist Party was the most forthright in its defense of the autonomy statutes of the Second Republic. As far as the historical regions of Spain (Basque provinces, Cataluña, and Galicia) were concerned, the PCE advocated simply the immediate restitution of their autonomy statutes that had been granted or under consideration at the time of the Civil War. For the other regions, whose nationalist sentiment was only beginning to reawaken (such as Andalucía or the Canary Islands), new statutes would have to be drafted, probably with their origin in some kind of popularly elected regional assembly. In any case, the PCE called for the constitutional guarantee of regional rights and autonomy, although Madrid would retain primacy in such areas as foreign policy and defense, and economic planning and coordination.

In sum, then, Spain's major parties disagreed on some of the important details of possible solutions to "the regional problem": whether the guarantees of regional rights would be built into the constitution, or whether they would be contained in an ordinary law passed by the Cortes; whether local officials would be freely elected or appointed by Madrid; whether there would be "decentralization" with increased powers for each province on an individual basis, or whether provinces would be clustered together in historically viable regions to receive their new powers; and so forth. Nevertheless, the campaign prior to the 1977 elections was notable for the degree of consensus of the country's major parties regarding regional rights. No major party or group advocated retention of the centralist Franco system; but none supported extreme movement in the other direction, toward full separation. The consensus position seemed to lie somewhere between a restitution of the autonomy statutes and some sort of federal experiment.

The blossoming of political parties in Spain following

Franco's death was matched by a similar growth in the Basque provinces. Before and during the period of the Second Republic, Basque nationalists had had to choose between only the PNV and the ANV among those parties with viable programs and chances of gaining success. After 1976, there were at least half a dozen political groupings of Basque nationalist persuasion, although several of these were certain to be swallowed up by coalitions after the 1977 elections. As these new parties emerged, the most striking development was the sharp turn to the left made by the usually conservative Basque electorate. The majority of the new parties were part of what was called the "generational answer" (*contestación generacional*) of Basque youth to the more cautious and conservative PNV. And the results of the 1977 elections showed with clarity the gains made by the parties of the left, at the expense first of the conservative right and to a much lesser degree of the centrist PNV.

Analysis of the Basque political spectrum after 1976 is made exceedingly difficult by the effect of four cross-cutting issues that dominated Basque political debate.[5] Probably the most attention was paid to the conflict between *abertzale* and *sucursalista* forces. *Abertzale* parties (derived from the word in Euskera meaning patriot) were those that eschewed any contact or cooperation with Spanish parties and restricted their activity entirely to the four Basque provinces. The *abertzale* parties included both moderate, centrist groups such as the PNV, as well as more radical socialist organizations, like *Euskal Herriko Alderdi Sozialista* (EHAS), and even Marxist-Leninist parties including some of the offspring of ETA. The word *sucursalista* was used (pejoratively) to describe those parties that had links with parties that operated throughout Spain. *Abertzale* political leaders were critical of such groups, arguing that they were allowing themselves to be used by Spanish parties that would betray the Basques once in power. The groups that cooperated with Spanish parties called themselves *estatal* groups, to signify their willingness to be a part of the overall political process of the Spanish state. Again, *sucursalista* parties spanned the gamut from conservative, right-wing groups like the *Partido*

Proverista Autónomo de Euskadi, to Trotskyite parties like the Communist Revolutionary League and ETA VI.

A second important question debated by Basques before the 1977 elections was the "true" territorial base of Euzkadi. The most restrictive interpretation was that of the Government of Euzkadi in Exile, which argued that the only real basis for negotiations had to be the Autonomy Statute of 1936, which covered only the provinces of Alava, Guipúzcoa and Vizcaya. Navarra could be included only after having gone through the same decision-making process experienced by the other provinces, and in truth it often appeared as if the government in Paris was not particularly eager to encourage Navarra to join. No doubt this was the case because of the weakness of the PNV in Navarra, and the consequent fear that other forces could take over the government if Navarra were included. The most frequently encountered position was that of the centrist and left *abertzale* parties, which held that Euzkadi should be based on the four Spanish provinces (including Navarra, the so-called Euzkadi Sur), and the three French provinces. Even these parties disagreed, however, on how much the citizens of these provinces should be consulted on the question. While the more moderate parties felt that there should be some sort of referendum to test popular sentiment in Navarra before incorporating it into Euzkadi, the more intransigent groups believed that the people there had already been so propagandized by Madrid that they were not capable of recognizing their true interests as Basques. The most extreme position was that taken by EHAS, which proclaimed itself in favor of recovering for Euzkadi the lands beyond the four Spanish provinces that had historically constituted the Basque homeland before the French Revolution and the redrawing of the map of Spain. (In fact, it is a curiosity of contemporary Basque politics that the parties farthest to the left also appear to be the ones most inclined to expansion of the customary territorial confines of the Basque nation.)

The third major issue that separated Basque parties was that of the exact nature of the links between Spain and Euzkadi. A small group of radical parties, such as EHAS and the Basque

Revolutionary Workers Party (*Langille Abertzale Iraultzaleen Alderdia,* or LAIA), favored complete separation of the Basque nation from Spain. A sovereign nation, recognized by other countries with full diplomatic relations, membership in the European Economic Community and the United Nations, with currency, armed forces and full dominion over internal affairs, would be the ultimate goal of parties in this category. Apparently, these parties are allowed to function in Spain only on the assumption that they do not advocate the use of force to achieve this goal, and that the goal itself be of such a long-range nature as not to attempt any near-term objectives such as specific legislative proposals in the Cortes or anything else that could enflame the passions of a shaky democratic Spain. The majority of Basque nationalist parties, however, support either return to the Autonomy Statute of 1936, or the re-negotiation of a more modern document that would include Navarra. Even under the most extreme proposals in this group, Spain would remain responsible for foreign policy, defense, customs duties, and the protection of political rights of non-Basque Spaniards living in Euzkadi. As in the Statute of 1936, the government of Euzkadi would be responsible for the maintenance of law and order, the system of justice and courts, education, welfare, taxation, economic coordination, and other more or less internal matters. This approach is clearly inadequate for the more radical socialist parties because they feel that it would perpetuate rule by the Basque bourgeoisie in league with the Spanish industrialists and capitalists. It must be noted, however, that there are a number of radical left-wing parties that do support integration of Euzkadi into Spain, mainly it seems because they believe that the cause of social revolution in Spain will fail unless the Spanish social revolutionary forces can count on full support from the working classes in Euzkadi and Cataluña. Thus, the Eurocommunist PCE, the Marcist-Leninist *Movimiento Comunista de Euzkadi,* and the Trotskyite ETA VI all are *integracionista* parties, at least until Spain has undergone a social revolution.

These last observations lead us, then, to the fourth major issue in the Basque political arena: the degree of social, economic, and political change advocated either for Spain as a whole, or only for the Basque region. I have already alluded to the convervative, centrist, and socialist positions on the political spectrum. In general, these positions correspond to the platform of each group as regards the need for change. A few of the small right-wing groups want to return to the period not only before Franco but to the medieval days of Ferdinand and Isabella and the *fueros*. The PNV and DCV follow the Christian Democrat position of reaffirming their faith in the free market and the sanctity of private property, although tempered substantially by a need to meet the social needs of a growing urban, working class population. Finally, a fairly large number of small parties have articulated a consistent left-oriented platform, advocating substantial social change, centering on nationalization of the Basques' major industries, and using workers' committees to run the firms. These measures would be accompanied by a tax and payment system that would seek to redistribute income, as well as social programs designed to alleviate the ills of blighted urban areas such as Bilbao.

Because of the rather large number of parties active in the Basque provinces in 1976 and 1977, I think it wise to try to represent them schematically, as is done in Table 15. What this chart loses in detail is, I hope, compensated for by the comparative clarity of party relationships which it highlights. As the reader reviews the chart, it should be clear that the Basque nationalist movement has proliferated its institutional expressions far beyond the limits of the PNV. Not only are there more choices for Basques of a nationalist persuasion, but the expansion seems to have taken place almost entirely to the left side of the political spectrum. As much as anything else, this leftward movement of Basque nationalist politics illustrates a growing sense of discontent with the cautious conservatism of the PNV. Later in this chapter, I shall discuss the implications of this phenomenon for the outcome of the 1977 parliamentary elections.

Table 15.
Political Party Structure in Basque Provinces, 1976-1977.

Initials	Basque Name	Spanish Name	Ideology
PNV	*Euzko Alderdi Jeltzalea*	*Partido Nacionalista Vasco* (Basque Nationalist Party)	Moderate, centrist, Christian Democrat. *Abertzale. Integracionista.* Territorial base defined by 1936 Autonomy Statute. Favors moderate socio economic reforms, regulation of industry, worker-owner joint management of firms.
ANV	*Euzko Abertzale Ekintza*	*Acción Nacional Vasca* (Basque National Action)	Moderate, left, no church affiliation. *Abertzale, Integracionista.* Territorial base defined by 1936 Autonomy Statute. Favors considerable socialist reform of industrial system.
DCV	—	*Democracia Cristiana Vasca* (Basque Christian Democrat)	Moderate, centrist, Christian Democrat. Branch of Spanish Christian Democrats Coalition. *Integracionista;* territorial base might include Navarra if they so choose. Believes in free market economy, some regulation, especially of monopolies.
KAS/EE	*Koordinadora Abertzale Sozialista/ Euzkadiko Ezkerra*	*Coordinadora Socialista Vasca/ Izquierda Vasca* (Basque Social Coordinator/ Basque Left)	Socialist coordinating council composed of two labor unions, *Langille Abertzaleen Batzordea* (LAB) and *Langille Abertzale Komiteak* (LAK), and three socialist parties: *Eusko Herriko Alderdi Sozialista* (EHAS), *Langille Abertzale Iraultzaleen Alderdia* (LAIA), and ETA-pm (ETA *politico-militar*). *Abertzale.* Opposed to any ties with Spain. Favors Euzkadi based

			on all seven provinces, closely tied to a general social revolution in both Spain and France. Contested 1977 elections under title *Euzkadiko Ezkerra* (EE).
ESB	*Euskal Sozialista Biltzarrea*	*Convergencia Socialista Vasca* (Basque Socialist Convergence)	Social democratic party, originally part of ETA but split off to pursue nonviolent socialist revolution. *Abertzale*. Favors autonomy of Euzkadi, program of far-reaching social reform including nationalization of industry, banks, etc. Considered about midway between KAS and PNV.
EKA	*Euskadiko Karlista Alderdia*	*Partido Carlista Vasco* (Basque Carlist Party)	Despite the party's dogmatic conservative origins of more than a century ago, it has now adopted as ideology a curious blend of socialism and hierarchical authoritarianism. Organized throughout Spain. Favors a federal solution to Spain's regional problem: a self-governing Euzkadi federated with other Spanish "peoples." Includes both Navarra and French provinces in Euzkadi.
PV	—	*Partido Proverista Euzkadi* (Autonomous Basque "Pro-Truth" Party)	A tiny, mystically religious right-wing faction that favors the monarchy and political protection of the Catholic Church. Organized throughout Spain. Favors a federated Spain with Euzkadi (including Navarra) given a self-governing status.

(*Table 15, cont'd*)

MCE; ORT; PT	—	*Movimiento Comunista de Euzkadi; Organización Revolucionaria de Trabajadores; Partido del Trabajo*	Tiny Marxist-Leninist factions that split off from ETA because of the latter's *abertzale* position. These parties are loosely associated with similar groups operating elsewhere in Spain. They favor socialist revolution throughout Spain which will bring as a consequence the liberation of Spain's historical region.
ETA VI-LCR	—	ETA VI - *Liga Comunista Revolucionaria* (Communist Revolutionary League)	Similar to three preceding groups, except adheres to Trotskyite line of "permanent revolution."

NOTE: In addition to the listed parties, most of the major Spanish parties presented candidates in the Basque Provinces in 1977. These parties included *Alianza Popular* (AP), *Unión del Centro Democrático* (UCD), *Partido Socialista del Obrero Español* (PSOE), and *Partido Comunista de España* (PCE).

1976-1977: The Road to Free Elections

Francisco Franco died on November 20, 1975. Even before his death, however, Prince Juan Carlos, soon to be elevated to the throne as king, let it be known that his regime would begin with conciliatory gestures toward the nation's restive regions. (It will be recalled from Chapter Seven that the period immediately preceding Franco's death was marked by very high levels of public unrest, mass demonstrations, and a number of ETA assassinations of police and Guardia Civil members.) For the next eighteen months, Juan Carlos and Premier Adolfo Suárez advanced a number of measures designed to placate the Basque provinces, and in the process to try to erode the base of popular support for ETA that had been building in Euzkadi because of Franco's harsh repression.

On November 11, 1975, nine days before Franco died, Juan Carlos announced that one of his first acts after becoming king would be to declare a general amnesty for all political prisoners except those convicted of violent crimes. The long awaited amnesty would affect about 1,000 prisoners, many of whom were Basque nationalists. Left unaffected, however, were some 250 persons convicted of terrorism, and these were overwhelmingly of Basque origin. From this point onward, the amnesty issue became one of the hottest sources of friction between Madrid and the Basques, as most nationalists argued for the release of all Basque prisoners regardless of their crimes.

On November 16, Juan Carlos issued a decree aimed at preserving and protecting Spain's regional languages, especially Euskera and Catalan. Reaction to the decree from the affected provinces was unexpectedly negative, however. For Juan Carlos had made the error of including in the decree a statement to the effect that the regional languages, while officially protected, would not enjoy equal status with Spanish in the regions' courts, municipalities, and administrative offices. At the same time, the soon-to-be king signed a proclamation creating a study commission to examine ways of restoring administrative and economic autonomy to Vizcaya and Guipúzcoa provinces, thus negating the effects of the 1937 decree intended to punish those two provinces for siding with the Republic. In this case, Basque response was cautious but generally approving.

There were other moves toward reconciliation during the first several weeks after Franco's death, but again they often displayed a lack of understanding in Madrid of Basque nationalist sentiment. At his coronation on November 22, King Juan Carlos tried to strike a middle position with regard to the regional problem with this formula: "A just order permits the recognition of regional peculiarities." Many Basques considered the statement to be something less than a ringing affirmation of their right to autonomy. On November 25, the amnesty program went into effect, releasing more than 1,000 political prisoners, and shortening the sentences of 700 more. The 250 prisoners convicted under the terrorism law remained outside the program, however. On December 11, Juan Carlos' first Premier, Carlos Arias Navarro, a Franco appointee, was allowed to dissolve the Cabinet and reassemble a government more in tune with the spirit of reconciliation. Much was made of the appointment of conservative Basque monarchist José María Areilza and former Interior Minister Manuel Fraga Iribarne, of Basque ancestry on his mother's side, to the Cabinet. In the Basque country, however, many remembered Areilza as Franco's appointee to be the first mayor of Bilbao after the city fell in the Civil War, and as the man responsible for the early policies of Spanish occupation. And Fraga Iribarne was remembered mainly for his statement made in an interview on a Caracas television station that the Basque flag would be flown in a Spanish province only "over his dead body." Not surprisingly, the naming of these two members of the Cabinet was not received in Basque nationalist circles as reassuring.

Of all the steps taken by Madrid in the early days to pacify Basque emotions, none was more significant than the decision to permit the public display of the Basque flag, called the *ikurriña,* whose use had been prohibited for nearly forty years. The decision was agreed upon in a meeting of Basque political leaders and Spanish Minister of Interior Martín Villa in September 1976. The decree was to be published and made official on September 19, but rumors began to filter into the Basque provinces in advance of the actual publication, and pressures began to build for displaying the flag before the official date. The central issue was not one of public display by individuals, such as from private balconies or in other non-official ways. Rather, passions became stirred over the question of whether the *ikurriña* should be flown on public buildings such as the seat of a municipal government, thereby sharing the honor and prestige of political symbolism with the Spanish flag. The first municipality to raise the *ikurriña* officially alongside the Spanish flag was the tiny town of Garay, in the province of Vizcaya, whose town council voted to display the flag on September 18, one day before the decree was to take effect. Eventually, by February 1977, about forty percent of all Basque municipal governments (146 out of 365) had agreed to display the *ikurriña* as a co-official symbol of political authority. As is generally true with all expressions of Basque nationalism, support for the *ikurriña* was distributed unequally across the four provinces. In Guipúzcoa, 79 out of 81 municipalities agreed to fly the flag, while in Vizcaya, the figure was 50 out of 96 (in itself, a remarkable decline in nationalist support at the town and village level). In Navarra and Alava combined, only 17 municipalities favored public, co-official display of the banner.[6] Many municipal governments before voting resorted to referenda of their citizens to determine popular sentiment for or against display, and the resultant campaigns were often highly charged with emotion and fiery rhetoric. For the individual Basque citizen of nationalist persuasion, however, there was little wavering or doubt. Stores such as the expensive Bilbao department store Corte Inglés quickly sold their stocks of items with the *ikurriña* embossed or affixed to them. Simple items like bottle openers were sold for as much as five dollars if they carried the Basque flag as an adornment. The *ikurriña* began to appear affixed to automobiles and displayed at sporting contests, in magazines and newspapers, and flying from telephone poles. Not all nationalists, however, greeted the event with unrestrained glee; many left parties criticized the PNV for attempting to convert their party's symbol into the flag for the entire Basque nation. But in the last analysis these criticisms were swept aside in one of the most fervent shows of emotional support for the idea of Basque nationalism that had been seen in Spain since the Civil War.[7]

As 1976 turned into 1977, the Suárez government undertook a series of high-level personnel changes designed to alter the impression many Basques had of the Spanish law enforcement authorities and military establishment. In late December, Suárez fired the heads of the Guardia Civil and the Armed Police (the force charged with urban security and riot control), and replaced them both with younger, more moderate generals who were known to be sympathetic to the cause of regional autonomy. In addition, a new chief was picked to head the National Security Directorate, Spain's version of the Central Intelligence Agency and the Federal Bureau of Investigation combined. These changes were intended to complement and support the naming of Lt. Gen. Manuel Gutierrez Mellado, whom Suárez had chosen to preside over the reorganization of the country's military and police. At the end of 1976, Suárez abolished the political court of the Franco era, the Tribunal of Public Order, and stripped the military of their right to try persons accused of terrorism (the Decree-Law on Terrorism had been revised earlier, in February 1976, to eliminate its more objectionable provisions). At about the same time, Madrid made it clear that right-wing vigilante squads like the Warriors of Christ the King would no longer receive official protection, and their criminal exploits would be punished as would any violations of the law. During the following months, Spanish police made good on their promise by breaking up a right-wing terrorist arms factory and arresting a number of Spanish and Italian neo-fascists, including the head of the Warriors, Mariano Sanchez Covisa.[8]

With all of these changes, it is noteworthy that the traditional Basque suspicion and mistrust of Spanish politics continued unabated. One must remember that the many reforms I have outlined here were interwoven with a series of mass demonstrations, accompanied by police violence, as well as with an increase in attacks by the harried remnants of ETA, all of which served to heighten the air of fear and unrest in the

Basque provinces. These events merely reinforced the age-old Basque feelings toward Spanish rule, making it that much more difficult for Juan Carlos and Premier Suárez to achieve their goal of conciliating the moderate Basque nationalist center.

The data presented in the following tables suggests the extent of discontent in the Basque provinces with the course of reform in Spain as of December 1976, one year into the process. In the first one, Table 16, we see the results of a public opinion survey reported in the magazine *Cambio 16,* which show that opinions favorable to the Suárez reforms were running about 20 percentage points behind the overall Spanish totals, and significantly behind percentages in the two other regions with historical grievances against Madrid, Galicia, and Cataluña. In the Basque provinces, only about one-third of the respondents felt more satisfied with Suárez' actions at that time than several months earlier, and less than one-third were prepared to vote for him in parliamentary elections. (Interestingly, Suárez' party, the UCD, received only 16.2 percent of the Basque vote in the June 1977 elections, indicating that the premier continued to lose ground badly after the December 1976 referendum.)

The second table, 17, reveals the vote in the Basque provinces in the December 1976 referendum in which Spanish voters were asked to ratify the proposed constitutional reforms that were generally interpreted as significant liberalization of the Franco regime. The data are shown compared with voting patterns on two earlier referenda, in 1947 and 1966, when voters were consulted about major organic laws proposed by Franco. Since there are many obstacles to casting a "No" vote in these referenda, many observers look at the figures for "Abstention" to determine the degree of popular opposition to the proposals. In Spain as a whole, abstention rates in the 1976 referendum were about double what they had been in 1947 and 1966, but they still totaled only about one-fifth of the total adult population, considerably lower than the non-voting adult population in U.S. presidential elections. In the Basque provinces, abstentions in earlier referenda had run rather low, ranging from 6.0 percent in Navarra in 1947 to 23.9 percent in

Table 16.
Support for Suárez Reforms, by Region, December 1976 (percent).

Questions	Answers	Galicia N=123	Cataluña N=248	Basque Provinces N=107	Madrid N=157	Total N=1,527
Now that the Cortes has approved the Suárez reform, are you more, the same, or less satisfied with Suárez than you were several months ago?	More	42	52	35	59	52
	Same	32	35	26	34	28
	Less	8	4	18	5	6
	Don't know	18	9	21	2	14
Suppose that elections were held in a month and Suárez were a candidate, would you vote for him?	Yes	40	37	28	57	49
	No	18	23	36	18	17
	Don't know	42	42	36	25	34

Source: *Cambio 16,* No. 261, December 12, 1976, p. 9.

Table 17.
Comparative Voting Patterns in Referenda of 1947, 1966 and 1976 (percent of adult population).

	Abstentions			Yes			No		
Province	1947	1966	1976	1947	1966	1976	1947	1966	1976
Alava	14.1	11.8	13.7	83.2	80.4	79.3	1.9	4.8	4.7
Guipúzcoa	8.4	23.9	55.1	88.4	66.4	41.1	3.2	6.5	2.6
Navarra	6.0	15.1	26.4	91.4	75.7	68.3	1.2	4.3	2.1
Vizcaya	21.9	12.7	46.8	66.0	78.4	48.3	4.5	5.9	2.1
All of Spain	11.4	11.1	22.6	82.3	85.2	72.8	4.2	1.6	2.0

Source: "Referendum: Vía Libre," *La Actualidad Española*, No. 1,303 (December 20-26, 1976), pp. 10-14.

Note: Percentages do not add to 100 percent because of ballots spoiled or cast blank.

Guipúzcoa in 1966. In 1976, however, abstentions rose to more than half (55.1 percent) in Guipúzcoa, and nearly reached that level in Vizcaya (46.8 percent). Abstentions in Navarra were higher than the national average (26.4 percent against 22.6 percent), but were lower than the national average in Alava (13.7 percent). "Yes" votes declined by only 3.9 percent in Alava between the 1947 and 1976 referenda; but in Navarra, the decline was 23.1 percent, in Vizcaya it was 17.7 percent and in Guipúzcoa, it was a significant 47.3 percent!

In sum, after one year of reform effort, the Suárez government had failed to convince the majority of Basques of its willingness or ability to meet the needs of their region.

* * * * * * *

One of the central developments of the 1976-1977 period was the re-emergence of the Basque Nationalist Party to legal electoral activity after nearly four decades in exile and in the underground. As the Party returned to legal status, it became clear that the organization's structure and leadership had remained remarkably intact despite the rigors of exile and clandestinity. In Vizcaya, for example, Juan Ajuriaguerra, who had been the leader of the Basque Provincial Council, or *Bizkai*

Buru Batzar, for more than forty years emerged as one of the chief spokesmen of the Party and was elected to the new parliament from Vizcaya in the 1977 elections. Many of the Party's former leaders and younger supporters began to return from exile in Europe and Latin America, lending their voices to the strength of the Party, but also creating new sources of friction and tension over the new directions the Party should be taking.

During the PNV's first year and a half of restored legality, a number of important policy issues arose that demanded debate and consideration, if not prompt resolution. Many of these issues had been successfully avoided while Franco was alive, and the PNV stood virtually alone as a spokesman for the cause of Basque nationalism. With the restoration of parliamentary democracy, however, came new challenges to the Party's leadership, to its stance on important contemporary policy questions, and even to its identity.

Perhaps the central issue for many leaders of the PNV was the source of its electoral strength, closely tied to the question of electoral alliances with Basque or Spanish parties. The core of PNV identity had always been its nationalist and Catholic character, rather than any kind of social class identification. The PNV has consistently maintained that it does not seek alliance with any specific class, but rather aims at organizing all Basque nationalists into a unified front for purposes of meeting Madrid on a more nearly equal basis. The slogan for this policy was "*Batasuna!*" which means "Unity!" in Euskera. In brief, the Party held that all Basque nationalists, regardless of social class, should support the PNV, at least until Basque autonomy was achieved. After the Basques became self-governing, then they could enjoy the luxury of dividing into class-based parties for the purposes of debating policy alternatives within Euzkadi. The PNV leaders argued, then, that even socialist Basques should join the PNV until autonomy was secured. From the left came the answer that the PNV should join a non-partisan "Patriotic Front," or *Frente Abertzale*, in which each party, the socialists as well as the PNV, would have equal voice and equal chance for election to the parliament. Since this would obviously have the effect of diluting the PNV's power, the Party declined this invitation to alliance.

Another alliance, with the Spanish Christian Democrats, arose to bedevil PNV leaders. How, asked many Basques, could the PNV presume to try to speak for all Basques when it was allied with a Spanish party, and one that introduced religion into politics, at that? While the Basque provinces remained undeniably Catholic, it was no longer clear whether many Basques wanted their politics and their religion mixed. Thus the PNV was put on the defensive as regards their links with the Catholic party in Spain. In addition, the rising surge of *abertzale* sentiment condemned *any* ties with Spanish parties, no matter how pragmatic or how valuable they might be in the near term. In their defense, the PNV asserted that they had associated with the Spanish Christian Democrats only because that was the only way they could deliver the Basque message to important liberal political circles in Western Europe, and that the alliance had no meaning as far as Spanish and Basque politics were concerned. To confirm that assertion, the PNV broke with the Christian Democratic *Equipo* over the question of running joint candidates in the 1977 elections, and the Christian Democrats retaliated by presenting their own candidates in a direct challenge to the PNV. (The Christian Democrats lost badly, not only in the Basque provinces but throughout Spain; and it appears that the PNV made a wise strategic decision not to cling to their larger sister party for electoral purposes.)

After all of these alliance-maneuverings, however, there remained major questions concerning the ideological position of the PNV on issues that it had never been forced to confront while in exile. In meeting these issues, it looks as if the Party has tried to steer a middle course between their Catholic principles on moral or ethical issues and the leftward drift of the Basque electorate on social and economic questions. On issues like abortion, divorce, and the rights of women, the PNV continues to adhere to its long-standing traditional linkages with Catholicism. However, the Party has moved considerably to the left on questions of economic significance: tax rates, control of industrial firms, regulation of monopolies, pollution control, welfare, housing, and so forth. Obviously there is a good deal of tension associated with the process of dealing with these issues, and many remain unsettled today. No doubt the Party will be struggling for most of the remainder of this decade to come to grips with social and economic issues that were unheard of when the PNV leaders went into exile.

Several other questions faced by the PNV are less cosmic than the identity or ideology of the Party but have still caused considerable friction within the Party, and between the Party and its electoral following. The relationship of Navarra to the government of Euzkadi has already been mentioned as causing great difficulty. The president of the Basque government, Jesús María Leizaola, has repeatedly taken the position that the mandate of the government is dictated by the Autonomy Statute of 1936, and that does not include Navarra. His position apparently has been that the Republic of Euzkadi should be reinstalled on Basque soil first, and then Navarra should be consulted on whether or not it wishes to join the Basque group. Other PNV leaders, however, have opposed this line of reasoning, saying that it deprives Navarra of any chance to participate in the formative stages of the new regional government, and that Navarra should be included until the region is given autonomy. Following that step, the people of Navarra can be consulted about whether or not they wish to leave the union, thus reversing the question to be put to the plebiscite.[9]

One of the most inflammatory issues in Basque politics in this period concerned the participation of the PNV in the *Comisión de los Nueve,* the nine-man commission established to negotiate with Premier Suárez the transition to parliamentary democracy. This commission represented virtually all of the significant opposition parties in Spain, including the socialists, PSOE and the *Partido Socialista Popular;* the communists, PCE; the social democrats, *Federación Social Demócrata;* the coalition of liberal parties and groups; the Christian Democratic party in Cataluña; and representatives from each of the three historically restive regions: Euzkadi, Cataluña, and Galicia. The objective of this group was to present to Suárez the unified and combined power of all of the centrist and left opposition in Spain, in order to insure that the center-right and right groups would not block the transition or stifle the new breath of reform. The Commission was empowered to deal with most of the major issues confronting Suárez as the 1977 elections neared: amnesty; the legalization of all parties (which meant, in practice, the communist PCE); constitutional guarantees, and other measures designed to insure that the campaign would be carried out with due respect for the right of dissent; economic and social questions, especially those involving labor unions; and finally, the regional problem. The PNV in general, and its representative on the Commission, Julio Jaúregui, in particular, were targets of serious criticism for having betrayed the most important rights of the Basques. In particular, it was felt by some that the Commission took a pragmatic and compromising position on the amnesty issue, and was satisfied with any move made by Juan Carlos to release small numbers of prisoners, even though many Basques remained in jail. The government and the PNV both voiced support for the work of the Commission, and for Jaúregui's participation in its labors.[10] Nevertheless, this stance was viewed by many radical Basques as just another example of the PNV's betrayal of the real interests of the Basque region.

The transition of the Basque Nationalist Party to legal and open status culminated in a series of meetings of the Party's municipal and provincial assemblies held during the first two months of 1977. As prescribed by Party regulations, this process resulted in the selection of fifteen delegates from each province who met in Pamplona on March 25-28 to prepare the Party's platform.[11] Although only 60 delegates were empowered to vote, the sports arena where the meeting was held was packed with several thousand invited guests, many of whom ended up sitting on the floor of the crowded gymnasium. The meeting was preceded by the emotional arrival from exile of Manuel Irujo, now 86 years old and as grand a symbol of Basque resistance as ever. For several days, the delegates debated the Party platform, which in final form focused on political objectives, economic and social principles, and cultural objectives of the Party. In addition, certain internal structural changes were introduced and ratified.

The PNV platform began the section on political objectives by proclaiming "the reality of Euzkadi as a nation, and the right of the Basque people to bring it into being in accord with its own personality." The Party dedicated itself to allowing each of the four provinces to retain its own peculiar personality and institutions, recognizing the underlying Basque culture that joined them all together. The PNV pledged itself to work "for an autonomous Basque State that would be a progressive political entity within a framework of political democratization, . . . and in a posture of solidarity with the liberty and rights of the other peoples of the [Spanish] State." The political section of the platform reaffirmed the Party's dedication to join with the Basque provinces on the French side of the border and to work for the eventual democratization of Europe, and of the European community.

In economic and social matters, the Party skirted some difficult issues by talking of "principles" rather than concrete "objectives." Nevertheless, the Assembly made it clear that it regarded the liberation of the Basques as having two component parts: national liberation and social liberation. The latter dimension of human liberation could be achieved only through a just social order based on a spirit of egalitarianism, which might on occasion require the socialization "of those enterprises that overcome the possibilities of private initiative, the activities or enterprises that fulfill a public service, the enterprises that might have acquired political or economic power that might impede the exercise of a free democracy, or the enterprises or sectors which by their importance constitute economic keys for the economy of the country." The platform also called for the democratization of businesses by bringing workers into participation in the management of firms. While the PNV remained committed to the free market system as the basis for the economic organization of Euzkadi, they also realized that this system must be brought into accord with the needs of the community as a whole.

The third section of the platform dealt with cultural matters, of which of course the most important was that of language. Accordingly, the PNV called for the establishment of Euskera as a co-official language with Spanish, the dedication of channels of mass communications media (especially radio and television) to programs in Euskera, free primary education in Euskera paid for by the state, and the building of a public supported Basque university that would serve all young people of the four provinces.

The Assembly closed with a series of resolutions concerning miscellaneous matters that did not fall into one of the other categories, such as a defense of the rights of women, or a call for restructuring the military service in Spain. Their last resolution called for immediate unconditional amnesty for all Basques, and for the immediate return of all exiles from abroad. These steps were termed "indispensable requisites for the normalization of the political and social life [of the country]."

The 1977 Elections: An Analysis

On June 15, 1977, voters in Spain went to the polls to choose the members of the first freely elected Cortes since 1936. Since this was the first test of the popular strength of Spanish political parties in this generation, politicians and analysts across the country paid especially close attention to the election returns for indications of any new and unexpected trends in the distribution of political forces. In the days following the election, no group scrutinized the results more closely than the leaders of the Basque Nationalist Party.

There were two clear winners from the June 15 elections. The center-right coalition of Premier Adolfo Suárez, the Union of the Democratic Center (UCD), won about 34 percent of the popular vote, but received a little more than 47 percent of the seats in the new parliament's lower house, the Congress of Deputies, because of the weighted voting system used in the elections.[12] The Spanish Socialist Worker's Party (PSOE) was the other big winner, with about 28.5 percent of the vote, and 33.7 percent of the seats in the Congress. The major losers were the Spanish Communist Party (PCE), which received only 9 percent of the vote; the neo-Francoist Popular Alliance (AP), 4 percent; and the moderately conservative Christian Democrats (EDC), about 1 percent. Of the 162 parties that contested the elections, only twelve succeeded in electing candidates.

Voters in the four Basque provinces cast slightly more than 1,315,000 ballots (about 7.7 percent of the total Spanish vote of 17.5 million), to choose 26 delegates to the Congress (about 7.4 percent of the 350 seats in the lower house). Voting turnout ranged from 71 percent in Guipúzcoa to 80.1 percent in Navarra, 81 percent in Alava and 85.9 percent in Vizcaya. Overall, 80.2 percent of the eligible voters in the Basque provinces voted, compared with about 77 percent nationwide.[13]

There are three important dimensions of the 1977 vote that should be considered in any complete analysis: the share of the vote captured by the Basque Nationalist Party; the electoral strength of the *abertzale* parties; and the percentage of the vote obtained by all parties of the left, whether Basque nationalist or Spanish.[14]

One of the most significant features of the 1977 elections was the decline in strength of the Basque Nationalist Party. For the first time in several generations, the PNV was no longer the leading party in the Basque provinces.[15] In terms of percentage of the vote, the PSOE carved out a narrow victory with 25.0 percent, followed closely by the PNV with 24.4 percent, and at a greater distance by the UCD, which won 16.2 percent (see Table 18). In terms of seats won, the PSOE led with nine (out of twenty-six), followed by the PNV with eight, and the UCD with seven. The remaining two seats were won by the *abertzale* socialist coalition, *Euzkadiko Ezkerra,* and by the right-wing Popular Alliance.

Tables 19 through 23 show the voting patterns arranged according to province. As has always been the case historically, the PNV vote was concentrated in Guipúzcoa and Vizcaya, which together accounted for 90.6 percent of all votes cast for PNV candidates for Congress. (The two provinces account for 71.2 percent of *all* Basque voters.) The PNV carried about 30 percent of the vote in both Vizcaya and Guipúzcoa, and won seven of its eight seats in these two provinces, four out of ten in Vizcaya and three out of six in Guipúzcoa. Their eighth seat came in Alava (out of four elected). The PNV did

Table 18.
Voting Patterns in Four Basque Provinces, 1977 Parliamentary Elections (showing percent of total vote).

		Left	PNV		Center/Right	Total
Abertzale	EE	69,526 (5.2)				
	ESB-ANV	54,860* (4.1)				
	Other	24,489 (1.8)				
		148,875 (11.2)	323,522* (24.4)			472,397 (35.6)
Spanish	PSOE	332,220 (25.0)		UCD	214,379 (16.2)	
	Other	145,488 (11.0)		Other	151,021 (11.4)	
		477,708 (36.0)			365,400 (27.6)	843,108 (63.6)
Total		626,583 (47.2)	323,522 (24.4)		365,400 (27.6)	1,315,505 (99.2)

*Vote in Navarra for UAN coalition (PNV-ANV-ESB) divided equally between ANV-ESB, and PNV.

Source: Summarized from Tables 20-23.

not present a separate slate of candidates for the Congress in Navarra, but instead joined in a coalition with ANV and ESB, two left *abertzale* parties. The coalition earned 6.8 percent of the vote in Navarra. On a comparative basis, the PNV defeated the PSOE and the UCD in Vizcaya and Guipúzcoa, but lost to both in Alava and Navarra. While UCD strength in these latter two provinces was expected to be significant, the socialists also did well there, winning 27 percent of the vote in Alava (and one seat), and 21 percent of the vote in Navarra (two seats).

In terms of their historical electoral strength, the PNV showed a decline in vote percentages in each of the four provinces, from 1933 to 1936 to 1977. In Alava, their share of the vote dropped from 29 to 20.3 to 17.1 percent; in Guipúzcoa, from 45.5 to 36.9 to 30.9; in Navarra, from 9.3 to 9.5 to 3.5; and in Vizcaya, from 46.3 to 37.3 to 31.1. Thus, from their position as nearly a majority party in Guipúzcoa and Vizcaya, the PNV has slipped to a little less than one-third of the vote, and their position in the two interior provinces has deteriorated accordingly (see Table 19).

Some PNV publications have asserted that the net *abertzale* vote remained high, suggesting that a portion of the PNV vote had been drained off by new nationalist parties that did not exist in the 1930s. The arrangement of the vote data in Tables 20 to 23 permits us to test this assertion, which is affirmed, but not overwhelmingly. Across the four provinces, the *abertzale* parties other than the PNV (all of which are socialist or social-democrat) won 11.2 percent of the vote. When added to the PNV count, this gives all *abertzale* parties 35.6 percent of the total Basque vote, or a little more than the share that the PNV won in 1933 (the Party's high point in electoral victories). Province-by-province comparisons show much the same pattern. In Alava, the *abertzale* vote was 21.4 percent of the total (17.1 for the PNV, 4.3 for the others), compared with 29 percent for the PNV in 1933 and 20.3 percent in 1936. In Guipúzcoa, the left *abertzale* parties won 15.5 percent of the vote, which, when added to the PNV total, gives Basque nationalist parties a total of 46.4, compared with the PNV total of 45.5 in 1933. In Navarra, the two *abertzale* parties, UNAI (EHAS) and the PNV-ANV-ESB coalition, won 16.5 percent, better than

Table 19.
Vote Distribution in Four Basque Provinces in Parliamentary Elections, 1933, 1936 and 1977 (percent of total vote).

Province	**Left Parties**			**PNV**			**Right Parties**		
	1933	1936	1977	1933	1936	1977	1933	1936	1977
Alava	19.0	22.2	41.9	29.0	20.3	17.1	52.0	57.5	40.4
Guipúzcoa	29.8	30.0	51.0	45.5	36.9	30.9	24.7	33.1	17.8
Navarra	19.9	21.3	50.7	9.3	9.5	3.5	70.8	69.2	41.7
Vizcaya	34.3	37.2	44.7	46.3	37.3	31.1	19.4	25.5	24.2
Four provinces	28.0	29.8	47.2	34.3	28.0	24.4	37.7	42.2	27.6

Sources: For 1933 and 1936, see José Miguel Azaola, *Vasconia y su destino, I: La Regionalización de España* (Madrid: Revista de Occidente, 1972), pp. 544-545. For 1977, see Tables 18 and 20-23.

the PNV ever did in the 1930s. And in Vizcaya, all *abertzale* parties won 40.7 percent (including 31.1 from the PNV), which compares with the party's 46.3 in 1933 and 37.3 in 1936. Apparently, the performance of the left *abertzale* parties in their first electoral contest, with scant resources and little time for organizational work, should convince observers that the decline in the PNV vote does not mean a similar decline in Basque nationalism generally.

These observations bring us, then, to an analysis of the vote performance of the left in general. As Table 19 makes clear, left parties have never achieved more than about one-third of the popular vote of any of the Basque provinces, or in the region as a whole, except in 1936, when the left captured a little more than 37 percent in Vizcaya. Yet if we consider both the *abertzale* and the Spanish left parties together in the 1977 elections, they received nearly half of all votes cast in the four provinces (47.2 percent, to be precise). Of this percentage, about 36 percent came from the Spanish parties, and a little more than eleven percent from the *abertzale* socialists. The Spanish and left *abertzale* parties combined received 41.9 percent of the vote in Alava, 44.7 in Vizcaya, 51.0 in Guipúzcoa and 50.7 in Navarra. The difference between 40 percent and 50 percent seems to be the performance of the left *abertzale* parties. The Spanish left received much the same kind of response across the region: 35.1 in Vizcaya, 35.5 in Guipúzcoa, and 37 each in Alava and Navarra. Yet, the *abertzale* socialists scored major gains in Guipúzcoa and Navarra (15.5 and 13.0, respectively), much less in Vizcaya (9.6), and made hardly a dent in the statistics in Alava (4.3).

There appears to have been, then, a shift of major importance in the Basque provinces from the bourgeois center and the oligarchic right to the socialist left. Part of the shift is reflected in the increased strength of the Spanish socialists, particularly the PSOE. The remainder of the swing is observed in the new phenomenon of *abertzale* left-wing parties which manage to combine socialist and Basque nationalist ideologies, mainly at the cost of the Basque Nationalist Party. The net result is that left-oriented parties find themselves quite close to becoming a majority in the Basque region. There are three

Table 20.
Voting Patterns in Alava, 1977 Parliamentary Elections (showing percent of total vote).

		Left	PNV		Center/Right	Total
Abertzale	ESB	2,757 (2.2)				
	EE	2,622 (2.1)				
		5,379 (4.3)	21,247 (17.1)			26,626 (21.4)
Spanish	PSOE	34,243 (27.7)				
	PC	3,888 (3.1)				
	PSOE(H)	3,337 (2.6)		UCD	38,446 (31.1)	
	FUT	2,347 (1.9)		AP	7,957 (6.4)	
	PSP	1,674 (1.3)		DCV	3,369 (2.7)	
	Other	1,303 (1.0)		Other	396 (0.2)	
		46,792 (37.6)			50,168 (40.4)	96,960 (78.0)
Total		52,171 (41.9)	21,247 (17.1)		50,168 (40.4)	123,586 (99.4)

Source: Talde Euskal Estudio Elkartea, *Euskadi, ante las elecciones municipales* (San Sebastián: Ediciones Vascas, 1978), p. 33.

Table 21.
Voting Patterns in Guipúzcoa, 1977 Parliamentary Elections (showing percent of total vote).

		Left	PNV	Center/Right		Total
Abertzale	EE	31,009 (9.5)				
	ESB	18,131 (5.5)				
	ANV	1,826 (0.5)				
		50,966 (15.5)	101,036 (30.9)			152,002 (46.4)
Spanish	PSOE	91,872 (28.1)				
	PCE	12,034 (3.7)				
	PSP	4,896 (1.5)		GU	26,802 (8.2)	
	FUT	3,913 (1.1)		DCV	16,358 (4.9)	
	Other	4,005 (1.1)		DIV	15,398 (4.7)	
		116,720 (35.5)			58,558 (17.8)	175,278 (53.3)
Total		167,686 (51.0)	101,036 (30.9)		58,558 (17.8)	327,280 (99.7)

Source: Talde Euskal Estudio Elkartea, *Euskadi, ante las elecciones municipales* (San Sebastián: Ediciones Vascas, 1978), p. 34.

Table 22.
Voting Patterns in Navarra, 1977 Parliamentary Elections (showing percent of total vote).

	Left		PNV	Center/Right		Total
Abertzale	UNAI	24,489 (9.4)				
	ANV-ESB	9,039 (3.5)*				
		33,528 (13.0)	9,040 (3.5)*			42,568 (16.5)
Spanish	PSOE	54,720 (21.2)				
	AETN	13,195 (5.1)				
	EKA	8,451 (3.2)				
	PSP	6,629 (2.6)				
	FDI	6,661 (2.6)		UCD	75,036 (29.1)	
	PC	6,319 (2.4)		AFN	21,900 (8.5)	
	FUT	1,361 (0.5)		FNI	10,606 (4.1)	
		97,336 (37.7)			107,542 (41.7)	204,878 (79.4)
Total		130,864 (50.7)	9,040 (3.5)		107,542 (41.7)	247,446 (95.9)**

* Votes cast for UAN coalition (PNV-ANV-ESB) are divided equally between PNV and ANV-ESB.

**About 4 percent of votes cast for independents.

Source: Talde Euskal Estudio Elkartea, *Euskadi, ante las elecciones municipales* (San Sebastián: Ediciones Vascas, 1978), p. 35.

Table 23.
Voting Patterns in Vizcaya, 1977 Parliamentary Elections (showing percent of total vote).

		Left	PNV		Center/Right	Total
Abertzale	EE	35,895 (5.8)				
	ESB	17,527 (2.8)				
	ANV	5,580 (0.9)				
		59,002 (9.6)	192,199 (31.1)			251,201 (40.7)
Spanish	PSOE	151,385 (24.5)				
	PCE	32,764 (5.3)				
	PSP	13,754 (2.2)		UCD	100,897 (16.4)	
	ASD	7,466 (1.2)		AP	41,063 (6.6)	
	Other	11,491 (1.9)		DCV	7,172 (1.2)	
		216,860 (35.1)			149,132 (24.2)	365,992 (59.3)
Total		275,862 (44.7)	192,199 (31.1)		149,132 (24.2)	617,193 (100.0)

Source: Talde Euskal Estudio Elkartea, *Euskadi, ante las elecciones municipales* (San Sebastián: Ediciones Vascas, 1978), p. 36.

obstacles in their path. First, they must somehow overcome their own internal schisms and divisions. The PSOE clearly dominates the Spanish left, winning about 70 percent of the total socialist vote in each province except Navarra (where they got about 56 percent), and in the region as a whole. Yet, there were at least seven other left parties that shared in the remainder, and some, such as the PCE and the Carlists, are not at all prepared to yield to some sort of broad popular front coalition, at least in the short run. Second, the Spanish left and the *abertzale* socialists must come to some kind of agreement that will permit them to cooperate in campaigns and in power, rather than fragment their power in direct confrontation. It is clear that the *abertzale* socialist parties now hold a sort of anti-Madrid balance of power in the Basque country. Much now depends on how they choose to lean in the coming years: will they begin to consider themselves more Basque than socialist, and join with the PNV in a *"Batasuna"* coalition of Basque nationalists? Or, will they emphasize their socialist ties, and merge into some sort of alliance with the PSOE? The answer to this question hinges on how the PSOE meets its third obstacle: the articulation of Basque nationalist grievances, as opposed to those of the working class. Although the PSOE has committed itself to a restoration of the Autonomy Statute of 1936, this falls far short of meeting the contemporary demands of Basque nationalists, particularly in cultural areas such as language and education. In addition, while no one seemed to mention the church-state issue during the 1977 campaign, one cannot forget that the socialists failed to solidify their gains in the Basque region to a large degree because of their anticlerical posture, which is anathema to many Basques, and which may still prevent Basques from cooperating with the Spanish socialists.

Whatever the future holds in store, the 1977 elections should have communicated at least one message to Madrid: that the Basque provinces remain overwhelmingly discontented with the current state of affairs in Spain. When one adds together the votes of the nationalist PNV, the *abertzale* left parties, and the Spanish socialists, the result is a solid rejection of Premier Suárez, the UCD and the reform efforts of Madrid.

This vote, which I may be permitted to label the anti-establishment vote, reached 71.6 percent in the four Basque provinces as a whole, and ranged from 54.2 in Navarra and 59.0 in Alava, to 75.8 in Vizcaya and 81.9 in increasingly restive Guipúzcoa.[16] For the short run, the impact of this discontent would be held down by the Basques' cultural aversion to violence, and by their internal disagreements over the true identity of the enemy (whether it should be Spain, capitalism, or both). If Madrid failed to move promptly after June 1977 to resolve the festering Basque regional issue, and if one of the several dissident forces began to exercise region-wide leadership in the Basque country, the electoral discontent of the Basques would be likely to flare up in some other form of frustrated action, with unhappy consequences for both Spaniards *and* Basques.

Chapter Twelve

1978: CONSTITUTION, ESTATUTO AND ETA

At about 1:00 on the morning of December 31, 1977, the Spanish Minister for Regions, Manuel Clavero Arévalo, emerged from a marathon closed-door meeting of Spanish and Navarrese political leaders of the UCD, the governing political party, to announce that the Suárez government had decided to decree the granting of a "pre-autonomy" legal and administrative status to the Basque provinces.[1] Almost exactly one year later, on December 29, 1978, in the historic Casa de Juntas in Guernica, the members of the Spanish parliament from the three provinces of Alava, Guipúzcoa and Vizcaya voted overwhelmingly (24 to one, with one abstention) to approve the draft Autonomy Statute, and to send it immediately to Madrid to begin the lengthy process of ratification.[2] This chapter, then, deals with the principal political events of 1978, a watershed year in Basque political history, in that it marked the beginning of the crafting of the juridical and administrative framework within which Basque nationalism would have to develop over the coming years and decades. Within this context, the most significant developments had to do with the establishment of the Basque General Council to administer the transition to autonomous status, the efforts of the Basque nationalist deputies in parliament to influence the drafting of the new Spanish Constitution in the direction of greater autonomy for their region, and finally the drafting of the Autonomy Statute itself. In Basque politics, however, violence is never far from the surface. In the midst of this intensely political process, ETA-*militar* went on a renewed offensive which was met with considerable counter-violence by the Suarez government. At year's end, not only the Spanish armed forces but the general public as well rated terrorism as one of the principal problems their nation faced. The upheaval caused by ETA's offensive, as well as by the economic and political uncertainties of the young Spanish democracy, meant that the future of Basque nationalism in post-Franco Spain could be discerned only in barest outline.

The Basque General Council

The Basque General Council (*Consejo General Vasco,* or CGV), the administrative organ created by the Spanish government to manage the transition of the region to autonomy, was born in controversy. Its very creation was delayed for more than three months after its Catalan counterpart began to operate; and even after the pre-autonomy decree had been issued, there continued to be delay and postponement before the Council could begin to assume its responsibilities. The Council was not formally constituted until February 17, 1978, or about a month and a half after its establishment was decreed.

The first source of controversy connected with the creation of the CGV had to do with the inclusion or exclusion of Navarra from the regional body. The ancient separation between Navarra and the other three Basque provinces that had bedeviled Basque nationalist politicians for nearly a century, emerged once again to test the patience and bargaining skills of Basques of all political leanings. Leaders of the Basque Nationalist Party urged inclusion of Navarra along with the other three provinces on the grounds that Navarra constitutes about half of the territory of the region, and is its principal source of agricultural production. Furthermore, by leaving Navarra outside the regional body, the Spanish government had retained a bargaining wedge that they could use to effect to frustrate the transition of the region to complete autonomy. The Navarrese, for their part, asserted that were they to join the regional unit, they would lose their special privileged relationship with the Spanish government dating back to the nineteenth century.[3] The conflict was aggravated somewhat by the fact that Spain's governing party, UCD, had been the major vote-getter in Navarra in the 1977 elections, winning 28.5 percent of the popular vote, and three of the province's five seats in the parliament's lower house. From that electoral victory, the UCD deputies from Navarra exercised a special degree of influence with their UCD colleagues in Madrid, and so were able to affect the Spanish government's decisions about regional autonomy more than would have been the case otherwise.

The very method of organizing and ratifying the CGV, and a province's presence in it, was the source of controversy. While there was a presumption that a province's participation in the Council should be the result of the actions of freely and democratically elected representatives, the fact was that in the period between Franco's death and the promulgation of the new Spanish Constitution (still a year into the future), there were no such democratically chosen leaders to which one could turn for ratification. The provincial and municipal governments had all been appointed from Madrid; and, while many were no doubt in close touch with the popular opinion of their jurisdictions and their constituents, many were equally far removed from the current of public attitudes. Worst of all, in the absence of provincial and municipal elections, there was no reliable way to determine which local leaders really represented their constituents and which were merely enjoying the appointed power from the Spanish government. Faced with this problem, the Suárez government left the task of ratification of each province's participation in the hands of the members of parliament from that province. Since they were the only democratically elected political leaders available to be consulted, it was felt that they would have to serve as the voice of the people until such time as a better and more responsive mechanism could be fashioned.

In Alava, Guipúzcoa and Vizcaya, the deputies and senators met on February 14 and officially ratified not only the general notion of the pre-autonomy decree, but accepted for their province a role in the new CGV. A few members from Alava did question briefly whether it might not be advisable for Alava to delay their joining until Navarra had become a member; but once it became clear that Navarra was not going to join (a decision formally ratified by Navarra's parliamentary representative on February 15), they hastened to reassure the other provinces that they could count on Alava's presence in the Council.[4]

In the case of Navarra, however, the members of parliament objected to the very method of joining the CGV, and held out for a special supplementary decree that would govern the adhesion of Navarra to the already-formed Basque regional unit. Instead of lodging decision making authority in the assembly of members of parliament from Navarra, the Navarrese proposal was to go first to the provincial government of the province, followed (if adhesion was approved) by a plebiscite of the people of Navarra, which had to be approved by two-thirds of the towns, cities and municipalities of the province in order to be passed. Because it would be impossible to carry out this process until after provincial and municipal elections, and because such elections could not be held until after the new constitution had been adopted, the Navarrese proposal was essentially to stay out of the CGV until after the constitution had come into effect, and to govern its adhesion by the terms of that document. The other major parties in the CGV, PNV and PSOE felt that the Navarrese suggestion left too much power in the hands of the several hundred municipal governments. Of the 500 *municipios* in the four Basque provinces, 264 are located in Navarra, even though Navarra has only about 19 percent of the population of the region. Of the 264 Navarra townships, 215 contain populations of fewer than 2,000 persons. These 215 *municipios* contain only about 21.5 percent of the total population of Navarra, and only about 4 percent of the total population of the Basque provinces.[5] According to the original Navarrese formula, this tiny segment of the Basque population could effectively thwart the intentions of the overwhelming majority by refusing their assent to Navarrese membership in the unit. Accordingly, PNV and PSOE representatives met with UCD leaders in Madrid to work out a compromise which would consider the plebiscite approved if carried by a simple majority of the total population. Predictably, the Navarrese members of parliament, as well as the provincial government of Navarra, rejected this solution and charged that they had been betrayed by UCD leaders.[6] As it was finally worked out, the Spanish Constitution incorporates *both* Navarrese formulas: for a province to join an already existing autonomous regional unit, the decision must be made by the provincial government, or (in the words of the Constitution) the "competent foral organ," and subsequently approved by a majority of the votes in a provincial plebiscite.[7] In any case, Navarra remained definitively outside the Basque pre-autonomy structure, and it seemed likely that the province would remain outside whatever regional government might emerge in the foreseeable future.

Apart from the question of Navarra, the second major source of controversy was the split between the PNV and the Basque socialists over control of the CGV. In addition to approving the province's adhesion to the CGV, the assembly of parliament members from each province was responsible for choosing five members of the Council. According to the pre-autonomy decree, each province was allowed five members of the Council, to be chosen by the assembly of deputies and senators from that province. The choice of these fifteen members was made roughly according to the strength of each political party in the Basque parliamentary delegation. Thus, the 1977 parliamentary elections came to be used as guidelines for selecting the members of the CGV. This method of selection resulted in the following composition of the Council: from Alava, two seats for UCD, one for the socialist PSOE, one for the PNV, and one independent; from Guipúzcoa, two seats for PNV, two for PSOE, and one for the left *abertzale* party, *Euzkadiko Ezkerra;* and from Vizcaya, two for PNV, two for PSOE, and one for UCD. As a whole then, the PNV and the PSOE each held five seats on the council, UCD had three, EE had one, and there was one independent.[8] This division of strength virtually guaranteed friction between PNV and PSOE, and put into the hands of UCD the power to act as an arbiter on close votes. This was not the most fortuitous balance of forces for the fledgling Council.

At the outset of the CGV's functioning, there was a spirit of cooperation between Basque nationalists and socialists, who together represented well over half of the population of the four Basque provinces. On the issue of the adhesion of Navarra, for example, the final compromise solution was struck by negotiation among representatives of PNV and PSOE together with leaders of the UCD. However, after a month or so this cooperative spirit began to suffer under the stresses and strains of competition for the scarcest of political resources: access to power.

During January and February of 1978, the central point of conflict between Basque nationalists and the PSOE was the presidency of the CGV. A subsidiary issue, and one whose solution depended entirely on the solution found for the first issue, was the disposition of Council seats, and the assignment of specific ministerial responsibilities among the various parties represented on the Council. The PNV proposed that their principal leader, Juan Ajurriaguerra, should be chosen president of the CGV because the Basque Nationalist Party had been the top party in the 1977 elections in the three provinces represented on the Council, gaining 30.6 percent of the vote, against 27 percent for the PSOE. The PNV's candidates had been the leading vote getters in Vizcaya and Guipúzcoa, and third in Alava; whereas the socialists had come in second in all three provinces. In addition, they argued, since the CGV was being formed expressly to pave the way for the transition to regional autonomy, it made no sense to place in the presidency of the Council a representative of what was essentially a Spanish political party and deny that post to the party that had been the traditional source of pressure for Basque regional autonomy for more than 80 years. Finally, since the candidate proposed by the PSOE did not speak Euskera, the PNV argued that it would be difficult for the CGV to advocate bilingualism in official matters if a person with that deficiency were chosen as the symbolic head of the transitional government. To counter these arguments, the PSOE asserted that their candidate, Ramon Rabial, should be selected because Spanish parties, i.e., non-Basque or non-*abertzale* parties, represented the majority of the Council (five from PSOE and three from UCD); a representative from that sector of Basque public opinion should be placed in the presidency. Further, it was felt that the CGV would have more success in Madrid if their leader were chosen from one of the two major Spanish parties and could therefore count on support from his colleagues in the rest of Spain. Finally, if one considered all four Basque provinces, the difference between the two parties' popular vote in 1977 was insignificant: 336 votes out of more than 1,200,000 cast; or about two-hundredths of a percent. Much of the time during the first two months of 1978 was spent trying to hammer out a compromise solution to these opposed positions. Finally, on February 7 PNV representatives proposed that the Council meet on February 17, whether or not the conflict had been resolved, and proceed to elect a president on the basis of sheer political strength.[9] The following day, February 8, representatives of UCD announced that, while they would prefer for PSOE and PNV to work out a suitable arrangement between themselves, if the vote went to the floor of the full Council, they (the UCD) would support the socialist candidate, Rubial.[10] This decision was an interesting reflection of the priorities of UCD: better to support the socialists, their arch enemies in the rest of Spain, than to give any sign of support for regional autonomy as advocated by the PNV. In the battle between class and ethnicity, UCD obviously felt that it was preferable to deal with the Basques in terms of class, and try thereby to defuse the ethnic dimension of the upcoming struggle over regional autonomy.

Further negotiations between the PNV and the PSOE were futile. On February 17, the CGV met formally for the first time, as convened and selected by the members of Parliament from the three provinces. There still had been no decision made about the Council's presidency, or about the disposition of any of the remaining posts. The election of the Council's president required eight separate votes, and more than six hours of negotiations before a definitive choice could be made. From the beginning, the two candidates, Rubial and Ajurriaguerra, abstained, as did the independent member from Alava, Juan Manual Lopez de Juan Abad, thus leaving twelve voting members. The first vote gave six votes to Ajurriaguerra, five to Rubial, and one ballot was left blank; but, since the pre-autonomy decree required that the first vote had to be by two-thirds majority, the Council passed on to successive votes. The second through seventh ballots ended in a series of six-to-six ties, meaning that one of the UCD Council members was voting for the PNV candidate. At about five o'clock in the afternoon, it was announced that there was a telephone call from Madrid for one of the UCD members, Juan Echevarria from Alava. Shortly after the call, there was a recess while members of the *Euzkadiko Ezkerra* coalition publicly criticized their delegate Juan María Bandrés for voting for Ajurriaguerra. Finally, at 7:45 pm, the eighth ballot produced the tie-breaking vote: six for Rubial, five for Ajurriaguerra, and one vote blank. Speculation abounded as to which pressure had broken the support for the PNV candidate, that on the UCD delegate from Madrid, or that on the EE delegate from the Basque left. In either case, the PSOE's support held fast, and the socialists gained the leadership position of the CGV at least until the next parliamentary elections.[11]

With the election of the president out of the way, the next major obstacle was the disposition of ministerial portfolios among the various parties. While there was supposed to be consensus between PNV and PSOE in principle over this distribution, in actual practice it turned out to be rather difficult to come to a definitive disposition, given the personal preferences of certain members of the Council. It was not until the first working session of the Council, on February 24, that these decisions were made and announced. PNV members were placed in four posts: Education; Health and Social Welfare; Industry, Commerce and Fishing; and Economy. Members of PSOE were given four posts as well: Labor, Culture, Justice, and Interior. To UCD went the positions dealing with Agriculture and with Public Works and Housing. The councilor from *Euzkadiko Ezkerra* was given the portfolio for Transportation and Communications. Three councilors were left without portfolio.[12]

After nearly two months, then, the Basque General Council was finally constituted, and could begin to function as an interim or transitional organ to facilitate the progress of the region to its autonomous status. While certainly not fatal, the delay and acrimonious fighting between PNV and PSOE did not bode well for the future of the Council. Once again, the clash between social class and ethnicity emerged as a chief obstacle to Basque unity. The new element in the whole process was the "divide and conquer" strategy of UCD. At least as seen by Basque nationalists, the first objective of UCD had been to fragment the Basque provinces by keeping Navarra out of the CGV. Successful in that, UCD had then acted as a wedge within the Council itself, first to aggravate the struggle between nationalists and socialists, and then to throw their weight on the side of the PSOE candidate, who, it was felt, would be more "reasonable" on the issue of regional autonomy. As long as UCD remained in power in Madrid, and as long as UCD and PSOE shared a general consensus about how to deal with the ethnic regions, then it appeared as if Basque nationalism would have a difficult time gaining the ascendancy, not only in Madrid but in the Basque region as well.

The third major problem confronting the Basque General Council had to do with the general issues of the transfer of actual governing responsibilities and the devolution of sufficient authority and resources to meet these responsibilities effectively. According to the terms of the decree that established the CGV, the Council would possess only those powers and responsibilities granted to it subsequently by the Spanish government. Within these limits, the Council would have the power to allocate resources that had been granted it by Madrid and to administer the local programs required to meet the needs of the Basque provinces in those areas assigned to it by the central government. All matters internal to the CGV would be left to its own control, and the Council would have authority to make recommendations to the Spanish government concerning problems that were of special importance to residents of the Basque region. Beyond these powers, however, the Basque General Council was basically a weak and transitory institution, virtually dependent on the Spanish central government for its power and the resources necessary to carry out its responsibilities.

To begin with, the Council could carry on its activities only according to a set of rules laid down by the Spanish government. Madrid would assign to the Council its basic functions and fields of authority and inform it of the services it was entitled and empowered to deliver to its constituents. It was foreseen in the decree that the Council and the Spanish government would establish a joint mixed-membership commission composed primarily of technicians who would negotiate the specific functions, tasks, and responsibilities to be accorded to the CGV. Despite the requests of the Basque nationalists, Madrid decided not to institute democratic elections in the Basque provinces at the time of the selection of the Council; but Madrid retained control over the formation of provincial and municipal governments in the Basque region, in order to preserve consistency across Spain's fifty provinces as far as the representativeness of local governments was concerned. In the case of Navarra, the Spanish government, in consultation with the Navarrese provincial government, would determine which institution within Navarra would be empowered to vote the province's adhesion to the Basque regional entity (a favorable vote would be followed by a referendum of Navarrese voters, according to the new Spanish Constitution).

The Spanish government reflected its basic mistrust of the Basque regional experiment most clearly in its retention of final control over the decisions and actions taken by the CGV. According to the decree, Madrid retains the right to suspend all acts of the Basque General Council, from which the Basques have no recourse or avenue of appeal. Finally, as an ultimate protection against unwarranted or excessive acts by the CGV, the central government can dissolve the organs of preautonomy "for reasons of state security."[13] In sum, it can easily be seen that the creation of the Basque General Council was at best only a very tentative step in the direction of regional autonomy, and much remained to be fleshed out through subsequent actions and decisions by the Suárez government.

It was at this point that it became clear that the government in Madrid chose to regard the Basque regional experiment as basically an exercise in administrative decentralization rather than as a response to the nationalist aspirations of the PNV and its followers. Over the course of the Franco era, Spain had become a modern industrialized state of more than 35 million people, with the substantial problems as are inevitably connected with such a development: urban congestion; scarcity of low income housing; environmental degradation; the need for mass education, health care, and communications; and many others. As other industrial countries have discovered, many of these problems cannot be resolved adequately if the central regime retains full control over policies that are nation-wide in scope. Thus, the new post-Franco elites in Spain sought to loosen the bonds of governmental regulation and administration by a policy of steady and controlled devolution of certain *administrative* responsibilities to the more heavily industrialized regions. These policies were pursued, however, not to foster an upsurge in regional ethnic sentiment, but rather to achieve greater efficiencies in the management of a complex industrial state. By placing the creation of the Basque General Council in this context, Madrid gave a clear indication that the transition to regional autonomy would not be allowed to edge closer to any sort of juridical or political framework that offered the Basques the opportunity to widen the economic gap between themselves and the rest of Spain.

As an integral part of this strategy to equate Basque regionalism with administrative decentralization, the Spanish government insisted that all autonomous regions would possess the same powers, resources and responsibilities during their transitional phase. While the establishment of a fully autonomous region would be a unique procedure in each case, and one that would be negotiated individually for Basques, Catalans, Galicians, and others, the transitional entities would be for all intents and purposes identical institutions. For this reason, the Catalan example proved to be the only one of negotiation over the transfer of powers. Since the Catalan regime was the first to be developed, its powers were subject to more bargaining. Subsequent regional entities, such as the Basque General Council, would have to follow the pattern established by the Catalan *Generalitat*. Thus, while the joint Spanish-Basque Mixed Commission was indeed established, it met only infrequently, and before long lapsed into nonexistence. Another mixed commission, established to study the restoration of the *Conciertos Económicos* for Vizcaya and Guipúzcoa met only once to be constituted formally. By the end of 1978, it was apparent that these special matters of interest to the Basque provinces would have to await the approval of a formal autonomy statute; and even then, it looked as if the solutions would be found only after long and arduous negotiation with Madrid.

In the absence of pressure from the proposed Mixed Commission, the transfer of power proceeded, as the Basques liked to say, "drop by drop." Despite the fact that each councilor had quickly drawn up comprehensive lists of possible powers to be transferred to the CGV, by the middle of the year Madrid had still not transferred a single authority, function, or service to the Council.[14] By the end of 1978, the Spanish government had transferred two "packages" of functions, including commerce, industry and fishing, and transportation. Shortly after the beginning of 1979, the following activities were also transferred in whole or in part: labor, health, culture, education, and agriculture. In certain sensitive areas that dealt with the maintenance of public order, such as interior and justice, Madrid kept tight control over all responsibilities. This control was symbolized dramatically in late December, when the Spanish Director of Prisons ordered the transfer of all Basque political prisoners from the various jails and prisons in the Basque provinces where they were being held to the maximum security prison in Soria. The move, made allegedly to prevent a massive escape of nearly 90 members of ETA, was executed in secrecy, and for a while after the move not even the families of the prisoners knew that they had been removed. The CGV and its Councilor for Justice complained heatedly, and there were demonstrations in San Sebastián and other Basque cities to protest this step. Nevertheless, on sensitive matters such as these, the Basques were still completely helpless to prevent the Spanish government from acting unilaterally and without prior consultation.

Still another source of weakness within the CGV was the low level of economic resources on which they could rely to carry out their functions. Since the Council had no independent taxing authority, it had to rely entirely on funds granted to it by the Spanish government. For the second half of 1978, Madrid made available to the CGV the sum of 131 million pesetas, the equivalent of a little more than $2,183,000, or about $363,000 per month. After dividing this sum evenly among the various Council portfolios, each councilor had a budget of about $100,000 to cover the expenses of his office's functions and activities for the six-month period.

The Council's Office of Commerce, Industry and Fishing illustrates many of the salient operational problems of the CGV during the first year of its existence. Despite the fact that this portfolio covered approximately 66 percent of the economic production of the three Basque provinces, and accounted for about 57 percent of the employment of the region, the physical and financial resources of the office were kept ridiculously low for the entire first year of operation. With the budget given him, the councilor for this office, Mikel Isasi, was able to employ only two persons other than himself, in addition to covering the operating expenses of the office. As late as July 1978, the councilor had no separate office from which to operate; he was forced to use the office set aside for him as a representative of the Basque Government-in-Exile. His one single professional assistant, the Director of the Office, operated from a separate location. The major personnel resource available to Isasi consisted of the 120 employees of the Spanish government's Vizcayan office for industrial and trade promotion. Even though they worked technically for Isasi, they continued to receive their salaries from Madrid, a fact that obviously influenced their commitment to the directives and policies of the Basque General Council. Technical assistance was extremely scarce. Few economists or engineers would be willing to commit themselves to employment that had such an obviously short life span. A number of Basque economists and other technicians worked on a volunteer basis to supply Isasi's office with advice; but these nuclei of experience suffered from a lack of research resources as well as from the usual problems of lack of leadership and discontinuity that most volunteer groups experience. Local chambers of commerce and other professional associations had little formal contact with the CGV in these early stages. All in all, Isasi estimated that his office would need at least four times the budget it had in order to begin to resolve some of the really grave economic problems affecting the Basque region, especially in Vizcaya and Guipúzcoa. But so long as the CGV lacked its own taxing powers, it seemed highly unlikely that it would ever be able to mount much more than a token operation.[15]

In sum, then, the experience of the first year of the Basque General Council was disappointing. Lacking vital human and fiscal resources, enjoying only those powers and authorities doled out little by little by the central Spanish government, and divided internally by the schism between class and ethnicity, the Council was a frustrated and ineffectual body. The CGV's frustration could easily have been translated into political disillusionment and protest, for many Basque nationalists deeply believed that the constitution of the CGV would lead easily to the establishment of regional autonomy. Working class Basques brought many of their complaints to the CGV for resolution; but in most cases they had to be turned away with the explanation that the Council lacked the resources even to begin to deal with their problems. That the level of frustration did not rise any higher than it did among Basque nationalists in these days was due probably to the relatively great strides that were made toward the drafting of a definitive autonomy statute under the terms of the new Spanish Constitution. Thus, it is to that aspect of the watershed year 1978 that we must now turn our attention.

The Constitution and the Estatuto[16]

The first two stages of the transition of Spain to democracy had been the December 1976 referendum on political reform, followed by the legalization of political parties and labor unions, and the June 1977 parliamentary elections to form the first freely elected Cortes since the Civil War. Although the 1977 elections had been conducted without explicit reference to the drafting of a new constitution, the logical flow of events from the 1976 referendum forward led to the newly formed Cortes being given responsibilities for writing and approving a new Spanish constitution. Thus, while the Basque General Council developed its approach to the problem of regional autonomy within the Spanish state, on another track the Basque nationalist members of the new parliament worked to insure that the new constitution would contain provisions that would be favorable for the establishment of an autonomous Basque region once the country's organic law was approved.

The new parliament had barely been formed when decisions of fundamental importance were taken that had significant bearing on the regional autonomy issue. On July 25, 1977, only a little more than a month after the elections, the parliament's lower house, the Congress of Deputies, created as one of its standing committees the so-called Constitutional Commission, which subsequently came to be known as the Committee on Constitutional Matters and Public Liberties. On August 1, the full Committee elected seven of its members to serve as a Subcommittee charged with preparing the first draft of a bill that would eventually become the new constitution.

At about this time, maneuverings to form the political coalitions within the Congress created a number of inescapable problems for the Basque nationalists. At the outset of the Congress' functioning, it was decided that seats on the various committees and subcommittees would be allocated according to the number of seats each party or bloc of parties held in the full body. However, in order to qualify as a party or a coalition of parties, each unit had to hold at least fifteen seats in the Congress. Since the PNV had only eight seats, they were forced to coalesce with their counterparts from Cataluña, who had 13 seats, and who were therefore also obliged to ally with other groups in order to gain representation. To this group was joined the single representative from *Euzkadiko Ezkerra,* Francisco Letamendia, who eventually left the coalition for reasons that were both ideological and personal. Before Letamendia's departure, however, the Basque-Catalan Parliamentary Group consisted of 22 members, which made it the third largest coalition in the Congress, but much smaller than the governing UCD or the socialists. The Basque members of UCD and PSOE naturally affiliated with their respective party's members and seldom participated with the PNV in matters having to do with regional autonomy questions.

Although the alliance with the Catalans added power to the PNV parliamentary delegation, it also had serious consequences for its representation on the key committees that dealt with constitutional questions. The full Constitutional Committee consisted of 36 deputies, of which 17 were from UCD, 13 from PSOE, two were communists, two were from the neo-Francoist AP, one was a Basque Nationalist, and one was from Cataluña. In the important Subcommittee that was charged with drafting the first version of the constitution, however, the Basques were without voice or vote. The seven members of the Subcommittee included three from UCD, one from PSOE, one from the communists, one from AP, and one from the Basque-Catalan coalition. Since the Catalans were the dominant force in that coalition, they naturally insisted on the right to occupy the single seat allocated to the coalition from the Subcommittee. Thus, the Basques found themselves helpless to affect the drafting of the first version of the constitution. From that point onward, they were forced to carry on their business by efforts to amend the original version. The defenders of the original version, on the other hand, were in much the stronger position. The absence of natural allies within the Congress and the Senate also hurt the PNV's cause. Even the Catalan nationalists had a less intransigent view of regional rights than did the Basques; and the Spanish socialists showed themselves more inclined to deal with Basque regionalism as a matter of administrative decentralization than as a question of ethnic nationalism. Thus, the Basque nationalist cause had little reason for optimism as the constitutional review and approval procedure went forward during late 1977 and all of 1978.

The Constitutional Subcommittee of the Congress began its deliberations in strict secrecy on August 22. By November 17, the first draft was completed, which was leaked to the press on November 23. After being subjected to two more readings within the Subcommittee, the final draft of the first version was submitted to the chairman of the full Constitutional Committee on December 23, and was published in the official bulletin of the Cortes on January 5, 1978.

Following the official publication of the draft version of the new constitution, parties in the Congress were given until the end of January to prepare their lists of amendments. The deputies from the PNV, together with the party's governing council, the *Euzkadi Buru Batzar,* gathered in a convent in Amorebieta and in a matter of days hammered out a complete set of amendments that would present the Basque nationalist case. In all, the PNV presented slightly more than 100 amendments to the draft constitution, out of a total of 3,100 amendments presented by all the members of the Congress.[17] The *abertzale* left, represented by the *Euzkadiko Ezkerra* coalition, presented 85 amendments, many of which were co-sponsored with other political parties, including the PSOE.

For sake of analysis, the PNV amendments can be clustered into six broad categories. The first of these sets of amendments, which proved to be the most controversial, had to do with the re-establishment of the framework of foral law for all four Basque provinces, including Navarra. Thus, according to these changes, the laws of September 6-19, 1837, October 25, 1839 and June 21, 1876 would all be canceled, and replaced with the foral laws that had governed relations between the Spanish Crown and the Basque provinces before the Carlist Wars. The second cluster of amendments focused on the symbolic statements in the first several articles of Title I, that had to do with nationality. For example, whereas Paragraph Two of Article One stated that "National sovereignty resides in the Spanish people, . . ." the PNV proposed altering this phrase to read "National sovereignty resides in the peoples that form the Spanish state." Article Two asserts that "The Constitution is based on the indissoluble unity of the Spanish Nation," while the PNV proposal would have read "The Constitution is based on the indissoluble union of the Spanish Nation." Much labor of the PNV went into defending the portion of the original version of Article Two which read, in part, that "The Constitution . . . recognizes and guarantees the right to autonomy of the nationalities and regions that make up [the Spanish Nation]", a phrasing that allegedly caused much consternation among Spanish rightists. In this same vein, the PNV fought to insure that regional languages would be treated in a protective manner by the new constitution, and would be given a status equal to that of Castillian, proclaimed as the official language of the Spanish state. Still another set of amendments consisted of concerns of Basque nationalists that were not directly linked to the issue of regional autonomy: elimination of the death penalty, recognition of the special rights of children and of the elderly, authorization of divorce, and other social matters.

At a somewhat more mechanical level, the PNV's amendments dealt with three sets of practical questions. The first had to do with the powers of the autonomous units still to be created under the terms of the constitution. The PNV argued generally that the list of such powers should be expanded as much as possible, especially in those fields related to economic and financial matters, including taxation and public spending. The second area of PNV concern centered on the procedure for establishing an autonomous regional unit. The original draft had stipulated that proposed autonomy statutes would originate in an assembly of deputies and senators from the provinces affected, pass through the Constitutional Committee of the Congress, be voted on by a popular referendum of the region, and be sent to the Cortes for ratification. The PNV sought to reduce the time requirements for this procedure by sending the proposed statute directly from the deputies and senators to a popular referendum, and thence to the Cortes for ratification. The third set of issues involved the possibility of links between and among autonomous territories. With this proposal, the PNV sought to open the possibilities of linking together the Basque provinces and Navarra, on the assumption that the latter would not be included in an autonomous Basque region in the foreseeable future. The principal Spanish concern with amendments of this sort lay in a fear that a union of autonomous regions could become the foundation for an eventual Spanish federal state, a solution that was anathema to many conservative Spaniards.

On February 9, 1978, the Constitutional Subcommittee of the Congress began to examine the several thousand amendments to their original draft. The PNV, effectively closed out of the deliberations of this Subcommittee, was restricted to public declarations and behind-the-scenes negotiations over issues of importance to them. Within the Subcommittee, the regional autonomy issue was so controversial that it was a major cause for the delay of the work of the Subcommittee far beyond the deadline of March 16 that had been set for its final report.[18] Finally, after the application of pressure from the Catalan deputies, a compromise wording of Title VIII of the constitution dealing with autonomous territories was reported out of the Subcommittee in late March.[19]

It would take us afield to discuss in much detail the ensuing process of negotiation, bargaining, and approval. Bare outlines will suffice. On May 5, the full Constitutional Committee of the Congress began debate on the draft constitution, a process that was completed by June 20. On July 4, the draft was taken up by the full Congress of Deputies. On July 13, representatives from PNV and UCD entered into a series of intensive discussions in order to reach consensus on a number of sensitive issues related to regional autonomy, especially the wording of the constitutional provision dealing with the reestablishment of foral law in the Basque provinces. The Congress began debating Title VIII of the draft on July 18, and the UCD-PNV discussions broke down in failure almost immediately thereafter, with both sides accusing the other of intransigence and of bargaining in bad faith. Shortly thereafter, the entire draft constitution was approved by the Congress and sent to the Senate, whose Constitutional Committee began discussion of its provisions on August 18. From the end of August to about the middle of September there was another round of PNV-UCD discussions at the Senate level, with the same dismal results as those at the earlier point in the process. On October 5, in a definitive vote on Title VIII, the Senate rejected the last of the PNV amendments concerning the mechanisms of regional autonomy. Even though the final vote of the Cortes on the new Constitution would not be taken until October 31, it was apparent at this point that the PNV had been defeated on nearly every point that it had tried to contest the draft. Accordingly, on October 29, at a meeting of the Party's National Assembly in Pamplona, the PNV formally decided to urge all Basques to abstain in the upcoming referendum on the Constitution, now scheduled for December 6.

The PNV decision to abstain from the referendum was a complex and controversial one that called for maximum party unity and discipline. There were, on the one hand, those who believed that the draft Constitution did at least make provision for the creation of autonomous communities in Spain's historical regions; and while their powers and authorities might be less than optimal for Basque nationalists, the new document offered the first step toward the restoration of regional autonomy so long denied them. For this reason, many leaders of the PNV felt that it would be harmful to vote against the new Constitution, especially if it looked as if the draft might fail in the December referendum. Inasmuch as the new Constitution took a radical position on such issues as abortion and divorce, and so had provoked the opposition of the Church, there were those who argued that the regional issue could not be allowed to drag down the new organic law and its opportunities, no matter how minimal, for regional autonomies. On the other hand, the PNV had been sharply dismayed by the rough treatment their representatives had received in Madrid, and by the Spanish government's insistence on dealing with the Basque issue as merely a question of administrative decentralization. Therefore, the Party determined that it would be necessary to send a message to Madrid to reaffirm their position that the Basque people were dissatisfied with the spirit of the new Constitution and of the process that produced it, even if they were minimally satisfied with its literal content.

It does seem to be the case that the new Spanish Constitution offered a mixed bag of advantages and disadvantages to the country's regional minorities. Article Two of Title I, for example, guarantees the right to autonomy for virtually any significant group that requests it; yet the procedures provided to lodge such requests seemed designed to prevent the actual granting of any significant degree of real self-government. Article Three of Title I exalts the linguistic pluralism that characterizes modern Spain; but the same article gives preeminent status to Castillian over the "other Spanish languages." Regional flags and other symbols are permitted if they are used alongside the Spanish flag. The first of the so-called "Additional Provisions" that were added at the end of the basic text of the Constitution affirms that the Constitution "shelters and respects the historic rights of the foral territories," but the second sentence of this provision asserts that the restoration of foral status to any region "will be carried out within the framework of the Constitution and of the Autonomy Statutes," which are basically political documents that emerge from a political process rather than some absolute grant of monarchical authority from an earlier time. The infamous Spanish decrees of 1837 and 1876 are formally done away with by the new Constitution; but, since nothing is put in their place, little is changed, as the Basque provinces of Alava, Guipúzcoa and Vizcaya continue to be governed from Madrid, while Navarra is not even mentioned in this passage in the new Constitution.

Title VIII of the new document addresses itself to "The Territorial Organization of the State." After affirming that no regional authority has the power to restrict the free circulation of Spaniards within the national territory, and after dedicating several articles to local administration, the Third Chapter moves on to consider the Autonomous Communities. Such communities are envisioned as arising out of one of two sources: either the provincial governments, together with two-thirds of the municipal governments, in the case of new regions that have never been so designated before; or, as in the case of the Basques, from the designated pre-autonomy organ, in this instance the Basque General Council, whose majority vote will be sufficient to initiate the process. The CGV, by majority vote, is empowered to convene the deputies and senators from the three member provinces who, in assembly, are responsible for drafting the proposed Autonomy Statute. The assembly of parliamentarians by majority vote will ratify the Statute and send it to the Constitutional Committee of the Congress of Deputies, where it will be examined for its accordance with the Constitution. If the Committee approves the form of the Statute, it will then be submitted to a referendum in each of the constituent provinces, where it must receive a majority vote in each province in order to be ratified. After this step, the Statute will be sent to both houses of the Cortes, where it must be approved by a majority of both houses. Following such approval, it will be ratified by the king and will take effect. According to an additional provision of the Constitution, Navarra can join later by means of a majority vote of the designated "foral organ" (in all likelihood, a democratically elected provincial assembly), followed by a majority vote in a popular referendum.

The powers and authorities of any given Autonomous Community may consist of the following (a partial list): regional planning, especially in such areas as land use; public works; transportation facilities; agriculture, livestock, raw materials, forests, etc.; economic development; education, especially in the case of the regional language; social welfare; health; sports, entertainment and recreation. Matters left strictly to the central government in Madrid include the following (again, a partial list): equality of personal and individual rights; international relations and armed forces; administration of justice; penal codes; labor legislation; civil legislation; tariffs and customs duties; monetary system, including exchange rates; the nation's Social Security system; public works, transportation facilities, and so forth that exceed the limits of the Community; public security, police and the maintenance of order. Any matters not dealt with expressly in the Constitution may be attributed to the Community by means of the Statute. The Spanish government retains the right to bring the laws of various Autonomous Communities into harmony with national legislation when necessary; and Madrid reserves the right to intervene with approval of a majority of the Senate to alter Community acts that threaten Spain's national interest.

The governing institutions of Autonomous Communities will consist of a popularly elected parliament, a president elected by the parliament, and a Supreme Tribunal of Justice. The government of the Community will enjoy considerable financial autonomy, including the right to levy its own taxes and to charge for its services in its territory, as well as the power to charge for licenses and permits, and to receive income from the rent or other use of public property such as buildings or land. Autonomous Communities are prohibited from levying taxes the effect of which is to impede the free circulation of people or goods throughout Spain; but autonomous regions may receive additional transfer payments from the central government if such are negotiated with Madrid.

In sum, while the provisions for regional autonomy in the new Spanish Constitution are not everything the Basque nationalists would want, they are not vastly different from similar provisions in the Constitution of the Second Republic, and in some cases go considerably beyond those provisions. Given a commitment to negotiate in good faith on both sides of the bargaining table, it was reasonable to anticipate that the Basques would soon enjoy a statute granting them substantial freedom to govern themselves in both cultural and economic matters according to their own needs and interests. It was precisely the fear of many Basque nationalists that the Spanish center and right would not negotiate in good faith, however, that prompted them to insist on one more clear signal from Euzkadi of their discontent with the prevailing Spanish approach to regional autonomy. It was in this context, then, that the PNV advocated abstention on December 6 in order to remind Madrid of the steadfastness of their commitment to meaningful regional self-governance.

As a means of sending a message, however, abstention or non-voting in a referendum is exceedingly complex, since the results almost always allow multiple or conflicting interpretations. It is true, on the one hand, that nearly a million residents of the Basque provinces chose not to vote in the 1978 referendum, slightly more than half of the total eligible Basque electorate (51.2 percent, to be exact). However, as Table 24 indicates, the inclination to abstain varies considerably across the provinces, with Alava and Navarra registering from one-third to about 40 percent non-voters, and Vizcaya and Guipúzcoa achieving much higher rates of more than 55 percent. Abstention data must be subjected to a comparative analysis that measures the results not only against the rest of Spain but across time as well. In this analysis, the Basque provinces did not achieve remarkable levels of abstention in 1978. Alava and Navarra abstained to about the same degree as the rest of Spain. While Vizcaya and Guipúzcoa abstention rates were about 1.7 to 1.8 times those of the rest of Spain, they represented an actual decline from the proportions seen in

Table 24.
Abstention Levels in Basque Provinces in Four Spanish Referenda.

Province	Abstentions as Percent of Eligible Voters				Ratio of Abstentions to Spanish Average			
	1947	1966	1976	1978	1947	1966	1976	1978
Alava	14.1	11.9	23.7	40.7	1.2	1.1	1.0	1.2
Guipúzcoa	8.4	24.2	55.1	56.6	0.7	2.2	2.4	1.7
Navarra	6.0	11.9	26.4	33.4	0.5	1.1	1.2	1.0
Vizcaya	12.7	21.3	46.9	57.6	1.1	2.0	2.1	1.8
Basque Provinces	9.8	19.4	42.8	51.2	0.9	1.8	1.9	1.6
Spain	11.4	10.8	22.6	32.9	—	—	—	—

Sources: For 1978: *Deia* (Bilbao), December 22, 1978. For other years: Luis C.-Nuñez Astrain, *La Sociedad Vasca Actual* (San Sebastián: Editorial Txertoa, 1977), Table 15, p. 51.

earlier referenda, particularly those of 1966 and 1976. And the four provinces as a whole actually achieved a lower ratio of abstentions to the rest of Spain, declining from a ratio of 1.9 : 1 in 1976 to 1.6 : 1 in 1978.

Beyond the raw data, however, lies a much more challenging question: to what extent was the Basque abstention level due to PNV mobilization of the voters, or to Basque nationalist discontent with the state of political affairs in Spain generally, or with the new Constitution in particular? Indeed, still other interpretations were possible. Some suggested that the high level of non-voting actually represented apathy, a general lack of interest in the issue; others asserted that many Basques were actually pleased with the regional autonomy provisions of the new law. Especially perceptive observers noted that 1978 had been a tumultuous year in Basque politics, full of street demonstrations and mass meetings, that had simply exhausted the Basque political community, and had satiated the mass of potential voters. In the more conservative areas of Navarra, some interpreted the abstentions as a message that the new Constitution had gone too far in the direction of liberalization of the Spanish political framework.

One of the most useful attempts to analyze the true meaning of the 1978 abstention appeared in a series of four articles in the Bilbao newspaper *Deia* in late December and early January following the referendum. Written by two sociologists, José Ignacio Ruiz de Olabuenaga and Javier Yarza, the articles represented the application of modern social science data analysis techniques to the question: what is the real significance of the 1978 vote (or non-vote) for Basque nationalism?[20] The authors contend, first, that abstention in the Basque provinces cannot be interpreted as apathy or inability of the voters to reach the polls. The intense propaganda activity surrounding the electoral process indicated that the referendum was of great interest to the great majority of Basque voters; and the densely populated urban character of Basque society made it relatively easy to reach a polling place. Thus, the abstention was an event with real political significance. Because of the nature of the propaganda used during the pre-referendum campaign, Ruiz and Yarza interpret the vote as a referendum over the true nature of Euzkadi, and the best way for Basques to organize their relations with Spain. The results of the referendum can thus be read as a portrait of Basque society in the 1970s.

When one attempts to interpret the abstention results for clues to the character of Basque nationalism, the first theme to appear is that of tremendous variation in voting patterns within the Basque provinces. The variation in vote among the Basque provinces was greater than that between the highest and lowest abstention rates in the other Spanish provinces. The "Yes" vote on the Constitution ranged from 6 percent to 80 percent across Basque townships and cities; "Abstain" was the choice of between 2 percent and 93 percent; and between one percent and 46 percent voted "No." Along the coast of the Bay of Biscay, abstention rates reached 70 percent; along the banks of the Ebro River, in southern Navarra, the rate dropped to 20 percent. As Ruiz and Yarza put it, "the social distance is greater from the Basque Coast to the Navarra *Ribera* than from Asturias to Cadiz, or from Extremadura to Valencia."[21]

Such great intra-region variation in abstention rates suggests that the Basque provinces are not an integrated or unified political entity but contain substantial internal differences. Actually, according to the Ruiz-Yarza study, there were five discernible levels of abstention, measured in concentric bands that ripple out westward, southward, and eastward from a densely concentrated center in the Guernica area. The significant feature of these various divisions in abstention rates has to do with the varying social forces that produce them. Areas of the Basque provinces that adjoin non-Basque provinces, such as Santander, Logroño and Burgos, tend to exhibit the same level of abstention as their neighboring provinces. Within the core provinces of Vizcaya and Guipúzcoa, the primary reason appears to lie in non-Basque immigration. Abstention in the two coastal provinces correlates .91 with the level of immigration from non-Basque provinces. In the two interior provinces, however, geography seems to be the controlling factor. In Alava and Navarra, abstention varies according to the distance one moves away from Vizcaya and Guipúzcoa. Even areas of Alava and Navarra that have significant concentrations of immigrants tended to have high levels of abstention if they were near the Vizcaya-Guipúzcoa borders. Ruiz and Yarza suggest that this means that Basque culture seems to be absorbing non-Basques, and converting Spaniards into Basque nationalists. An additional supporting datum for this point of view is seen in the close correlation between abstentions and the use of Euskera. In general, the greater the use of Euskera, the greater also tends to be the rate of abstention, a fact not lost on the Basque nationalists or on the groups working to restore Euskera to a modern working language.

Notwithstanding the Basque abstentions, the Spanish Constitution was approved by about 60 percent of the nation's eligible voters in the December 6 referendum; and King Juan Carlos officially promulgated the document as Spain's organic law on December 28, 1978, thereby initiating a new era in Spanish political history. Although the Basque nationalists had opposed the Constitution, they lost no time in developing their draft Autonomy Statute to present before the Congress as prescribed by the new law.

Shortly after the December 6 referendum, the Basque General Council formally convened the assembly of deputies and senators from its three constituent provinces to prepare the draft Statute. Working in marathon sessions, the representatives were able to overcome considerable differences among themselves to develop the draft proposal for presentation soon after King Juan Carlos promulgated the new Constitution. Despite the emergence of schisms between PNV and the two Spanish parties, UCD and PSOE, a spirit of consensus prevailed long enough to permit the drafting of a document for presentation to the Congress. The final version of the draft was completed on December 26. On the following Friday, December 29, the deputies and senators gathered in Guernica in the historic Sala Juradera to vote their ratification of the draft Statute. The vote was nearly unanimous, with only one abstention and one vote against. Shortly thereafter, two delegates from the assembly flew by chartered plane to Madrid to deliver the draft in person to the president of the Congress of Deputies. By doing so, the Basques managed to deliver their

Statute proposal several hours before the Catalans, and thus ensured that the Congress would consider the Basque draft first.[22]

Despite the prompt action taken by the Basques, it quickly became apparent that the draft Autonomy Statute would face considerable delay in moving toward approval and promulgation. The same day that the Basque parliamentarians met in Guernica to ratify the draft proposal, Spanish Premier Adolfo Suárez signed the decree dissolving the Cortes and ordering new elections, not only for the parliament but for all municipalities and provincial governments as well. The Cortes elections were scheduled for March 1, 1979; the municipal and provincial elections, for April 3. This action created several problems for the Basque nationalists and their draft proposal. From the point of view of timing, the Suárez decision meant that the new Cortes could not be formed until late winter or early spring, thus forcing delay in the consideration of all legislation, including the Basque Statute. There were political unknowns as well. The new Cortes could well take on a more conservative configuration if the center-right party, UCD, and the neo-Francoist right, AP, gained votes at the expense of the PSOE and the various regional parties. Still another potential political obstacle could develop out of the doubts about Basque regional autonomy held by the members of the Spanish parties, PSOE and UCD, who had participated in the drafting of the Statute. The socialists pledged their support of the draft in votes in the Congress. The Basque socialist deputy Enrique Múgica promised that the PSOE would "support in Madrid what we have voted for here."[23] The Basque delegates from UCD made no such pledge, however; if in the new Cortes UCD retains its majority status, the future of the Basque Autonomy Statute could be very doubtful. In sum, at this writing (March 1979), the most appropriate attitude for the outside observer would appear to be a guarded optimism.

ETA and Political Violence

In December 1977 a poll[24] taken by the Spanish magazine *Cambio 16* revealed that slightly more than one Spaniard in five (22.7 percent) was seriously worried about terrorism, compared with the more than 50 percent of the respondents who expressed serious concern about the twin economic problems of unemployment (51.5 percent) and inflation (56.5 percent). Eleven months later, in November 1978, the balance of public concerns had shifted dramatically. Now, terrorism ranked as the second most serious problem faced by the Spanish people. More than half (53.1 percent) now expressed grave worries about terrorism, which according to most respondents was synonymous with ETA. A clear majority (63.1 percent) still worried considerably about unemployment, and somewhat fewer (43.0 percent) were concerned about inflation. No matter that unemployment and inflation touched virtually every Spanish family, while ETA's terrorist attacks affected only a tiny fraction of the nation's population. In matters of this sort, a person's rational calculations of their effects upon himself seldom determine attitudes toward potential dangers. The fact remains that in the midst of what nearly every observer regarded as a fairly successful attempt at building a functioning democracy in Spain, ETA not only survived but rose to new heights of violence. Not only did the numbers of ETA victims increase; they now began to include persons who could only remotely be identified as instruments of an oppressive state policy toward dissent. Police, Guardia Civil troops, and military figures continued to be targets for ETA assault; but the attacks also caused the death of construction workers in the Lemóniz nuclear plant, and the fiancée of a Guardia Civil soldier. Clearly, the phenomenon that was ETA had entered a new phase in the third year after Franco's death.

The recrudescence of ETA violence could certainly not be attributed to an absence of counter-measures. Indeed, 1978 was notable for the wide variety of forces that attempted to cause ETA to turn its revolutionary ardor into non-violent channels. Some forces were rightist or centrist and sought to use counter-terror and police tactics to subdue ETA's commando units. Others, leftist or Basque nationalist, tried to launch conciliatory efforts at negotiation, or to mobilize middle class Basque opinion against the insurgents. No matter what the technique, no matter what its source, they all failed.

From Madrid, the Spanish government launched a series of

counter-attacks against ETA that included not only new decrees against terrorism, but the establishment of special anti-terrorist units whose mission was to crush ETA once and for all. In early February, the Director General of the Ministry of Justice, Fernando Cota y Marquez de Prado, announced that the government was preparing special anti-terrorist measures to deal with the growing threat to internal stability in the country.[25] By late March, the government was ready to send to the Cortes its proposed set of laws, which would give to the police special powers for dealing with supposed terrorist groups.[26] Police were to be given the right to wiretap telephone conversations, to intercept mail, to investigate places of residence without prior court approval, and to lengthen the period permitted for detention without charge of suspected terrorists. Certain checks were placed on the government's use of these extraordinary measures, particularly in the way in which the parliament and the courts were to monitor the use by the government of its newly proposed powers. Following the assassination of the Bilbao newspaper publisher José María Portel on June 28, the Suárez government withdrew its legislative proposals for a new anti-terrorist law, and announced its powers in a cabinet decree.[27] Although the Congress of Deputies expressed its unanimous support for such energetic government action, Basque nationalist deputies withheld their approval, arguing that it was not necessary to act through a decree imposed by executive fiat, and that the matter should have been dealt with through legislative debate and action. Other political forces, including the PSOE deputies, were similarly inclined. Thus, after the government's decree had gone into effect, the Cortes continued its consideration of the proposed anti-terrorist law, which was approved and entered into force on August 30. While leftist Basques continued to criticize the new law as neo-Francoist, and as implying a new "state of exception" for the Basque provinces, it was clear that virtually all democratic political forces in Spain wanted the government to have the necessary juridical authority to deal aggressively with ETA.

Even before the Portel assassination and the resultant anti-terrorist law, however, the Spanish government had demonstrated its resolve and commitment to the anti-terrorist struggle. Shortly after the ETA bombing of the Lemóniz nuclear plant in Vizcaya, which produced the deaths of two workers at the plant, the Spanish government dispatched to Bilbao the Assistant Director General of Security, José Sainz Gonzalez, to become the new police chief of the Vizcayan capital.[28] Widely regarded as one of the Spanish police's major experts on ETA, Sainz Gonzalez announced shortly after his arrival in Bilbao that he wanted to establish a dialogue with the Basque insurgent group, and that he recognized that the problem of ETA was basically a political one and not a simple matter of law enforcement.[29] Nevertheless, his invitation fell on deaf ears. ETA apparently wanted no part of any dialogue with one of its chief opponents. A week later, the Spanish cabinet acted to create a special anti-terrorist police force, with extra pay incentives to attract the desired number of qualified agents, and endowed with special weapons and tactics to deal with an insurgent threat.[30]

The creation of a special counter-insurgent force began to gain new momentum after August 30, when the parliament's anti-terrorist law went into effect.[31] Spanish Interior Minister Martín Villa had traveled to West Germany in July to gather first-hand information on how the Germans were combatting their own insurgent groups. Armed with this knowledge, he returned to advocate a fifteen-point package of measures designed to suppress ETA. After August 30, when the government's actions could be justified by reference to the new law, the government's program began to take shape. Under the command of anti-insurgent expert Roberto Conesa, more than 50 experienced police officers were gathered together in Bilbao to form the nucleus of the anti-ETA strike force. Police files were combed carefully to develop new leads or special patterns of action that might point out specific individuals for special concern. According to unofficial sources, the Conesa group began to infiltrate ETA, a task previously thought to be so difficult that it had never been achieved for any appreciable period. Former ETA members were routinely detained and interrogated, sometimes for several days, without being charged with any specific crime. The government especially began to crack down on former ETA members who had remained active in politics, through membership in one of the more radical left *abertzale* parties.

From September 1 through December 25, the Conesa group registered numerous gains in their blows against the ETA organization. A report issued by the Spanish government at the close of this four-month period lists these impressive statistics:[32]

> . . . Forty-six ETA operating units, called *comandos,* had been uncovered and arrested. (Assuming an average of four to five persons per group, this would suggest that between 180 and 230 ETA members or supposed ETA members had been arrested in this series of raids.) Of this figure, 38 were so-called *legales,* which meant that they conducted their political activities in addition to being employed at a regular job. Of these 38 groups, 25 were "action" groups (engaged in violent activities), and 13 were support or "information" *comandos.* Of the 46 groups that had been destroyed, eight were *ilegales,* meaning that they were dedicated completely to insurgent actions.
>
> . . . The Government did not announce the exact number of persons arrested, saying only that there were about 200. This would correspond to the estimated number presented earlier. Of those arrested, 132 had already been released.
>
> . . . Numerous weapons had been confiscated, including 30 sub-machine guns, 21 shotguns, 63 pistols, 66 kilos of plastic explosive, and other artefacts such as cartridges, detonators, and chemicals for explosives.
>
> . . . In addition, the raids had uncovered three "people's prisons," where kidnapping victims had been kept, several "safe houses," used by ETA to hide members who were being sought by police, six automobiles, false documents and license plates, and 48 million pesetas (about $800,000), identified as part of the funds stolen during ETA robberies.

Anti-ETA measures were not restricted to the passage of anti-terrorist laws or the creation of anti-terrorist police units. On both the official and the unofficial levels, anti-terrorist forces carried on the struggle against ETA using a variety of tactics. In Spanish prisons, for example, the plight of Basque political prisoners arose again as a burning political issue. As a result of the earlier amnesty policies, the number of such prisoners had declined to practically zero by the fall of 1977. Yet when the renewed counter-insurgent tactics of the Spanish police began to take effect, the consequence was an increase in the number of alleged ETA members in prison. By the end of 1978, the number had increased to 111, out of a total of about 243 political prisoners in Spanish jails.[33] Torture of political prisoners was no longer the problem it had been during the Franco era; but there were enough signs of its continued use to be of concern to the families of Basques in prison.[34] The most worrisome condition for Basque political prisoners, however, was the tendency of the Spanish government to move them from one prison to another without notice, and without informing their attorneys. In late December, 97 prisoners were moved to the maximum security prison at Soria, according to the Spanish Interior Ministry because of a planned mass escape from the Basque prisons in which they were being held. The street demonstrations caused by this removal produced a number of serious clashes with police in San Sebastián on December 28, 1978, and again on January 7, 1979.[35]

Still another source of anti-ETA pressure came from rightist vigilante groups such as the Triple AAA and the Warriors of Christ the King. The actions of these and other similar ultraconservative groups were evidenced in both mass demonstrations and in counter-terror bombings against ETA members. On repeated occasions, during street demonstrations in Basque cities, these groups (called *incontrolados*) appeared to attack the demonstrators with chains, clubs, and stones. One such attack took place in San Sebastián on the night of March 10-11, when a number of groups of ten to fifteen *incontrolados* each assaulted participants in a demonstration, and then turned their anger toward the customers of bars, restaurants, and a motion picture theater. In all, three persons were injured in this attack, and there were explosions or fires in several bars and commercial establishments.[36] The most dramatic of the individual attacks was that in the French Basque city of Bayonne on July 4 against ex-ETA member Jon Etxabe and his wife, who were machine gunned from a passing automobile. The rightist Triple AAA claimed responsibility for the attack, which caused the death of Sra. Etxabe and left the former ETA militant in grave condition with two bullets in the abdomen.[37]

The Spanish government's strategy for dealing with ETA was not solely one of suppression and intimidation. Through a number of direct and indirect channels, the Suárez government let it be known that it was disposed to enter into a dialogue with ETA leaders to achieve peace in the Basque country. In early February, an ETA communiqué established five minimum requirements for a cease fire from their point of view. These were total amnesty for all political prisoners, who at that time must have been very few in number; legalization of all political parties (there were still at least two leftist Basque parties that had not been granted legal status); expulsion from Euzkadi of all Spanish law enforcement authorities, including the Guardia Civil; measures to improve the standard of living of the workers in the Basque provinces; and an Autonomy Statute that would reserve for Basque authorities the control of the law enforcement entities in the Basque provinces.[38] The response from the Spanish government to these demands was to reject them as a group but to accept the negotiable nature of them collectively and the immediate approval of several of them individually. The question of the Autonomy Statute, for example, could not be negotiated outside the framework of the Constitution; but the government expressed its willingness to meet with ETA leaders to continue the dialogue.[39]

There were other clues throughout 1978 to indicate some possible movement toward a less intransigent position on the part of the government. No sooner had he been elected president of the Basque General Council than Ramon Rubial announced his desire to communicate with ETA leaders to arrange a cease fire.[40] In May, the president of the Catalan regional pre-autonomy government, Josep Tarradellas, met with the president of the Basque Government-in-Exile, Jesús María Leizaola, to discuss the possibility of the latter's serving as an intermediary between the Spanish government and ETA to begin conversations and negotiations. Rumors in the press contended that Tarradellas had gone to France to meet with Leizaola at the request of King Juan Carlos, but the government denied such rumors. In the Basque country, nationalists both within and without the PNV hotly suggested that Sr. Tarradellas should stay out of Basque matters, and the incident provoked considerable tension within the Basque government in Paris.[41]

In June, key developments seemed to indicate the genuine possibility that the government and ETA would finally get down to the business of negotiation. Over the weekend of June 24-25, the Minister of the Interior of the Basque General Council, the socialist Txiki Benegas, met with representatives of the left *abertzale* parties, LAIA and HASI, to begin laying the basis for a dialogue between ETA and Madrid. As colleagues with ETA in the KAS (the coordinating organ of all Basque left *abertzale* parties), the LAIA and HASI were well placed to be able to negotiate such a beginning with Benegas. It was believed that the ETA leadership was at that time split over the desirability of negotiating with the Spanish government. The advocates of negotiation were led by José Miguel Beñaran Ordenana, also known as "Argala," best known for his leadership role in the assassination of Prime Minister Carrero Blanco in 1973. The "hard line" position was reportedly taken by Miguel Angel Apalategui, "Apala," recently escaped from a French prison, and still exercising considerable influence within the more radical ETA-m forces.[42] Apparently, a key figure in these early negotiations was the Bilbao journalist José María Portel, who had written several works on ETA and was thought to be in close touch with the group's leaders. On Wednesday, June 28, Portel was shot to death; and the ensuing reaction against ETA (detailed above) meant the end of negotiations. Although it is highly speculative, there are many who believe that the assassination was the work of ETA intransigents determined to prevent any kind of negotiated cease fire. In any case, after the anti-terrorist law went into effect and the Spanish police stepped up their enforcement efforts,there was really no opportunity for a negotiated settlement. Some six months later, on December 18, the CGV offered once again to serve as intermediary between ETA and the government to discuss a cease fire. Three days later, the ETA leader more inclined toward conciliation, Argala, was blown up by a bomb placed in his car. ETA figures argued that the killing was the work of Spanish rightists or the Spanish secret police who did not want conciliation to take place. Others believed that the Argala killing was carried out by the same people who had assassinated Portel, again to block negotiation.

Throughout the entire year, while ETA and the Spanish government shadow boxed with one another, the Basque center and left looked on relatively helplessly. In February, certain parties, including the PNV, had attempted to bring all Basque nationalist groups together to form a unified committee that would seek to engage ETA in discussions about the prospects for peace in Euzkadi. With the failure of this group to achieve participation by several important left parties, the effort dissolved. The PNV, for its part, continued to speak out against the violence of ETA, particularly when it involved innocent bystanders; but the Party also condemned the institutional violence imposed on the Basque people by the Spanish police, the Guardia Civil, and the armed forces. This double-edged use of the word "violence" meant that the PNV could never attract the contending forces in Basque politics: the left rejected the criticism of ETA; the right denounced the implied criticism of the law enforcement actions of the Suárez government.

As time went on, however, and as ETA's attacks grew in ferocity, the PNV found itself devoting most of its criticism to ETA, and less and less to Madrid. Following the ETA attack on five Guardia Civil soldiers in Vitoria in early March, the PNV denounced the insurgents in harsh terms and called once again for all violence to cease in the Basque region.[43] After the Lemóniz bombing incident, in mid-March, the PNV communiqué read in part: "The Basque Nationalist Party manifests its most energetic repudiation of such acts, considering them directly directed at the creation of a climate of political instability and evolution toward the liquidation of the incipient democracy in Euzkadi." The PNV went on to urge all Basques to push ETA out to the margin of political life and to deny them the support they would need to carry on their struggle. After the assassination by ETA of the Military Governor of Madrid in January 1979, the president of the PNV, Carlos Garaicoechea, issued a communiqué that said in part: "We are with neither ETA nor with Martín Villa [the Spanish Minister of Interior]." This position of condemning both sides in the struggle was characteristically Basque nationalist but became increasingly difficult to maintain in the face of such violence.

The most controversial act taken by the PNV to establish its position was its convoking a mass meeting in Bilbao on October 28, 1978, to condemn all violence, including terrorism, and to call for a restoration of peace to Euzkadi. Although the meeting was labeled a convocation "For a Euzkadi Free and in Peace," and PNV made clear its belief that violence on all sides had to end, the call for the meeting was one of the acts most hotly opposed by PNV rank and file members in the Party's recent history. In the end, the PNV leadership invoked strict party discipline to mobilize many tens of thousands of supporters for the meeting. But there were many more who remained home in defiance of their party, calling the meeting little less than a betrayal of their comrades in arms who were carrying on the same struggle for which the PNV claimed to be committed.[44]

We may ask, then, what support ETA had among the Basque population at the end of 1978. Unfortunately, the question is unanswerable. Conventional survey research techniques simply are not up to the task of probing for so emotional a sentiment. Table 25 presents the results of an opinion poll taken by *Cambio 16* magazine at the end of 1978. It is apparent from studying this table that about one-third of the people residing in the Basque provinces consider ETA a terrorist organization whose violence has no justification; but another one-third believe that ETA is a national liberation force whose members are fighting for the freedom of the Basque people. Significantly, between 45 and 50 percent of the Basque respondents refuse to answer any questions on the subject. One cannot argue, as did the *Cambio 16* article which was based on the poll, that this means that Basques really oppose ETA but

Table 25.
Attitudes Toward ETA, 1978 (answers in percentages).

Statement	Agree		Don't Agree		No Answer	
	All of Spain	Basque Provinces	All of Spain	Basque Provinces	All of Spain	Basque Provinces
ETA members are patriots fighting for the liberation of the Basque people.	19.4	31.9	39.3	22.4	31.4	45.7
ETA represents only a minority of the Basque people.	52.6	43.6	15.3	10.6	32.0	45.7
ETA's violence has no justification today.	62.7	37.2	11.8	16.0	25.6	47.9
A majority of Basques support ETA.	28.8	19.2	38.9	35.1	32.5	47.9
ETA is the only organization that really represents the aspirations and interests of the Basque people.	13.4	12.8	50.9	43.6	35.8	44.7
ETA members are terrorists who should be pursued and eliminated.	47.8	17.0	22.3	37.3	29.9	45.7

Source: *Cambio 16*, No. 370, January 7, 1979, p. 31.

are afraid to say so. The real meaning could be exactly the opposite: they support armed struggle but fear reprisals if they were to express such support.

Despite the wide variety of counter-pressures against them in 1978, ETA managed to raise armed struggle to new levels. As Table 26 shows, the number of ETA victims increased dramatically in 1978 to 60, from only eleven the year before. Whereas only 74 people had lost their lives to ETA attacks during the entire period between 1968 and 1977, nearly that many were killed by ETA violence in only one year. The 50 to 60 deaths registered during the first six months of 1979 indicate a still higher rate of ETA violence if the level of killing is projected forward throughout the year. (It should be noted that these data are police statistics, which in turn are based on messages from individuals claiming to be ETA members, claiming responsibility for the killings. Since few of these murders are ever tried and resolved in a conventional homicide trial in a court of law, it is impossible to rely heavily on the data. Nevertheless, the increase in claimed ETA killings in 1978 reflects a basic upward shift in political violence in the Basque provinces, even though the "true" statistics might be

Table 26.
ETA Victims per Year and Cumulative, 1968-1978.

Period	**No. of victims**	**Annual Average**	**Cumulative Total**
Prior to 1968	None recorded	—	—
1968-1973	8	1.3	8
1974-1975	36	18.0	44
1976	19	19.0	63
1977	11	11.0	74
1978	60	60.0	134
January-June, 1979	50-60 (estimated)	100-120.0*	184-194

*Projected.

Sources: For period from 1968 to middle of 1977, see José María Portel, "E.T.A.: Objetivo, La Insurrección de Euzkadi," *Blanco y Negro,* June 29-July 5, 1977, pp. 25-29. Period from middle of 1977 to January 4, 1979, calculated from *Diario Vasco* (San Sebastián), January 4, 1979, p. 32. For January-June 1979, see Washington *Post,* May 26 and May 27, 1979, pp. 22 and 32.

slightly different in one direction or the other.) In addition to the assassinations, ETA carried out bank and other robberies during 1978 that netted them approximately 250 million pesetas (about $4,166,000 at 1978 exchange rates).[45]

Not only did ETA's actions increase in number in 1978; they also grew in dramatic impact, as well. A number of ETA killings involved senior Spanish military officials, especially toward the end of the year, when ETA in effect declared war on the Spanish armed forces. Their victims included the Military Governor of Madrid, and the assistant to the Military Governor of Guipúzcoa province. In other actions, Guardia Civil troops were the chief target. The most dramatic of these attacks was that in Vitoria in April, when a Guardia Civil truck carrying five soldiers was ambushed and riddled with machine gun fire, leaving two dead and three wounded. ETA bombings took their toll as well. The bombing at the Lemóniz nuclear plant under construction killed two workers and wounded several others and was answered by universal condemnation of ETA by labor unions in Vizcaya. Following the Lemóniz explosion, which was produced by at least 70 kilos of plastic explosive, a series of bomb scares throughout the Basque provinces led to what newspapers labeled a "bomb psychosis," aggravated by an average of three false bomb alarms daily.[46] The police announcement that ETA had stored more than 600 kilos of explosives in the French Basque country did little to pacify public concerns about this aspect of ETA violence.[47] Still another ETA tactic that caused little damage but was disconcerting to the victims involved was what came to be called "momentary kidnappings." The objective of these actions apparently was to obtain the victims' automobiles. In a large number of cases, the victims chosen for capture were taxi drivers. The typical kidnapping of this sort began with the theft of the automobile with driver; then the vehicle was driven to a remote spot where the driver was bound and abandoned; the stolen car was then used to carry out some other planned ETA action, such as an armed assault or robbery. In the 17-month period ending in February 1978 there were 32 such kidnappings recorded by police in the four Basque provinces.

Finally, ETA adopted a tactic that has been employed in other insurgent settings, including Uruguay and Northern Ireland: the revolutionary tax. In 1978, ETA was able to force several banks in Bilbao to make available to them lists of their depositors, along with the size of their deposits. These lists then became the basis of requests from ETA to the larger depositors for contributions to their group's treasury. If contributions were not forthcoming, ETA threatened reprisals. According to one source, the revolutionary tax was responsible for the flight of much capital from Euzkadi, as major depositors moved their funds to banks in other Spanish provinces where they would be less vulnerable to such pressure from ETA.

In sum, ETA was far from eliminated as a powerful force in Basque politics despite all of the changes in the group's operating environment since Franco's death. The transition of Spain to a relatively free parliamentary democracy, the increased counter-insurgent pressure on the group from the Spanish government, and the virtually complete abandonment of ETA by non-violent Basque political groups were insufficient to cause ETA to veer from its chosen course. In a communiqué following the Lemóniz bombing, an anonymous ETA spokesman tried to respond to the question "Where is ETA going?" "Many people," he wrote, "are asking today, why is ETA continuing to be active after Franco's death, and with the democratizing process begun in Spain? The answer is that ETA has not changed. What has changed is the consciousness of a sector of the people toward what our organization represents and defends. These people have thought that we were simple anti-Franco patriots, and they never stopped to reflect on the meaning of the definition of our title: a Basque revolutionary socialist organization for national liberation. During Franco's lifetime, we abandoned in good measure the ideological struggle, and our field of action was anti-Francoism. This is one reason that explains in part the lack of understanding by a sector of the Basque people of our present struggle. The other reason is that certain people, confusing reality with their desires, have seen ETA as they wanted, and not as it was. ETA will try to struggle in the most adequate way possible until the creation of a Basque state, independent, socialist, reunified [with the French Basque provinces] and Basque-speaking."[48]

Given this revolutionary socialist commitment by ETA members, and ETA's seeming ability to survive even the hardest blows from the Spanish law enforcement agencies, it is probable that ETA and its violent strategy will continue to play a key role in Basque politics for months and perhaps years to come. After all of the police activity of 1978, much of which is related above, observers estimated that there were still approximately 70 ETA *comandos* operating in the sphere of armed action, and another group of similar size operating in the realm of propaganda and support activities. If these figures are correct, then there were still between 600 and 750 ETA militants active in the struggle against Spain, as well as against their own bourgeois class. Only time would tell how their impact would be felt, and answered, by Basque and Spanish political leaders who had a stake in a peaceful solution to the problem of Basque regionalism.

Chapter Thirteen

SOME CONCLUDING REMARKS: THE CENTRAL ISSUES IN BASQUE NATIONALIST POLITICS

In the summer of 1973, after spending ten weeks in the Basque country talking with leaders of the Basque Nationalist Party, I came away with the impression that they believed that General Franco was the primary source of their difficulties and that after his death the way would be cleared for them to realize their long-standing aspirations for regional self-governance. At this writing, more than three years after Franco's death, I am now convinced that Basque nationalism faces a number of severe obstacles that are both structural in character and profound in extent. To be sure, some of these problems date from the Franco era, and indeed can be traced to the nature of the Franco regime's approach to governance in the Basque region. Nevertheless, there are obstacles to Basque nationalism that are deeply rooted and will not dissolve soon, and perhaps not for a number of years, if at all.

One of the central themes of this book has been the continuing clash between Basque ethnicity and economic class as a determinant of Basque politics. This struggle dates back at least to the beginning of this century, and in certain instances even before that. Nevertheless, it is apparent to me that in the ebb and flow of history, the clash between ethno-nationalism and class origin has yet to run its course in the Basque region. Indeed, there are solid signs that the schisms in Basque politics are just as strong now as they were at the turn of the century, and may even be intensifying.

A second major theme of this study has centered on the ill effects of unbridled industrialization, especially in Vizcaya and

Guipúzcoa. Stimulated and protected by Spanish industrialization policies, the Basque industrial elite has carried on a program of manufacturing expansion that has been the cutting edge of the so-called Spanish economic miracle over the past several decades. Such economic prosperity has not been bought cheaply, however; and the Basque provinces are now the scene of most of the ill effects known to other industrial societies: air and water pollution, inadequate social services, a badly overloaded social and economic infrastructure, and a glaring absence of urban amenities such as parks and playgrounds. To these relatively long-run ills one must now add a skyrocketing unemployment figure more than double Spain's average, a sharp increase in business failures, and the opening stages of capital flight, sure signs of a drop in corporate confidence in what was once one of Spain's most powerful economic regions.

Closely tied to the preceding problem is, of course, the problem that refuses to go away: the recrudescence of terrorist violence, and the continued intransigence of ETA. Nothing seems to daunt or blunt ETA's revolutionary ardor. Counterviolence seems futile; efforts at negotiation never reach fruition; condemnation by non-violent Basque political groups apparently masks continuing real support for ETA by the average Basque citizen. It appears as if the suppression of the Franco years bred a generation of revolutionary youth who combine a commitment to both socialist change and nationalist liberation with a hardened willingness to kill to achieve their goal. As other countries have discovered, intransigence breeds intransigence. The ill effects of these policies will be around to poison relations between Basques and Spaniards for a long time to come.

Finally, this brief inventory of obstacles facing Basque nationalists would not be complete without some mention of the view from Madrid. Spain is changing. Industrialization, social ferment and political democratization cannot help bringing in their wake substantial transformations in attitudes among significant centers of Spanish public opinion. All the parties concerned — Basques, Spaniards, and outside observers — must take care not to misinterpret these changes as signifying support for regional separatism. If the Spanish government is now slightly more willing than was Francisco Franco to grant some kind of regional autonomy to Basques, Catalans, and others, in all probability it is because the new industrial order in Spain both permits and requires decentralization of administration. I see no signs that the Spanish government is now inclined to let the Basques slip away from the national union any more than they were willing to do so under Franco. The concessions to autonomy in the new Spanish Constitution are concessions to efficiency and economics, not to the romance of nationalism and language. Nevertheless, as in most political matters, success and failure are relative. Regardless of the motivation, the Basques are now closer to some form of regional autonomy than they have ever been before (unless one excludes the highly unstable period from July 1936 to June 1937); and it is ardently to be hoped that their understandable desire for full autonomy not deflect them from their short term objective of achieving some measure of control over their own lives and futures. As a Basque friend once put it to me, "The perfect is the enemy of the good."

There is in all these developments a historical irony of enormous proportions: just as Spain seems willing and able to permit the Basques some small degree of their long sought autonomy, the social and economic changes of the last century are beginning to erode the base of Basque nationalism. After one hundred years of industrial growth, and economic and social modernization and urbanization, the Basque working class has become unwilling to accept without question continued rule by bourgeois classes and politicians, whether Basque or Spanish. After forty years of suppression by Madrid, emigration of workers from other parts of Spain, growth of the industrial labor force, and the radicalization of the youth of the region, many Basques now think that class is more important than ethnicity. It seems, then, that the Basque Nationalist Party may have achieved its greatest victory — the restoration of its regional autonomous status — at the very moment when it is seeing its electoral base drained away by those of its former supporters who no longer define their world in terms of ethnic symbols. If the PNV is unable to meet the challenges of their new political and economic surroundings, if they cannot redefine Basque nationalism to grapple with the tangible grievances of the Basque workers in areas such as income, housing, transportation, and education, then in all likelihood the Basque workers will shift their allegiance toward the Spanish left parties, especially the socialist PSOE, or toward one of the new *abertzale* left parties that may still emerge as the new power in Basque politics. If, on the other hand, the PNV is able to fashion a new alliance of ethnicity and class, one that recognizes that there *are* very real links between the symbolic and tangible in the life of Basque workers, then Basque nationalism will survive and flourish in the new Spanish political environment, and may even go on to demonstrate to a watching Europe how small ethnic groups can retain their identity and their viability in the midst of continental-sized economies without sacrificing economic efficiency or social services that meet human needs.

During the transition to regional autonomy, however, a number of imponderables will intrude to direct the course of history either toward a progressive resolution of Spain's seemingly interminable regional problems, or away from genuine accommodation of interests and toward increased levels of terroristic violence and counter-violence. I have already cited one of these factors: the ability of the PNV to deal creatively with class and ethnicity issues in a single framework. In addition, successful solution of the Basque-Spanish struggle rests on these developments:

. . . the ability of the intransigent Spanish right (neo-Franco groups and the military) to avoid being provoked into self-defeating over-reaction;

. . . the ability of the Suárez government and the Spanish center-right to withstand pressures from their more conservative challengers;

. . . the willingness of the Spanish left to eschew the use of the regional issue to gain political advantage over Suárez and the center;

. . . the patience of the non-violent Basque left, including the Basque labor movement;

. . . the ability of ETA to understand that their historical role has come to an end and no longer fills a need in Basque politics, and a willingness of ETA members to accept less than total solutions to Basque problems;

. . . an ability and willingness of the Basque people in general, and of the Basque middle class in particular, to support moderate solutions to their problems, and to reject the violence of both right and left.

As the poet C. Day-Lewis wrote, freedom *is* more than a word — it is a state of being. But just as there are many different dimensions of one's being, there are many different directions in which free men and women can turn. The real challenge to Basque nationalists today is to decide for themselves what it means to be both free and Basque in democratic Spain and industrial society.

Postscript

In the spring of 1979, while the manuscript for this book was in its final stages, two more elections were held in Spain. On March 1 Spaniards went to the polls to choose members of the first parliament elected under the terms of its new Constitution; on April 3 they voted again to choose members of town or city councils and provincial legislative assemblies. These latter elections were the first such exercises in democracy in Spain since before the Civil War.

Taken together with the results of the 1977 parliamentary election, reported above in Chapter Eleven, the outcomes of the two 1979 elections enhance our understanding of post-Franco politics in the Basque provinces. Thus, while I do not wish to lengthen this particular study unnecessarily by undertaking a major analysis of the 1979 elections, I do think it valuable to conclude with some of the basic electoral data from this period. It may assist others who wish to pursue further studies of this new era in Spanish politics.

The tables that follow portray the electoral trends of the three elections by major party, by major political grouping, and by province. The figures within the parentheses are the number of seats won by each party in the given election. For obvious reasons, the number of seats at stake in the municipal elections of 1979, here designated "1979(m)," were much more numerous than the seats involved in the two Cortes elections of 1977 and 1979. Each party's electoral performance is given in terms of its percentage of the total vote. Vote totals are given in thousands at the bottom of each table.

For the reader with a scholarly interest in this subject, a few notes on methodological problems and sources may be in order. Scholars who like their research neat and well ordered, with few "loose ends," would do well to avoid working with contemporary Spanish electoral data, at least until official figures are published. The primary source for the 1977 data is

Relative Strengths of Major Parties and Groupings in the Basque Provinces, 1977 and 1979 (strength is expressed as a percent of the total vote earned by each party or grouping).

	Alava			Guipúzcoa		
Party	**1977**	**1979(p)**	**1979(m)**	**1977**	**1979(p)**	**1979(m)**
PNV	17.1 (1)	21.3 (1)	36.4 (170)	30.9 (3)	26.1 (3)	35.0 (338)
Abertzale Left	4.3	13.0	14.6	15.5	30.3	29.8
EE	2.1 (0)	1.8 (0)	NA	9.5 (1)	13.2 (1)	10.3 (60)
HB	NA	9.8 (0)	14.5 (55)	NA	17.1 (1)	14.8 (106)
Spanish Left	37.6	24.7	17.6	35.5	25.2	19.6
PSOE	27.7 (1)	19.8 (1)	17.5 (33)	28.1 (3)	18.5 (1)	15.0 (79)
Spanish Right	40.4	23.8	28.0	17.8	17.4	3.9
UCD	31.1 (2)	23.8 (2)	28.0 (106)	NA	16.8 (1)	3.9 (0)
Total Vote (000s)	123.5	113.3	100.2	327.3	298.5	320.2
Total Seats	4	4	419	7	7	746

Party	Navarra			Vizcaya		
	1977	1979 (p)	1979 (m)	1977	1979 (p)	1979 (m)
PNV	3.5 (0)	3.3 (0)	2.5 (3)	31.1 (4)	27.9 (4)	39.0 (543)
Abertzale Left	13.0	15.0	28.3	9.6	20.1	23.4
EE	NA	NA	NA	5.8 (0)	6.2 (0)	5.2 (25)
HB	NA	7.3 (0)	11.1 (9)	NA	13.9 (2)	17.3 (134)
Spanish Left	37.7	34.7	26.3	35.1	24.0	20.9
PSOE	21.2 (2)	23.8 (1)	19.0 (15)	24.5 (3)	18.0 (2)	15.2 (90)
Spanish Right	41.7	47.0	42.9	24.2	15.1	9.3
UCD	29.1 (3)	36.3 (3)	26.8 (20)	16.4 (2)	15.1 (2)	9.3 (21)
Total Vote (000s)	247.4	232.9	253.9	617.2	570.2	516.4
Total Seats	5	5	70*	10	10	1,074

*Provincial legislature.

Party	Four Provinces 1977	1979 (p)	1979 (m)
PNV	24.4 (8)	22.2 (8)	29.9 (1,054)
Abertzale Left	11.2	21.0	25.4
EE	5.2 (1)	6.3 (1)	5.0 (85)
HB	NA	13.0 (3)	15.1 (304)
Spanish Left	36.0	26.4	21.4
PSOE	25.0 (9)	19.4 (5)	16.1 (217)
Spanish Right	27.6	22.6	16.6
UCD	16.2 (7)	20.4 (8)	13.2 (147)
UPN	NA	2.3 (1)	3.4 (13)
AP	3.7 (1)	NA	NA
Total Vote (000s)	1,315.5	1,215.0	1,190.7
Total Seats	26	26	2,309

Talde Euskal Estudio Elkartea, *Euskadi, ante las elecciones municipales* (San Sebastián; Ediciones Vascas, 1978), Chapter 2. Despite the fact that this is a secondary source that summarizes such original sources as contemporary press reports, there are still a number of discrepancies within the study itself. Too frequently, global provincial figures for a particular party are not the same as the sum of the votes for that party from all the cities and towns in the province. Nevertheless, the sources of data for the 1977 study are a model of clarity compared with those for the two 1979 elections. In the 1979 parliamentary election, for example, the principal sources I have relied on are *El País* (Madrid), March 3, 1979; *Egin* (San Sebastián), March 2, 1979; and *Diario de Navarra* (Pamplona), March 11, 1979. Not only do these three sources not agree on certain critical matters, such as the total number of votes cast in each province, but there are many internal discrepancies in each report, and several glaring omissions, most serious of which are the vote totals from Bilbao and Vitoria. The sources for the 1979 municipal elections are somewhat better, especially for Navarra. These sources include *Egin,* April 5, 1979; *Diario de Navarra,* April 5, 1979; *Deia* (Bilbao), April 5, 1979; and *El Correo Español - El Pueblo Vasco* (Bilbao), April 4, 1979. Here the principal conceptual problem had to do with the enormous number of independent candidates for local office in Navarra. Unable to do any kind of party comparison at the town level in Navarra because of this, I have chosen to work with the election for the provincial legislature (the *Parlamento Foral*) in the case of Navarra, even though that makes the Navarrese case not exactly comparable with the other three provinces. In sum, this kind of study requires the creative use of empirical data by the analyst and a considerable degree of tolerance on the part of the reader. That is one important reason why I have chosen not to provide raw vote statistics at this point, preferring to deal here with percentages which are not likely to be grossly wrong.

The conclusions that seem to emerge from the data of these three elections can be quickly summarized, with the understanding that full analysis of these conclusions would expand this research note far beyond what seems called for here. First, the Basque Nationalist Party (PNV) has returned to its traditional position as the leading party in the Basque provinces, although it has yet to reach the level of votes that it received in the 1930s. The party continues to be strong in Guipúzcoa and Vizcaya and shows steady improvement in Alava; but the PNV has declined to almost insignificance in Navarra, and indeed does not even present its candidates alone there, preferring to cluster together with other groups in electoral coalitions.

Second, the *abertzale* left parties, *Euskadiko Ezkerra* (EE) and *Herri Batasuna* (HB), have shown steady growth to the point where they are now the second strongest political force in the Basque provinces. *Herri Batasuna,* regarded by many observers as the political arm of ETA-*militar*, accomplished striking results in 1979, winning three seats in the Spanish parliament, and nine out of seventy seats in the Navarrese provincial legislature. That fact alone would mark the Basques as one of the most radicalized ethnic minorities in any industrial democracy in the world. If we treat the PNV and the *abertzale* left as the combined voice of Basque political ethnicity, then that voter sentiment has risen from 35.6 percent in 1977 to 43.2 percent in the 1979 parliamentary elections to 55.3 percent in the municipal elections. Since the PNV has traditionally been extremely strong at the town and village level, the last of these figures may not represent a genuine commitment to Basque ethnicity as the touchstone of Basque voters. Further, many *abertzale* left votes may be more class oriented than ethnic. Whatever the case, the Spanish government will ignore this vote only at great risk.

Both sets of Spanish parties have seen their fortunes decline as those of the Basque parties have risen. The PSOE has dropped from 25 percent in 1977 to 19.4 and 16.1 percent in the two 1979 elections. While the UCD rallied slightly in the second parliamentary election, it dropped again in the municipal vote to only 13.2 percent. Other expressions of rightist sentiment, such as the neo-Francoist *Alianza Popular,* have faded completely from the Basque political spectrum.

I shall close this summary of conclusions with one set of statistics that should make dreary reading in Madrid: the sum of anti-Suárez votes in the Basque provinces has hovered around 70 percent through the three elections (71.6 in 1977; 69.6 and 76.7 in 1979). Whatever judgment history may make about President Suárez' contributions to Spanish democracy, the Basques seem to evaluate most negatively the policies of his government for the three and a half years following the death of Francisco Franco.

Notes

Notes to Prologue

1. The spelling of the ship names, "Nabara" instead of "Navarra," for example, illustrates the idiomatic Basque substitution of B for V and K for C.

2. George L. Steer, *The Tree of Gernika* (London: Hodder and Stoughton, 1938), pp. 142-148. The story is told from the Basque point of view for the first time in Sarria, *De Arrantzales a Gudaris del Mar* (Bilbao: Gráficas Lorono, 1978), pp. 99-154.

3. "The *Nabara*" first appeared in Day-Lewis's book *Overtures to Death* (1938), and was reissued in *Collected Poems 1954* (London: Cape, 1954), paper edition, 1970, pp. 191-200. The poem is discussed by Joseph N. Riddel in his book *C. Day-Lewis* (New York: Twayne, 1971), pp. 77, 90-91.

Notes to Chapter One

1. José Miguel de Azaola, *Vasconia y su Destino: I, La Regionalización de España* (Madrid: Ediciones de la Revista de Occidente, 1972), pp. 305-307.

2. Edward E. Malefakis, *Agrarian Reform and Peasant Revolution in Spain: Origins of the Civil War* (New Haven: Yale University Press, 1970), pp. 35-50.

3. Manuel de Terán Alvarez, "País Vasco," in Manuel de Terán, Luis Sole Sabaris, and others, *Geografía Regional de España* (Barcelona: Ediciones Ariel, 1968), Chapter III.

4. Luis C.-Nuñez Astrain, *Clases Sociales en Euskadi* (San Sebastián: Editorial Txertoa, 1977), Chapter 1.

5. William A. Douglass, "Borderland Influences in a Navarrese Village," in William A. Douglass, Richard W. Etulain and William H. Jacobsen, Jr., eds., *Anglo-American Contributions to Basque Studies: Essays in Honor of Jon Bilbao* (Desert Research Institute Publications on the Social Sciences, No. 13, 1977), pp.135-144.

6. These conclusions are derived from data in Instituto Nacional de Estadística, *España: Panorámica Social, 1974* (Madrid: INE, 1975), p. 60, Table 1.12.

7. Basques have the highest rate of blood type O and the lowest rate

of blood type B in Europe. They also have the highest rate of the Rh negative factor of any population in the world. See William A. Douglass and Jon Bilbao, *Amerikanuak: Basques in the New World* (Reno, Nevada: University of Nevada Press, 1975), p. 10.

8. Pedro de Yrizar, "Los dialectos y variedades de la Lengua Vasca: Estudio Linguístico-Demografico," *Separata del Boletín de la Real Sociedad Vascongada de los Amigos del Pais,* 29, 1/2/3 (1973).

9. Douglass and Bilbao, pp. 15-16.

10. Amando de Miguel, *Manual de Estructura Social de España* (Madrid: Editorial Tecnos, 1974), p. 390, Table 25.

11. Selma Huxley Barkham, "Guipúzcoan Shipping in 1571 with Particular Reference to the Decline of the Transatlantic Fishing Industry," in Douglass, Etulain and Jacobsen, eds., pp. 73-82.

12. de Miguel, p. 407, Table 32.

13. de Miguel, pp. 64-65, Table 3.

14. Since the liberalization of Spanish society, there has been a flurry of sociological analyses of the Basque people and the groups into which they are divided. Of these, the following have been useful in this section: Beltza, *Nacionalismo Vasco y Clases Sociales* (San Sebastián: Editorial Txertoa, 1976). Luis C.-Nuñez Astrain, *Clases Sociales en Euskadi.* Luis C.-Nuñez Astrain, *La Sociedad Vasca Actual* (San Sebastián: Editorial Txertoa, 1978). Ortzi, *Los Vascos: Síntesis de su Historia* (San Sebastián: Hordago, 1978).

15. Only about 100 kilometers to the west, in the province of Santander, is the more famous cave of Altamira, near Santillana del Mar. The Altamira cave contains drawings made by Cromagnon men about 15,000 years before the birth of Christ. See Rafael Altamira, *A History of Spain from the Beginnings to the Present Day,* trans. by Muna Lee (New York: D. Van Nostrand, 1949), pp. 2-4.

16. Martín de Ugalde, *Síntesis de la Historia del País Vasco* (San Sebastián: Ediciones Vascas, 1977), pp. 11-45.

17. Stanley G. Payne, *Basque Nationalism* (Reno, Nevada: University of Nevada Press, 1975), pp. 10-11. Douglass and Bilbao, pp. 10-11.

18. Maximiano García Venero, *Historia del Nacionalismo Vasco,* 3rd. ed. (Madrid: Editora Nacional, 1969), p. 34.

19. Rodney Gallop, *A Book of the Basques* (Reno, Nevada: University of Nevada Press, 1970; reissue of original 1930 version), pp. 9-10.

20. García Venero, pp. 27-28.

21. García Venero, pp. 30-31.

22. Douglass and Bilbao, p. 23.

23. Altamira, p. 79.

24. Douglass and Bilbao, pp. 30-31.

25. Altamira, pp. 170-172.

26. Payne, p. 13.

27. Douglass and Bilbao, pp. 38-45.

28. The process of absorption of the three Basque provinces into the Kingdom of Castilla is dealt with in detail in Ugalde, pp. 95-106.

29. Rachel Bard, "The Decline of a Basque State in France: Basse Navarre, 1512-1789," in Douglass, Etulain and Jacobsen, pp. 83-84.

30. Barkham. Douglass and Bilbao, pp. 49-60.

31. Altamira, pp. 332-338.

32. Elena de la Souchere, *An Explanation of Spain,* trans. by Eleanor Ross Levieux (New York: Vintage, 1965), pp. 34-42, esp. pp. 36-37.

33. García Venero, p. 77.

34. García Venero, pp. 77-78.

35. Altamira, p. 336.

36. Ortzi, Chapters 1 and 2.

37. Hills, p. 86.

38. García Venero, p. 97.

39. Ugalde, p. 140.

40. For a discussion of the powers of the Spanish government as inscribed in the Constitution of 1812, see Raymond Carr, *Spain: 1808-1939* (London: Oxford University Press, 1970), pp. 97-101. Also, Altamira, pp. 537-538.

41. García Venero, pp. 135-143.

42. A valuable source on these developments is Beltza, *El Nacionalismo Vasco, 1876-1936* (San Sebastián: Editorial Txertoa, 1976), Chapters 1 and 2.

43. García Venero, pp. 161-166.

44. García Venero, p. 188.

45. García Venero, pp. 230-231.

Notes to Chapter Two

1. Andoni de Soraluze, *Riqueza y Economía del País Vasco* (Buenos Aires: Editorial Vasca "Ekin," 1945), Chapters 5, 6, and 7.

2. Stanley Payne, *Basque Nationalism* (Reno, Nevada: University of Nevada Press, 1975), p. 64.

3. Rodney Gallop, *A Book of the Basques* (Reno, Nevada: University of Nevada Press, 1970; reissue of original 1930 version), p. 26.

4. Milton M. da Silva, "Modernization and Ethnic Conflict: The Case of the Basques," *Comparative Politics*, 7, 2 (January, 1975), pp. 227-251.

5. James E. Jacob, "The Basques of France: A Case of Peripheral Ethnonationalism in Europe," *Political Anthropology*, I, 1 (March, 1975), pp. 67-86.

6. This section follows the analysis in these works: Beltza, *El Nacionalismo Vasco, 1876-1936* (San Sebastián: Editorial Txertoa, 1976), especially Chapters 1-7. Ortzi, *Los Vascos, Síntesis de su Historia* (San Sebastián: Hordago, 1978), especially Chapters 1-4. The following articles also contain general treatments of the subject: Pedro Gonzalez Blasco, "Modern Nationalism in Old Nations as a Consequence of Earlier State-Building: The Case of Basque-Spain," in Wendell Bell and Walter E. Freeman, eds., *Ethnicity and Nation-Building: Comparative, International and Historical Perspectives* (Beverly Hills: Sage, 1974), pp. 341-373. Also, Juan Linz, "Early State-Building and Late Peripheral Nationalisms against the State: The Case of Spain," in S. N. Eisenstadt and Stein Rokkan, eds., *Building States and Nations: Analyses by Region, Volume II* (Beverly Hills: Sage, 1973), Chapter Two.

7. Raymond Carr, *Spain: 1808-1939* (London: Oxford University Press, 1966), p. 394.

8. The following is based on Ofa Bezunartea, "Hoy, centenario del primer concierto económico," *Deia* (Bilbao), February 28, 1978. See also, Vicente Llona, "El Concierto Económico," *Euzkadi*, No. 63, February 16, 1978, pp. 14-15.

9. Maximiano García Venero, *Historia del Nacionalismo Vasco* (Madrid: Editora Nacional, 1969), p. 270.

10. Hugh Thomas, *The Spanish Civil War* (New York: Harper & Row, 1961), p. 61.

11. Carr, p. 205.

12. García Venero, pp. 239-251. See also, Beltza, *Nacionalismo Vasco y Clases Sociales* (San Sebastián: Editorial Txertoa, 1976), esp. Chapter Four.

13. García Venero, pp. 259-262. See also, Carr, pp. 447-449.

14. The standard work in Spanish on Sabino Arana and the origins of Basque nationalism is by Jean-Claude Larronde, *El Nacionalismo Vasco: Su Origen y Su Ideología en la Obra de Sabino Arana-Goiri* (San Sebastián: Ediciones Vascas, 1977), trans. by Lola Valverde. See also, García Venero, Part Three, Chapters I-IV.

15. Javier Tussell, "La Democracia Cristiana en España," *Actualidad Económica* (Madrid), (791), May 12, 1973, pp. 55-69.

16. Cited in García Venero, p. 325.

17. Cited in García Venero, p. 317.

18. García Venero, p. 398.

19. Carr, p. 568.

20. The role of the Basque provinces in the voting patterns in Spain's parliamentary elections during the 1930s has been exhaustively analyzed in two articles that appeared in the *Revista Española de la Opinión Pública,* 48 (1977). The first was by Juan J. Linz and Jesus M. de Miguel, "Hacia un analisis regional de las elecciones de 1936 en España," pp. 27-68; and the second was by Javier Tussell Gomez and Genoveva García Queipo de Llano, "Introducción a la sociología electoral del País Vasco durante la Segunda República," pp. 7-25. Both of these articles contain extensive bibliographies on the subject, and impressive amounts of electoral data from the period.

21. George Hills, *Spain* (New York: Praeger, 1970), p. 151.

22. García Venero, p. 561.

23. The Autonomy Statute and the procedures surrounding its drafting and adoption are discussed extensively in Manu Escudero and Javier Villanueva, *La Autonomía del País Vasco desde el Pasado al Futuro* (San Sebastián: Editorial Txertoa, 1976). These other sources may also be consulted: *La gestión del Gobierno de Euzkadi desde 1936 hasta 1956* (Paris: Basque Government in Exile, 1956). Alzibar, "Los Estatutos Vascos de Autonomía," *Alderdi* (Boletín del Partido Nacionalista Vasco), No. 284 (May-June, 1973), pp. 8-13. "Constitución del Gobierno de Euzkadi," *Garaia,* I, 6 (October 7-14, 1976), pp. 26-28.

24. Cited in Rafael Altamira, *A History of Spain: From the Beginnings to the Present Day* (New York: D. Van Nostrand, 1949), p. 618.

25. The reader may consult José Antonio de Aguirre y Lekube, *Entre la Libertad y la Revolución, 1930-1935* (Bilbao: Editorial Geu, 1976) for the Basque leader's personal account of this tumultuous period. The celebrated meeting between Aguirre and General Orgaz in the summer of 1931 to discuss a possible *coup* against the Republic resulted in publicity but little else. During the labor violence of October 1934, the PNV official position was opposed to revolution, although Aguirre and several others were arrested for conspiracy. These are isolated incidents, however, in an overall strategy of parliamentary maneuver and non-violence.

26. It should be remembered that the Constituent Cortes had undertaken a major program to drive the Catholic Church out of its privileged status almost from the beginning of the Republic. The pro-Church stance of the draft Statute was, under these circumstances, quite inflammatory to the Spanish left. The Basques, on the other hand, wanted autonomy precisely in order (among other

reasons) to be able to protect the Church from Madrid. See Hills, pp. 144-146.

Notes to Chapter Three

1. Brian Crozier, *Franco* (Boston: Little, Brown, 1967), pp. 167-168.

2. George Hills, *Spain* (New York: Praeger, 1970), p. 207.

3. Raymond Carr, *Spain: 1808-1939* (London: Oxford University Press, 1966), p. 652.

4. Hills, pp. 205 and 218. The approximate population of Navarra in 1936 was 350,000.

5. "El Partido Nacionalista Vasco," a mimeographed report issued by the Basque Nationalist Party sometime in the late 1960s, pp. 19-20.

6. Hills, pp. 212-213.

7. This account is based on Maximiano García Venero, *Historia del Nacionalismo Vasco,* 3rd ed. (Madrid: Editora Nacional, 1969), pp. 571-573, 576-580.

8. George L. Steer, *The Tree of Gernika: A Field Study of Modern War* (London: Hodder and Stoughton, 1938), pp. 68-69.

9. Hugh L. Thomas, *The Spanish Civil War* (New York: Harper and Row, 1961), pp. 194-195.

10. Thomas, pp. 194-195.

11. This and subsequent accounts of the military operations against the Basques lean heavily on George Steer's classic, *The Tree of Gernika.* The salient facts surrounding the campaigns in Guipúzcoa and Vizcaya are summarized in Thomas' *The Spanish Civil War.*

12. Steer, pp. 74-77.

13. The negotiations between the Basques and the Republic during September 1936 are reported in García Venero, pp. 591-592. See also Thomas, p. 290.

14. García Venero, pp. 615-617.

15. Steer, pp.189-209.

16. José Antonio de Aguirre, *De Guernica a Nueva York Pasando por Berlin* (Buenos Aires: Editorial Vasca "Ekin," 1944), pp. 21-22.

17. Steer, pp. 157-158, 288.

18. Juan de Iturralde, *El Catolicismo y la Cruzada de Franco: Tomo III* (Toulouse, France: Editorial Egi-Indarra, 1965), pp. 226-238.

19. Steer, p. 159.

20. These events are discussed in Aguirre, pp. 31-39.

21. The sea evacuation from Bilbao is discussed in great detail in Iturralde, pp. 270-272.

22. Aguirre, pp. 58-61.

Notes to Chapter Four

1. Quoted in Luis de Ibarra Enziondo, *El Nacionalismo Vasco en la Paz y en la Guerra* (ediciones "Alderdi", n.d.), p. 65.

2. Juan de Iturralde, *El Catolicismo y la Cruzada de Franco,* Volume III (Toulouse, France: Editorial Egi-Indarra, 1965), p. 288.

3. Hugh Thomas, *The Spanish Civil War* (New York: Harper & Row, 1961), p. 448.

4. Thomas, pp. 449-451.

5. Ibarra Enziondo, pp. 67-72.

6. Elena de la Souchere, *An Explanation of Spain,* trans. by Eleanor Ross Levieux (New York: Vintage, 1965), p. 248.

7. Iturralde, p. 288.

8. George Hills, *Spain* (New York: Praeger, 1970), pp. 230-231.

9. Iturralde, p. 290. Ibarra Enziondo, p. 91.

10. The following account is based on a remarkable diary kept by one of the prisoners, Rafael de Gárate, *Diario de un Condenado a Muerte* (Bayonne, France: Editorial Axular, 1974). See also, Joseba Elósegi, *Quiero Morir por Algo* (Barcelona: Plaze & Janes, 1977), pp. 201-231.

11. *Garrote Vil* is a method of execution which strangles the victim, and snaps his spinal cord at the same time. Death is long in coming, and the process is an extremely painful way to die. Typically, such executions were conducted before the entire prison population.

12. Ibarra Enziondo, pp. 114-116. Also, José Antonio de Aguirre, *De Guernica a Nueva York Pasando por Berlin* (Buenos Aires: Editorial Vasca Ekin, 1944), pp. 66, 348.

13. Aguirre, p. 74. See also Luis de Aranguren, *Memorias de un Exilado Vasco* (Mexico City: Editorial Vasca, n.d.), p. 485.

14. Ibarra Enziondo, pp. 88-89.

15. Vicente Escudero, "Ivonne Dutard, la 'madre' de los pilotos aliados," *Deia* (Bilbao), March 1, 1978.

16. Vicente Escudero, "Emilio Ithurria pasó los planos de las bases de submarinos alemanes," *Deia* (Bilbao), February 28, 1978.

17. Vicente Escudero, "Por el Pais Vasco se pasaron muestras de arena de las playas francesas," *Deia* (Bilbao), February 9, 1978.

18. Antonio Vilanova, *Los Olvidados: Los Exilados Españoles en la Segunda Guerra Mundial* (Paris: Ruedo Ibérico, 1969), p. 73.

19. Aguirre, pp. 73-330.

20. These assurances were contained in a telegram sent by Eden to

the Duke of Alba, Spanish Ambassador in London, in 1940. The telegram's contents were made known to American officials in October 1947, at the height of the controversy over foreign intervention in Spanish domestic affairs. See U.S. Department of State, *Foreign Relations of the United States, 1947: Volume III, The British Commonwealth; Europe* (Washington, D.C.: USGPO, 1972), pp. 1088-90.

21. This account is based on the article by Manuel de Irujo, "De Gaulle y los Vascos, "*Alderdi* (Boletín del Partido Nacionalista Vasco), No. 282 (February, 1973), pp. 3-12.

22. Of the hundred or so Basques who ended up in the death camp at Gusen, only one survived until the end of the war. See, " 'Yo escapé al exterminio,' " *Euzkadi*, No. 94, September 21, 1978, pp. 9-13.

23. This account is based on Vilanova, pp. 235-310.

24. Hills, pp. 252-253.

25. U.S. Department of State, *Foreign Relations of the United States, 1945: Volume V, Europe* (Washington, D.C.: USGPO, 1967), pp. 667-668.

26. *Foreign Relations of the United States, 1945*, pp. 670, 686-687, 702-703, 707.

27. U.S. Department of State, *Foreign Relations of the United States, 1946: Volume V, The British Commonwealth; Western and Central Europe* (Washington, D.C.: USGPO, 1969), p. 1045.

28. *Foreign Relations of the United States, 1946*, pp. 1033-36.

29. *Foreign Relations of the United States, 1946*, pp. 1038-42.

30. *Foreign Relations of the United States, 1946*, pp. 1044-45.

31. *Foreign Relations of the United States, 1946*, pp. 1077-78.

32. *Foreign Relations of the United States, 1947*, pp. 1091-97.

33. Theodore J. Lowi, "Bases in Spain," in Harold Stein, ed., *American Civil-Military Relations: A Book of Case Studies* (Birmingham, Alabama: University of Alabama Press, 1963), pp. 667-702.

34. The two best examples of this approach are Ortzi, *Los Vascos: Síntesis de su Historia* (San Sebastián: Hordago, 1978), esp. pp. 169-172; and, Beltza, *El Nacionalismo Vasco en el Exilio, 1937-1960* (San Sebastián: Editorial Txertoa,1977), esp. Parts Two and Three. The latter book, by the way, contains a number of interesting documents most useful for studying and understanding this period.

35. Material on the guerrilla war in Spain can be found in Hills, pp. 433-440. See also Ibarra Enziondo, p. 175.

36. *Alderdi* (Boletín del Partido Nacionalista Vasco), No. 37 (April, 1950), p. 10.

37. "Leizaola: 'La autonomía es fundamental para el pueblo vasco'," *La Actualidad Española,* February 14-20, 1977, pp. 30-34.

38. *Alderdi* (Boletin del Partido Nacionalista Vasco), No. 46 (January 1951), p. 7. See also the interview with one of the founders of Radio Euzkadi, Jokin Intza, in *Euzkadi,* No. 90, August 24, 1978, pp. 20-22.

39. Ibarra Enziondo, pp. 214-220. For some interesting anecdotes on this period, see the speech of one of the early resistance figures, Primi Abad, welcoming back from exile one of his comrades of that struggle, Andoni de Ormaetxe, in *Euzkadi,* No. 63, February 16, 1978, pp. 16-17.

40. Ibarra Enziondo, pp. 220-221. See also Max Gallo, *Spain under Franco: A History,* trans. by Jean Stweart (New York: Dutton, 1974), pp. 176-177.

41. Ibarra Enziondo, pp. 220-226.

42. Gallo, pp. 210-213. Ibarra Enziondo, pp. 186-192, 226.

Notes to Chapter Five

1. Since there never has been a definitive study made on the Basque Nationalist Party, in developing this section I have had to rely on a more or less systematic perusal of a number of PNV publications, including mimeographed reports and, most importantly, a number of issues of its monthly bulletins, first *Alderdi* and later *Euzkadi.* These sources have been supplemented by about fifty interviews with PNV members, including both leaders and rank and file members, conducted during two trips to the Basque country, in 1973 and in 1978-79. Also of interest is the second half of the book by Luis de Ibarra Enziondo, *El Nacionalismo Vasco en la Paz y en la Guerra* (Ediciones "Alderdi," n.d.).

2. *Alderdi* (Boletín del Partido Nacionalista Vasco), No. 295, November-December, 1974, pp. 24-25.

3. See Ortzi, *Los Vascos: Síntesis de su Historia* (San Sebastián: Hordago, 1977), pp. 170-173. Also, *Euzkadi,* No. 83, July 6, 1978, p. 13. For a general treatment of this period, see Beltza, *El Nacionalismo Vasco en el Exilio, 1937-1960* (San Sebastián: Editorial Txertoa, 1977), Part Four.

4. The standard reference on the ideology of the PNV during the 1950s and 1960s is Francisco Javier de Landaburu, *La Causa del Pueblo Vasco,* 3rd edition (Bilbao: Editorial Geu Argitaldaria, 1977).

5. *Alderdi* (Boletín del Partido Nacionalista Vasco), No. 102, September, 1955, p. 2.

6. *Alderdi* (Boletín del Partido Nacionalista Vasco), No. 292, April-May, 1974, pp. 3-5.

7. This account is based on several lengthy interviews held by the author during the summer of 1973. At the time, I agreed to keep my informant's identity secret for political reasons. I choose to do so now to protect his privacy.

8. See Max Gallo, *Spain under Franco: A History,* trans. by Jean Stewart (New York: E. P. Dutton, 1974), pp. 210-216.

9. Ibarra Enziondo, pp. 114-116.

10. Even well into the post-Franco period, when the PNV had returned to legal parliamentary activity, those of its leaders who had lived during much of the Franco period in Venezuela were referred to, somewhat pejoratively, as "los venezolanos," and had still not been fully accepted back into the inner circles of the Party.

11. Rodney Gallop, *A Book of the Basques* (Reno, Nevada: University of Nevada Press, 1970; reissue of the original 1930 version), pp. 10-11.

12. Gallop, p. 46.

13. Charlotte Crawford, "The Position of Women in a Basque Fishing Community," in William A. Douglass, Richard W. Etulain and William H. Jacobsen, Jr., eds., *Anglo-American Contributions to Basque Studies: Essays in Honor of Jon Bilbao* (Desert Research Institute Publications on the Social Sciences, No. 13, 1977), pp. 145-152.

14. Julio Caro Baroja, *Los Vascos* (Madrid: Ediciones Minotauro, 1958), pp. 302-303, 322-323, 339-345. See also William A. Douglass, *Muerte en Murélaga: El Contexto de la muerte en el País Vasco* (Barcelona: Barral Editores, 1963), Chapter Two.

15. Gallop, p. 65.

16. Douglass, p. 29.

17. It is worth pointing out here that one of the sources of the remarkable staying power of the Basque nationalist leadership was their comparative youth at the outbreak of the Civil War. President Aguirre and many of the other PNV leaders were in their early thirties, and a few were even in their late twenties. Since they lived quite long lives — and a few survive even at this writing — they provided that rare continuity of leadership in clandestine political movements that can link a struggle to its historical roots, but which can also block the recognition of new or altered circumstances that may call for changes in strategy.

18. Gallop, p. 68.

Notes to Chapter Six

1. Although it is beyond the scope of this study to examine the origins and structure of the little known Basque language, the reader

interested in pursuing this subject further may begin by consulting some of the following works. Of major interest would be the work by Rodney Gallop, *A Book of the Basques* (Reno, Nevada: University of Nevada Press, 1970; reissue of original 1930 version). The book has an extensive bibliography listing many works of interest on the Basque language. The Basque publishing house in Buenos Aires, called Editorial Vasca "Ekin," has published a number of important works on Euskera, many of which contain extensive bibliographies which will lead the reader on to additional sources. Three of these works are Vicente de Amezaga, *El Hombre Vasco* (1967), Isaac Lopez Mendizabal, *La Lengua Vasca* (1949), and Martin de Ugalde, *Unamuno y el Vascuence* (1966). See also the six articles on Basque linguistics in William A. Douglass, Richard W. Etulain and William H. Jacobsen, Jr., eds., *Anglo-American Contributions to Basque Studies: Essays in Honor of Jon Bilbao* (Desert Research Institute Publications on the Social Sciences, No. 13, 1977), pp. 163-217.

2. Gallop, pp. 2-5.

3. Maximiano García Venero, *Historia del Nacionalism Vasco,* 3rd edition (Madrid: Editora Nacional, 1969), pp. 435-436.

4. Juan Linz, "Early State-Building and Late Peripheral Nationalisms against the State: The Case of Spain," in S. N. Eisenstadt and Stein Rokkan, eds., *Building States and Nations: Analyses by Region* (Beverly Hills and London: Sage Publications, 1973), Volume II, Chapter Two, p. 76. 

5. Gallop, p. 79.

6. Beltza, *El Nacionalismo Vasco: 1876-1936* (San Sebastián: Editorial Txertoa, 1976), p. 220.

7. Manu Escudero and Javier Villanueva, *La Autonomía del Pais Vasco desde el Pasado al Futuro* (San Sebastián: Editorial Txertoa, 1976), pp. 105-106, and Appendix I.

8. This letter from Aguirre to UNESCO is reproduced as an appendix in Beltza, *El Nacionalismo Vasco en el Exilio, 1937-1960* (San Sebastián: Editorial Txertoa, 1977), pp. 135-136.

9. George Hills, *Spain* (New York: Praeger, 1970), pp. 283-284.

10. In May 1973, according to a count made by the author, 30 of the weekly 153 masses celebrated in San Sebastián (or about 19.6 percent) were said in Euskera. In January 1979, when I made a second count, the percentage had declined to 18.2 percent (36 masses in Euskera out of a total of 198).

11. A copy of the draft Autonomy Statute is found in *Diario Vasco* (San Sebastián), December 26, 1978.

12. Javier Angulo, "La Universidad vasca propugna la institucionalización del euskera," *El País* (Madrid), July 9, 1978.

13. *Diario Vasco* (San Sebastián), January 5, 1979.

14. Milton M. da Silva, "Modernization and Ethnic Conflict: The Case of the Basques," *Comparative Politics,* 7, 2 (January 1975), pp. 227-251, esp. 228-229. On the use of Basque on the French side of the border, see Raymond and Françoise Mougeon, "Basque Language Survival in Rural Communities from the Pays Basque, France," in Douglass, Etulain and Jacobsen, pp. 107-115.

15. Meic Stephens, *Linguistic Minorities in Western Europe* (Llandysul, Wales, England: Gomer Press, 1976), p. 643.

16. Pedro Gonzalez Blasco, "Modern Nationalism in Old Nations as a Consequence of Earlier State-Building: The Case of Basque-Spain," in Wendell Bell and Walter E. Freeman, eds., *Ethnicity and Nation-Building: Comparative, International, and Historical Perspectives* (Beverly Hills and London: Sage Publications, 1974), pp. 341-373, esp. p. 362. See also, Stanley G. Payne, "Regional Nationalism: The Basques and the Catalans," in William T. Salisbury and James D. Theberge, eds., *Spain in the 1970s: Economics, Social Structure, Foreign Policy* (New York: Praeger, 1976), Chapter 6, esp. p. 85. Further discussion is found in the Linz and da Silva articles cited above.

17. Beltza, *Nacionalismo Vasco y Clases Sociales* (San Sebastián: Editorial Txertoa, 1976), p. 33.

18. Pedro de Yrizar, "Los dialectos y variedades de la Lengua Vasca: Estudio Linguístico-Demográfico," *Separata del Boletín de la Real Sociedad Vascongada de los Amigos del País,*Vol. 29, Nos. 1, 2 and 3 (1973).

19. Salustiano del Campo, Manuel Navarro and Felix Tezanos, *La cuestión regional española* (Madrid: Edicusa, 1977). The section on the Basque language is found on pp. 211-216.

20. Stephens, p. 644.

21. *Deia* (Bilbao), December 9, 1978.

22. "El euskera, olivdado en Televisión," *Deia* (Bilbao), March 9, 1978.

23. Iñaki de Zabala, "Informe Sobre Euzkadi," typed report issued by the Basque Nationalist Party, dated February 1972. "Las ikastolas infantiles propias pueden salvar a los vascos," *Euzkadi,* No. 35 (1974), p. 12. "El movimiento de las ikastolas," *Garaia,* 1, 24 (February 10-17, 1977), p. 32. Stephens, p. 645.

24. Toward the end of the 1970s, it was thought that the Spanish Government, through its Ministry of Education, would begin to offer direct financial support to the *ikastolas*. However, as late as 1978, the Federation of *Ikastolas* in Vizcaya had to go on strike to force the Ministry to provide the 404 million pesetas (about $6.7 million) it had promised. See *Deia* (Bilbao), May 9, 1978; and *El Pais* (Madrid), June 24, 1978.

25. Txillardegi, "El Problema del Bilinguismo," *Garaia,* 1, 3 (September 16-23, 1976), pp. 32-33. See also the interview with a leader in Euskera teaching, Xabier Mendiguren, in *Garaia,* 1, 6 (October 7-14, 1976), pp. 7-8.

26. Gallop, p. 82. García Venero, p. 427.

27. Beltza, *Nacionalismo Vasco y Clases Sociales,* p. 33.

28. Escudero and Villanueva, pp. 110-111.

29. del Campo, Navarro and Tezanos, pp. 45, 221-223.

30. Beltza, *Nacionalismo Vasco y Clases Sociales,* pp. 160-161.

Notes to Chapter Seven

1. *Christian Science Monitor,* April 25, 1974.

2. The assassination is described in detail in Julen Agirre, *Operation Ogro,* trans. by Barbara Probst Solomon (New York: Ballantine, 1974).

3. Luis Ruiz de Agirre, "A.N.V. y el Estatuto de 1936," *Garaia,* September 16-23, 1976, p. 8.

4. Gisele Halimi, *El Proceso de Burgos,* trans. by Mercedes Rivera (Caracas: Monte Avila Editores, 1972), pp. 262-290.

5. New York *Times,* December 23, 1973. According to one set of calculations, which the author admits may be inexact, industrial workers represented about 40 percent of all ETA militants imprisoned in Spain and France during the late 1960s and early 1970s, while lower ranking office employees and technicians represented an additional 20 percent. See Beltza, *Nacionalismo Vasco y Clases Sociales* (San Sebastián: Editorial Txertoa, 1976), p. 153.

6. " 'Marietta,' La Asesina de Acero," *La Actualidad Española,* February 7-13, 1977, pp. 20-22. See also, "A 'marietta' limpia," *Cambio 16,* February 20, 1977, p. 5.

7. Frederick Forsyth's recent novel *The Dogs of War* (New York: Bantam, 1974) describes in great detail the workings of this arms traffic, and has much information about the flow of weapons into and through Spain. Although it is fictional, the book is reputed to be based on fact.

8. *Diario Vasco,* May 8, 1973.

9. The Spanish government used countless numbers of such spies or informers to gain information about Basque nationalist activities. Their presence became so onerous that many Basques who had no separatist sentiments and no political connections came to fear that they would be informed on by spies eager to gain favor with the authorities. The efforts by an ETA cell to discover which of their members is informing the police of their activities are the central

theme of a recent novel by Martin de Ugalde, *Las Brujas de Sorjin* (Saint Jean de Luz: Editorial Axular, 1975).

10. José María Portel, "E.T.A.: Objectivo, La Insurrección de Euzkadi," *Blanco y Negro,* June 29-July 5, 1977, pp. 25-29.

11. Federico de Arteaga (pseud.), *ETA y el Proceso de Burgos* (Madrid: Editorial E. Aguado, 1971), pp. 345-350.

12. The most significant work in this area has been done by Phillip A. Karber. See his article, "The Psychological Dimensions of Bombing Motivations," *Bomb Incident Bulletin,* 1, 12 (June, 1973). Also his article "Urban Terrorism: Baseline Data and a Conceptual Framework," *Social Science Quarterly* (December, 1971), pp. 521-533.

13. Portel, p. 28.

14. Portel, p. 29. Full data on all the states of exception declared in Spain between 1956 and 1975 are available in Luis C.-Nuñez Astrain, *La Sociedad Vasca Actual* (San Sebastián: Editorial Txertoa, 1978), pp. 121-128.

15. See, for example, the New York *Times,* September 28, 1972. The report by Iñaki de Zabala, *"Informe sobre Euzkadi,"* contains a complete list of all known Basques in prison for political crimes as of February 1972. However, in the work by Luis C.-Nuñez Astrain cited earlier, it is reported that the number of Basques arrested each year between 1968 and 1975 never dropped below 315 and rose as high as 862. (See *La Sociedad Vasca Actual,* p. 121.) In order to reconcile these two sets of figures, one must presume that most of the Basques arrested for political crimes were held for such a short time that they never appeared on any official list of prisoners.

16. Based on press reports. See particularly, the New York *Times,* November 12, 1975, and the Washington *Post,* July 31, 1976.

17. Instituto Nacional de Estadísticas, *España: Panorámica Social, 1974* (Madrid: INE, 1975), p. 401.

18. *Cambio 16* (Madrid), June 2, 1975, p. 26.

19. *Cambio 16* (Madrid), May 26, 1975, p. 25.

20. New York *Times,* May 28, 1975.

21. *Cambio 16* (Madrid), June 2, 1975.

22. The Amnesty International findings are contained in its publication, *Report of an Amnesty International Mission to Spain* (London: Amnesty International, 1975).

23. This discussion, and much of what follows, is based on Kepa Salaberri, *El Proceso de Euzkadi en Burgos: El Sumarísimo 31/69* (Paris: Ruedo Ibérico, 1971), especially Part I.

24. This trial attracted a good deal of attention and several books were written about it. The best known are those already cited earlier,

by Halimi, de Arteaga, and Salaberri. The discussion here is based on these sources.

25. Carol Edler Baumann, *The Diplomatic Kidnappings: A Revolutionary Tactic of Urban Terrorism* (The Hague: Martinus Nijhoff, 1973), pp. 86-89.

Notes to Chapter Eight

1. On the general subject of Spanish regionalism, the reader may begin by consulting these works: Amando de Miguel, *Recursos Humanos, Clases y Regiones en España* (Madrid: EDICUSA, 1977). Salustiano del Campo, Manuel Navarro and J. Felix Tezanos, *La cuestión regional española* (Madrid: EDICUSA, 1977). José Miguel de Azaola, *Vasconia y su Destino, I: La Regionalización de España* (Madrid: Revista de Occidente, 1972), esp. Chapter 6. For an earlier version of the work of de Miguel, see Juan Linz and Amando de Miguel, "Within-Nation Differences and Comparisons: The Eight Spains," in Richard L. Merritt and Stein Rokkan, eds., *Comparing Nations: The Uses of Quantitative Data in Cross-National Research* (New Haven: Yale University Press, 1966), Chapter 13.

2. Ramón Tamames, *Introducción a la Economía Española,* seventh ed. (Madrid: Alianza Editorial, 1972), Table 11-5, p. 413.

3. Edward E. Malefakis, *Agrarian Reform and Peasant Revolution in Spain: Origins of the Civil War* (New Haven: Yale University Press, 1970), Appendix C, p. 416.

4. Amando de Miguel, *Sociología del franquismo* (Barcelona: Euros, 1975).

5. The ideological proposals of the Falange have been studied exhaustively in Stanley Payne, *Falange* (Stanford, California: Stanford University Press, 1961). See also Charles W. Anderson, *The Political Economy of Modern Spain: Policy-Making in an Authoritarian System* (Madison: University of Wisconsin Press, 1970).

6. Tad Szulc, "The Politics of Church-State Relations in Spain," in William T. Salisbury and James D. Theberge, eds., *Spain in the 1970s* (New York: Praeger, 1976), Chapter Five.

7. Paul H. Lewis, "The Spanish Ministerial Elite, 1938-1969," *Comparative Politics,* 5, 1 (October, 1972), pp. 83-106.

8. Richard Herr, *The Eighteenth-Century Revolution in Spain* (Princeton, N. J.: Princeton University Press, 1958), pp. 91-98.

9. Jaime Vicens Vives, *An Economic History of Spain,* trans. by Frances M. Lopez-Morillas (Princeton, N.J: Princeton University Press, 1969), p. 491.

10. Tamames, p. 57.

11. Malefakis, *Agrarian Reform and Peasant Revolution in Spain.*

12. Tamames, pp. 98, 377.

13. Richard Gunther, "The Removal of Policy Constraints in Post-Franco Spain," paper delivered to the International Studies Association, St. Louis, Missouri, 1977, p. 11.

14. Vincente R. Pilapil, "Franco's Rule: Institutionalization and Prospects of Succession," in Salisbury and Theberge, eds., Chapter 7.

15. Benjamin Welles, *Spain: The Gentle Anarchy* (New York: Praeger, 1965), p. 319.

16. James D. Theberge, "Spanish Industrial Development Policy in the Twentieth Century," in Salisbury and Theberge, eds., Chapter 2.

17. Anderson, p. 146.

18. Max Gallo, *Spain under Franco,* trans. by Jean Stewart (New York: Dutton, 1974), esp. pp. 346-348.

19. Amando de Miguel, *Manual de Estructura Social de España* (Madrid: Editorial Tecnos, 1974), Table 30, p. 398.

20. Anderson, p. 198.

21. Stanley G. Payne, *Politics and the Military in Modern Spain* (Stanford, California: Stanford University Press, 1967), p. 452.

22. Payne, p. 396.

23. The Acoca story is from the Washington *Post* of September 24, 1977. See also stories in the *Post* on August 21, 1977 and September 28, 1977.

24. As quoted in Linz and de Miguel, p. 318.

25. The following data are drawn from José Miguel de Azaola, Statistical Tables following p. 403. See also, Tamames, *Introducción a la Economia Española.* See also, "Armamento en polvo," *Cambio 16,* June 1, 1975, pp. 16-17.

26. "Las Regiones-Bisagra Nos 'Abren' a Europa," *Hoja del Lunes de San Sebastián,* May 28, 1973.

27. These data are taken from Iñaki de Zabala, "Informe sobre Euzkadi," a typed report issued by the Basque Nationalist Party in 1972.

28. This analysis is based on data from *Alderdi* (Boletín del Partido Nacionalista Vasco), No. 292, April-May, 1974, p. 29.

29. *Alderdi* (Boletín del Partido Nacionalista Vasco), No. 289, December, 1973-January, 1974, pp. 8-16.

30. At least, the percentage of taxes returned to the Basque provinces seems to be increasing. From 1958 to 1964, Vizcaya province received from the Spanish government contributions that varied be-

tween 10.5 percent and 16.2 percent of what Vizcaya had contributed to the Spanish treasury. These data are found in *Gudari,* a publication of Euzko Gaztedi (EGI) in Caracas, No. 37, 1966, p. 5.

31. Tamames, pp. 450-459.

32. During the 1930s, it appears, Basque capital amounted to about five billion pesetas, or roughly 25 percent of the entire capital supply of Spain. Of this sum, three billion pesetas (or about 60 percent) were invested in Basque industries and businesses. For further data, consult Andoni de Soraluze, *Riqueza y Economia del Pais Vasco* (Buenos Aires: Editorial Vasca "Ekin," 1945), esp. Chapter IX. There is little reason to believe that these proportions changed much during the 1940s and 1950s. See also, "Decide Bilbao," *Cambio 16,* May 26-June 1, 1975, p. 50.

33. de Azaola, pp. 143, 549.

Notes to Chapter Nine

1. For a good discussion of the regional development program, see James D. Theberge, "Spanish Industrial Development Policy in the Twentieth Century," in William T. Salisbury and James D. Theberge, eds., *Spain in the 1970s: Economics, Social Structure, Foreign Policy* (New York: Praeger, 1976), Chapter 2. See also, Amando de Miguel, *Manual de Estructura Social de España* (Madrid: Editorial Tecnos, 1974), pp. 223-233.

2. de Miguel, Table 33, p. 409.

3. Edward E. Malefakis, *Agrarian Reform and Peasant Revolution in Spain: Origins of the Civil War* (New Haven: Yale University Press, 1970), pp. 104-106.

4. Instituto Nacional de Estadística, *Anuario Estadístico de España* (Madrid: INE, 1971 and 1974).

5. *ABC* (Madrid), June 27, 1973.

6. de Miguel, p. 189.

7. The preceding data are drawn from de Miguel, pp. 185-193.

8. Manuel de Terán Alvarez, "País Vasco," in Manuel de Terán, Luis Sole Sabaris, and others, *Geografía Regional de España* (Barcelona: Ediciones Ariel, 1968), pp. 86-87.

9. Instituto Nacional de Estadística, *Anuario Estadístico de España* (Madrid: INE, 1974), p. 470.

10. Blanca Rodriguez and Beatriz Iraburu, "El siquiatrico de Bermeo: Un verdadero manicomio," *Deia* (Bilbao), June 19, 1977, p. 9. See also "Los hospitales siquiatricos del Pais Vasco," in the same issue of the newspaper.

11. "Vizcaya: miles de niños se quedarán sin escuelas por falta de puestos," *Deia* (Bilbao), June 25, 1977, p. 7. In the same issue, see also Ana Garabati, "Vitoria: más de 5,000 niños en la calle," p. 7. For a good general discussion of the problems of educational policy in Spain, see de Miguel, Chapter 5.

12. Juan Manuel Idoyaga, "Los Vecinos de Bilbao Impugnan el Reglamento de Parques," *Sábado Gráfico* (Madrid), April 26, 1975, pp. 37-39.

13. *Alderdi* (Boletín del Partido Nacionalista Vasco), No. 287, October, 1973, p. 29.

14. "Why the Basques are singling out Dow," *Business Week*, July 28, 1975, pp. 32-34.

15. "Bilbao es la ciudad más contaminada del Estado español," *Deia* (Bilbao), June 23, 1977, p. 10.

16. Kepa Salaberri, *El Proceso de Euskadi en Burgos* (Paris: Ruedo Ibérico, 1971), p. 66.

17. "Baracaldo: 650 familias pueden quedar en la calle," *Deia* (Bilbao), June 25, 1977, p. 11.

18. Fermin Goni, "Estudios Belagua: un movimiento ecologista para Euzkadi que cumple un año en lucha," *Deia* (Bilbao), June 25, 1977, p. 9.

19. Beltza's three most important works are *El Nacionalismo Vasco: 1876-1936* (San Sebastián: Editorial Txertoa, 1976); *El Nacionalismo Vasco en el Exilio: 1937-1960* (San Sebastián: Editorial Txertoa, 1977); and *Nacionalismo Vasco y Clases Sociales* (San Sebastián: Editorial Txertoa, 1976).

20. Beltza, *El Nacionalismo Vasco: 1876-1936*, Chapter 15.

21. One of the most important sources of information on the Basque labor movement from 1900 to the Civil War is the two-volume work by Policarpo de Larrañaga, *Contribución a la Historia Obrera de Euskalerría* (San Sebastián: Editorial Aunamendi Argitaldaria, 1977). See also the following for useful data: Beltza, *El Nacionalismo Vasco: 1876-1936*, Chapters 15, 21, 26. Also, "Breve Historia del Sindicalismo Vasco," *Garaia*, 1, 3 (September 16-23, 1976), pp. 24-27. Also, "Atlas Político Sindical de Euzkadi Sur," *Garaia*, 1, 2 (September 9-16, 1976), pp. 22-28.

22. Ortzi, *Los Vascos: Síntesis de su Historia* (San Sebastián: Hordago, 1977), p. 66.

23. Beltza, *Nacionalismo Vasco y Clases Sociales*, pp. 164-165.

24. Larrañaga, Volume 2, Chapter 13.

25. Robert Moss, *Revolutionary Challenges in Spain* (London: Institute for the Study of Conflict, June 1974), pp. 25-31.

26. Amando de Miguel, *Recursos Humanos, Clases y Regiones en España* (Madrid: Editorial Cuadernos para el Dialogo, 1977), Table 3.7, p. 137. Also, *La Actualidad Española,* No. 1,298 (November 15-21, 1976), p. 41. Also Beltza, *Nacionalismo Vasco y Clases Sociales,* pp. 137-138. Also, Manu Escudero and Javier Villanueva, *La Autonomía del País Vasco desde el Pasado al Futuro* (San Sebastián: Editorial Txertoa, 1976), p. 115.

27. *La Actualidad Española,* No. 1,323 (May 9-15, 1977), p. 35.

28. "Una manifestación 'desconvocada'," *La Actualidad Española,* No. 1,297 (November 8-14, 1976), p. 31. Also, "No sólo contaban las cifras," *La Actualidad Española,* No. 1,298 (November 15-21, 1976), p. 40.

29. *Deia* (Bilbao), September 17, 1977.

30. "I Congreso de la USO de Euskadi," *Punto y Hora,* No. 19 (January 1-15, 1977), p. 9.

31. Kepa Salaberri, *El Proceso de Euskadi en Burgos* (Paris: Ruedo Ibérico, 1971), p. 39.

32. Max Gallo, *Spain under Franco: A History,* trans. by Jean Stewart (New York: Dutton, 1974), p. 240. Also, Hills, p. 290. Also, *Alderdi* (Boletín del Partido Nacionalista Vasco), No. 110 (May, 1956), p. 14.

33. Gallo, p. 259; Hills, p. 300.

34. Gallo, pp. 289-290.

35. Gallo, pp. 295-296; Hills, p. 345.

36. Gallo, p. 345.

37. Moss, pp. 29-30. See also, *Diario Vasco,* June 23, 1973.

38. *Alderdi* (Boletín del Partido Nacionalista Vasco), No. 293 (June-July, 1974), pp. 26-28; and No. 294 (August-October, 1974), p. 30.

39. "La huelga de los 200,000," *Cambio 16,* No. 162 (December 23, 1974), pp. 24-25. Also, *Alderdi* (Boletín del Partido Nacionalista Vasco).

40. "Construcción: La huelga mas larga," *La Actualidad Española,* No. 1,298 (November 15-21, 1976), p. 42.

41. "Que viene el despido," *Cambio 16,* No. 278 (April 10, 1977), p. 38.

Notes to Chapter Ten

1. Out of a working class population of about 650,000. See Amando de Miguel, *Recursos Humanos, Clases y Regiones en Espana* (Madrid: Editorial Cuadernos para el Diálogo, 1977), Table 3.7, p. 137. See also,

La Actualidid Española, No. 1,298 (November 15-21, 1976), p. 41; "Beltza," *Nacionalismo Vasco y Clases Sociales* (San Sebastián: Editorial Txertoa, 1976), pp. 137-138.

2. Miguel Acoca, "Police Battle Basque Strikers," Washington *Post,* March 9, 1976.

3. "Manuel Gaztelumendi: 'Así nos fugamos de la cárcel de Segovia'," *Cambio 16,* No. 262 (December 19, 1976), pp. 18-19.

4. Miguel Acoca, "Spain Permits Parties after 37-Year Ban," Washington *Post,* June 10, 1976.

5. Miguel Acoca, "Spain Agrees to Amnesty, Wide Reform," Washington *Post,* July 17, 1976. See also, Miguel Acoca, "Police, Demonstrators Clash During King's Santiago Visit," Washington *Post,* July 26, 1976.

6. "Amnesty for Political Prisoners," Washington *Post,* July 31, 1976.

7. *García,* Vol. 1, No. 3 (September 16-23, 1976), pp. 9-16. See also, *La Actualidad Española,* No. 1,291 (September 27-October 3, 1976), pp. 15-16. Washington *Post,* September 14 and September 15, 1976.

8. "Continúa la violencia," and "Funeral por Araluce," in *La Actualidad Española,* No. 1,294 (October 17-24, 1976), pp. 28-29. See also, articles in the Washington *Post,* October 5, 6 and 8, 1976.

9. "Los que regresaron," *La Actualidad Española,* No. 1,298 (November 15-21, 1976), p. 11. See also, "Euskadi insiste: amnistía," *Cambio 16,* No. 262 (December 19, 1976), pp. 18-19.

10. "Está 'Carlos' en Madrid?" *La Actualidad Española,* No. 1,299 (November 22-28, 1976), p. 44. The nature of the division between ETA-m and ETA-pm is discussed in Alberto Pérez Calvo, *Los Partidos Políticos en el País Vasco* (San Sebastián: Luis Haranburu Editor/Turner Ediciones, 1977), pp. 106-110.

11. "El deshielo de ETA," *La Actualidad Española,* No. 1,313 (February 28 - March 6, 1977), pp. 14-19.

12. "A por votos etarras," *Cambio 16,* No. 278 (April 10, 1977), p. 22. For other aspects of this debate see "Los partidos se definen," *García,* Vol. 1, No. 24 (February 10-17, 1977), pp. 16-17. "Una Meta: Euskadi Socialista," *Punto y Hora,* No. 19 (January 1-15, 1977), pp. 30-32. "Atlas Político Sindical de Euzkadi Sur," *García,* Vol. I, No. 2 (September 9-16, 1976), pp. 22-28.

13. This is the central theme of the important interview with ETA-pm members in "El deshielo de ETA," in *La Actualidad Española,* cited in footnote 11 above.

14. The rescue is described in *La Actualidad Española,* No. 1,311 (February 14-20, 1977).

15. "GRAPO & Cía," *Cambio 16,* No. 271 (February 20, 1977), pp. 4-9. See also, "EL GRAPO, una nueva 'estrella' para el terror," *La Actualidad Española,* No. 1,303 (December 20-26, 1976), pp. 26-27. "Los hombres de GRAPO," *La Actualidad Española,* No. 1,312 (February 21-27, 1977), pp. 39-40.

16. A complete description of the Oriol kidnapping, with a list of the 15 prisoners whose release was demanded, is contained in *La Actualidad Española,* No. 1,303 (December 20-26, 1976).

17. "No todos a casa," *La Actualidad Española,* No. 1,304 (December 27, 1976-January 2, 1977), p. 15.

18. "La cita europea de Euskadi," *Punto y Hora,* No. 19 (January 1-15, 1977), pp. 12-13.

19. "Navidad Sin Amnistía," *Punto y Hora,* No. 19 (January 1-15, 1977), p. 5. See also, "Pro-amnistía en bizkaia," *García*, Vol. I, No. 24 (February 10-17, 1977), p. 36.

20. "Adíos, Tribunal de Orden Publico," *La Actualidad Española,* No. 1,305 (January 3-9, 1977), p. 9.

21. "La 'Oferta Suárez'," *La Actualidad Española,* No. 1,307 (January 17-23, 1977), pp. 6-7.

22. *La Actualidad Española,* No. 1,308 (January 24-30, 1977), p. 7.

23. "Vitoria: Uno año despues," *La Actualidad Epañola,* No. 1,314 (March 7-13, 1977), pp. 26-29.

24. Washington *Post,* March 6 and 7, 1977.

25. "San Sebastián: A las barricadas," *La Actualidad Española,* No. 1,315 (March 14-20, 1977), pp. 22-24.

26. *Diario de Navarra,* March 29, 1977.

27. "Luto Vasco," *La Actualidad Española,* No. 1,316 (March 21-27, 1977), pp. 23-26.

28. "El terror apunta a Fraga," *La Actualidad Española,* No. 1,318 (April 4-10, 1977), pp. 16-18.

29. "Gota a gota," *Cambio 16,* No. 278 (April 10, 1977), pp. 16-19.

30. New York *Times,* April 11, 1977.

31. *La Actualidad Española,* No. 1,324 (May 16-22, 1977), pp. 9-10.

32. "Explota el País Vasco," *La Actualidad Española,* No. 1,325 (May 23-29, 1977), pp. 28-34. See also, Miguel Acoca, "Basques Near Rebellion on Eve of Mondale Visit," Washington *Post,* May 17, 1977.

33. "Industrialist kidnapped by Basques," *The Times* (London), May 21, 1977. See also, Miguel Acoca, "Spain Set to Free Basques After Industrialist Abducted," Washington *Post,* May 21, 1977.

34. "Libertad, a medias," *La Actualidad Española,* No. 1,326 (May 30 - June 5, 1977), pp. 30-34.

35. "La amnistía de nunca llegar," *La Actualidad Española,* No. 1,328 (June 13-19, 1977), pp. 22-23. The matter of the numbers of remaining prisoners was complicated by two facts. First, there was in prison a Basque who had been convicted of political activities as a member of a Spanish radical group and who occasionally appeared on Basque nationalist lists although he was not a member of ETA. In addition, a small group of ETA-pm members (six in all) had been arrested in early June in connection with an unsuccessful attempt to blow up a bus carrying Guardia Civil members. If these seven are counted in the list, there were in fact twelve Basques in prison on June 10, 1977, although only five were from the basic list of 23 that had figured so much in the news. See for a list of all the names: *Deia* (Bilbao), June 10, 1977.

36. Unknown to most of the outside world, the French government had placed a number of Basque exiles in confinement on two of its prison islands, Yeu in the Atlantic, and Porquerolle in the Mediterranean, despite the fact that they had violated no French law and had been charged with no crime by the French government. See "Yeu, Cada Vez Peor," *Punto y Hora,* No. 19 (January 1-15, 1977), pp. 33-35. See also, "Porquerolles, la nueva Yeu," *La Actualidad Española,* No. 1, 326 (May 30 - June 5, 1977), p. 35.

37. *Deia* (Bilbao), June 23, 1977. See also, "Ybarra: Otro Episodio Sangriento," *Blanco y Negro,* No. 3400 (June 29 - July 5, 1977), p. 30. Also, "Ybarra, ejecutado," *La Actualidad Española,* No. 1,330 (June 27 - July 3, 1977), p. 8.

38 "El entierro eel rencor," *Cambio 16,* No. 307 (October 30, 1977), p. 28.

Notes to Chapter Eleven

1. "Los 333 días de Adolfo Suárez," *La Actualidad Española,* No. 1,330 (June 27-July 3, 1977), pp. 22-42.

2. *La Actualidad Española,* No. 1,323 (May 9-15, 1977), pp. 16-21.

3. *Cambio 16,* No. 271 (February 20, 1977), pp. 14-15.

4. "Las ambiguas ofertas electorales," *La Actualidad Española,* No. 1,327 (June 6-12, 1977), pp. 19-20.

5. The following analysis leans heavily on a recent essay on Basque political parties: Alberto Perez Calvo, *Los Partidos Políticos en el País Vasco* (San Sebastián and Madrid: Luis Haraburu Eds. and Turner Ediciones, 1977). See also, Idoia Estornes Zubizarreta, *Que Son Los Partidos Abertzales* (San Sebastián, 1977). Also of value is "Atlas Político Sindical de Euzkadi Sur," *Garaia,* I, 2 (September 9-16, 1976),

pp. 22-28. See also, "A por votos etarras," *Cambio 16,* No. 278 (April 10, 1977), p. 22.

6. *La Actualidad Española,* No. 1,310 (February 7-13, 1977), p. 10. See also, "La 'Ikurriña' al viento," *La Actualidad Española,* No. 1,291 (September 27-October 3, 1976), pp. 22-23.

7. "Entre la ikurriña y la amnistía," *La Actualidad Española,* No. 1,309 (January 31-February 6, 1977), pp. 36-40.

8. Based on various articles in the Washington *Post,* September 28, December 24, December 25, December 31, 1976; and February 21 and March 2, 1977.

9. See the important interview with Leizaola, "La Continuidad del Pasado," in *Punto y Hora,* No. 19 (January 1-15, 1977), pp. 18-21. The matter is also discussed in the interview with PNV leader Xabier Arzallus in *Garaia,* Vol. 1, No. 24 (February 10-17, 1977), pp. 10-13.

10. "Leizaola: 'La autonomía es fundamental para el pueblo vasco,' " *La Actualidad Española,* No. 1,311 (February 14-20, 1977), pp. 30-34.

11. "El Partido Nacionalista Vasco vuelve a la carga," *La Actualidad Española,* No. 1,317 (March 28-April 3, 1977), p. 35. "Mitin de Clausura del Congreso del PNV," *Diario de Navarra,* March 29, 1977, pp. 15-16. "Amnistía, erre que erre," *Cambio 16,* No. 278 (April 10, 1977), pp. 23-25.

12. General election data are taken from Spanish press accounts of June 18, 1977, as supplied by the Office of Information, Spanish Embassy, Washington, D. C. More specific data from the Basque provinces are from *Euzkadi* (Boletin Informativo del Partido Nacionalista Vasco), No. 29 (June 23, 1977), p. 9.

13. In the following section, all analyses are based on the vote data contained in Talde Euskal Estudio Elkartea, *Euskadi, ante las elecciones municipales* (San Sebastián: Ediciones Vascas, 1978), pp. 33-36. A few words of caution are in order regarding these data. First, the cited study uses vote data drawn essentially from press accounts of the elections in each of the four Basque provinces. These data may differ slightly from official statistics in some respects. Second, even within the study there are internal inconsistencies, and some vote totals do not add correctly, or do not match other tables in other places of the study. Despite these problems, I do not feel that the data are grossly incorrect; and they have the important virtue of being comprehensive and comparable across the four provinces.

14. There are certainly other ways of arranging the 1977 vote data in order to make analytical judgments about the elections. See, for example, the aforementio ed study, *Euskadi, ante las elecciones*

municipales, Chapter 2. See also, Luis C.-Nuñez Astrain, *La Sociedad Vasca Actual* (San Sebastián: Editorial Txertoa, 1978), Chapter 8.

15. Calculations of the PNV's share of the 1977 vote are complicated by the fact that the party joined in a three-party coalition (with ANV and ESB) in Navarra. For the sake of analysis, I have given half of the Navarra vote to PNV, and half to the left *abertzale* combination, ANV-ESB. This was arbitrary, but necessary, in order to carry out the desired kind of analysis.

16. Alberto Perez Calvo, writing before the 1977 elections, observed that while Bilbao had traditionally been the center of PNV support, in the future that support might shift eastward to San Sebastián, in part, he thought, because Spanish emigration to Guipúzcoa had been less than that to Vizcaya (*Los Partidos Políticos en el País Vasco,* p. 15). The election results from 1977 seem to bear out that prediction. See also, Luis C.-Nuñez Astrain, *Clases Sociales en Euskadi* (San Sebastián: Editorial Txertoa, 1978), especially Chapter 8.

Notes to Chapter Twelve

1. "Fruto de años de lucha y diplomacia: Llegó la Preautonomía," *Euzkadi* (Boletín Informativo del Partido Nacionalista Vasco, No. 57, January 5, 1978), p. 20. See also, Miguel Acoca, "Self-Rule Agreement Alleviates Fears of Violence in Spain's Basque Region," Washington *Post,* January 7, 1978.

2. *Deia* (Bilbao), December 30, 1978.

3. These arguments are dealt with comprehensively, although not sympathetically, in Joseba-Koldo Narbarte, *Mil Dias: De la dictadura a la preautonomía en Euskadi* (San Sebastián: Ediciones Vascas, 1978), pp. 142-215.

4. *Deia* (Bilbao), Feburary 4, 14, and 15, 1978.

5. Talde Euskal Estudio Elkartea, *Euskadi, ante las elecciones municipales* (San Sebastián: Ediciones Vascas, 1978), p. 11.

6. *Deia* (Bilbao), January 29, January 31, February 1, and February 2, 1978.

7. The question of Navarrese adhesion is the subject of the fourth "Transitory Disposition" of the new Spanish Constitution.

8. Beatriz Iraburu, "El Consejo General Vasco: Una herramienta para empezar a trabajar," *Deia* (Bilbao), February 18, 1978, p. 36.

9. *Deia* (Bilbao), February 8, 1978.

10. *Deia* (Bilbao), February 9, 1978.

11. *Deia* (Bilbao), February 18, 1978.

12. *Deia* (Bilbao), February 25, 1978.

13. Narbarte, Chapter 6, esp. pp. 218-220.

14. *Deia* (Bilbao), May 30, 1978.

15. This discussion is based on interviews with Mikel Isasi in Bilbao in January 1979. See also *Euzkadi*, No. 83, July 6, 1978, pp. 10-13.

16. This section is based on press accounts which are cited individually, as well as the publication of the Basque Nationalist Party, *El Partido Nacionalista Vasco ante la Constitución: Historia y alcance de unas negociaciones* (Zarauz, Vizcaya: 1978).

17. The PNV amendments are discussed generally in *Deia* (Bilbao), February 1 and February 3, 1978, as well as in *El Partido Nacionalista Vasco ante la Constitución,* Chapter III. See also *Deia* (Bilbao), February 24, 1978.

18. *Deia* (Bilbao), March 16 and March 18, 1978.

19. *Deia* (Bilbao), March 19, 1978.

20. These four articles are found in the issues of *Deia* (Bilbao) of December 29, 30, and 31, 1978, and January 3, 1979.

21. *Deia* (Bilbao), December 30, 1978.

22. The complete text of the draft Autonomy Statute is found in *El Diario Vasco* (San Sebastián), December 26, 1978.

23. *El País* (Madrid), December 27, 1978.

24. As reported in *Cambio 16,* No. 370, January 7, 1979, p. 28.

25. *Deia* (Bilbao), February 4, 1978.

26. *Deia* (Bilbao), April 1, 1978.

27. *El País* (Madrid), June 29, July 1 and July 6, 1978.

28. *Deia* (Bilbao), March 22, 1978.

29. *Deia* (Bilbao), March 23, 1978.

30. *Deia* (Bilbao), March 31, 1978.

31. The following is from *Cambio 16,* No. 370, January 7, 1979, pp. 18-21.

32. A preliminary version of this report is found in *Deia* (Bilbao), December 21, 1978. A more complete report is in *Cambio 16,* No. 370, January 7, 1979, p. 21.

33. *Diario Vasco* (San Sebastián), January 4, 1979.

34. *El País* (Madrid), July 1, 1978.

35. *Deia* (Bilbao), December 29, 1978.

36. *Deia* (Bilbao), February 11, 1978.

37. *El País* (Madrid), July 6, 1978.

38. *Deia* (Bilbao), February 1, 1978.

39. *Deia* (Bilbao), February 5, 1978.

40. *Deia* (Bilbao), February 19, 1978.

41. *Deia* (Bilbao), May 16, 1978. *El País* (Madrid), May 17 and May 20, 1978.

42. *El País* (Madrid), June 28, 1978.

43. *Deia* (Bilbao), March 7, 1978.

44. For an explanation of the PNV position, see "Cronología de una Decisión Importante," *Euzkadi,* No. 98 (October 19, 1978), pp. 20-22.

45. *Deia* (Bilbao), January 5, 1979.

46. *Deia* (Bilbao), April 2, 1978.

47. *Deia* (Bilbao), January 3, 1979.

48. *Deia* (Bilbao), March 21, 1979.

Glossary

POLITICAL TERMS AND ORGANIZATIONS

Abertzale Derived from the Basque language word for "patriotic," in the 1970s this word came to mean any political party or movement that opposed association or affiliation with Spanish parties with similar class origins or ideologies. In the lexicon of Basque nationalism, *abertzale* parties are considered the only true ethnic Basque parties; the others have chosen to place class origin above ethnicity in importance. The opposite of *abertzale* would be *sucursalista* (derived from the Spanish word for "branch office," *sucursal*), *estatal* (associated with the Spanish State), or *españolista* (literally, "Spanish-ist").

Abertzale parties With the passage of the Franco dictatorship, there has emerged a bewildering variety of political parties, only a few of which manage to survive the intense electoral competition. The following list is an attempt to supply the reader with all of the principal *abertzale* parties (other than the PNV, the Basque Nationalist Party, which is treated separately below) that appeared to be significant as of 1979. There will no doubt continue to be many changes in this list through the 1980s.

ANV *Acción Nacionalista Vasca* (Basque Nationalist Action)

EE *Euzkadiko Ezkerra* (Basque Left)

ESB *Euskal Sozialista Biltzarrea* (Basque Socialist Convergence)

UNAI *Unión Navarra de Izquierda* (Navarrese Left Union)

KAS *Koordinadora Abertzale Sozialista* (Basque Socialist Coordinator)

EIA *Euskal Iraultzarako Alderdia* (Basque Revolutionary Party)

LAB *Langille Abertzaleen Batzordea* (Basque Workers' Council)

LAK *Langille Abertzale Komiteak* (Basque Workers' Committee)

LAIA *Langille Abertzale Iraultzaleen Alderdia* (Basque Revolutionary Workers' Party)

EHAS *Eusko Herriko Alderdi Sozialista* (Socialist Party of the Basque People)

HB *Herri Batasuna* (Unity of the People)

CGV *Consejo General Vasco* (Basque General Council). The organization created in 1979 by the Spanish government to act as the interim administration in the Basque region to facilitate the transfer of power to a regional government.

ELA-STV *Eusko Langileen Alkartasuna-Solidaridad de Trabajadores Vascos* (Solidarity of Basque Workers). The first ethnic Basque labor union, founded in 1911, and still the principal representative of Basque nationalism among Basque workers. Since the 1950s there have been a number of splits within the Basque labor movement, leading to the creation of splinter groups that have spun off from the parent organization (now known as ELA-*oficial*) Some of these groups are:

ELA-BERRI (New-ELA)

ELA-MSE (ELA-Socialist Movement of Euzkadi)

ELADIOS (the labor arm of the Basque Nationalist Party)

ELA-AUTOGESTIONARIA (roughly, "ELA-Selfgoverning")

EZKER BERRI (a socialist political party)

ETA *Euzkadi ta Askatusuna* (Euzkadi and Freedom). The principal Basque insurgent group responsible for much of the politically oriented violence in the Basque provinces since 1968. Founded in 1959, ETA has experienced a number of splits in recent years, leading to the creation of the following splinter groups (among others):

ETA-m ETA-*militar*, the armed insurgent group within ETA

ETA-pm ETA-*politico-militar,* the propaganda and political arm of ETA

ETA-BERRI and **ETA-ZARRA** New ETA and Old ETA, the products of one such split

ETA-V and **ETA-VI,** or **ETA-Quinta** and **ETA-Sexta** Groups resulting from struggles at the Fifth and Sixth Assemblies of ETA

Euzkadi The name coined by Sabino de Arana y Goiri to describe the geo-political entity that was to be the national home for Basques. In its most all-encompassing form, Euzkadi includes not only the four Spanish Basque provinces of Alava, Guipúzcoa, Navarra and Vizcaya (referred to as *Euzkadi Sur,* or South Euzkadi), but also the three French provinces of Labourd, Basse Navarre and Soule (known as *Euzkadi Norte,* or North Euzkadi). Although the Basque region today is officially called Euskadi (spelled with an *s*), in this book we have retained the traditional spelling, Euzkadi. Organizational names derived from Euzkadi are spelled here with *s* or *z* according to each organization's preference.

Euzkadi, Government of The official Government-in-Exile of the Basque region. Created in October 1936 by the Spanish parliament, the government's original area of jurisdiction covered Alava, Guipúzcoa and Vizcaya, since Navarra chose not to be included. Because of the outbreak of the Spanish Civil War, however, Alava and most of Guipúzcoa were already in the hands of the insurgent military forces by the time of its creation. The Government of Euzkadi remained in Bilbao until the city fell in June 1937, when the government went into exile, where it has remained ever since. The government presently resides in Paris; its president is Jesús María Leizaola. To aid in its task of keeping the Basque political unit alive, and to coordinate the various arms of the resistance movement, the Government of Euzkadi created several auxiliary bodies:

Consejo Consultativo (Consultative Council)

Junta de Resistencia (Resistance Committee)

CEVA *Confederación de Entidades Vascas de América* (Confederation of Basque Entities in America)

ASE *Alianza Sindical de Euzkadi* (Basque Labor Alliance)

PNV *Partido Nacionalista Vasco* (Basque Nationalist Party). Also referred to by its name and letters in the Basque language: EAJ, or *Eusko Alderdi Jeltzalea.* The first political organization to espouse the cause of Basque nationalism. Founded in 1895, although divided from 1917 to 1930. Has remained the foremost exponent of Basque nationalism, and has customarily been the strongest single political party in the Basque region, except Navarra where it has always been rather weak. The party is organized along federal lines, with the primary decision making bodies being called *Buru Batzar.* Over the entire region there sits a general council called *Euzkadi Buru Batzar.* Within each of the four Spanish provinces there is a provincial body: *Araba Buru Batzar, Guipuzkoa Buru Batzar, Napar Buru Batzar,* and *Bizkai Buru Batzar.* There are also municipal units, called *Uri Buru Batzar.*

Index

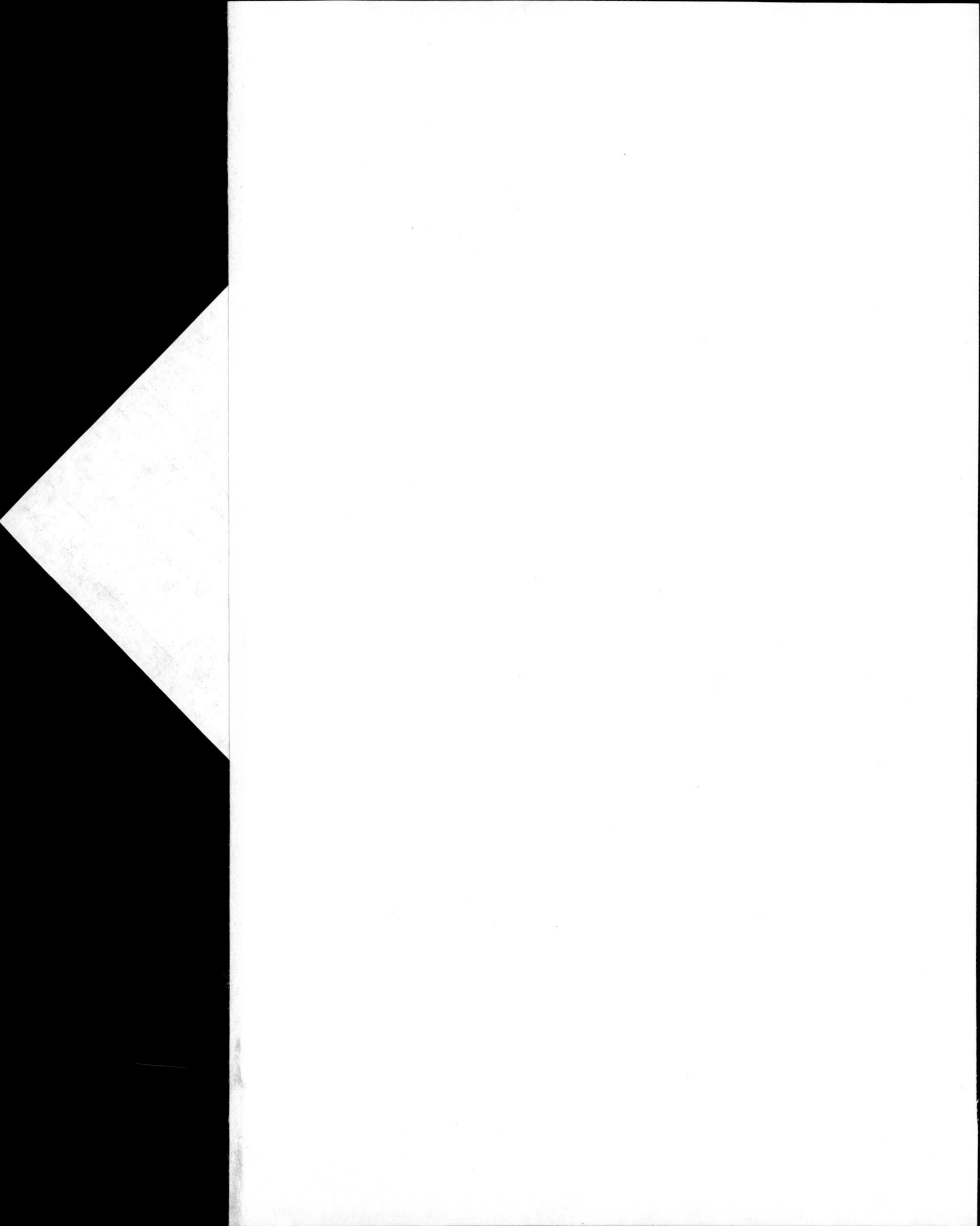

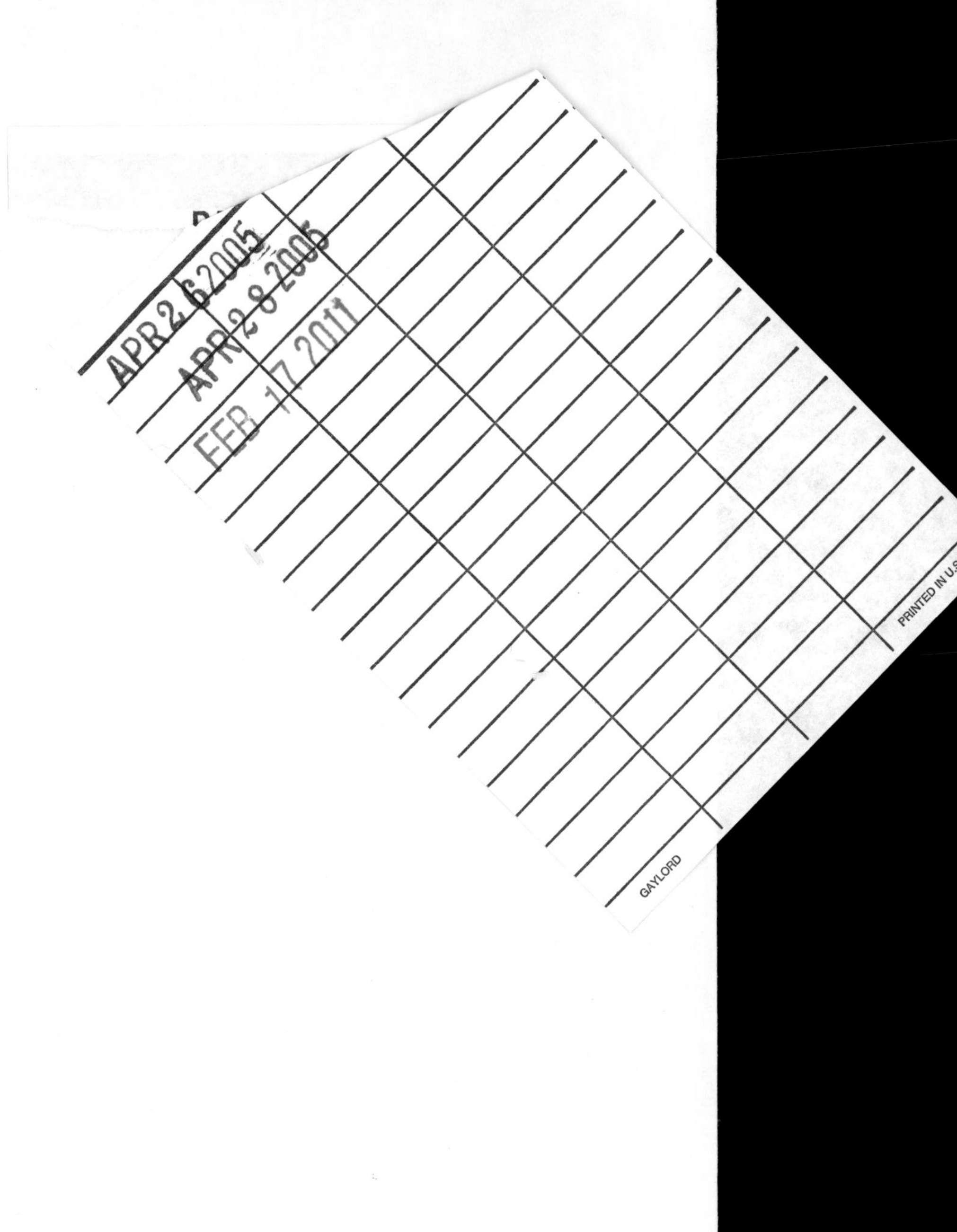